How to Do Everything™

iPhone® 5

Jason R. Rich

New York Chicago San Francisco Lisbon
London Madrid Mexico City Milan New Delhi
San Juan Seoul Singapore Sydney Toronto

The *McGraw·Hill* Companies

McGraw-Hill books are available at special quantity discounts to use as premiums and sales promotions, or for use in corporate training programs. To contact a representative, please e-mail us at bulksales@ mcgraw-hill.com.

How to Do Everything™: iPhone® 5

1234567890   QFR QFR   1098765432

ISBN   978-0-07-180333-5
MHID   0-07-180333-5

Cover photograph used by permission from Jason Rich Photography © 2012.

Sponsoring Editor Megg Morin	**Technical Editor** Janet Cloninger	**Composition** Fortuitous Publishing Services
Editorial Supervisor Janet Walden	**Copy Editor** William McManus	**Illustration** Fortuitous Publishing Services
Project Editor Howie Severson, Fortuitous Publishing Services	**Proofreader** Paul Tyler	**Art Director, Cover** Jeff Weeks
Acquisitions Coordinator Stephanie Evans	**Indexer** Jack Lewis	**Cover Designer** Jeff Weeks
	Production Supervisor Jean Bodeaux	

This book is dedicated to my niece, Natalie Shay Emsley Skehan, and to the late Steve Jobs, without whom there would be no Apple iPhone to write about.

About the Author

Jason R. Rich (www.JasonRich.com) is the bestselling author of more than 56 books, covering a wide range of topics. Some of his recently published books include *How to Do Everything: MacBook Air, How to Do Everything: Digital Photography, How to Do Everything: iCloud,* and *How to Do Everything: Kindle Fire* (all with McGraw-Hill Professional), and *Your iPad at Work: Third Edition, OS X Mountain Lion Tips and Tricks,* and *iPad and iPhone Tips and Tricks: Second Edition* (all with Que).

Jason has written more than 100 feature-length, how-to articles about the iPhone and iPad that you can read by visiting www.iOSArticles.com (click on the Articles tab). His work also appears in a wide range of national magazines, major daily newspapers, and popular websites. You can follow Jason on Twitter (@JasonRich7).

About the Technical Editor

Janet Cloninger worked as a chemist and a programmer for many years before becoming a work-at-home mom. Janet has written more than 2,000 articles and product reviews for The Gadgeteer, a well-respected website for reviews of gadgets and gear. Her love of gadgets came from her father, who never met anything he couldn't fix or improve. Janet lives in North Carolina with her husband, Butch, her daughter, Rachel, and their Shiba Inu, Teddy.

Contents at a Glance

PART I   **Get to Know Your iPhone 5**

1   Discover What's Great About the iPhone. 3
2   Set Up and Configure Your iPhone 5 19
3   Use iPhone's Basic Functions. 43
4   Backup, Sync, and Import Your Existing Data into Your iPhone. 79

PART II   **Learn the Basics of iOS 6**

5   Discover the Apps That Come Preinstalled with iOS 6 99
6   Customize Your iPhone 125

PART III   **Use Your iPhone's Built-in Apps**

7   Make and Receive Calls 159
8   Manage Contacts on Your iPhone 187
9   Send and Receive E-mail Using the Mail App 217
10   Surf the Web with Safari. 235
11   Shoot, Edit, and Share Photos and Videos 263
12   Use the New Maps App to Navigate Your World 289
13   Organize Your Life with the Calendar, Reminders, and Notes Apps 307
14   Communicate Using Video Conferencing and Text Messaging. 335

PART IV   **Your iPhone Is a Portable Entertainment System**

15   Use Your iPhone to Experience Multimedia Entertainment 355
16   Use Your iPhone as an E-book Reader 385
17   Play Games on Your iPhone. 407

PART V   **Extend the Capabilities of Your iPhone**

18   Find and Install Additional Apps 427
19   Protect Your iPhone 457

Appendix A: Troubleshoot iPhone Problems 467
Index 473

Contents

Acknowledgments xv
Introduction xvii

PART I   Get to Know Your iPhone 5   **1**

CHAPTER 1   Discover What's Great About the iPhone **3**
Get to Know Your New iPhone 5   3
   Battery Life of the iPhone 5   6
   Acquaint Yourself with the Anatomy of the iPhone 5   6
   Discover the Many Ways to Interact with Your iPhone   8
   Learn About the iPhone 5's Useful New Features   9
Choose the Perfect iPhone 5 for Yourself   12
   Choose the Color of Your iPhone   13
   Choose a Storage Capacity   14
   Select a Wireless Service Provider and Service Plan   14

CHAPTER 2   Set Up and Configure Your iPhone 5 . . . .   **19**
Charge Your New iPhone's Battery   20
Activate and Set Up Your New iPhone   20
   Set Up as New iPhone   24
   Restore from iCloud Backup   29
   Restore from iTunes Backup   29
Set Your Phone in Sleep or Airplane Mode   30
   Place Your iPhone in Sleep Mode So It Can Continue to Function with the
      Display Turned Off   30
   In Airplane Mode, Your iPhone Can't Transmit   31
   Turn Wi-Fi On and Off Separately   32
   Enjoy Peace and Quiet by Silencing Your iPhone   33
Customize the Notification Center   34
   Get to Know the Notification Center Screen   35
   Customize the Notification Center   37

CHAPTER 3   Use iPhone's Basic Functions. **43**

Get Acquainted with the iPhone's Virtual Keyboard.   44
   Configure the Virtual Keyboard Options   49
   Create and Use Custom Keyboard Shortcuts   52
Learn When and How to Tap, Swipe, Flick, or Pinch the iPhone's
Multi-Touch Display.   54
Discover the Multiple Functions of the iPhone's Home Button   57
   Run Multiple Apps Simultaneously and Easily Switch Between Them   59
   Access Music Controls and Rotation Lock Using the Home Button.   61
Use Siri to Control Your iPhone Verbally   62
   Initiate a Call with Siri   64
   Launch Apps Using Siri   66
   Use Siri to Communicate via the Messages App   67
   Tell Siri to Enter Meeting and Schedule Info into the Calendar App.   69
   Query Siri About Sports, Movies, and Restaurants.   69
   Get Directions Using Siri's Full Integration with the Maps App   71
   Control the Music App with Your Voice   71
   Prepare for the Weather with Siri.   72
   Let Siri Help You Manage Your To-Do Items or Notes   73
   Use Siri to Get Stock Prices, Update Your Facebook Page, Send Tweets, and
      Much More   74
   Ask Siri Questions and Get Quick Answers   74
   Fine-Tune Siri's Performance Through Practice.   74
   Deactivate Siri.   75
Enter Text into Apps via Your iPhone Using the Dictation Feature   75
Interact with Your iPhone However You'd Like   76

CHAPTER 4   Back Up, Sync, and Import Your Existing Data into Your iPhone . .   79

Create and Maintain a Backup of Your iPhone   80
   Create and Maintain an iTunes Sync Backup.   81
   Create and Maintain an iCloud Backup   83
   Restore Data from a Backup   85
Sync Data, Documents, Files, and Photos Using iTunes Sync   87
Use iCloud to Wirelessly Sync Data, Documents, Files, and Photos.   88
   Sync Purchased Content via iCloud   90
   Set Up Your iPhone to Auto-Sync New Purchases   91
Share Files Using Other Cloud-Based File-Sharing Services   92
Sync Other Data and Files Between Your Computer, Network, and iPhone   93
Share Data and Files with Online-Based Applications   94
Use the Share Button Incorporated into Many Apps.   95

PART II   Learn the Basics of iOS 6   **97**

CHAPTER 5   Discover the Apps That Come Preinstalled with iOS 6 . . . . **99**

Explore the Apps That Come Preinstalled on the iPhone 5 101
   App Store. 101

Calculator 102
Calendar 103
Camera 104
Clock 105
Contacts 106
Facebook 107
FaceTime 107
Find My iPhone 108
Game Center 108
iBooks 108
iTunes 108
Mail 109
Maps 110
Messages 111
Music 111
Newsstand 112
Notes 113
Passbook 113
Phone 113
Photos 113
Reminders 115
Safari 115
Stocks 116
Twitter 116
Videos 116
Voice Memos 116
Weather 117
New and Improved iPhone Functions That Work with iOS 6 and Your
    Favorite Apps 117
Siri 118
Notification Center 118
Location Services 119
Facebook and Twitter Integration 119
Share Capabilities 120
iCloud 121
Dictation 121
AirPrint 122
AirPlay 122
iOS 6's Other Features 122

CHAPTER 6   Customize Your iPhone **125**
Customize Your iPhone's Lock Screen and Home Screen 125
Turn On the Passcode Lock Feature 126
Customize the Passcode Lock Feature's Functionality 127
Select a Wallpaper Graphic for Your Lock Screen and Your Home Screen 128
Rearrange the App Icons on the Home Screen 132

x Contents

Create Custom App Folders to Organize Your Home Screen 136
Remove App Icons from a Folder 137
Delete Apps from Your iPhone 138
Purchase Additional iCloud Online Storage Space 144
Back Up Your iPhone Using iCloud Backup 145
Personalize the Sound and Vibration Options of Your iPhone 146
Temporarily Turn Off All Sound Generated by Your iPhone 148
Assign Custom Ringtones to Specific Contacts 148
Use Your iPhone with a Wide Range of Bluetooth Accessories 151
Adjust iPhone Settings to Help Maintain Your Privacy 151
Configure Privacy Settings 151
Configure Restrictions 153
Adjust App-Specific Settings to Customize Their Functionality 154

PART III   Use Your iPhone's Built-in Apps   157

CHAPTER 7   Make and Receive Calls 159
Launch the Phone App 159
Choose How You'll Speak with Someone on the Phone 161
Hold the Phone Up to Your Ear 161
Use the Built-In Speakerphone Feature 161
Use a Corded Headset 163
Use a Wireless Bluetooth Headset 163
Answer Incoming Calls 165
Answer an Incoming Call While Using the iPhone 165
Answer an Incoming Call from the Lock Screen 169
Answer an Incoming Call When Already Engaged in a Call 171
Manage Incoming Calls Using New iOS 6 Features 172
Use the Reply With Message Feature 172
Use the Remind Me Later Feature 173
Manage Voicemails 173
Make Calls from Your iPhone 176
Create Favorites and Initiate Calls from Your Favorites List 176
Call People from Your Recents List 179
Find and Call Anyone in Your Contacts Database 180
Dial Any Phone Number Manually Using the Keypad 180
Initiate FaceTime Calls from the Phone App 181
Use Other Options While You're Engaged in a Call 181
Participate in Conference Calls 182
Customize the Phone App from Within Settings 184

CHAPTER 8   Manage Contacts on Your iPhone 187
Create a Customized Contacts Database Using the Contacts App 188
Let's Take a Closer Look at the Contacts App 189
Add New Entries to Your Contacts Database 192
Add Pictures to Your Contacts Entries 200

Add Contact Entries from the Maps App 200
Add Contact Entries from the Phone App 201
Edit Existing Contact Entries.. 203
Find and Access Contacts Data 206
Use the Interactive Fields in a Contact Entry 208
Share Your Contacts Data Manually 209
Sync Your Contacts Database with iCloud........................ 211
Sync Your Contacts Database with Other Services 212

CHAPTER 9   **Send and Receive E-mail Using the Mail App** **217**
Set Up Your Existing E-mail Accounts to Work with the Mail App 217
Customize the Mail App 220
Read and Manage Incoming E-mails Using the Mail App.................. 222
View the Contents of One Inbox or All Inboxes.................. 222
Switch Between E-mail Accounts 222
Create a Custom Mailbox 223
Access E-mail from Your Inboxes 224
Read Individual E-mails 226
Reply To or Forward Incoming E-mails 228
Flag Incoming E-mails and/or Mark Them as Unread 229
Delete Incoming E-mails 229
Move Incoming E-mails to Another Mailbox or Folder 230
Add an E-mail's Sender to Your VIP List........................ 230
Compose and Send a New Outgoing E-mail 231
Stay Connected via the Mail App, Wherever You Are. 234

CHAPTER 10   **Surf the Web with Safari**............................... **235**
Get Acquainted with the Latest Version of the Safari Web Browser 236
Make Webpages Easier to Read Using the Reader Feature............... 239
Utilize Safari's Share Button 240
Access Your Web Surfing History 245
Manage Safari Bookmarks 245
Read Webpage Content Offline Using the Reading List Feature 251
Switch Between Open Browser Screens............................ 253
Discover the New iCloud Tabs Feature............................ 253
Customize the Safari App from Settings.......................... 255
Use Other Web Browsers to Surf the Web 257
Stay Active on the Online Social Networking Services 257
Use the Official Facebook App 258
Use the Official Twitter App.. 259
Use an Unofficial Facebook or Twitter App 260
Use Optional Apps for Google +, Instagram, LinkedIn, and More........ 261

CHAPTER 11   **Shoot, Edit, and Share Photos and Videos**................ **263**
Become Familiar with Your iPhone's Built-In Cameras 264
Shoot Photos Using the Camera App.................................... 265

Launch the Camera App and Locate Its Controls 265

Snap Clear, Vibrant Photos Using Your iPhone 5 267

Shoot Videos Using the Camera App. 272

Use the Photos App to View, Edit, and Enhance Your Photos 273

Navigate the Albums Screen of the Photos App. 273

View and Edit the Contents of an Album. 275

View Individual Photos Stored in an Album 276

Edit and Enhance Individual Photos 278

Geo-Tag Your Photos and Video. 279

Share Your Photos and Videos. 280

Share Your Contents of an Album 280

Share Individual Photos Stored in an Album 282

Use Other Options to Share Your Photos Online 282

Sync Your Photos Using iCloud's Photo Stream 283

Discover the Hundreds of Other Photography-Related Apps Available from
the App Store 287

CHAPTER 12 Use the New Maps App to Navigate Your World 289

Turn On Location Services and Siri Before Using Maps 290

Get Acquainted with the Newly Revamped Maps App. 291

Obtain Turn-by-Turn Directions Between Start and End Locations. 291

Change Your Map View 297

View a Map of Any Location 301

Access the Maps App from the Contacts App. 304

Use the Maps App with Siri. 304

Find Third-Party Maps Apps 305

**CHAPTER 13 Organize Your Life with the Calendar, Reminders, and
Notes Apps 307**

Manage Your Schedule Using the Calendar App. 309

View One Calendar at a Time, or View Multiple Calendars Simultaneously. . 312

Add a New Calendar or Edit or Delete an Existing Calendar. 312

Manually Enter New Events into the Calendar App 314

View, Edit, and Delete Events 317

Access Calendar Information Using Siri. 317

Set Up the Calendar App to Work with the Notification Center. 318

Create and Manage To-Do Lists Using the Reminders App. 321

View, Search, Create, Edit, or Delete a List 322

Manage and View a Specific List 324

Customize Each To-Do Item in a List from Its Details Screen 326

Compose, View, Organize, and Share Text-Based Memos Using the Notes App. . . 329

Useful Features of the Notes App. 329

Create a New Note from Scratch. 331

Managing Your Notes 333

CHAPTER 14 Communicate Using Video Conferencing and Text Messaging . . 335

Use FaceTime for Video Conferencing 336

Accept FaceTime Calls 338
Initiate a FaceTime Call 339
Initiate a FaceTime Call via Your Favorites List. 340
Participate in a FaceTime Call 342
Use FaceTime Alternatives for Video Conferencing 345
Use the Messages App for Text Messaging and Instant Messaging. 345
Set Up the Messages App to Work with Apple's iMessage Service. 347
Send and Receive Text/Instant Messages Using the Messages App. 348
Use Alternative Options to iMessage and the Messages App. 352

PART IV   Your iPhone Is a Portable Entertainment System   353

CHAPTER 15   Use Your iPhone to Experience Multimedia Entertainment. . . .   355
Gather Entertaining Content Using the iTunes App. 357
Shop for Music Using the iTunes App 358
Purchase or Rent Movies from Your iPhone. 362
Purchase Single Episodes or Entire Seasons of Your Favorite TV Shows. . . . 366
Search the iTunes Store for Whatever You're Looking For 368
Discover What Else You Can Access from the iTunes App. 368
Discover the Cost of Purchasing, Renting, or Streaming Content 371
Experience Your Digital Music Library with the Music App. 373
Enjoy Your Digital Music On Your iPhone 373
Control the Music App from the Lock Screen and While in
Multitasking Mode 376
Use the Music App with External Speakers 377
Watch Video Content Acquired from the iTunes Store Using the Videos App 380
Discover the New Passbook App. 382

CHAPTER 16   Use Your iPhone as an E-book Reader   385
Customize the iBooks App from Settings 386
Explore the iBooks Library Screen 388
Shop for E-books at iBookstore 392
Find Details on an E-book's Info Screen. 395
Read an E-book Using iBooks 397
Manually Set Bookmarks as You Read 398
Interact with the Book Through the Table of Contents 399
Adjust the Look of an E-book's Text on the iPhone's Screen 400
Perform a Keyword Search Within an E-book 402
View PDF Files Using iBooks 402
Read Newspapers and Magazines Using the Newsstand App 403

CHAPTER 17   Play Games on Your iPhone.   407
Discover iPhone 5 Games Suitable for People of All Ages 409
Distinguish Between Single-Player and Multiplayer Games 411
Discover Games You'll Love 411
Sample 12 Awesome Games Worth Playing. 412
Experience Multiplayer Games on Game Center. 421

PART V   Extend the Capabilities of Your iPhone   **425**

CHAPTER 18   Find and Install Additional Apps **427**

Discover New Apps in the App Store 428
 Quickly Locate a Specific App Using Its Name or a Keyword 428
 Browse the App Store's Featured Offerings 430
 View Charts of the Most Popular Apps. 432
 Rely on the Genius to Help You Find Apps 434
Learn All About an App on the App's Info Screen 435
 Get All the Details About an App 435
 Read Reviews for an App Before Acquiring It 437
 Find Related Apps 439
 Acquire an App from Its Info Screen 439
Discover the Difference Between Paid and Free Apps 440
 Acquire Free Apps 441
 Acquire Apps by Paying for Them 442
Keep Your Apps Up to Date 442
Obtain Apple's Own 'Must Have' Apps That Are Optional 444
Discover Additional Ways to Use iPhone Apps to Improve Your Life 449
 Use Your iPhone with Other Gadgets and Technology 450

CHAPTER 19   Protect Your iPhone **457**

Select a Clear Protective Film for the iPhone's Screen 458
Apply a Custom "Skin" to Encase the Entire iPhone 460
Choose the Perfect Case or Cover for Your iPhone 460
Discover the Benefits of Investing in AppleCare + ... 462
Evaluate Third-Party iPhone Insurance Options 463
Discover What to Do if Your iPhone Gets Damaged 464
 Strategies for Replacing a Lost, Stolen, or Damaged iPhone 465

APPENDIX A   Troubleshoot iPhone Problems **467**

Fix Common iPhone-Related Problems 467
 What to Do if Your iPhone Gets Lost or Stolen 468
 What to Do if Your iPhone Gets Damaged 468
 What to Do if Your iPhone Starts Acting Sluggish 468
 What to Do if Your iPhone Won't Make or Receive Calls 469
 What to Do if Your iPhone Can't Access the Internet 469
 Dealing with Other iPhone-Related Problems 470
Try to Prevent Problems, but Be Prepared if Any Arise 470

Index **473**

Acknowledgments

Thanks to Megg Morin at McGraw-Hill for inviting me to work on this book. Thanks also to Stephanie Evans, Janet Cloninger, Howie Severson, William McManus, Paul Tyler, Jack Lewis, and everyone else who contributed their talents and publishing know-how as this book was being created.

Thanks also to my friends and family for their endless support and encouragement; to Frankie Donjae, for being patient during his visit to Boston while I was writing this book; and to you, the reader, for choosing this book as your guide as you discover the power and capabilities of the Apple iPhone 5.

Introduction

The Apple iPhone 5 is much more than just another run-of-the-mill smartphone. When it was released in October 2012, it quickly became a worldwide phenomenon, a device that people from all walks of life wanted to get their hands on.

While the iPhone product line has been around for a few years now, the iPhone 5 represents a somewhat significant redesign, with its larger Multi-Touch Retina display, faster processor, and enhanced cameras. Plus, the iPhone 5 runs iOS 6, which is Apple's most advanced operating system for its smartphones yet. (iOS 6 also operates Apple's other mobile devices, including the iPad, iPad mini, and iPod touch.)

As you're about to discover if you're a new convert to the iPhone, you can use your iPhone 5 for much more than just making and receiving calls. For example, thanks to the newly enhanced Safari web browser that comes preinstalled on the device, your iPhone 5 is also a powerful tool for surfing the Internet. And thanks to many other apps that either come preinstalled on the iPhone or are available for it at Apple's App Store, your iPhone can help you to stay informed, stay entertained, and handle a wide range of tasks in your everyday life. For example:

- Using the Mail app, you can manage your e-mail accounts.
- With the FaceTime app, you can participate in real-time video conferences.
- The Camera and Photos apps enable you to use your iPhone to take and share photos and videos.
- The Maps app helps you to get to whatever destinations you set out for without getting lost, and if you're driving, Siri can give you your Maps directions verbally so that you can keep your hands on the steering wheel and your eyes on the road.
- The Contacts, Calendar, Notes, and Reminders apps help you to manage your contacts, schedule, and to-do lists with incredible efficiency.
- To help you relax and entertain yourself, several other apps enable your iPhone to serve as a feature-packed e-book reader, a handheld gaming device, or a portable entertainment system on which you can watch TV shows and movies or listen to your favorite music.
- If you're active on Facebook, Twitter, or any of the other popular online social networking services, you can use a corresponding app on your iPhone to stay in touch with your online friends and share details about your life as it unfolds, from wherever you happen to be.

And that's just the beginning! Using specialized apps, your iPhone can help you handle your online banking from almost anywhere, manage your credit card accounts, keep up to date on the latest news, and perform thousands of other tasks using the more than 500,000 optional, third-party apps that are available from the App Store. In addition, using Siri (another iPhone feature that's been enhanced with iOS 6), you can interact with and control your iPhone using voice commands and requests.

The iPhone 5 is truly a remarkable device that you can utilize throughout your day to help you communicate more efficiently, better manage your time, improve your organization, juggle a wide range of personal and work-related tasks, become more productive, stay well informed, and entertain yourself and others.

How to Do Everything: iPhone 5 not only helps you to start using your new iPhone 5 quickly, it also teaches you how to fully utilize the many different apps that are part of iOS 6 and that come preinstalled on your iPhone, while also introducing you to some of the optional apps that can dramatically increase what the iPhone is capable of.

Even if you're a veteran iPhone user, *How to Do Everything: iPhone 5* will teach you everything you need to know about iOS 6, and help you to discover the new features added to many of the core apps you use most often, like Phone, Contacts, Calendar, Reminders, Safari, Camera, Photos, Mail, Maps, FaceTime, Passbook, Music, Videos, iTunes, Notes, Facebook, and Twitter. You'll also get up to speed on the latest new features and enhancements made to the iPhone's built-in functions, like Notification Center and Siri.

What Does This Book Cover?

This book covers all you need to know to get the most out of your iPhone 5 and its iOS 6 operating system. The book contains 19 chapters, broken up into five parts.

Part I: Get to Know Your iPhone 5

- Chapter 1, "Discover What's Great About the iPhone," focuses on the evolution of the iPhone and the new features and functions this latest iPhone model offers when used in conjunction with iOS 6.
- Chapter 2, "Set Up and Configure Your iPhone 5," shows you how to set up and activate your new iPhone 5, turn it on, get it connected to the Internet, and then configure some of the core apps that come preinstalled.
- Chapter 3, "Use iPhone's Basic Functions," gets you up to speed using your iPhone with its Multi-Touch Retina display and teaches you how to effectively use Siri and the Dictation feature.
- Chapter 4, "Back Up, Sync, and Import Your Existing Data into Your iPhone," explains how to quickly and easily import and sync data, files, and content to your iPhone 5 from your primary computer, Apple's iCloud service, and/or your other iOS mobile devices.

Part II: Learn the Basics of iOS 6

- Chapter 5, "Discover the Apps That Come Preinstalled with iOS 6," introduces you to many of the apps that are available to you as soon as you turn on your iPhone 5 for the first time. You'll also learn how to use the Share function that many apps offer, and you'll discover how many of the popular apps now work seamlessly together to help you better manage information and content.
- Chapter 6, "Customize Your iPhone," focuses on how to personalize your iPhone 5's Lock screen and Home screen and customize your new smartphone in several other ways.

Part III: Use Your iPhone's Built-In Apps

- Chapter 7, "Make and Receive Calls," explains how to use your iPhone 5 to make and receive calls using the Phone app, how to use your iPhone's voicemail feature, and how to customize its ringtones.
- Chapter 8, "Manage Contacts on Your iPhone," teaches you how to efficiently use the Contacts app to manage your contacts, with a focus on how to sync your personal contacts database with your primary computer and other iOS mobile devices, as well as with iCloud, Facebook, and/or online-based contact management applications.
- Chapter 9, "Send and Receive E-mail Using the Mail App," shows how to use your iPhone 5 to manage one or more e-mail accounts, and explains how to use many of the new features added to the Mail app.
- Chapter 10, "Surf the Web with Safari," shows you how to use your iPhone to visit and keep track of your favorite websites, and helps you to become proficient surfing the Web using the iPhone's Multi-Touch display.
- Chapter 11, "Shoot, Edit, and Share Photos and Videos," teaches you how to get the most out of the cameras that are built into your iPhone 5, and explains how to shoot, edit, and share awesome photos and videos using the Camera and Photos apps (or some of the many other photography apps available for the iPhone 5).
- Chapter 12, "Use the New Maps App to Navigate Your World," explains how to use the newly revamped Maps app to obtain turn-by-turn directions between two locations, look up businesses and points of interest, and utilize this app in a variety of other ways.
- Chapter 13, "Organize Your Life with the Calendar, Reminders, and Notes Apps," offers an introduction to these three powerful apps that can help you manage your schedule, keep track of your to-do lists, and jot down and share text-based notes.
- Chapter 14, "Communicate Using Video Conferencing and Text Messaging," delves into some of the additional ways you can use your iPhone to communicate efficiently with friends, relatives, coworkers, customers, and clients, including using real-time video conferencing via FaceTime or Skype and exchanging text messages or instant messages via iMessage.

Part IV: Your iPhone Is a Portable Entertainment System

- Chapter 15, "Use Your iPhone to Experience Multimedia Entertainment," explains how to use the iTunes app to acquire music, TV shows, movies, and other content from Apple's online-based iTunes Store, and then shows you how to enjoy that content on your iPhone using the Music and Videos apps. You'll also discover what the new Passbook app is capable of.
- Chapter 16, "Use Your iPhone as an E-book Reader," shows you how to use the iBooks app to find, purchase, and download e-books from Apple's iBookstore, and then read those e-books on your iPhone. You'll also learn about the Newsstand app, which you can use to read digital editions of popular newspapers and magazines.
- Chapter 17, "Play Games on Your iPhone," introduces you to some of the exciting, challenging, and highly entertaining games you can play on your iPhone, and then demonstrates how to use Game Center to experience multiplayer games and compete against other people.

Part V: Extend the Capabilities of Your iPhone

- Chapter 18, "Find and Install Additional Apps," explains how to access Apple's App Store from your iPhone in order to find, download, and install optional apps that can dramatically enhance what your iPhone 5 is capable of.
- Chapter 19, "Protect Your iPhone," explains what you can do to protect your iPhone from damage, and then focuses on the importance of investing in AppleCare+ or third-party insurance for your iPhone.
- The Appendix, "Troubleshoot iPhone Problems," helps you to overcome common problems you may encounter when using your iPhone 5, and provides simple solutions to address or solve these problems.

Conventions Used in This Book

To help you better understand some of the more complex or technical aspects related to using your iPhone 5, and to help focus your attention on particularly useful features and functions offered by the device, throughout this book, you'll discover Note, Tip, and Caution paragraphs that highlight specific tidbits of useful information.

Plus, throughout this book, you'll discover "How To..." and "Did You Know?" sidebars that provide additional, topic-related information and advice that pertains to what's being covered in the chapter you're reading.

PART I

Get to Know Your iPhone 5

1

Discover What's Great About the iPhone

HOW TO...

- Get acquainted with the iPhone 5
- Choose the best iPhone 5 hardware configuration
- Evaluate your options when choosing a wireless service provider
- Manage your wireless account directly from your iPhone

Just like its predecessors, Apple's iPhone 5 represents a cutting-edge piece of technological hardware that's capable of handling a wide range of tasks right out of the box. However, when you combine the iPhone 5 with wireless Internet access, some optional apps (there are more than 700,000 to choose from), and potentially one or more of the optional iPhone accessories that are available, the possibilities for what this handheld device can do are truly limitless.

You should be proud of yourself for getting your hands on one of the most advanced smartphones ever created. Don't worry! Just because the technology behind the iPhone is extremely complex, as you'll soon discover, actually using the iPhone is often a straightforward process once you understand how the iOS 6 operating system and various apps work.

From this book, you'll learn about the iPhone 5, iOS 6, and related app features that are readily accessible to you, and that will dramatically enhance your experience using this phone. Now, let's get started by focusing on how to actually use the basic functionality of your new iPhone 5.

Get to Know Your New iPhone 5

When compared to previously released iPhone models, the iPhone 5 is 18 percent thinner and 20 percent lighter weight, but it offers a slightly taller design that now houses a stunningly vibrant 4-inch Retina Multi-Touch display. The iPhone 5 also offers a faster A6 processor, two improved built-in cameras, and a nice collection of other enhancements, such as Bluetooth 4.0 compatibility and the ability to provide faster Wi-Fi Internet connections. Plus, the iPhone 5 runs iOS 6, which offers not only more than 200 new features (compared to iOS 5.1), but also a selection of totally redesigned apps and a few new core apps.

Yes, like virtually all smartphones on the market, the iPhone 5 (shown in Figure 1-1) enables you to make and receive phone calls, surf the Internet, manage multiple e-mail accounts simultaneously, and send and receive text messages. It also includes a powerful digital camera, and it can be used as a tool for managing your schedule, contacts, to-do lists, notes, and a wide range of other important data and tasks.

With its larger screen, the iPhone 5 is also an amazingly robust portable entertainment system that gives you access to your digital music library, TV show episodes, movies, audiobooks, e-books, digital editions of newspapers and magazines, and a vast selection of streaming multimedia content from the Internet. Your new iPhone 5 is also capable of playing games, real-time video conferencing, and so much more.

FIGURE 1-1 Apple's iPhone 5

In addition to offering state-of-the-art hardware, Apple's latest smartphone operates using the company's proprietary iOS 6 operating system, which is the most advanced, versatile, and feature-packed mobile operating system ever created for Apple devices. iOS 6 offers full integration with Apple's iCloud service, which makes syncing data and files between your iPhone, iPad, iPad mini, iPod touch, and Mac or PC-based computers an extremely easy process.

Note Apple's iCloud service is a free, cloud-based file sharing service that is fully integrated into iOS 6, but it also works seamlessly with Macs (and can be used with PCs). Using this service makes it easy to sync and transfer data, files, and content between your iPhone and other devices and computers wirelessly, via the Internet. Once it's set up, the data syncing process happens in real time, automatically, and in the background. iCloud offers a handful of features that are not offered by other cloud-based file sharing services. Setting up an iCloud account takes just a minute or two, and it includes 5GB of online storage space, free additional storage space for purchased content, and a personal e-mail address.

Did You Know?

From 2007–2012: A Look Back at the iPhone's Past

In just five or so short years, Apple has dramatically changed the way people communicate while on the go. Back in 2007, *Time* magazine referred the original iPhone as the innovation of the year and as "the phone that has changed phones forever." The original iPhone quickly became the bestselling smartphone in the world. But that was just the beginning.

If you were to compare the original iPhone with the iPhone 5, the iPhone released just over five years ago might seem as antiquated as a rotary dial landline phone, with functionality that doesn't come close to rivaling what today's iPhone model is capable of. Each generation of iPhone has met and often exceeded a new level of expectations among consumers.

With each new iPhone model that's been introduced, the iOS operating system has also taken great strides forward. Also, no other line of smartphones in the history of global telecommunications has been supported by so many third-party apps and optional accessories.

At the same time, no other smartphone has been so popular among consumers in countries all over the world. Just days after Apple released the iPhone 5, the company announced it sold more than 5 million units within the first week of its availability. That same week, radio personality and *America's Got Talent* judge Howard Stern talked about his new iPhone 5 and said, "It's more than a phone. It's a lifestyle."

If you're a first-time iPhone user, it won't be long before the iPhone 5 becomes an indispensible tool that you use in many aspects of your personal and professional life. However, if you're a veteran iPhone user who has upgraded to the iPhone 5, between the new technology that's packed into the iPhone itself and the new iOS 6 operating system, you should prepare yourself to be amazed at what's now possible.

Battery Life of the iPhone 5

Even with all of the new features packed into the iPhone 5, its battery life provides about 8 hours of web browsing on a 3G or 4G cellular network (or up to 10 hours using Wi-Fi), or 8 hours of talk time, up to 10 hours of video playback, up to 40 hours of audio playback, or up to 225 hours of standby time. However, since you'll probably use a handful of these different functions daily, how long the battery lasts in between charges will vary.

As you'll discover in Chapter 21, a variety of optional external battery packs and other charging options are available, so you can keep your iPhone fully operational all day, whether you're at home, at work, in your car, or while on the go.

Acquaint Yourself with the Anatomy of the iPhone 5

If you've used a previous iPhone model, when you first look at the iPhone 5 in your hand, you'll immediately notice that it has a larger, 4-inch (diagonally measured) touch screen compared to the 3.5-inch screen of previous models, as shown in Figure 1-2. The width of the screen remains the same. All iPhone-compatible apps will work flawlessly on the iPhone 5, including those not specifically designed for the iPhone 5's larger display. Thanks to the larger display size, the Home Screen benefits by being able to display an extra row of icons.

Apps not specifically designed for the iPhone 5 will be surrounded by a small black frame on the screen.

However, many app developers are quickly updating their apps so that the apps automatically detect when they're being used on an iPhone 5 and adjust the graphics and onscreen menus and content accordingly.

 Tip   If you're upgrading from an older iPhone model, all of the apps you've purchased to date from the App Store will be fully functional on your iPhone 5, starting immediately.

On the front of the iPhone, near the bottom center, is the Home button. Near the top center of the iPhone's front is one of its built-in speakers and microphones, above which is the FaceTime camera (which can also be used for snapping photos, shooting video, or participating in video calls via the Internet).

The very bottom of the iPhone 5, shown next, sports the new Lightning connector port (which can be used for connecting the iPhone to other devices or charging the

FIGURE 1-2   Compared to the previous iPhone models, the iPhone 5 has a larger, more vibrant screen. Shown here is the iPhone 4S (left) and the iPhone 5 (right).

iPhone), the headphone jack, an additional built-in speaker (on the far right), and one of the iPhone's built-in microphones (next to the headphone jack).

Taking a look at the iPhone 5's left side, shown in Figure 1-3, you'll find the Ring/Silent switch, as well as the Volume Up and Volume Down buttons. Figure 1-3 also shows the Power button (also referred to as the Sleep/Wake button) on the top of the iPhone 5. On the opposite side of the iPhone is a tiny Micro-SIM port. It's within this slot that your iPhone's Micro-SIM chip, provided by your selected wireless service provider, comes preinstalled.

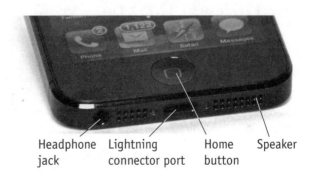

Headphone   Lightning   Home   Speaker
jack   connector port   button

On the smooth back of the iPhone 5, you'll discover the second built-in camera. This one offers 8MP resolution and a tiny but powerful built-in flash, as well as yet another built-in microphone.

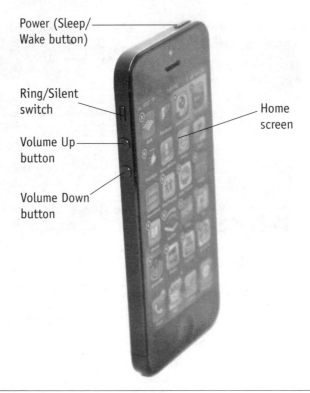

Power (Sleep/
Wake button)

Ring/Silent
switch

Home
screen

Volume Up
button

Volume Down
button

FIGURE 1-3   The left side of the iPhone 5 is where you'll find the Ring/Silent switch and the Volume Up and Volume Down buttons. On the top of the iPhone (to the right) is the Power (Sleep/Wake) button.

Discover the Many Ways to Interact with Your iPhone

Just like all of the previous iPhone models, the iPhone 5 offers a virtual onscreen keyboard that pops up on the screen only when it's needed for data entry. However, thanks to iOS 6, you also have access to Siri and the Dictation feature, which allow you to issue voice commands and requests to your iPhone, or enter text by speaking into your iPhone.

In Chapter 2, you'll learn all about how to interact with your iPhone. It includes an introduction to some of the optional, external keyboards that are compatible with the iPhone, which can make data entry faster and more accurate, especially when you're using a word processing app, such as Pages.

Much of your interaction with your iPhone will be done using a series of finger taps, swipes, flicks, and pinches applied with your finger(s) directly on the Multi-Touch display.

Learn About the iPhone 5's Useful New Features

At the time of writing, Apple still offers the iPhone 4 and iPhone 4S models (older iPhone models have been discontinued, but may be available as used or refurbished phones on the secondhand market). Starting with the iPhone 3GS, all later versions of the iPhone are capable of running iOS 6. However, only the iPhone 5 offers the most advanced technology and features, which is why so many people are opting to upgrade to this iPhone model.

Some older iPhone models are not able to utilize all of iOS 6's latest features and functions. For that, you'll need the iPhone 5.

In a nutshell, some of the reasons to upgrade to or choose the iPhone 5 are these advanced features:

- A larger (4-inch diagonal), more vibrant, and higher-resolution Retina Multi-Touch display. (All previous iPhone models have featured a 3.5-inch diagonal display.) The 44 percent greater color saturation that's offered by the new display becomes obvious when viewing movies, TV shows, streaming HD video, your own digital photos, or the graphics displayed within apps.
- A taller, thinner, and lighter design. The iPhone 5 is 9 mm (about .35 inches) taller than other iPhone models, which gives you more onscreen real estate to view your favorite apps and access the onscreen virtual keyboard, for example. It is also 18 percent thinner and 20 percent lighter than previous iPhone models.

The newly designed iPhone now fits more ergonomically in your hand, and can be used more efficiently with your thumb(s) and finger(s) to type and navigate using one or both hands.

- Higher-resolution front and back cameras with more built-in features for taking photos and shooting video in various lighting situations. The iPhone 5 offers a Panorama photography mode, and can record video in 1080p HD. Figure 1-4 shows a sample photo shot using Panorama mode on the higher-resolution, rear-facing camera that's built into the iPhone 5.
- The new Lightning connector port on the bottom. This replaces the older, 30-pin Dock Connector port (which was first introduced in 2003 for the iPod). A Lightning to USB Cable (shown in Figure 1-5) is included with the iPhone 5. You can use it to connect your iPhone to your primary computer and to charge your iPhone from an electrical outlet (using the supplied adapter). In the near future, many optional devices, such as external speakers, will support the Lightning connector port. In the meantime, the Apple Store sells an optional Lightning to 30-Pin Adapter ($29, http://store.apple.com/us/product/MD823/lightning-to-30-pin-adapter), so you can easily connect your iPhone 5 with any other optional accessories that were designed for the older iPhone models.

FIGURE 1-4 The iPhone's Camera app now allows you to shoot vibrant, full-color, panoramic photos.

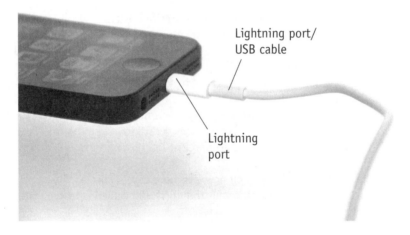

Lightning port/
USB cable

Lightning
port

FIGURE 1-5 The Lightning connector port on the bottom of the iPhone 5 connects to the USB cable that comes with the iPhone. Use it to charge the iPhone or to connect your primary computer to your iPhone.

- A faster A6 processor chip, which doubles the speed of the iPhone's processing and graphics power, compared to the iPhone 4S.
- An additional (third) built-in microphone (one on the front, one on the back, and one on the bottom). These microphones are used to capture the best audio quality possible, whether you're participating in a phone call, recording a video, or using the FaceTime or Skype app, for example, to do real-time video conferencing. These microphones also enhance Siri's accuracy when it comes to understanding your voice commands and requests, or translating your spoken words into text using the iPhone's Dictation feature.

Noise cancellation and what Apple refers to as "wide-band audio technology" have been incorporated into the iPhone 5's microphones and speakers, ensuring you'll be heard by and be able to hear the people you're speaking or video conferencing with.

- Apple's newly designed EarPod headphones with a built-in remote and microphone. (The EarPod headphones can be purchased separately for other iPhone models for $29.)
- Faster Wi-Fi Internet connectivity, plus Bluetooth 4.0 compatibility.

 Many people opt to use a Bluetooth wireless headset to enhance clarity and hands-free functionality of the iPhone when participating in phone calls or listening to music, for example. You'll learn more about these optional accessories in Chapter 7.

- Full iOS 6 support. This includes integration with Siri and Apple iCloud, as well as Facebook and Twitter, plus a collection of preinstalled apps that add a tremendous level of functionality to the iPhone, right out of the box. From within the Notification Center (shown in Figure 1-6), for example, you can now compose and post Facebook status updates and compose and send tweets to your Twitter

FIGURE 1-6   Using iOS 6, you can now update your Facebook status or send a tweet directly from the Notification Center, regardless of which apps are running on your iPhone.

followers, regardless of which apps are running on your iPhone. There's no need to first launch the Facebook or Twitter app.

 While Siri was introduced with iOS 5 for the iPhone 4S, this functionality has since been improved. Siri can now provide sports- and movie-related information, launch apps, and respond to many more types of questions, commands, and other spoken requests. You'll learn all about how to access and use Siri in Chapter 2. In subsequent chapters, you'll learn how to use the iPhone 5's other built-in apps, such as Contacts, Calendar, Reminders, Notes, Safari, Messages, Passbook, Camera, Photos, and Maps.

- Improved core app integration. With iOS 6 running on the iPhone 5, apps can now more seamlessly share app-specific data with each other. Plus, many of these same apps can tap into the iPhone's Location Services feature to pinpoint your exact location and use it to provide you with details that you need about the world around you, such as the local weather forecast, or how to get from your current location to any destination of your choosing, using real-time, turn-by-turn directions displayed in conjunction with stunningly detailed maps.
- The Passbook app (which is new to iOS 6). Passbook enables you to manage many of your tickets, store cards, gift cards, airline boarding passes, digital coupons, and other related information from one centralized app. This app can detect your location and display relevant data. For example, when you get to the airport, your airline boarding pass will automatically pop up on your iPhone's screen. Or, when you enter into any Starbucks, your prepaid Starbucks card (which can now be stored on your iPhone) will appear on the iPhone's display, so you can quickly and easily pay for your purchases.

Choose the Perfect iPhone 5 for Yourself

If you haven't yet purchased your iPhone 5, let's take a few minutes to review your various options so that you're certain to select the best hardware configuration to meet your needs. Once you purchase an iPhone 5, it is not upgradable in terms of its internal storage space, and you can't switch wireless service providers without buying a new phone, so you need to consider how you'll use your iPhone in the long term.

Unless you purchase an unlocked version of the iPhone 5 (and pay full price for it), you'll need to commit to a two-year contract with the wireless service provider you choose (which in the United States could be AT&T Wireless, Verizon Wireless or Sprint PCS). Other wireless service providers may, however, add support for the iPhone 5 in the future.

Whether you visit an Apple Store, Apple.com, an Apple authorized reseller, or an authorized agent for AT&T Wireless, Verizon Wireless, or Sprint PCS, when purchasing your iPhone 5, you'll need to make a few decisions, several of which are rather important.

Did You Know?

The iPhone 5 Integrates with Apple's iCloud Service in Many New Ways

In the past, to sync and back up your iPhone, it was necessary to connect the iPhone to your primary computer via a supplied USB cable, and then use the iTunes software on your computer to perform an iTunes sync. The iTunes sync process backs up your iPhone's content onto your primary computer and simultaneously syncs apps, files, and data between the iPhone and your Mac or PC. However, most people now use wireless iCloud functionality to back up and sync app-specific data between their iPhone, iPad, iPad mini, iPod touch, Mac(s), and/or PC(s) that are linked to the same Apple ID account.

In conjunction with the release of iOS 6 and the iPhone 5, iCloud integration was again enhanced, allowing for real-time, app-specific data syncing for the Contacts, Calendar, Reminders, Notes, and Safari apps. Plus, the functionality of the iCloud Photo Stream feature has been improved, and the new Shared Photo Stream feature has been introduced.

iCloud also works with the optional iWork for iOS apps (Pages, Numbers, and Keynote), so your Microsoft Word–compatible documents, Excel-compatible spreadsheets, and/or PowerPoint-compatible digital slide presentations can all automatically remain synced between your computer(s), tablet, and iPhone.

Once app-specific data is synced with your free iCloud account, that same data can also sync in real time with your other iOS mobile devices (including your iPad and iPod touch), as well as your Mac or PC-based computers, as long as they are linked to the same Apple ID account. Thus, when you update an entry within the Contacts app, for example, that change is almost immediately reflected within your contacts database on your primary computer and other mobile devices.

Once you have your iPhone app-specific data being synced in real time with iCloud, you can also access the data for free using online-based apps through the iCloud website (www.icloud.com). Simply go to this website from any computer or mobile device that can connect to the Internet, and log in using your Apple ID and password. So, if you accidentally forget your iPhone at home or at work, or leave it in your car, you can always use another device or computer to look up a contact, access your to-do lists, check your schedule, or access document files, for example.

Choose the Color of Your iPhone

Each hardware configuration of the iPhone 5 is currently available in a white or black casing. The operation of a black or white iPhone is absolutely identical, so it's a matter of personal preference as to which color you select.

When considering color, keep in mind that, to protect your iPhone 5 investment, you'll probably want to use a case or some type of optional cover with the iPhone, both while it's in use and during transport, so chances are, the back and sides of the iPhone itself will be covered up anyway.

Cases and covers for the iPhone 5 come in a wide range of designs and colors, so you can easily find one that fits your budget, offers an appropriate level of protection based on how active your lifestyle is, and fits nicely with your personality and sense of style.

Choose a Storage Capacity

The second decision you'll need to make when purchasing an iPhone is how much internal storage space it should contain. Ultimately, this determines how many apps, how many files, and how much data it can hold. As you make this decision, think about how you'll be using your iPhone in the future and the type of content that you'll store on it.

The iPhone 5 is available with 16GB, 32GB, or 64GB of internal storage. The iPhone's storage capacity also determines how much you'll pay for it. Assuming you're signing up for a two-year service agreement with a wireless service provider, the subsidized price of a new iPhone 5 is $199 (16GB), $299 (32GB), or $399 (64GB). However, without the subsidized pricing, expect to pay anywhere from $649 to $849 (or more) for a new iPhone 5 that has no long-term wireless service contract (with a monthly fee) associated with it.

 Apps, digital photos you shoot, digital files associated with TV show episodes, movies, music, e-books, digital publications, audio books, files associated with videos you shoot, your data and files associated with apps, and other content that's stored within your iPhone will all take up some of its internal storage space. The more storage space you have on your iPhone, the more apps, content, files, and data it'll be able to hold.

Select a Wireless Service Provider and Service Plan

At the time you purchase your iPhone, you'll need to select a wireless service provider. Currently, in the United States, your options include AT&T Wireless, Verizon Wireless, and Sprint PCS. The internal hardware configuration of the iPhone 5 for each wireless service provider is slightly different, and they are not compatible.

 If you purchase an iPhone that's compatible with Sprint PCS, for example, you will not be able to switch to another wireless service provider in the future without purchasing a new iPhone.

Before you select a wireless service provider, look closely at the plans being offered. Each wireless service provider offers at least several different service plans (at different price points) for the iPhone, as well as additional add-on services, all of which are fee based.

When you choose a wireless service provider and choose a service plan, a monthly fee will be associated with that plan, and you'll be making a two-year commitment to that service provider (although, during that time, you can change service plans).

Caution   If you cancel your wireless service plan early, you will typically incur an early termination fee of up to $350.

The specific service plan you choose will have three main components:

- **Talk time**   How many minutes you have per month to talk on your iPhone.
- **Text messaging**   The number of text messages you can send and receive each month using the provider's 3G/4G-based text messaging service, which allows you to communicate with any other cell phone or smartphone. Apple's iMessage service, however, is free of charge and is web based. It allows you to send and receive unlimited text messages and instant messages with other iPhone, iPad, iPad mini, iPod touch, and Mac users.
- **Wireless Web**   The amount of wireless data you can send and receive using the cellular service provider's 3G or 4G wireless data network.

Note   In addition to these three components, one of the extra options you can pay for (where available) is the ability to use your iPhone while outside the country to make/receive calls, send/receive text messages, and/or surf the Web.

Before deciding which wireless service provider to go with, visit Apple's website and access the iPhone 5 information page (http://store.apple.com/us/browse/home/shop_iphone/family/iphone). Click the View Rate Plans option to compare the various plans offered by AT&T Wireless, Verizon Wireless, and Sprint PCS in one place, or visit each company's website separately by pointing your web browser to

- **AT&T Wireless**   www.att.com
- **Verizon Wireless**   www.verizonwireless.com
- **Sprint PCS**   www.sprintpcs.com

In addition to the wireless service plans available to individuals, each wireless service provider offers special family plans (for use with multiple phones). They also offer separate plans for individuals who want to use multiple wireless devices (such as an iPhone and an iPad) on the same plan.

Note   While your wireless data plan may limit how much wireless data usage on a 3G or 4G network you're allowed per month, you always have the option to connect to a Wi-Fi hotspot or home wireless network, or use the Personal Hotspot feature of another wireless device to connect to the Internet via your iPhone, without utilizing any of your monthly 3G/4G wireless data allocation.

The wireless data plan component of your service agreement may include 1GB, 2GB, or 5GB of wireless data usage per month. If you go above that usage, you'll incur a per-gigabyte fee, unless you sign up for a plan that includes unlimited wireless data usage.

When comparing plans, ideally, you want one that offers unlimited voice, unlimited texting, and unlimited data for a flat monthly fee. However, you will typically find less expensive plans that offer one component on an unlimited basis and predetermined allocations for the other components, such as wireless data usage. For example, a plan might offer 500 minutes of talk time, unlimited text messaging, and 2GB of wireless data usage per month.

Along with analyzing the service plans being offered by the various service providers, look carefully at their coverage maps, and make sure wireless service is readily available in the cities or regions where you'll be using the iPhone the most. As you do this comparison, look for 4G (or preferably 4G LTE) wireless coverage, as opposed to 3G coverage.

 Many of the iPhone 5's core features, including surfing the Web, streaming web content, managing e-mail, video conferencing, using Siri, using the iPhone's Dictation feature, and using many apps (such as Maps, Facebook, and Twitter, for example), all rely heavily on Internet access. If no Wi-Fi Internet connection is available, you could quickly use up your monthly wireless data allocation if you're not careful, so plan accordingly when choosing a wireless data plan to avoid unexpected fees. Keep in mind, streaming video content from the Internet using Netflix, YouTube, or a television network's proprietary app (such as ABC Player or HBO Go) requires a tremendous amount of wireless data usage.

4G (4G LTE) wireless data service is up to ten times faster than 3G service. Some wireless service providers, however, do not yet have 4G (4G LTE) service in many areas of the country, except for within major U.S. cities and metropolitan areas. Especially if you'll be using your iPhone a lot to access the Internet using the wireless data network offered by your wireless service provider (as opposed to a Wi-Fi hotspot or wireless home network), the ability to connect at 4G (or 4G LTE) speeds is highly beneficial.

How to Use a Specialized App to Manage Your Wireless Service Plan Directly from Your iPhone

Once you've activated your iPhone 5 with the wireless service provider of your choice and have selected a wireless data plan, be sure to download the free app from AT&T Wireless, Version Wireless, or Sprint PCS that allows you to manage your account directly from your iPhone. The app enables you to pay your monthly bill from your iPhone and, more importantly, view your usage so that you don't exceed your allocated talk time, number of text messages sent or received, or wireless data allocation, any of which will result in additional (and sometimes hefty) fees.

 How to set up and activate your new iPhone 5 and (if you're upgrading) how to easily transfer data from an older iPhone model to your iPhone 5 are covered in Chapter 3 and Chapter 4. Chapter 20 covers how to use the App Store to find, download, and install optional apps onto your iPhone 5.

To find, download, and install the free app that's offered by your wireless service provider, from your iPhone, launch the App Store app when your iPhone has access to the Internet. Next, tap the Search icon that's displayed at the bottom of the screen. Within the Search field that appears, enter the name of your wireless service provider (AT&T Wireless, Verizon Wireless, or Sprint PCS).

The app preview window for the proprietary iPhone app available from that service provider will be displayed. For AT&T Wireless, you'll want to download and install the free myAT&T app, shown in Figure 1-7. For Verizon Wireless, you'll want to

FIGURE 1-7   Use the myAT&T app to manage your AT&T Wireless account from your phone.

download and install the free My Verizon Mobile app. If you've become a Sprint PCS customer, download and install the free Sprint Zone app.

Once the app is installed on your iPhone, set up the Alert feature that's built into the app to remind you when your monthly payments are due. Most importantly, however, you'll want to refer to the app periodically to make sure you aren't close to exceeding or haven't already exceeded the various voice calling, texting, and/or wireless data allocations associated with your account.

2

Set Up and Configure Your iPhone 5

HOW TO...

- Turn on and activate the iPhone
- Set up your iPhone 5 for the first time
- Discover the difference between Sleep mode, Airplane mode, and Wi-Fi only mode
- Set up an Apple ID account
- Customize the Notification Center

When you purchase your iPhone, you are given a slick-looking box that fits in the palm of your hand. Within this box is everything you need to begin using your iPhone 5: the iPhone itself, a small printed information packet, official Apple stickers, your new Apple EarPods, a white Lightning to USB Cable, and an AC power adapter. However, before you can begin using your iPhone's functions, you first need to activate and set up the device after registering it.

Regardless of where you purchased your iPhone 5, if you're within the United States, at the time of purchase, you'll set up a new wireless service account with AT&T Wireless, Verizon Wireless, or Sprint PCS, or upgrade your old phone and swap it for the iPhone 5 (potentially keeping your old service plan and transferring your mobile phone number). Either way, at the time of purchase, the iPhone was registered to you and assigned a phone number.

 If you purchased an unlocked iPhone 5 at full price, with no service plan associated with it, you'll need to insert a compatible micro-SIM chip into the phone to associate a phone number and wireless service plan with it. In some cases, the unlocked phone will come with a micro-SIM chip installed.

Charge Your New iPhone's Battery

At the time of purchase, the iPhone's battery will be partially charged. If you plan to sync the iPhone with your primary computer and transfer data to it from your older-model iPhone using iTunes Sync, you'll want to connect the iPhone to the computer using the supplied Lightning to USB Cable. Your iPhone 5 can recharge its battery from power supplied by your primary computer when the computer and iPhone are connected via the supplied USB cable.

If you plan to use iCloud to transfer content to your iPhone, or set up the iPhone 5 as a new device, to begin charging the device, attach the supplied AC power adapter to the Lightning to USB Cable, and then plug the adapter into an electrical outlet and the opposite end of the cable into the Lightning port on the bottom of your iPhone.

As long as the iPhone is plugged into an external power source and charging, you can continue to use it in order to activate and configure it for the first time. Keep the iPhone charging until the battery indicator that's displayed near the top-right corner of the screen displays it as fully charged. You're now ready to activate and set up your new iPhone 5!

Activate and Set Up Your New iPhone

Begin the activation and setup process by turning on your iPhone. To do this, press and hold down the Power button for about three seconds. (The Power button is also referred to as the Sleep/Wake button.) It's located at the top of the device near the right corner. The Apple logo will appear on the screen, and the iPhone will power up.

 The activation and setup process only needs to be done once.

After between 10 and 15 seconds, the Apple logo will be replaced by a gray screen that simply says iPhone (shown in Figure 2-1). Place your finger on the slider that's displayed near the bottom of the screen, and slide your finger from left to right.

The Welcome screen is now displayed (shown in Figure 2-2). Choose your language by tapping your selection. The default option is English. However, if you tap the downward-pointing arrow, dozens of additional language options are displayed. After selecting your language option, tap the right-pointing arrow icon that's displayed near the top-right corner of the screen to continue.

Next, choose your country or region (shown in Figure 2-3). If you purchased the iPhone within the United States, that will be your default option. You can, however, tap the Show More option to choose another country or region. Tap the Next button that's displayed near the top-right corner of the screen to continue.

You're now asked to choose a network (shown in Figure 2-4). If you're within a Wi-Fi hotspot or the signal radius of a wireless network, a listing of available networks will be displayed. Select one to continue. If, however, no Wi-Fi hotspot is present, or

FIGURE 2-1   This is what is displayed the very first time you turn on your iPhone 5.

FIGURE 2-2   Begin the activation process by choosing a default language.

FIGURE 2-3 Select a country or region where you'll primarily be using your iPhone.

FIGURE 2-4 Your iPhone needs access to the Internet (via Wi-Fi, 3G/4G, or an iTunes connection with a computer that has access to the Internet) to continue the activation process.

you do not have the password to access a locked hotspot, you'll be given the option to use a cellular connection or connect your iPhone to iTunes (via your primary computer). To continue, you'll need to select a method for your iPhone to connect to the Internet. Once the connection is established, tap the Next icon to continue.

A message appears on the screen that says, "Activating Your iPhone.... It may take a few minutes to activate your iPhone." Within between 15 seconds and two minutes, the Location Services screen will be displayed (shown in Figure 2-5).

Tap the Enable Location Services option, and then tap the Next button to continue. You are asked how you want to set up your iPhone, as shown in Figure 2-6. You're given the following three options: Set Up As New iPhone, Restore From iCloud Backup, and Restore From iTunes Backup. These options are described, in turn, in the following sections, with instructions on how to proceed after choosing each.

 Choose Restore From iCloud Backup or Restore From iTunes Backup if you're a current iPhone 3Gs, iPhone 4, or iPhone 4S user who is upgrading to the iPhone 5 and you want to easily transfer the older iPhone's content and settings to the new iPhone. If you need to transfer and sync data from other (non-Apple) smartphone or tablet models, as well as data from software running on your computer(s), from your network, or from online-based apps, you can do that later, as explained in Chapter 4.

FIGURE 2-5   Turn on the master Location Services feature now. You can later customize which apps can utilize it (and how) from within Settings.

FIGURE 2-6 Set up the iPhone 5 as a new device or restore data from another iPhone's backup files.

Did You Know? **Your iPhone Can Track Your Location**

Your iPhone has built-in GPS capabilities. Many core iPhone functions, as well as the apps you'll soon be using, rely on the iPhone's ability to pinpoint and track your exact location. None of these tracking capabilities function if you turn off the master Location Services option during the activation process. For now, turn on this option. Later, you can customize this option from within Settings and determine specifically which apps and iPhone functions are allowed to access your location information (and potentially share it).

Set Up as New iPhone

Choose this option if you're a new iPhone user and do not plan to restore data, apps, content, and phone preferences from a backup you created using your previous iPhone model. If you select this option, once the iPhone is activated, only the apps that come preinstalled with iOS 6 will be loaded on your iPhone, and all iPhone settings will be set at their factory defaults.

If you want to continue activating the iPhone using this option, tap the Set Up As New iPhone option and then tap the Next button. You'll be asked whether you want to sign in with your Apple ID account or create a new, free Apple ID (shown in Figure 2-7). Signing in with an Apple ID will allow you to link your new iPhone with your other Mac(s), PC(s), and iOS mobile devices in order to share and sync data and iTunes content wirelessly via iCloud.

If you have an established Apple ID account, tap the Sign In With An Apple ID option and then enter your Apple ID and password. If you do not have an Apple ID account, you can set one up by tapping the Create A Free Apple ID option. You also have the option to Skip This Step by tapping the option displayed near the lower-right corner of the screen. You can then later provide this information within Settings, when you're required to enter Apple ID information in order to use iCloud, the iTunes Store, the App Store, iBookstore, Newsstand, iMessage, or FaceTime.

When you supply your Apple ID information, all of your Contacts, Calendar, Reminders, Notes, Photos, and Safari data from other computers and iOS mobile devices that are linked to that account, as well as your previous Apple content purchases (including purchases from the iTunes Store, App Store, iBookstore, and Newsstands) and your Photo Stream content, can be downloaded and synced

FIGURE 2-7   When prompted, proceed to enter your existing Apple ID account information or set up a new Apple ID account.

How to... Set Up or Manage a Free Apple ID Account

As you'll discover, apps with which you can make online purchases from Apple—for music, TV shows, movies, audiobooks, e-books, digital publications, or apps, for example—require that you to have an active Apple ID account. That account needs to be linked to a credit card or debit card account if you want to make one-tap online purchases from your iPhone. It's possible to set up an Apple ID without using a credit or debit card, but to make online purchases through any of Apple's online business ventures, you'll then need to acquire and redeem iTunes Gift Cards, which are available from Apple Stores, Apple.com, and just about anywhere gift cards are sold. To learn more about iTunes Gift Cards, visit www.apple.com/gift-cards.

Beyond just allowing you to make purchases, however, your Apple ID is used by other apps, like Messages and FaceTime, and is typically used for your iCloud account as well. When creating an iCloud account (which is Apple's online file sharing, data syncing, and data backup service), most people opt to use their Apple ID and password as their iCloud username and password. However, you can set up your iCloud account using a different username (e-mail address) and password if you want to be able to share apps and content purchased from Apple with other computers and iOS mobile devices that are linked to the same Apple ID account, but you do not want app-specific data (from Contacts, Calendar, Reminders, Notes, Photos, Safari, and so on) to be synced with those other computers or devices.

To get the most functionality out of your iPhone and the apps you'll be using with it, you'll ultimately need an Apple ID account and an iCloud account associated with your iPhone. If you already own or use another Apple product, such as a Mac, iPad, iPad mini, iPod, or Apple TV, you probably have an Apple ID account established. To set up a new Apple ID, manage your account, or recover your forgotten username or password, visit https://appleid.apple.com.

automatically with your iPhone 5. This happens almost instantly, assuming your iPhone has Internet access. You can, however, determine which iCloud features and functions to activate. To do this, launch Settings and tap on the iCloud option.

After you sign in with your Apple ID or tap Skip This Step, the Siri screen shown in Figure 2-8 appears. You're given the choice of whether or not you want to activate the iPhone's Siri feature. This feature allows you to handle a wide range of tasks using voice commands and requests, as covered in Chapter 3. Tap the Use Siri option to turn on this feature, or tap Don't Use Siri to deactivate it altogether. You can always adjust this option from within Settings. For now, tap the Use Siri feature, and then tap the Next button to continue.

FIGURE 2-8   Turn on the Siri feature if you want to be able to issue commands and utilize many iPhone features using your voice.

On the Diagnostics screen, you're given two options—Automatically Send or Don't Send. If you tap the Automatically Send option, this helps Apple track the operation of the iOS operating system and apps, and automatically track problems you and other iPhone users encounter. Tap either option, followed by the Next button to continue.

The iPhone 5 activation process is now completed. The Thank You screen is displayed (shown in Figure 2-9). Tap the Start Using iPhone button to access the Home screen (shown in Figure 2-10).

At this point, you can begin making or receiving calls or using any of the apps that come preinstalled with iOS 6. If this is your first iPhone, and you have a new phone number associated with it, now's also a good time to set up your voicemail options and record your outgoing message. See Chapter 7 for details. You'll then want to customize some of the iPhone 5's settings and functions, starting with the Notification Center (as described later in this chapter).

When you activate a new iPhone (with its factory settings intact), the Home screen displays the core apps that come preinstalled with iOS 6, as well as generic wallpaper for the Lock screen and Home screen. You can customize the look of the Lock screen and Home screen, as well as the ringtones and sounds the iPhone generates for alerts and alarms, for example, by following the directions in Chapter 6.

FIGURE 2-9 Tap the Start Using iPhone button to begin using your new iPhone. The activation process is completed.

FIGURE 2-10 The iPhone's Home screen with just the preinstalled apps and the default wallpaper displayed

Restore from iCloud Backup

If you're upgrading from an older iPhone model and have used the iCloud Backup feature to create a full backup of that device in conjunction with your existing iCloud account, you'll be able to wirelessly transfer and restore all of your apps, data, photos, files, and preferences from your old iPhone to your new one by selecting the Restore From iCloud Backup option. To use the Restore From iCloud Backup option, your iPhone 5 must have access to a Wi-Fi Internet connection.

If you select this option, you'll be prompted to enter your Apple ID and password (or your iCloud username and password) and agree to Apple's Terms and Conditions. Next, you'll be asked to select which version of the backup you want to use to restore your data onto your new iPhone. The dates and times of previous iPhone backups will be displayed on the Choose Backup screen. Tap your selection, and then tap the Restore button to begin the process. Depending on the amount of data that needs to be restored, this process could take up to an hour, so be patient.

At the same time that iCloud Backup restores your iPhone preferences, apps, photos, and files, all of your app-specific data that was also set up to sync with iCloud from your old iPhone, as well as your Mac(s), PC(s), iPad, and other iOS mobile devices that are linked to the same iCloud account, will also sync with your new iPhone 5.

 When you use the free iCloud Backup feature to create and maintain a complete backup of your iPhone's contents, the backup data files are stored "in the cloud" within your iCloud account. The backup files created will utilize some of the free 5GB of online storage space that Apple provides you with when you create your iCloud account. The benefit to using the iCloud Backup feature is that you can then restore your data to an iPhone wirelessly, from anywhere a Wi-Fi Internet connection is available.

Restore from iTunes Backup

The Restore From iTunes Backup option allows you to transfer your iPhone settings, apps, data, content, and files from your old iPhone to your new iPhone 5 using the iTunes sync process. For this option to work, you'll need to have created a backup of your old iPhone using the iTunes sync process in conjunction with your primary computer.

 The iTunes sync process allows you to back up and transfer data between your iPhone and your primary computer (a Mac or PC) using Apple's free iTunes software that's running on your computer. When you choose the iTunes Sync or iTunes Wireless Sync option, your iPhone's backup files are stored on your primary computer's hard drive. Thus, to access those files and restore an iPhone from a backup, the iPhone needs to be connected to the primary computer where the backup files are stored.

After selecting this option, you'll be prompted to connect your iPhone 5 to your primary computer running the latest version of iTunes. You can connect your iPhone to your computer either by using the supplied Lightning to USB Cable or by using a wireless connection if your iPhone and computer are connected to the same wireless network. Once the connection is made, your iPhone 5 will be activated and all of your iPhone settings, apps, content, files, photos, and data will be transferred to your new iPhone. Depending on how much data needs to be transferred and restored, this process could take 30 minutes or longer.

 When the Restore From iCloud or Restore From iTunes Backup process is completed, your iPhone 5 will be activated, and all of your iPhone settings, apps, data, content, and files will be transferred from your old iPhone onto your iPhone 5, which will be running iOS 6.

Place Your Phone in Sleep or Airplane Mode

Aside from simply being powered on or off, your iPhone has several other "states," like Sleep mode and Airplane mode, that you'll want and need to utilize in various situations.

Place Your iPhone in Sleep Mode So It Can Continue to Function with the Display Turned Off

When you place your iPhone into Sleep mode, the screen is turned off but the device itself remains functional. The iPhone can transmit data and receive incoming phone calls, text messages, and e-mails, and self-running apps have the ability to access the Internet. Any apps that are running in the background, such as the Notification Center, also continue operating unhindered.

While in Sleep mode, the wireless transmission functions of your iPhone remain operational. So, if you receive a phone call, text message, or incoming e-mail, or if one of the apps you're running (such as Calendar or Reminders) generates an alert, alarm, or notification, you'll be alerted immediately and the iPhone will "wake up" automatically.

To place your phone into Sleep mode at any time (which conserves battery life), press and release the Power button once (don't hold it down). The iPhone's screen will go dark. To then manually wake up the iPhone, press either the Power button or the Home button once.

Regardless of how you wake up your iPhone from Sleep mode, the Lock screen will appear. If you have the Passcode Lock feature turned on, you will need to enter the correct passcode to continue using the device. However, specific functionality, such as answering an incoming call, snapping a photo, controlling the Music app, or activating and using Siri, can be done directly from the Lock screen while the iPhone is still locked. You will, however, have limited access to these features until you enter the proper passcode.

To turn off the iPhone entirely, so it returns to its state of doing absolutely nothing and not being able to transmit or receive anything, press and hold down the Power (Sleep/Wake) button for about five seconds, until the Slide To Power Off slider appears at the top of the screen. Using your finger, move this red and white slider from left to right. The iPhone will shut down within about five seconds.

In Airplane Mode, Your iPhone Can't Transmit

Sometimes you'll want to use some of the functionality of your iPhone but not allow it to transmit or receive data or calls. For example, while you're aboard a commercial airplane, the iPhone must be kept in Airplane mode or powered off altogether.

While in Airplane mode, many of your iPhone's apps will function, but it will be unable to connect to the cellular network. Thus, it will not be able to make or receive calls, access the Internet, or send/receive text messages. Any calls you receive will go directly to voicemail. When you turn off Airplane mode, you will be alerted about any calls, incoming text messages, or e-mails you missed.

To place your iPhone into Airplane mode, from the Home screen, launch Settings by tapping on the Settings icon that's displayed on the Home Screen. Near the top of the Settings screen (shown in Figure 2-11) is a virtual Airplane mode switch. When set to Off, all features of your iPhone will function normally. As long as you're within range of a 3G/4G wireless signal, the iPhone can make and receive calls, access the Internet, and send and receive text messages and e-mails.

FIGURE 2-11   To place your iPhone into Airplane mode, tap the Airplane mode virtual switch to turn it On.

When Airplane mode is turned on, the iPhone itself will function, but any apps or features that require it to transmit will be inactive. A small airplane-shaped icon will appear in the upper-left corner of the screen (replacing the 3G/4G signal strength indicator) when the iPhone is in Airplane mode.

Turn Wi-Fi On and Off Separately

When you initially turn on Airplane mode, your iPhone's ability to transmit is turned off. However, you can then turn on Wi-Fi Internet connectivity separately while in Airplane mode. Thus, your iPhone can still connect to a Wi-Fi hotspot or wireless network even while its 3G/4G connectivity is deactivated.

You also have the option to turn off Wi-Fi while the iPhone is not in Airplane mode. Wi-Fi functionality is independent of your iPhone's ability to access the 3G/4G cellular network operated by your wireless service provider (such as AT&T Wireless, Verizon Wireless, or Sprint PCS).

To turn on or off your iPhone's ability to connect to a Wi-Fi hotspot or wireless network, access the Settings screen (refer to Figure 2-11) and tap the Wi-Fi option. As soon as you turn on this feature, a list of available wireless networks you can connect to is displayed on the Wi-Fi screen within Settings (see Figure 2-12). Tap a network to connect to it.

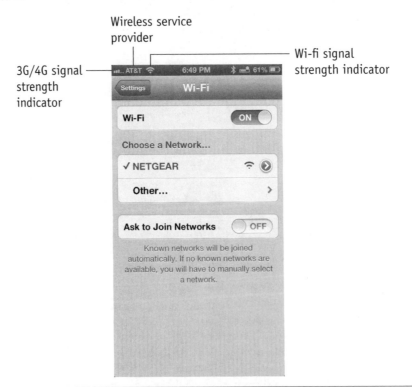

FIGURE 2-12   From the Wi-Fi screen, tap the Wi-Fi hotspot or wireless network you want to connect to.

When Wi-Fi is turned on, the Wi-Fi signal strength indicator is displayed in the upper-left corner of the screen, next to the 3G/4G cellular signal strength indicator. Also, when Wi-Fi is turned on, your iPhone defaults to accessing the Internet using Wi-Fi, to help you reduce your 3G/4G wireless data usage.

Keeping Wi-Fi turned on at all times, even when not within the radius of a Wi-Fi hotspot or wireless network, helps to improve the accuracy of your iPhone's Location Services functionality (when it comes to pinpointing your location and offering GPS navigation). However, keeping Wi-Fi turned on drains your iPhone's battery faster. Likewise, if you keep your iPhone's 3G/4G connectivity turned on when you're not within the signal radius of your wireless service provider's network, this too will drain your iPhone's battery faster, as the iPhone will waste power continuously looking for a signal.

If you attempt to connect to a Wi-Fi hotspot or wireless network that's locked (password protected), you'll be prompted to enter the appropriate password for that network, before you can initially access it.

Enjoy Peace and Quiet by Silencing Your iPhone

Even if your iPhone is in Airplane mode, individual apps, such as Calendar and Reminders, can still generate alerts, alarms, or notifications, either by generating audible alarms or by displaying Banners or Alerts on the screen. (Banners and Alerts are described later in the chapter, in the section "Set Up Alert Options for Each Listed App.")

If you don't want your iPhone to alert or notify you of an incoming call, go to the Settings screen (refer to Figure 2-11) and slide the Do Not Disturb switch to Off, and you will be left alone. Depending on how you have this feature set up, all or most of your calls will go to voicemail. (The section "Customize the Do Not Disturb Feature," later in the chapter, explains how you can customize this feature.) Make sure to turn off the Do Not Disturb feature when you want to start receiving calls again. A tiny, crescent moon–shaped icon appears on the status bar (at the very top of the iPhone's screen, to the immediate left of the time display) to remind you that the feature is turned on.

If you want to silence alerts, alarms, or notifications generated by apps running on your iPhone, instead of using Do Not Disturb, you also have the option to simply mute your iPhone and put it in vibrate mode. Thus, if you're in a meeting or a theater, for example, it will not play a ringtone in conjunction within incoming calls, nor play alarms or other sounds. To mute your iPhone, adjust the switch that's located on the left side of your iPhone (above the Volume Up button) to the off position. You can also mute or lower the speaker volume by accessing Settings and tapping the Sounds option. On the Sounds screen (see Figure 2-13), move the Ringer And Alerts slider to the left to lower the master volume of your iPhone or turn off the sound entirely. Another option is to use the Volume Down button on the side of the phone to lower the ringer until it is silent.

FIGURE 2-13 On the Sounds screen, you can adjust the master volume of your iPhone. This can also be done using the Volume Up and Volume Down buttons on the side of the iPhone.

Customize the Notification Center

The Notification Center continuously runs in the background, regardless of what you're doing on your iPhone. The purpose of this app is to monitor other apps that are running and to manage and display all alerts, alarms, and notifications generated by those apps in one centralized place, the Notification Center screen.

The time you spend initially customizing the Notification Center will allow you to be more productive using your iPhone on an ongoing basis, because you'll be alerted about your most important or time-sensitive tasks, deadlines, appointments, calls, messages, and other information immediately, in a way that you personally find most beneficial.

For example, you can set up the most important alerts, alarms, and notifications to generate a sound or audible alarm, display an Alert on the screen, and include a listing within the Notification Center screen. For app-related items that aren't critical, you can have those apps just display information on the Notification Center screen (or using a Banner), and for items that have no importance to you whatsoever, you can turn off all alerts, alarms, and notifications and have Notification Center ignore that app altogether.

Keep in mind, if the Notification Center is monitoring just 10 apps, and each app can generate up to 10 alerts, alarms, or notifications, at any given time, your Notification Center screen could display up to 100 separate listings that require your attention, in addition to displaying data from the Weather and Stocks widgets and buttons for updating your Facebook and Twitter accounts. Each app that's capable of generating alerts, alarms, or notifications also has the ability to display Alerts or Banners on the screen, generate audible alarms, and/or display a Badge within its respective app icon on the Home screen. (Banners, Alerts, Banners, and Badges are described later in the chapter, in the section "Set Up Alert Options for Each Listed App.")

Thus, to avoid being inundated and annoyed by endless alerts, alarms, and notifications, and to stay well organized and efficient using your iPhone, you'll want to invest a few minutes to fully customize the Notification Center app to determine which apps are monitored and display information on the Notification Center screen, as well as whether or not each compatible app will be able to generate Alerts, Banners, Badges, and/or audible alarms.

Get to Know the Notification Center Screen

At any time, regardless of what you're doing on your iPhone, you can manually access the Notification Center screen by swiping your finger from the very top of the screen in a downward direction. You then use your finger to scroll down or back up within the Notification Center screen. Depending on how you have Notification Center set up, the local weather (based on your current location) will be displayed, thanks to the Weather widget (shown in Figure 2-14). Also, information from the Stocks widget can be displayed, allowing you to showcase current quotes from your own investments. You can turn on or off the Weather and Stocks widget by launching Settings, tapping on the Notifications option, and then tapping on the Share Widget option. If you opt to turn On the Share Widget option, from the Notifications menu screen within Settings, tap on the Edit button that's displayed near the top-right corner of the screen and then use the Move icon to determine where the widget information will be displayed within the Notification Center screen.

 Some of the options that can appear within the Notification Center screen, such as Facebook and Twitter integration, the Weather widget, and the Stocks widget, may need to be turned on before they'll be displayed.

Just below the Weather widget are the Tap To Tweet and Tap To Post buttons. The Tap To Tweet button is used to compose and send a text-based tweet (with no attachments) from the Notification Center screen directly to your Twitter followers online. After tapping the button, type your 140-character (or fewer) message and then tap the Send button to publish your tweet online, without having to first launch the official Twitter app. Use the Tap To Post button to compose and publish a status update to your Facebook page. Compose your message and tap the Post button to publish it online.

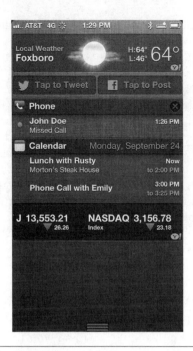

FIGURE 2-14 The Notification Center screen

 When composing either a tweet or a Facebook post, tap the Add Location option that's displayed in the lower-left corner of the screen to attach your current location to the outgoing message. For this feature to work, the Location Services feature for Facebook or Twitter, respectively, must be turned on. To adjust this, launch Settings, tap the Facebook or Twitter option, and then turn on the feature by entering your account information where prompted.

Based on how you customize the Notification Center screen, below the Tap To Tweet and Tap To Post buttons is a heading for each compatible app that the Notification Center is monitoring, such as Phone, Mail, Calendar, Reminders, Messages, Facebook, Twitter, and/or Game Center. Under each heading will be between one and ten alerts, alarms, or notifications generated by that app.

 When a blue dot appears to the left of a listing on your Notification Center screen, this indicates that the alert, alarm, or notification is new and still requires your attention.

Each individual listing on your Notification Center screen is interactive. For example, if you tap a listing under the Phone heading, the Phone app will launch and the iPhone will automatically dial the number of the missed call. Similarly, if it's a listing for a new incoming e-mail, the Mail app will launch and that particular e-mail will be displayed on the iPhone's screen. If an alarm is generated by the Calendar app or Reminders app, tap its respective listing to launch the app and view pertinent information related to the event, deadline, or alarm.

To return to whatever you were doing and close the Notification Center screen, place your finger on the close icon at the bottom of the screen (it looks like three horizontal lines) and flick your finger upward.

As the following section explains, you can customize the order in which app-specific information is displayed within the Notification Center screen, set the maximum number of alerts, alarms, or notifications that will be listed per app, and configure many other options.

Customize the Notification Center

Customizing the Notification Center enables you to determine the following:

- The behavior of the Do Not Disturb feature
- The order in which apps-related listings are displayed on the Notification Center screen
- Which compatible apps the Notification Center will monitor and display alerts, alarms, and/or notifications for
- How many alerts, alarms, and/or notifications the Notification Center will display at one time for each monitored app
- Whether the Weather widget and Stocks widget will display information
- Whether the Tap To Tweet and Tap To Post buttons will be displayed
- The alert options for each monitored app
- Whether Badge app icons are displayed for Badge-compatible apps
- Whether to display app-specific alerts, alarms, and notifications on the Lock screen

To customize the Notification Center, launch Settings and tap the Notifications option to open the Notifications screen.

Customize the Do Not Disturb Feature

As discussed earlier in the chapter, the Do Not Disturb feature can be used to make incoming calls go directly to voicemail. If you turn on this feature in the Settings screen, by default, you will not be alerted about incoming calls (they'll go right to voicemail). A crescent moon–shaped icon appears on the status bar to remind you that the feature is turned on. From the Notifications screen, you can customize the Do Not Disturb feature so that you still receive essential calls.

To do this, launch Settings, tap the Notifications option, and then tap the Do Not Disturb option. On the Do Not Disturb screen, you can preset a specific period each day or night when the Do Not Disturb feature will automatically activate and then deactivate. To use this feature, slide the Scheduled virtual switch to On, and then select the From and To times you want Do Not Disturb to activate, such as daily, from 11:00 P.M. to 7:00 A.M. the following morning.

You also have the option to allow specific calls to come through, even when the iPhone is in Do Not Disturb mode. To choose which callers can get through (your options are Everyone, No One, Favorites, or a specific Group within your Contacts database), tap the Allow Calls From option and make a selection.

With the Repeated Calls option, it's also possible to customize the Do Not Disturb feature to allow a caller to get through to you if they call once and then call back a second time from the same number within a three-minute period, perhaps indicating the call is an emergency or some other urgent matter.

When you're finished with the Do Not Disturb screen, tap Notifications in the upper-left corner to return to the Notifications screen.

Sort Apps Manually or By Time

You can decide whether you want to sort apps-related information to be displayed on the Notification Center screen manually or based on the time specific alerts, alarms, and notifications are generated.

Customize App-Specific Notification Settings

Scroll down the Notifications screen and you'll see the In Notification Center heading. Below it are listings for all of the compatible apps that Notification Center is currently monitoring. Tap each listing, one at a time, to customize options pertaining to that app. Continue to scroll down the Notifications screen and you'll discover the Not In Notification Center heading. Below this heading are the compatible apps that the Notification Center is not currently monitoring, but could monitor if you alter the settings for each app.

For each app listed under the In Notification Center or Not In Notification Center heading, tap it to customize the way Notification Center will manage that app and get your attention when alerts, alarms, or notifications are generated.

When you tap each app-specific listing, a Notification Center customization screen appears that is specific to that app. As an example, start by tapping the Phone app's listing to customize how the Notification Center will alert you about missed calls and voicemails. The Notification Center customization screen for the Phone app is shown in Figure 2-15.

At the top of the app-specific Notification Center screen is a virtual switch associated with the Notification Center option. Turn the virtual switch to On if you want the app's alerts, alarms, and notifications to be displayed on the Notification Center screen. If you turn this option to Off, the Notification Center will not display information about the app on the Notification Center screen, but can still get your attention in other ways using Alerts, Banners, and Home Screen icon Badges, for example. The apps you turn off will then be listed under the Not In Notification Center heading.

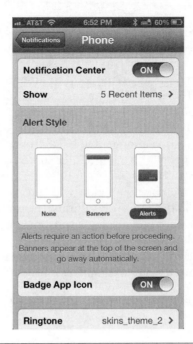

FIGURE 2-15   Customize the Notification Center options separately for each compatible app that can generate alerts, alarms, or notifications.

If you want to display local weather information within the Notification Center screen, tap the Weather widget listing under the Not In Notification Center heading and move the Notification Center switch to On. You can do the same for the Stocks widget. To display the Tap To Tweet and Tap To Post buttons near the top of the Notification Center screen (assuming you have these features turned on), tap the Share widget and move the Notification Center switch to On.

 Turn on the Notification Center feature only for apps that are most important to you. Otherwise, you will receive alerts, alarms, and notifications from apps that you don't necessarily use or that aren't important to your everyday life.

Below the Notification Center virtual switch on each app's customization screen is the Show option. If you turn on the Notification Center feature for the app, the Show option determines the maximum number of listings that app can display on the Notification Center screen at any given time. To change the setting, tap the Show option. Your choices include 1 Recent Item, 5 Recent Items, or 10 Recent Items.

So, for each app listed, one at a time, decide whether or not information from it will be displayed on the Notification Center screen, and how many alerts, alarms, and notification listings each app can display at once.

Set Up Alert Options for Each Listed App

In addition to, or instead of, displaying alerts, alarms, and notifications on the Notification Center screen, each app can also display Banners or Alerts on the iPhone's screen when the app requires your attention.

Under the Alert Style heading on each app's Notification Center customization screen (refer to Figure 2-15 to see the Phone app's screen), you can choose None, Banners, or Alerts. If you tap the None option, the app will display neither Banners nor Alerts, but could still generate audible alarms, utilize Badge icons, and/or display information within the Notification Center screen.

If you tap the Banners option, each time the app generates an alert, alarm, or notification, a separate pop-up window will appear at the top of the iPhone's screen (regardless of what app is currently running) or on the Lock screen if the iPhone is in Sleep mode. This Banner will display a short message pertaining to what needs your attention, but it will disappear automatically after several seconds.

If you tap the Alerts option, each time the app generates an alert, alarm, or notification, a pop-up window will appear on the iPhone's screen (regardless of what app is currently running), but the alert message will not disappear until you manually tap a command button to either address what needs your attention or dismiss the message.

Turn On or Off Badge App Icons for Badge-Compatible Apps

If an app is capable of generating Badge icons, a Badge App Icon virtual switch will be displayed on the app's Notification Center customization screen. When this switch is set to On, each time an alert, alarm, or notification is generated by that app, either a new Badge icon (for the first alert, alarm, or notification) will be displayed on the iPhone's Home screen as part of that app's icon (as shown for the Facebook, Phone, and Mail apps in Figure 2-16) or the number displayed within an existing Badge icon will increase.

For example, if you turn on the Badge App Icon feature for the Mail app, each time you receive a new incoming e-mail, the number displayed within the red and

FIGURE 2-16   Badges are displayed here in conjunction with the Facebook, Phone, and Mail app icons on the Home screen.

white Badge icon for the Mail app on the Home screen will increase by one. (When you choose to read the e-mail or delete it, the number displayed within the Badge will decrease by one.)

You can set up Badge icons to be displayed in addition to or instead of having the app display alerts, alarms, and notifications within the Notification Center screen and/or display Banners or Alerts.

Customize Audible Alarms or Tones

Also from the Notification Center customization screen for each app, you can customize the audible ringtone or sound that will be used in conjunction with that app, if it's capable of generating sound and is customizable from within Settings.

For example, when customizing the Phone app (refer to Figure 2-15), you can tap the Ringtone option and choose a ringtone to be the master ringtone for all incoming calls. For the Messages app, you can customize the Text Tone, and for the Reminders and Calendar app, for example, you can select the audible Reminder Alerts or Calendar Alerts tone, respectively.

Decide Whether to Display App-Specific Alerts, Alarms, and Notifications on the Lock Screen

One additional, app-specific customization you can make in regard to the Notification Center is whether or not Banners or Alerts, for example, will be displayed on the Lock screen when the iPhone is in Sleep mode. Scroll down to the bottom of each app-specific Notification Center customization screen and turn on or off the View In Lock Screen option. Figure 2-17 shows this option for the Calendar app.

The Notification Center Customization Options for Each App Will Vary

Each app that's compatible with Notification Center serves a different purpose and will offer slightly different options when it comes to getting your attention in conjunction with alerts, alarms, or notifications generated by that app. For example, when you tap the Mail app option, you can treat each e-mail account that the Mail app is managing as a separate entity, with separate customization settings. Thus, you can have work-related e-mails generate Alerts and Badges, in addition to being displayed within the Notification Center screen, and have your personal e-mail account display Banners and a listing within the Notification Center screen.

When customizing how the Notification Center will handle the Messages app and individual incoming text/instant messages, you can utilize a handful of extra options to fine-tune which incoming messages get your attention, and how you'll be notified.

FIGURE 2-17 Turn on the View In Lock Screen option to determine if an app's Alerts or Banners will "wake up" the iPhone and be displayed on the Lock screen when the iPhone is in Sleep mode.

 As you later install additional apps onto your iPhone, it will be necessary to customize their respective settings associated with the Notification Center. When applicable, listings for these apps will appear on the Notifications screen within Settings.

Although you need to set up how each app functions with the Notification Center only once, you can adjust your customized settings anytime later by returning to the Notifications screen within Settings.

3

Use iPhone's Basic Functions

HOW TO...

- Use your iPhone's virtual keyboard
- Navigate your iPhone using finger gestures on the Multi-Touch screen
- Use the Home button for various purposes
- Multitask on the iPhone 5
- Use Siri to control the iPhone with your voice

Before you activate your new iPhone 5 and learn how to begin using it in your everyday life, this chapter introduces you to some of the ways you'll be interacting with it using the virtual keyboard, Multi-Touch display, and your voice. These three interaction methods apply to all aspects of the iPhone 5's operation, regardless of which apps you'll be using.

Once you become familiar with how to use the virtual keyboard and how to use your fingers as input tools to tap, swipe, flick, and pinch the Multi-Touch screen, you'll become much more efficient using your iPhone 5. Then, you can focus on utilizing Siri and the iPhone's Dictation feature as an alternate way of interacting with your iPhone and the apps you'll soon be using with it.

 Siri and Dictation both allow you to speak directly to your iPhone. Using Siri, you can issue commands, questions, and requests, while Dictation is used to translate your spoken words into text that gets immediately inserted into apps, documents, or files. To use Siri or Dictation, your iPhone must be connected to the Internet using a Wi-Fi or 3G/4G connection. You'll discover that these features work faster with a Wi-Fi connection, however.

Yet another method for entering data into your iPhone is to connect it to an optional, external keyboard. As you'll discover later in this chapter, an external keyboard can be connected to the iPhone using its Lightning port or a wireless Bluetooth connection. There are dozens of iPhone-compatible keyboards available, some of which are small but offer tactile keys, others of which provide a full-size

QWERTY keyboard that's portable. People who are accustomed to using a physical keyboard, as opposed to the iPhone's virtual keyboard, often find that an external keyboard allows them to type faster and more accurately.

Get Acquainted with the iPhone's Virtual Keyboard

The virtual keyboard pops up on the screen whenever you need to use it to enter information into your iPhone. What you'll quickly discover about the iPhone 5's keyboard is that it adapts to the app it's being used with, so while a traditional QWERTY, typewriter-style keyboard will appear when using some apps, a more customized keyboard, often with specialized keys, will appear when using other apps.

You'll also discover that, for the many apps that work in both portrait mode and landscape mode, when you hold the iPhone in landscape mode and access the virtual keyboard, the keys are noticeably larger (shown in Figure 3-1), making it easier to type quickly and more accurately.

The traditional keyboard layout is displayed, for example, when you're entering a new event into the Calendar app (shown in Figure 3-2) or using the Notes app. Use your thumbs, a finger, or an optional pen-shaped stylus to type, based on whichever is most comfortable to you and how you're holding the iPhone in your hand(s).

Safari is an example of an app that displays a slightly different keyboard layout depending on the context. When you tap the address field to manually enter a website address (URL), as shown in Figure 3-3, the bottom of the keyboard's layout changes to display dot (.), /, and .com keys, as well as the blue and white Go key. As another

FIGURE 3-1 The layout of the iPhone 5's virtual keyboard is larger when used in landscape mode.

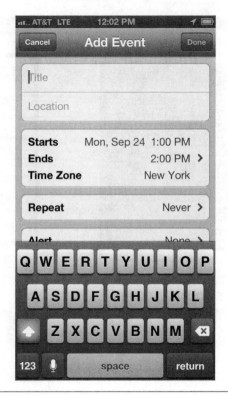

FIGURE 3-2   The virtual keyboard changes based on the app that's being used.

example, if you access the Spotlight Search feature on your iPhone, the virtual keyboard that appears when entering a keyword or search phrase displays a Search key (shown in Figure 3-4).

Many apps, such as the optional Numbers app, require extensive numeric data entry. In these cases, the virtual keyboard again adapts accordingly (shown in Figure 3-5).

When looking at the basic virtual keyboard layout (see Figure 3-2, for example), you'll see several keys that have specialized functionality. For example, tapping the 123 key that's displayed in the lower-left corner of the keyboard changes the keyboard's keys from letters to numbers, punctuation marks, and common symbols, as shown in Figure 3-6. The 123 key changes to ABC. Tap the ABC key to again display letters.

 When looking at the number and symbol version of the virtual keyboard, tap the #+= key to reveal a different selection of commonly used symbols.

The up-arrow key that's displayed within the standard alphabet keyboard layout serves as the Shift key for capitalizing letters. The left-pointing arrow key with an

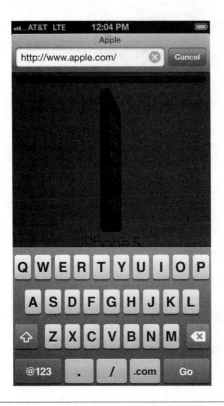

FIGURE 3-3 When using Safari, the virtual keyboard offers keys suited for entering website URLs.

FIGURE 3-4 The Search key is used to initiate a search when using the iPhone's Spotlight Search feature.

× within it is your Backspace key, and the key labeled Space is your Spacebar. The Return key (when present) serves as your carriage return. See Figure 3-7.

 You can lock the Shift key by double-tapping it. It turns blue and white to indicate it's locked. You'll then be able to type in all capital letters until you tap the Shift key again to unlock it. This feature, however, must be turned on from the Keyboard screen within Settings, which you'll learn about a bit later in this chapter.

One key that appears almost always (if you have the Siri feature turned on) is the Microphone key (refer to Figure 3-7). Tap this key to enter into Dictation mode and use your voice to input text instead of typing.

When using the virtual keyboard, you can use your finger(s) or thumb(s) to type, whichever is more comfortable based on how you're holding the iPhone. As you tap each key, an enlarged version of that key is displayed for a fraction of a second. This helps you quickly determine that you've tapped the correct key. At the same time,

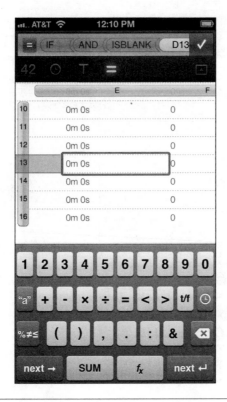

FIGURE 3-5   When numeric data entry is required, such as when using the Numbers app, the virtual keyboard adapts.

FIGURE 3-6   Tap the 123 key to access numbers, punctuation, and symbols. Tap the ABC key to switch back to letters.

if you have your iPhone set up to emit keyboard clicks, you'll hear a click with each key you tap. Certain letter keys also have special characters associated with them. To access these additional key options, press and hold the applicable letter key, such as n, z, c, l, a, e, u, i, or o.

Tip   To activate audible keyboard clicks in conjunction with the virtual keyboard so that you hear an audible click each time you tap any key, launch Settings (by tapping on the Settings icon that's found on the Home Screen) and tap the Sounds option. Scroll to the bottom of the Sounds screen and set the Keyboard Clicks option to On. If you turn off this feature, the keyboard remains silent as you type.

Often, when it's necessary to manually enter data into an iPhone app, the virtual keyboard appears without your prompting and displays an applicable keyboard layout. However, anytime you see a blank field within an app that requires data to be entered manually, simply tap that field and the virtual keyboard will appear. For example,

Dictation key

FIGURE 3-7   Use the Shift key to capitalize letters, the Backspace key to delete characters, the Space key as your spacebar, and the Return key as a carriage return.

if you opt to create a new entry within the Contacts app, after tapping the + icon to create an entry, the New Contact screen appears (shown in Figure 3-8). This app screen includes a handful of empty data fields. One at a time, tap each field, starting with the field labeled First to enter the contact's first name. As soon as you tap each field, the virtual keyboard appears.

Notice that when you tap one of the phone number fields, a different, numeric keyboard layout is displayed, which makes it faster and easier to enter phone numbers into the iPhone's Contacts app (shown in Figure 3-9).

As you're typing, if you need to back up and insert or delete characters within a particular word (or between words), press and hold down your finger on the screen directly over where you want to insert or delete characters or text. A large circular magnifying glass will appear over that area (shown in Figure 3-10). Slowly drag your finger right, left, up, or down to display areas of magnified text and move the cursor to the exact location it's needed in order to insert or delete text. This feature gives you a quick and precise way to move the cursor around on the touch screen, since navigational arrow keys (like you'd find on a traditional computer keyboard) are not available when using the iPhone's virtual keyboard.

FIGURE 3-8 On the New Contact screen within the Contacts app, tap any field to make the virtual keyboard appear.

FIGURE 3-9 When you tap a field to enter a phone number within the New Contact screen, the virtual keyboard displays a numeric keypad.

Configure the Virtual Keyboard Options

From within Settings, if you tap the General option and then tap the Keyboard option, you can customize other keyboard-related settings that work regardless of which apps are being used. From the Keyboard screen (shown in Figure 3-11), you can turn on or off the Auto-Capitalization, Auto-Correction, Check Spelling, Enable Caps Lock, and "." Shortcut features. You can also select a keyboard layout for a different language with the Keyboards setting, and you custom edit a listing of keyboard shortcuts (as explained in the next section). Here's a quick overview of these keyboard-related functions:

- **Auto-Capitalization** The iPhone 5 has an extensive dictionary built in and understands basic grammar rules. When this feature is turned on, the iPhone will automatically capitalize words, when appropriate, such as the first word of every sentence or common names.

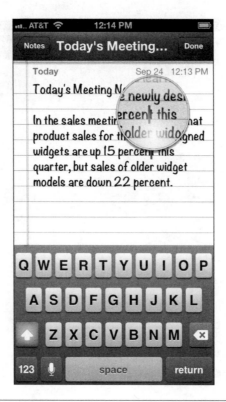

FIGURE 3-10 The magnifying glass allows you to move the cursor around on the screen with precision and insert characters in the middle of a word, for example.

- **Auto-Correction** Using the iPhone's built-in dictionary, as you type words that the iPhone recognizes, it displays matches to that word. Instead of typing the entire word when a match appears, tap the Space key, and the word is automatically entered into the field you're typing in. Also, if you incorrectly type a word when the Auto-Correction feature is turned on, the iPhone automatically replaces the incorrect word with what it believes is the correct one.

 Auto-Correction can be a very useful feature. However, be sure to proofread all text carefully after it's been entered to make sure that the Auto-Correction feature did not insert the wrong word into your text (which does happen somewhat frequently). The wrong word could dramatically change the meaning of a sentence, or result in embarrassing situations if what you were typing was part of an e-mail, text message, or business document, for example. Always proofread whatever text you enter into your iPhone, regardless of which app you're using, before sending, posting, or publishing that text.

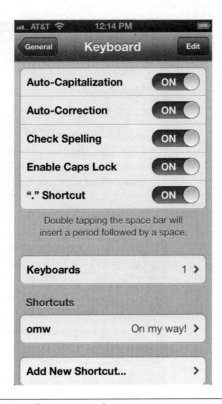

FIGURE 3-11 The Keyboard screen within Settings

- **Check Spelling** As you type, the iPhone determines if the words you enter are spelled correctly. If a word is misspelled, a dotted red line appears under that word. Tap the underlined word, and potential correctly spelled words are displayed in a bubble above the misspelled word (see Figure 3-12). Tap the correctly spelled word within the bubble to quickly replace the misspelled word without having to retype it.
- **Enable Caps Lock** When this setting is switched to On, you can turn on the Caps Lock feature on the virtual keyboard so that all the letters you type appear in uppercase. To activate Caps Lock, quickly double-tap the up-arrow (Shift) key that appears on the left side of the virtual keyboard. When Caps Lock is activated, the Shift key turns blue. To turn off Caps Lock, double-tap the Shift key again.
- **"." Shortcut** Use this feature to customize keyboard shortcuts that can be stored within the iPhone and can be later used in virtually any app that requires use of the virtual keyboard. These keyboard shortcuts can be used for phrases or sentences that you use often on the iPhone, but that you don't want to manually type over and over again.

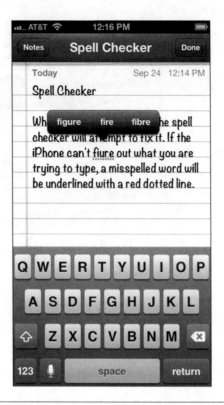

FIGURE 3-12 Hold your finger on a misspelled word to see potential correct spellings and replace the misspelled one. In this example, you'd tap the word "figure."

Create and Use Custom Keyboard Shortcuts

If you commonly use particular multiword phrases, you can create a shortcut for each of them so that you don't have to type those phrases repeatedly. Then, you can simply type the shortcut's letter combination to enter the entire phrase into whatever app you're using. For example, you can assign the shortcut "omw" to be "On my way" or "iam" to be "In a meeting." This makes entering commonly used phrases a faster process and reduces typos.

To create new, custom shortcuts that will work anytime the virtual keyboard is displayed (regardless of which app you're using), launch Settings, tap the General option, and tap the Keyboard option. Near the bottom of the Keyboard screen, the keyboard shortcuts that are already programmed into your iPhone are displayed under the Shortcuts heading, shown in Figure 3-13.

To create new keyboard shortcuts, tap the Add New Shortcut option. The Shortcut screen appears and displays two empty fields, labeled Phrase and Shortcut (shown

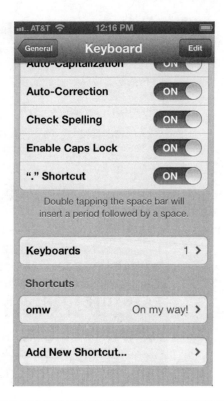

FIGURE 3-13   Look at the bottom of the Keyboard menu screen within Settings for the Shortcuts heading.

in Figure 3-14). First, enter the phrase you want to appear when you type a specific keyboard shortcut. For example, you could enter "I will call you back shortly. I am busy at the moment." Then, within the Shortcut field, enter a unique three-letter combination (not an actual word) that you'll type to make that shortcut phase appear. In this field, you could enter "iab" (for "I Am Busy").

Be sure to choose for each shortcut a letter combination that is easy to remember. Next, tap the Save button in the upper-right corner of the screen to save the newly created shortcut. Now, anytime you're using the iPhone's virtual keyboard and simply type "iab," the phrase "I will call you back shortly. I am busy at the moment." will appear and be inserted into whichever app you're working with.

 You can create a separate listing of phrases to be used as text messages from the Incoming Call screen if you opt to avoid answering an incoming call. How to use this new iOS 6 feature with the Phone app is explained in Chapter 7.

FIGURE 3-14 Create custom keyboard shortcuts from within Settings, but use them in any app that utilizes the virtual keyboard.

Learn When and How to Tap, Swipe, Flick, or Pinch the iPhone's Multi-Touch Display

You'll do much of your interaction with the iPhone using the phone's Multi-Touch display. This means using a series of taps, swipes, flicks, and pinch motions to launch apps, access features, and navigate your way around.

Here's a rundown of the most common figure gestures you'll need to use when working with your iPhone:

- **Tap** A tap is similar to a mouse click on a traditional computer. You can tap icons, menu options, and active links, for example. A tap requires a quick and gentle connection between your finger and the touch screen. There is never a need to press down hard on the touch screen.

How to...

Select an Optional, External Keyboard for Your iPhone

If you have difficulty typing quickly or accurately using the virtual keyboard that's built into the iPhone (a skill that takes practice) and you need to do a lot of data or text entry, one option is to connect an external keyboard to your iPhone. A handful of third-party accessory companies manufacture iPhone 5–compatible keyboards that come in a variety of shapes and sizes. Ideally, you want to choose a keyboard that's battery powered and that works wirelessly with your iPhone using a Bluetooth connection.

There are some pocket-size keyboard accessories that are tiny but offer tactile keys, which makes typing with your thumbs faster and more accurate. However, you'll also discover optional full-size keyboards that in some cases are foldable for easy transport and storage when they're not in use. For example, the Freedom Pro Keyboard ($99, www.freedominput.com) is a full-size, Bluetooth keyboard with tactile keys, but the unit folds up into a pocket-size package for easy transport when it's not in use.

If you have an iMac that uses an Apple wireless keyboard, you can easily "pair" that Bluetooth-compatible keyboard for use with your iPhone as well, or purchase this keyboard separately for use with your iPhone ($69, http://store.apple.com/us/product/MC184LL/B/apple-wireless-keyboard-english).

Brookstone (www.brookstone.com) is one example of a company that offers a variety of different portable keyboards that are compatible with the iPhone. The company's Bluetooth Silicone Keyboard ($59.99) is made from flexible silicone and is extremely thin. This full-size QWERTY keyboard can actually roll up when it's not in use, making it easy to store and take with you. Perhaps the most technologically advanced optional keyboard for the iPhone 5 is also available from Brookstone. It's called the Virtual Keyboard ($99.99). This keyboard is actually shaped like a tiny box and fits on a keychain. When turned on, paired with your iPhone, and placed on a flat surface, it uses a laser to project a full-size keyboard on that surface (such as a desk, or the tray in front of an airplane seat). Using a Bluetooth connection, the Virtual Keyboard tracks the movement of your fingers on the projected keyboard. While this keyboard does not offer tactile keys, it does offer a full-size keyboard that's incredibly portable.

Using any Internet search engine, enter the search phrase "iPhone 5 keyboard," and you'll find other external keyboards. Keep in mind, the majority of these keyboards are battery powered and need to be recharged periodically.

Your iPhone's Multi-Touch display will not respond to your finger gestures if you're wearing a glove. Instead of using their fingers, some people opt to use a pen-shaped stylus to interact with the touch screen. This option works well for taps and swipes, plus you can use the stylus with apps that allow you to write or draw on the iPhone's screen.

- **Double-tap**   Instead of using a single tap, some functions or options require a double-tap. Quickly tap on the same icon, menu option, or link, for example, twice in a row in quick succession.
- **Hold**   Place your finger on a particular word, icon, graphic, link, or menu option and hold it there for a second or two, applying minimal pressure. In some cases, while holding your finger down on the touch screen, you'll need to move it around on the screen to handle a specific task. In these situations, your finger should maintain contact with the Multi-Touch display as you drag it around.
- **Swipe/flick**   Using your thumb or index finger, quickly swipe from left to right, right to left, upward, or downward on the screen to activate or use a specific feature. Scrolling, switching between screens, turning the pages of an e-book, or switching between photos you're viewing are some of the tasks that require a swipe or flick of the finger. For example, from the main Home screen, swipe your finger from right to left to switch from the main Home screen to one of the other Home screens. Or, from the main Home screen, swipe your finger from left to right to access the Spotlight Search screen. To access the Notification Center screen, regardless of what else you're doing on the iPhone, swipe your finger from the very top of the display in a downward direction. Then, to make the Notification Center screen disappear, swipe your finger from the bottom of the display in an upward direction.

When performing a flick or swipe, your finger needs to maintain light contact with the touch screen.

- **Pinch**   Starting with your thumb and index finger apart on the touch screen, bring them together using a pinching motion. This is used to zoom out on whatever you happen to be looking at on the screen when using many apps.
- **Reverse pinch**   Starting with your thumb and index finger together on the touch screen, move them apart (away from each other) to create a reverse-pinch motion. This is often used to zoom in on what you're looking at on the screen.

Instead of using a pinch or reverse-pinch motion, you can often double-tap on a particular area of the screen to zoom in or out, depending on the app.

Discover the Multiple Functions of the iPhone's Home Button

The only physical or tactile button that can be found on the front of your iPhone 5 is the Home button, the large, round button below the touch screen. The Home button has several functions:

- Press the Home button once to wake up the iPhone 5 from Sleep mode.
- When the iPhone is active, press the Home button once at any time to return to the Home screen you last viewed (such as the example shown in Figure 3-15) and exit the app you're currently using. Doing this, however, typically does not shut down the app; it will continue running in the background.
- From any of the secondary Home screens, press the Home button once to return to the main Home screen.
- From the main Home screen, press the Home button once to access the Spotlight Search screen.
- From the Lock screen, double-press the Home button to access the Music app's controls. Without first unlocking the iPhone, you can play, pause, fast forward, or

FIGURE 3-15   Press the Home button to return to the Home screen.

rewind when listening to the preselected song, or switch between songs within a preselected Playlist. These controls are shown in Figure 3-16. You'll learn more about how to use them in Chapter 16.

- At any time, press and hold down the Home button in conjunction with the Power button for about ten seconds to reboot the iPhone (as opposed to simply powering it off and then turning it back on). On rare occasions when the iPhone crashes, rebooting the device may become necessary. This action, however, will not delete or erase apps from your iPhone.

- From the Home screen, double-press the Home button to access the Multitasking bar, a feature that is explained in the next section. It allows you to quickly switch between multiple apps that are running simultaneously on the iPhone. At any given time, one app can be active and multiple apps can be running in the background.

- Press and hold down the Home button for two to three seconds anytime (regardless of which apps are running) to activate Siri. The "What can I help you with?" message and circular microphone icon that's associated with Siri will appear, as shown in Figure 3-17. When you hear Siri's tone and the microphone within the icon turns purple, speak your command, question, or request, either

FIGURE 3-16 From the Lock screen, double-press the Home button to access the Music app's controls without first launching the Music app or even unlocking the iPhone.

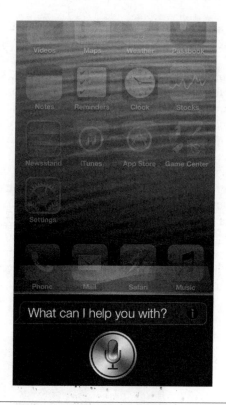

FIGURE 3-17   Press and hold down the Home button for two to three seconds to activate Siri.

into the iPhone itself or into a headset that's connected to the iPhone. How to use Siri as a virtual, voice-controlled assistant is explained later in this chapter.

 If you want to capture a screenshot of what's displayed on your iPhone's screen and have that image automatically stored within the Camera Roll folder within Photos, press the Home button and Power button simultaneously. You will hear a camera shutter sound effect, indicating the screenshot has been captured and saved.

Run Multiple Apps Simultaneously and Easily Switch Between Them

Your iPhone is capable of running multiple apps at the same time. Although only one app can be used at a time, others can be running in the background. For example, at all times, the Notification Center app is running and monitors the other apps for newly generated alerts, alarms, and notifications. At the same time, the Phone app is constantly waiting for new incoming calls, while the Messages app is waiting for new incoming text messages (unless the iPhone is in Airplane mode).

The Music app can continue running and playing your favorite songs or Playlists in the background while you are working with other apps.

When multiple apps are running, you can quickly switch between them by accessing the Multitasking bar. Regardless of which apps are running or what you're doing on the iPhone, at any time, quickly press the Home button twice in quick succession to access the Multitasking bar. As soon as you do this, a line of icons representing all of the apps currently running in the background is displayed along the bottom of the screen (shown in Figure 3-18).

If more than four apps are running, you won't be able to see all the icons, so swipe your finger from right to left across the line of icons to see the hidden ones. To quickly switch between apps, tap the icon for the app you want to use at that moment. When you tap its icon, the selected app appears onscreen, and the app you were using continues to run in the background. To return to the original app, return to the Multitasking bar and tap the original app's icon.

Also while viewing the Multitasking bar, you can manually shut down one or more apps that are currently running if you no longer need to use those apps or if you notice your iPhone is acting sluggish due to too many apps being open at the same

FIGURE 3-18   The iPhone 5's Multitasking bar allows you to quickly switch between apps.

time. Press the Home button twice in quick succession. When the Multitasking bar
is displayed and you see the lineup of app icons that represents the apps currently
running, press and hold down any of these app icons until they all start to shake and
a red and white negative sign (–) icon appears in the upper-left corner of each icon
(shown in Figure 3-19). To shut down an app, tap its (–) icon. Doing this shuts down
that app but does not delete it from your iPhone.

Access Music Controls and Rotation Lock Using the Home Button

Accessing the Multitasking bar is also a way to gain quick access to the Music
app's music controls. To do this, quickly press the Home button twice to view the
Multitasking bar. When the lineup of active apps icons is displayed, swipe your finger
from left to right across the app icons. The app icon lineup will be replaced with the
Music app's music controls (shown in Figure 3-20).

Tap the icon on the extreme left to turn on the iPhone's auto-rotation lock. With
this lock turned on, when you physically rotate the iPhone from portrait mode to

FIGURE 3-19   Press the negative sign icon associated with an app while viewing
the Multitasking bar to shut down that app.

FIGURE 3-20   Access Music app controls from the Multitasking bar without first launching the Music app.

landscape mode (or vice versa), what's displayed on the screen will not automatically rotate as well. When the lock rotation feature is turned on, a small lock icon appears within the auto-rotation lock icon.

Tap the Track Forward and Track Back icons (double arrows) to jump between tracks in a preselected Playlist. Tap and hold these icons to fast forward or rewind within a particular song. Tap the Play icon (the center icon) to play or pause the preselected song from the Playlist that's loaded into the Music app. You can also tap the Music app icon to launch the full Music app and take full control over your music. From the Music control screen (refer to Figure 3-20), swipe your finger from left to right to reveal a separate Volume Control slider that offers one way to adjust the volume of the music that's playing.

Use Siri to Control Your iPhone Verbally

By combining voice recognition technology with artificial intelligence, the knowledge that's available on the Internet, and your own app-specific data, and then integrating it all with the iPhone and its functionality, Apple has created Siri—a way to communicate directly with your iPhone using your voice to issue commands, make requests, or ask questions. In conjunction with iOS 6 and the launch of the iPhone 5, Apple made major enhancements to Siri's capabilities.

For Siri to function, your iPhone needs access to the Internet via a Wi-Fi or 3G/4G connection. Much of Siri's functionality is actually handled on Apple's remote, online-based servers, which allows the company to constantly improve upon Siri's technology, functionality, and accuracy.

To activate Siri at any time, regardless of what you're currently doing on the iPhone, press and hold down the Home button for two to three seconds. As soon as you activate Siri, near the bottom of the iPhone's screen, Siri's "What can I help you with?" message appears, along with a circular icon that displays a microphone. To the right of this icon, a speaker icon appears if your iPhone is connected to a headset (see Figure 3-21) either wirelessly or via a cable. Tap this speaker icon to select whether you'll use the iPhone's built-in microphone or the optional headset's microphone when communicating with Siri.

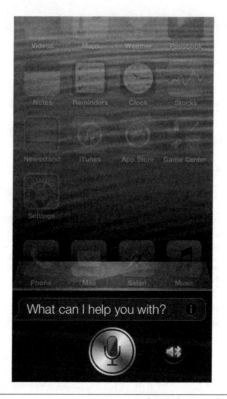

FIGURE 3-21   When Siri is active, you can use the iPhone's built-in microphone or an optional headset's microphone, assuming one is connected to the iPhone via a cable or Bluetooth.

Siri Does Not Offer Entirely Hands-Free iPhone Operation

It's important to understand that, while Siri allows you to use your voice to control many different features and functions of your iPhone and to access information from your apps and the Internet, this feature is not a totally hands-free solution for using your iPhone.

While Siri speaks certain responses, related information is also typically displayed on the iPhone's screen. Thus, just as you should refrain from texting while driving, for example, you should also avoid using the majority of Siri's features while driving. Only some of Siri's functions offer truly hands-free operation that do not require you to view the iPhone's screen at all. These are the only features you should consider using when driving or when your attention and eyes should be focused elsewhere.

Tip   To help improve Siri's accuracy when it comes to understanding your spoken requests, commands, or questions, this feature is best used when there is little or no background noise.

Upon activating Siri, the microphone icon turns purple and you hear a special tone indicating that Siri is waiting for you to speak. If you don't begin speaking within a few seconds, the feature will deactivate. To reactive Siri, simply tap the microphone icon. When speaking to Siri, use a normal voice and speak as clearly as possible.

When you activate Siri, a small Info ("i") icon appears to the immediate right of the "What can I help you with?" message. Tap this icon to view an interactive menu that contains examples of how to use Siri in different situations and with different apps (shown in Figure 3-22).

The following sections provide a rundown of the various ways you can use Siri to interact with your iPhone verbally.

Initiate a Call with Siri

You can tell Siri to initiate a phone call via the Phone app. To do this, activate Siri and say, "Call [insert name]." If the person you want to call has an entry within the Contacts database, Siri will access that person's phone number and dial the number for you if only one number is listed. If that person's Contacts entry has multiple phone numbers listed, Siri will ask you to specify which number to call (shown in Figure 3-23). You can avoid this intermediate step by expanding your initial request to specify which of the person's numbers you want to call, such as "Call [insert name] at home" or "Call [insert name]'s mobile phone."

If you need to dial a phone number that isn't in your Contacts database, you have several options. If you already know the phone number that needs to be dialed,

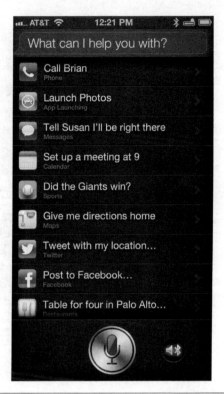

FIGURE 3-22   When Siri is active, tap the Info ("i") button for an onscreen primer about the different commands, requests, and questions you can pose using your voice.

activate Siri and speak the complete phone number, such as "Call 2 1 2 5 5 5 5 1 2 3 4." Or, if you need to locate the phone number for a business, ask Siri to "Look up [insert company name] in [insert city and state]," and then follow Siri's prompts when the search results are read to you one at a time and you're given the opportunity to initiate a call to any one of the search results.

Anytime you start a command with the word "Call" or "Dial," Siri will know to use the Phone app to initiate a call. However, if you begin the command with the word "FaceTime" and say, for example, "FaceTime [insert name]," Siri will attempt to initiate a FaceTime call (video conference) with that person.

If certain people within your Contacts database have names that are difficult for Siri to understand, you can complete the Phonetic First Name and Phonetic Last Name fields in their Contacts entries to help improve Siri's name recognition capabilities. How to use the Contacts app and create entries is covered in Chapter 8.

If you have an entry for yourself in your Contacts database that lists your own home, work, and iPhone numbers and your addresses, you should link that entry to Siri so that you can issue commands such as "Call home" and "Call work" and Siri will know which number to call. To do this, launch Settings, tap the General option, tap the Siri option, and then tap the My Info option. Select your own Contacts entry. By

FIGURE 3-23 Use Siri to initiate a phone call. Here, the command "Call Sue Martinez" was used.

doing this once, Siri will also now be able to address you by name, plus know where your home and work are located for purposes such as giving you driving directions from home or work to your designated destination.

 As part of your own Contacts entry, also include information in the Related People field, and create a detailed entry for each of those people. Be sure to include, where applicable, people such as your wife, husband, mother, father, sister(s), brother(s), and grandparents. This enables Siri to respond to requests like "Call my wife" or "Call mom's cell phone" without your referring to them by name.

Launch Apps Using Siri

Use Siri to launch iPhone apps. To do this, activate Siri and say, "Launch [insert app name]" or "Open [insert app name]." If that app is installed on your iPhone, Siri will launch it for you. Likewise, if you have a particular game installed on your iPhone, you can use the command "Play [insert game title]," and Siri will launch that game app. In most cases, launching apps using Siri is simply a time saver. However, if you need to use your iPhone on a hands-free basis, it's also useful for launching and then controlling certain apps without having to look at or touch the display.

Use Siri to Communicate via the Messages App

The Messages app that's built into your iPhone is used to send and receive text messages and instant messages. Upon activating Siri, you can compose and send a message via the Messages app by starting your command using the word "Tell" or "Send." For example, if you activate Siri and say "Tell Natalie that I am on the way," Siri will look up Natalie in your Contacts database and send her a text message that says "I am on the way."

After composing the message, you'll be able to proofread it before sending it (shown in Figure 3-24). Proofreading anything and everything Siri composes is essential, especially if it's related to an e-mail, text message, instant message, tweet, or Facebook status update. You can also use a command like "Send Ryan a message

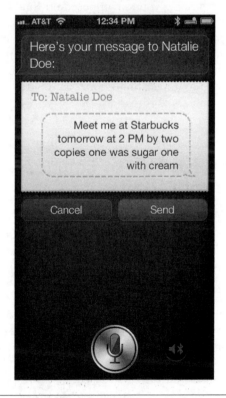

FIGURE 3-24   Always be sure to proofread the outgoing messages that Siri composes before sending them. This message to Natalie was supposed to say, "Meet me at Starbucks tomorrow at 2 P.M. Buy two coffees, one with sugar and one with cream."

that says let's meet for lunch today at 2 P.M." This too will alert Siri to compose a text message addressed to Ryan, assuming there is an entry for him within your Contacts database.

Keep in mind, you can also dictate punctuation marks with Siri. For example, you can say things like "comma," "period," "open quote," "close quote," "question mark," or "exclamation point." So, if you want to dictate the sentence, *"John said, 'I love the iPhone!'"*, what you'd say is *"John said comma open quotes I love the iPhone exclamation point close quote."*

Note If you refer to someone by name when using Siri, and that name has multiple entries within your Contacts database, Siri gives you the list of people with that name and asks you to select the appropriate one. For example, this will occur if you say "Call Emily" and there are five different people named Emily in your database. In this case, save a step by referring to the person using their first and last name. For example, say "Call Emily Robinson," not just "Call Emily."

In addition to allowing you to compose and send text messages or instant messages using the Messages app, Siri will read incoming messages to you. For example, when you use the command "Read my new messages," Siri will read aloud your latest incoming messages. Use a command that begins with "Reply" to compose a response and send it. Or, if you receive an incoming text message from someone and you want to respond to it over the iPhone, simply tell Siri to "Call her" or "Call him" after the incoming message is read to you.

Did You Know?

Siri Allows You to Compose, Send, and Read E-Mails

Siri works with the Mail app and allows you to compose and send e-mail messages using your voice. You can also command Siri to read your incoming e-mails and compose responses. Use the command "Check mail" to launch the Mail app and have Siri check for new, incoming e-mails. You can also ask Siri specific questions, like "Did I receive an e-mail from [insert name] today?," or issue a command, like "Show me the last e-mail from [insert name]."

To compose a new e-mail, begin a command by saying "E-mail [insert name]" or "New e-mail to [insert name]." If you say something like "E-mail John O'Brien at work about the sales meeting," Siri will create a new e-mail to John O'Brien using his work-related e-mail address and automatically fill in the Subject field with "Sales Meeting." Siri will then ask you what you want the body of the e-mail message to say.

As you're reading an e-mail message on the iPhone's screen, if you want to reply to that message, activate Siri and begin your command by saying "Reply."

Tell Siri to Enter Meeting and Schedule Info into the Calendar App

One of the ways Siri can save you time is by helping you enter new events into the Calendar app. To create a new event, such as an appointment or meeting, activate Siri and say, for example, "Set up a meeting at 9 A.M. with [insert name] at [insert location]." You can also begin this type of command by saying "Meet with," "New appointment with," or "Schedule a meeting with," and Siri will know you want to create a new event within the Calendar app.

It's also possible to use Siri to access the Calendar app to display upcoming meetings and appointments. For example, say "Show me my schedule for today" or "Show me my schedule for [insert date]." You could also ask Siri, "When is my next meeting?" or "When is my next appointment with [insert name]?" and Siri will seek out this information from the Calendar app and then tell you the details aloud while displaying the results on the iPhone's screen.

As you're looking at event-related details pertaining to the Calendar app, use commands like "Reschedule my 3 P.M. meeting...," "Cancel my appointment with [insert name]," or "Move my 3 P.M. meeting to 4:30 P.M.," and Siri will handle these requests without your having to manually edit the event using the iPhone's virtual keyboard.

 When creating new events, the more information you enter into the various fields, the more helpful Siri can be. For example, if you use the Location field for an event, ask Siri "Where is my next meeting?" and you'll get a location-based response. Or, if you list attendees to a meeting, ask Siri "When is my next meeting with [insert name]?" and view the results.

Query Siri About Sports, Movies, and Restaurants

Upon activating Siri, you can ask any sports-related question about a particular team, player, or event, for example, to obtain scores, stats, or other information. For example, you could ask Siri "Which New York Yankee has the most home runs this season?" In addition to displaying a response to your question, Siri will often display pertinent information on the iPhone screen (see Figure 3-25). You could also say "Show me the baseball scores for yesterday" to view the scores of all MLB games played yesterday, or ask "What football games are on today?" to discover which teams are playing.

You can also ask Siri to provide information about which movies are playing near you. Siri will pinpoint where you are, find the closest theater, and then tell you what's playing. Or, you can ask for movie times at a particular theater, ask when a particular movie is playing, ask to see reviews for a particular movie, or ask for information about a particular actor, director, or cast member (for example, "What movies has William Shatner starred in?" or "Who directed the movie *Star Trek: Nemesis*?").

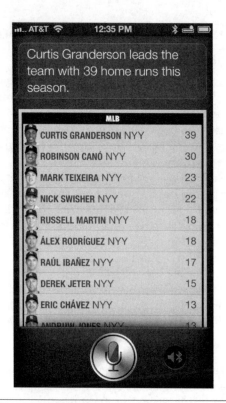

FIGURE 3-25   Depending on the request, Siri's response will sometimes be spoken. Other times, pertinent information will be displayed on the iPhone's screen.

If you get hungry, Siri has access to restaurant listings and works in conjunction with Yelp! and Open Table to provide restaurant details, reviews, and the ability to make a reservation for you. For example, ask "Where is the closest Chinese restaurant?" or say "Find me a steak restaurant in [insert city and state]." If you know where you want to make a reservation, say something like, "Table for two at [insert restaurant name] in [insert city and state] at [insert time and day]."

 Siri can access any online restaurant reviews for a particular restaurant if you say, "Show me the reviews for [insert restaurant name] in [insert city and state]." Siri can also locate a restaurant for you and provide turn-by-turn driving directions to it from your current location, allow you to initiate a call to that restaurant, or, in many cases, display the restaurant's menu on the iPhone's screen.

Get Directions Using Siri's Full Integration with the Maps App

You can access through Siri just about any function that the Maps app is capable of (see Chapter 12). For example, from wherever you happen to be, you can activate Siri and say "Give me directions home." Or, you can choose an address from your Contacts database, speak an address, or name a landmark, and Siri will provide directions to that location or display that location on a map, depending on your instructions.

Note As you'll discover, the new Maps app has access to a vast and ever-growing database of businesses and landmarks, so if you ask something like "How do I get to the Empire State Building in Manhattan?" or "How do I get to Boston Logan Airport?," Siri will be able to find that location, display it on a map, and provide you with directions to it.

If you want Siri to simply show you a destination on a map instead of providing directions to that destination, use a request like "Show me [location or landmark]," and Siri will display the location on the Maps app's screen. For example, say "Show me the White House in Washington, DC," and Siri will display it on a map (shown in Figure 3-26).

To find a particular type of business, ask Siri "Where is the closest gas station?" or instruct Siri to "Find the closest Apple Store." Again, by tapping into reviews published on Yelp!, Siri can also respond to a request like "Find me the best hair salon in [insert city and state]."

Tip While Siri is providing turn-by-turn directions, ask questions like "Are we there yet?" or "What's my ETA?" to determine when you'll be there based on your current driving speed.

Control the Music App with Your Voice

Use a command like "Play [insert artist or band name]" or "Play [insert Playlist name]" to make Siri locate particular music that's stored on your iPhone and play it. You can also use a request like "Play pop music [or another music genre]."

Tip When used in conjunction with the Music app, Siri understands and will respond to commands like "Play," "Pause," "Skip," "Stop," and "Repeat," and also understands song titles, Playlist names, music genres, and artists' names, for example.

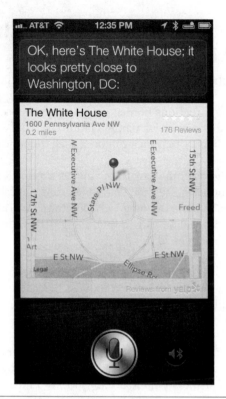

FIGURE 3-26 Ask Siri to display a particular landmark, address, or location on a map. Here, the command "Show me the White House in Washington, DC" was used.

Prepare for the Weather with Siri

With a simple request, Siri will tell you the current weather forecast for wherever you are, provide an extended forecast, or tell you the weather for any other location in the world. This is particularly helpful if you're planning a trip and need to know what to pack. Ask questions like "What's the weather forecast for today?," "Is it going to rain today?," "What is the extended forecast for Boston, Massachusetts?," or "Check next week's forecast for New York City."

You could also ask, for example, "What is the current temperature outside?" or "What is the current weather in Orlando, Florida?" (a sample of Siri's response to which is shown in Figure 3-27).

FIGURE 3-27   Siri will tell you the weather forecast you request, but also display related information on the screen using much more detail.

Let Siri Help You Manage Your To-Do Items or Notes

The Reminders app that comes preinstalled on your iPhone is a to-do list manager that's packed with features. Siri fully integrates with Reminders as well. To add a reminder or a new to-do item to the app, begin your command by saying "Remind me to" or "Add [insert item] to my [insert list time] list."

 Be as detailed as you'd like when creating new reminders. For example, if you say "Remind me to pick up my dry cleaning tomorrow at 2 P.M.," Siri not only adds this to your to-do list, but also sets an audible alarm for tomorrow at 2 P.M.

If you begin a command with "Remind me to," Siri will know to utilize the Reminders app. However, if you begin your command with the word "Note" and then dictate the contents of a note, Siri will utilize the Notes app to compose a new note based on what you say. You can then use a command like "Show me my Notes from..." or "Find my [insert title] Notes" in order to view notes stored within the Notes app.

Use Siri to Get Stock Prices, Update Your Facebook Page, Send Tweets, and Much More

As you'll soon discover, you can use Siri to access the latest information about the stock market and your specific investments. For example, ask, "What's Apple's stock price?" or "What did Facebook close at today?" It's also possible to ask more general questions, like "How are the markets doing?" or "What is the Dow at?"

If you want to quickly update your Facebook Status or compose and send a tweet to your Twitter followers, tell Siri to do this for you. For example, use a command like "Post to Facebook…" or "Write on my Facebook wall…" To compose and send a tweet, begin your command by saying "Tweet," followed by your message, which, as always, can be up to 140 characters.

 Siri is fully integrated with many of the iPhone's built-in apps, including Clock. You can request that Siri set an alarm or timer, for example.

Ask Siri Questions and Get Quick Answers

Siri is capable of looking up information on the Internet for you. To do this, begin your request by saying "Look up" or "Search the Web for." You could also say "Google [insert topic]" or "Search Wikipedia for…"

Another way to utilize Siri is to ask almost any type of question that has an answer Siri can look up on the Internet. For example, ask "What is Florida's state bird?" or "What were yesterday's winning lottery numbers in New York?" If you need the definition of a word, use the command "Define [insert word]."

Siri is an expert mathematician. Activate Siri and provide a math-based question, such as "What is 5 plus 5?" or "What is 15 percent of $62.50." Anything that the Calculator app built into the iPhone can handle, so too can Siri by responding to your voice commands.

 If you have the Find My Friends app installed on your iPhone, Siri can pinpoint and report to you the exact location of your friends and/or display their whereabouts on a map. As long as that person is active within your Find My Friends app, all you need to say is "Where's [insert name]?" Or, if you use the optional Apple Store app, Siri can help you find details about specific Apple products. For example, you could ask, "How much is Apple TV?"

Fine-Tune Siri's Performance Through Practice

As you begin using Siri, experiment by using different commands to accomplish various tasks, keeping in mind that Siri can control apps and iPhone functions, access app-specific data, and pull information from the Internet to provide the desired results. The trick to using Siri is discovering the best way to verbalize your requests in order to generate the desired result.

While Siri uses advanced artificial intelligence to understand not only the words you're saying but also the meaning or context behind your words, you sometimes need to be more specific about what you want Siri to do. For example, if you ask about the weather, restaurants, movies, or businesses, Siri's default behavior is to respond to your question based on your current location unless you provide an alternate location in conjunction with your request. (Siri relies on your iPhone's Location Services feature to pinpoint your location and the Maps app to find other locations and destinations.)

 The more information you include within your Contacts database, event listings (Calendar), to-do lists (Reminders), and notes (Notes), for example, the more information Siri will be able to provide to you when your request it.

In addition to discovering creative ways to issue questions, commands, or requests to obtain the desired results, if you want to have some fun while practicing using Siri, test out Siri's sense of humor. For example, activate Siri and say "Tell me a joke." Or, ask a question like "What is the best cell phone on the market?" You could also ask "Am I attractive?" or "Siri, what do you look like?" When it comes to using Siri, the possibilities are as limitless as the capabilities of the iPhone itself.

Deactivate Siri

As you've read, Siri can be a powerful tool to help you be productive and efficient using your iPhone. However, using this feature is 100 percent optional. In fact, from within Settings (or when you first activate your iPhone 5), you can deactivate the Siri feature altogether. To do this, launch Settings, tap the General option, and then tap the Siri option. To deactivate Siri, move the virtual switch that's associated with the Siri option to the Off position.

Enter Text into Apps via Your iPhone Using the Dictation Feature

As you just learned, you can use Siri to issue commands, make requests, or get questions answered. However, if you want or need to input text into virtually any app that requires the virtual keyboard, instead of typing that text, you can use iOS 6's Dictation feature.

 To use the Dictation feature, your iPhone must have access to the Internet. If you're using this feature with a 3G/4G Internet connection, it will use up some of your monthly wireless data allocation. You can use Dictation free of charge on an unlimited basis, however, by using a Wi-Fi connection. Dictation also tends to transcribe spoken words to text much faster when you're using Wi-Fi.

Dictation mode allows you to speak in a normal voice into your iPhone for up to 30 seconds at a time. Dictation mode records what you say, quickly transcribes your words into text, and inserts that text into the app you're currently using.

To activate Dictation mode, anytime the virtual keyboard appears, tap on the microphone key that's displayed between the 123 and Space keys. As soon as you enter into Dictation mode, the virtual keyboard disappears and the bottom of the iPhone's screen displays a large microphone icon and a Done button.

When using Siri, there is no need to tap a Done button (or tap the microphone button) when you're finished speaking. This is only necessary if there is too much background noise and Siri can't figure out when you've finished speaking. Tapping the Done button when using the Dictation feature, however, is required.

When the microphone icon turns slightly purple, begin speaking. Try to speak in your normal voice, as clearly as possible. (This feature works much better if it's used in an area that doesn't have a lot of background noise or loud music playing, for example.) As soon as you're done dictating your text, tap the Done key. Your iPhone translates your spoken words into text and inserts that text into the app you're currently using. How long this takes will depend on the speed of your Internet connection and how long you spoke for, but usually it's a matter of a few seconds.

Be sure to proofread the text carefully before sharing it with other people. You'll discover Dictation offers a high level of accuracy, but it's seldom 100 percent accurate. Chances are, you'll need to go back and manually correct errors in the text.

The Dictation mode understands basic rules of grammar and often knows when to capitalize words. While you're speaking, you can't tell the iPhone when to capitalize a specific word. You can, however, add punctuation as you're speaking.

Interact with Your iPhone However You'd Like

Between using the iPhone's virtual keyboard, touch-screen finger motions, Siri, and the Dictation feature, you have a variety of ways to interact with your iPhone. While each of these methods requires some practice, in no time you'll find each offers an efficient, fast, and pretty accurate way to enter information or interact with the iPhone and the apps you're utilizing.

If you are a veteran iPhone user who's recently upgraded to the iPhone 5, expect a slight learning curve before you become fully proficient using the new features, such as the larger touch-screen display and improved Siri functionality. After all, the new iPhone will feel different in your hands, and the size of the keys displayed as part of the virtual keyboard are slightly different, as is the iPhone 5's reaction time to key presses.

How to... **Incorporate Punctuation into Your Dictation**

As you're speaking into your iPhone using the Dictation feature, you can add punctuation to the text by saying that punctuation. For example, say the words "open quote," "close quote," "comma," "period," "exclamation point," etc., and your iPhone will insert that punctuation into the text when it's transcribed.

If you wanted to dictate a sentence that contains punctuation using the Dictation feature, here's what you'd say:

Sample Sentence	What You'd Actually Say When Using Dictation
I love using my new iPhone. Movies on the large display look amazing! I keep thinking to myself, "Wow!"	I love using my new iPhone period movies on the large display look amazing exclamation point I keep thinking to myself comma open quote wow exclamation point close quote

As you use the iPhone's various features, functions, and apps, you can often choose between manually entering information using the virtual keyboard, using an external keyboard for data entry, using finger gestures to navigate around, and/or verbally interacting with your iPhone through Siri and/or the Dictation feature. The choice is typically based on your personal preferences and whether you need to use the iPhone with one hand, two hands, or on a hands-free basis.

4

Back Up, Sync, and Import Your Existing Data into Your iPhone

HOW TO...

- Create and maintain an iTunes Sync backup
- Create and maintain an iCloud Backup
- Restore from an iTunes Sync backup or iCloud Backup
- Sync data and files with iTunes
- Sync data and files with iCloud
- Sync data and files using other cloud-based services
- Share data and files with software running on your computer or online-based apps

The folks who design the iPhone and the apps for it understand something very important—that for the iPhone to offer you, the user, the most functionality and versatility in your own personal and professional life, it needs to provide you with unhindered access to your own data and files, when and where you need that information. As a result, you have a variety of options when it comes to backing up, syncing, and importing data from your primary computer, your other devices, and the Internet.

In the past, for most data, files, and content that you needed to import into or sync with your iPhone, you had to use the iTunes Sync process. This involved connecting your iPhone (using the supplied USB cable) to your primary computer and using the free iTunes software on your computer to establish the link and be the conduit for the data exchange. While the iTunes Sync process is still a viable option for backing up and/or syncing data on your iPhone with your primary computer (whether it's a Mac or a PC), thanks to faster wireless Internet speeds and cloud-based file-sharing services, including Apple's iCloud, you now have other options that are more versatile and convenient. These other options are particularly useful for syncing files between your computer(s), your iPhone 5, and your other iOS mobile devices (such as an iPad), as well as any online-based applications you may utilize to manage your schedule, contacts, or to-do lists, for example.

 There are some good reasons to use your iPhone with a cloud-based file-sharing service: to back up (archive) app-specific data to a safe and remote location; to sync app-specific data or files between your iPhone and your other computers or mobile devices; and to share app-specific data and files with other people wirelessly.

The iOS 6 operating system that runs your iPhone 5 is now fully integrated with Apple's iCloud service. This online file-sharing service offers many different functions beyond just allowing you to upload, store, and share files in the "cloud." As you'll discover in this chapter, many of the core apps that come preinstalled with the iPhone 5, as well as Apple's own iWork and iLife apps (Pages, Numbers, Keynote, iPhoto, iMovie, and GarageBand, for example), all fully integrate with iCloud seamlessly. You'll also discover that many of the popular third-party apps that you can opt to use with your iPhone support other cloud-based file-sharing services, and you can choose to use those services as well (or instead of iCloud).

This chapter explores some of the ways to create and maintain a backup of your iPhone and some of the methods you can use to sync data, files, and content between your iPhone 5, primary computer, other iOS mobile devices, and/or any online-based applications you may be using.

Create and Maintain a Backup of Your iPhone

Regardless of what you use your iPhone for, chances are it will hold a lot of information and data that's very important to you. Just like your computer, the iPhone is a complex, technological device that should be backed up regularly. Thus, if something goes wrong, you can always restore your iPhone data onto your existing iPhone or onto a replacement iPhone with relative ease and minimal frustration.

 It's not uncommon for an iPhone to get lost, stolen, or damaged. If this happens, as long as you have a backup of your iPhone's content, you can restore that backup onto a replacement iPhone easily.

Apple has made it very easy to create and maintain a backup of your iPhone—its apps, data, files, photos, content, and personalized settings. However, you must get into the habit of regularly using one of the available backup methods.

You can create and maintain a backup of your iPhone using the iTunes Sync process or iTunes Wireless Sync process. Either of these methods allows you to store your iPhone's backup files on your primary computer's hard drive. You also have the option to use the iCloud Backup feature, which allows you to store your iPhone backup data "in the cloud," wirelessly via the Internet. This section describes how to use each backup method.

When you use the iTunes Sync process, you can set up iTunes to not only back up your iPhone, but also, at the same time, copy new apps, music, eBooks, photos, and other content from your primary computer to your iPhone. You can also tell the iTunes software which particular content you want synced in addition to the backup process. The section "Sync Data, Documents, Files, and Photos Using iTunes Sync," later in the chapter, describes how to do this. Similar syncing options are available with iCloud, as explained in the section "Use iCloud to Wirelessly Sync Data, Documents, Files, and Photos."

Note If you use iTunes Sync to create a backup of your iPhone, to later restore your iPhone using the saved backup files, you'll need to be able to connect your iPhone directly to your primary computer (either using the supplied Lightning to USB Cable or wirelessly if the iPhone and the computer are connected to the same wireless network via Wi-Fi). If you use iCloud Backup, however, you can create or restore your iPhone from anywhere a Wi-Fi Internet connection is available.

Create and Maintain an iTunes Sync Backup

You can create and maintain an iTunes Sync backup of your iPhone either by connecting your iPhone to your primary computer or by synching wirelessly. For both methods, begin by downloading, installing, and running the latest version of the iTunes software on your primary computer (www.apple.com/itunes).

For the wired method, connect your iPhone directly to your primary computer, using the supplied Lightning to USB Cable. This cable connects from the Lightning port on the bottom of your iPhone 5 to the USB port (or USB hub) on your Mac or PC. Once the computer and iPhone are connected, and the iTunes software is running on your computer, a link between the two devices will automatically be established. You can then customize the iTunes software to create and maintain a backup of your iPhone each time this connection is made. Keep in mind, the iTunes software for your Mac or PC is different from the iTunes app for your iPhone (which is not used for the syncing process).

Tip You'll need to get into the habit of connecting your computer to your iPhone often in order to maintain an up-to-date backup of the phone.

Instead of using the wired iTunes Sync process, if the iPhone and computer are connected to the same wireless network via Wi-Fi, you can use the iTunes Wireless Sync feature. To turn on this feature for the first time, launch the iTunes software on your computer and connect the iPhone using the supplied Lightning to USB Cable. Once the connection is made, on your computer, click the iPhone option displayed under the Devices heading on the left side of the iTunes screen. When the iPhone

Summary screen (shown in Figure 4-1) is displayed on the computer, look near the center of the screen, under the Options heading, and place a check mark next to the Sync With This iPhone Over Wi-Fi option.

Now, each time the computer and iPhone are connected to the same wireless network (via Wi-Fi), the iTunes software on your computer can create and maintain a backup of your iPhone. Just as with the iTunes Sync process, from the iTunes software running on your computer, you can custom configure how and when the iTunes Wireless Sync process will function. For example, when the iPhone and computer are linked to the same Wi-Fi network and you plug your iPhone into an external power source, it will automatically back up and sync with the computer. You also have the option to perform a manual sync wirelessly.

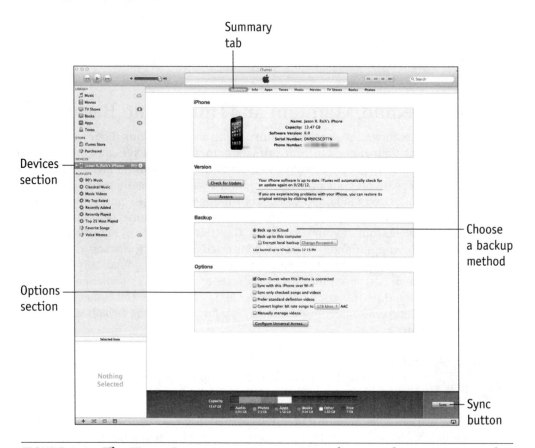

FIGURE 4-1   The iTunes Summary screen on a Mac when an iPhone is connected to it via the supplied Lightning to USB Cable. The PC version looks very similar.

How to...   Customize the iTunes Backup Process

While the iTunes software is running on your computer and your iPhone is connected, displayed along the top of the iTunes window are several tabs, labeled Summary, Info, Apps, Tones, Music, Movies, TV Shows, Books, and Photos. One at a time, click each tab to customize what content or data will be backed up, transferred, or synced between your iPhone and computer. You only need to customize these options once, but you can make changes to the configuration anytime. For example, instead of storing on your iPhone all of your TV show episodes or movies that you've purchased from the iTunes Store, you can pick and choose specific episodes or movies to transfer to your iPhone. This is also the case with your digital music (including your Playlists), e-books, ringtones, apps, and photos.

 Whether you're using iTunes Sync or iTunes Wireless Sync, click the Sync button near the lower-right corner of the iTunes screen to manually create a new or updated backup.

If you store private information on your iPhone, it's possible to encrypt the backup files from your iPhone that will be stored on your primary computer when you use iTunes Sync. To encrypt these files, check the Encrypt Local Backup check box under the Backup heading on the Summary screen in iTunes (refer to Figure 4-1). You'll be required to create a password so that you can access the encrypted files later if you need them to restore your iPhone. Make sure you do not forget the password you create—you will have to jump through a bunch of hoops to recover it.

As long as you maintain a backup of your iPhone on your computer, you can later restore those backup files onto your existing iPhone (or a replacement iPhone) with ease.

Create and Maintain an iCloud Backup

If you have an iCloud account, have your iPhone linked to that account, and have access to a Wi-Fi Internet connection for your iPhone, you can use iCloud to create and maintain a backup of your iPhone. When you turn on the iCloud Backup feature, your iPhone will attempt to automatically create an updated backup every day. For this feature to work, however, the iPhone needs to be in Sleep mode and connected to both a Wi-Fi network and an external power source. You also have the option to manually create an iCloud backup anytime.

 Unlike the iTunes Sync process, the iCloud Backup feature does not automatically check for new versions of apps stored on your iPhone, nor does it sync app-specific data. These features are handled through other iCloud features that work in conjunction with iCloud Backup but are managed separately.

To turn on the iCloud Backup feature, launch Settings, tap the iCloud option, and then tap the Storage & Backup option near the bottom of the iCloud screen. On the Storage & Backup screen (shown in Figure 4-2), slide the iCloud Backup virtual switch to On.

A Start iCloud Backup pop-up window is displayed on the screen. Tap the OK button to continue. This information window offers a reminder that you can use either iTunes Sync or iCloud to maintain a backup of your iPhone, not both methods.

With the iCloud Backup option turned on, from this point forward, the iPhone will attempt to make an automatic backup of your device on a daily basis. To manually create a backup anytime, tap the Back Up Now button that's now displayed near the bottom of the Storage & Backup screen. When creating a manual backup, a Wi-Fi Internet connection is required, but the iPhone does not need to be connected to an external power source.

 Displayed just below the Back Up Now button is the time and date that the last successful backup was created using the iCloud Backup feature.

FIGURE 4-2   The Storage & Backup screen within Settings on the iPhone 5

FIGURE 4-3   Manually updating an existing backup with the latest content on your iPhone shouldn't take more than one to three minutes.

The first time you create an iCloud Backup, the process will take a while to complete. However, all subsequent backups will take just one to three minutes, since the existing backup will be updated with only the latest additions or changes to your iPhone. Figure 4-3 shows the manual iCloud Backup process underway.

Restore Data from a Backup

Maintaining a backup of your iPhone's content allows you to restore files, data, apps, content, photos, and personalized iPhone settings if, for whatever reason, you need to reset your iPhone and erase its contents, or you need to replace or upgrade your iPhone.

 Whether created using iTunes Sync, iTunes Wireless Sync, or iCloud Backup, an iPhone backup can be used to transfer data from your old iPhone onto a new iPhone, such as when you upgrade from the iPhone 4 or iPhone 4S to the iPhone 5. These procedures were described in Chapter 2.

Restore Your iPhone from an iTunes Backup

To restore iPhone backup files onto an iPhone using iTunes Sync, connect the iPhone to your primary computer using the supplied Lightning to USB Cable. Once the connection is made, click the iPhone device displayed under the Devices heading on the left side of the iTunes screen (on your computer).

On the Summary screen within iTunes, click the Restore button near the center of the screen, below the Version heading, as shown next. You'll be prompted to choose which version of the backup file you want to load onto the connected iPhone. Depending on the amount of information that needs to be transferred to the iPhone and then installed, this process could take up to 30 minutes, maybe longer.

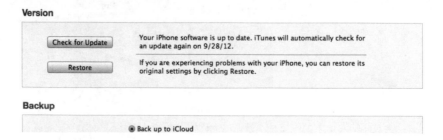

 When you use the Restore option, all data, files, and content currently stored on your iPhone will be deleted and replaced with the data, files, content, and personalized iPhone settings that are included within the backup files.

Restore Your iPhone from an iCloud Backup

You can manually delete all content currently on your iPhone and then restore everything from an iCloud backup. To do this, launch Settings on your iPhone, tap the General option, scroll down to the bottom of the General screen, and tap Reset. On the Reset screen, tap the Erase All Content And Settings option, and then confirm your decision when prompted.

Doing this will erase everything on your iPhone and restore its factory settings. Repeat the activation and setup procedure and, when prompted, select the Restore From iCloud Backup option. As long as your iPhone has access to a Wi-Fi Internet connection, the Restore process will begin. Depending on how much data and content need to be transferred, it could take up to 30 minutes or longer for the Restore process to finish.

 As described in Chapter 2, if you are activating your iPhone 5 for the first time, you can use the Restore From iCloud Backup option during the activation and setup process to transfer the content from your old iPhone model to your iPhone 5.

Sync Data, Documents, Files, and Photos Using iTunes Sync

A complete backup of your iPhone is a process that's designed to happen periodically and copy all files from your iPhone to another source (such as your computer's hard drive or iCloud). However, there are many apps you'll soon be using that allow you to sync app-specific data or files between your iPhone and computer. When you use the iTunes Sync process, the sync of app-specific data or files can happen as often as you desire, as long as the iPhone and computer are linked together.

When you sync app-specific data or files with your computer or another source, some information gets imported to and merged with the data already stored on your iPhone, while data on your iPhone gets exported to and merged with data already stored on your other devices. Using the iTunes Sync process, if you want to sync data between your computer, iPhone, and iPad (or iPod touch), for example, you need to first perform the sync process with your other device(s), and then perform the iTunes Sync process with your iPhone. This ensures that all of the most current data and content from your computer and other device(s) are transferred to your iPhone.

As you're looking at the iTunes Summary screen on your computer, click on each of the tabs near the top center of the screen (Info, Apps, Tones, Music, Movies, TV Shows, Books, or Photos) to determine which app-specific data will sync between your computer and iPhone. For example, to transfer to your iPhone some app-specific data, such as Microsoft Word or Pages for Mac documents (for use with Pages on your iPhone), tap the Apps tab near the top center of the iTunes window on your computer to open the Apps screen (see Figure 4-4). In the top-left corner of the Apps screen, check the Sync Apps check box and then choose which of the apps stored on your computer you want to sync with your iPhone. If you add a checkmark to the Automatically Sync New Apps check box that's found under the Sync Apps list on the left, the newly purchased or acquired apps not only will be installed on your iPhone but will be synced automatically in the future as well.

 You can also customize your iPhone's Home screen layout from your computer by using the top-right area of the Apps screen. You can always customize the iPhone's Home screen directly from the iPhone, of course, which is covered in Chapter 6.

Near the bottom of the Apps screen, in the File Sharing section, you'll see a listing of apps (under the Apps heading) that are capable of transferring documents from your computer to your iPhone (or vice versa). Click one app at a time and then manually select the data file(s) or documents that you want to sync under Documents (refer to Figure 4-4). The apps listed with the File Sharing section are capable of syncing app-specific data, such as Pages documents, between the iPhone and your computer via the iTunes Sync process.

For example, if you want to transfer to your iPhone a Microsoft Word document that's stored on your computer, and then access that document using the Pages app

FIGURE 4-4   In the File Sharing section of the Apps screen within iTunes, you can export software-specific documents and files directly into compatible apps on your iPhone.

on your iPhone, click the Pages app in the Apps list. Then, in the lower-right corner of the Pages Documents window (on the right side of the computer screen), tap the Add button. Select the Word files that are currently stored on your computer that you want to transfer to your iPhone. When the files are displayed within the Pages Documents window, tap the Apply button that's located near the bottom-right corner of the screen. The selected files are sent to your iPhone and become accessible via the Pages app.

Repeat this process for each compatible app that requires files from your computer (such as iPhoto, Numbers, Keynote, GarageBand, or iMovie).

Use iCloud to Wirelessly Sync Data, Documents, Files, and Photos

One of the biggest benefits to using iCloud to sync app-specific data between your iPhone and iCloud (and in turn with your other computers and iOS mobile devices that are linked to the same account) is that the sync process happens automatically and in real time, once the feature is activated. Thus, if you update an entry within the Contacts database on your iPhone, for example, that update will almost immediately be uploaded to iCloud and synced with your primary computer and/or other iOS mobile devices that are linked to the same iCloud account. Or, if you update an entry on your iPad, that change will be sent via iCloud to your iPhone, as long as both devices have access to the Internet.

From Settings, you can decide which app-specific data you want to automatically sync with iCloud. To do this, launch Settings, tap the iCloud option, and then turn On the virtual switch associated with, respectively, Mail, Contacts, Calendars, Reminders, Safari, Notes, Passbook, Photo Stream, and/or Documents & Data (shown in Figure 4-5).

iCloud is great for automatically syncing app-specific data, documents, and files related to compatible apps on your iPhone with your iCloud account. Once this data is stored "in the cloud," it can automatically sync with your other computer(s)—Macs or PCs—as well as with other iOS devices that are linked to the same account.

What iCloud is not so good at yet, except for when it comes to photos, is sharing data, documents, and files with other people, or with computers and devices that are not linked to the same iCloud (Apple ID) account. To do this, you'll need to use the

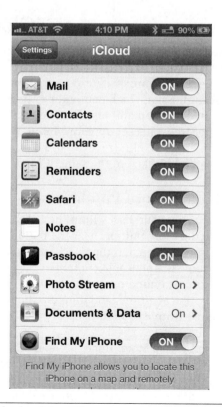

FIGURE 4-5   Choose which of the iPhone's preinstalled apps should be able to sync automatically with your iCloud account.

Turn On iCloud Syncing Functionality for Optional Apps

In addition to the core apps preinstalled on your iPhone, some optional apps that you install on your iPhone, like Numbers, Keynote, and Pages, can also use iCloud to back up their data. If you use these or other compatible apps and would like to sync them via iCloud automatically, you first have to turn on the Documents & Data option found on the iCloud screen (see Figure 4-5).

To do this, return to the main Settings menu and scroll down to each iCloud-compatible app listing. As an example, tap the Pages app and then tap the Use iCloud virtual switch displayed near the top of the Pages screen within Settings to turn it On. Repeat this process for each compatible app.

Share options found within the app, or utilize an alternate cloud-based file-sharing service that a particular app is compatible with (as described later in the chapter).

Sync Purchased Content via iCloud

All of your previous purchases from Apple's iTunes Store (music, movies, TV show episodes, audiobooks, music videos, and ringtones), as well as your App Store, iBookstore, and Newsstand purchases, are permanently stored online within your iCloud account, regardless of which computer or device the content was purchased from. Thus, you can download and install any of your previously purchased content onto your iPhone for free, plus set up your iPhone to automatically download and install any new content in the future, even if the purchase is made from another computer or device that's linked to the same iCloud (Apple ID) account.

Access Past iTunes Store Purchases

To access any of your past purchases from the iTunes Store, from your iPhone, launch the iTunes app, tap the More button (near the bottom-right corner of the screen), and then tap the Purchased option. On the Purchased screen, select Music, Movies, or TV Shows (or another type of applicable content).

A listing of your past online purchases from the iTunes Store will be displayed. Tap your selections, one at a time, and then tap the iCloud icon for that selection to download the content from iCloud directly to your iPhone.

While visiting the App Store, iTunes Store, Newsstand, or iBookstore, instead of accessing past purchases from the Purchased screen, you can locate that content in the main store. You'll be allow to re-download it onto your iPhone for free. Instead of a price icon, an Install button will be displayed. Or, if the price icon remains visible, as soon as you initiate the purchase, you'll be informed that it's a previous purchase and you will not be charged.

Access Past App Store Purchases

To access any of your past purchases from the App Store, from the iPhone, launch the App Store app, and then tap the Updates button near the lower-right corner of the screen. On the Updates screen, tap the Purchased option. When the Purchased screen appears, tap the Not On This iPhone tab that's displayed near the top of the screen.

A listing of all previously purchased iPhone-compatible apps that are stored within your iCloud account, but that are not installed on your iPhone, will be displayed. One at a time, tap the iCloud icon that's associated with each app listing to download and install (or reinstall) that app.

Access Past iBookstore and Newsstand Purchases

To access any of your past iBookstore e-book purchases, from your iPhone, launch the iBooks app. Next, tap the Store button near the upper-right corner of the main Library screen (which looks like a virtual bookshelf). When your iPhone accesses the online-based iBookstore via the iBooks app, tap the Purchased button near the bottom-right corner of the screen. Select the previously purchased e-book titles that you want to load onto your iPhone by tapping the iCloud icon that's associated with each listing.

The downloaded e-books will then be displayed within the Library screen of the iBooks app, which you can access once again by tapping the Library button near the upper-right corner of the Purchased screen.

To access any of your past Newsstand purchases (digital editions of newspapers or magazines), launch the Newsstand app, and then tap the Store button on the right side of the Newsstand window. The App Store will launch. Tap the Updates button, followed by the Purchased option, and then the Not On This iPhone tab. Within the listing of previously purchased apps will be apps related to the digital newspapers and magazines you've acquired in the past. From the publication-specific app, in most cases, you can then download and read previously purchased issues of that publication.

Set Up Your iPhone to Auto-Sync New Purchases

As you make new content purchases from the iTunes Store, App Store, iBookstore, or Newsstand, regardless of which computer or device is used to make the purchase, as long as that computer or device is linked to the same iCloud (Apple ID) account as your iPhone, you can set up the iPhone to automatically download any and all new purchases, within seconds after the purchase is made (or the next time the iPhone has access to the Internet).

To set up this auto-download feature, launch Settings on the iPhone and tap the iTunes & App Store option. On the iTunes & App Store screen, turn on the virtual switch associated with Music, Apps, and/or Books. These options are displayed below the Automatic Downloads heading.

You can then turn on or off the Use Cellular Data option. When turned on, if no Wi-Fi Internet connection is available, your iPhone will download content purchases using a 3G/4G Internet connection, but this will utilize some of your monthly wireless data allocation. When turned off, your iPhone will download new purchases only if a Wi-Fi connection is present.

 To download TV shows, movies, and music videos, launch the iTunes app and tap the Purchased option. Due to the large file sizes of this content, it can't be automatically downloaded to your iPhone unless it's purchased from your iPhone.

On the iTunes & App Store screen within Settings, you can also turn on (or off) the optional iTunes Match service, which allows you to sync your entire digital music library between all of your computers and iOS mobile devices that are linked to the same iCloud account, even if the music was not purchased from iTunes.

Share Files Using Other Cloud-Based File-Sharing Services

Many of the popular third-party apps that you can opt to use with your iPhone support other cloud-based file-sharing services, such as Dropbox (www.dropbox.com) or Microsoft SkyDrive (http://windows.microsoft.com/en-US/skydrive/home). These third-party apps typically allow you to use a free service such as Dropbox to back up app-specific data or files, share that information with others, and/or sync the information with your other computers and/or iOS mobile devices. Popular cloud-based file-sharing services such as Dropbox and SkyDrive also have their own proprietary iPhone apps that are available from the App Store, and they offer seamless integration with third-party apps.

As an iPhone user, you'll probably want to use iCloud because of all the unique features it offers for backing up, syncing, sharing, and archiving your data, files, documents, photos, and other content related to the iPhone's core preinstalled apps (including Contacts, Calendars, Reminders, Notes, Photos, and Safari) and optional apps (such as Pages, Numbers, Keynote, and iPhoto). Plus, iCloud is used to sync and share your purchased online content from the iTunes Store, App Store, iBookstore, and Newsstand between all computers and devices that are linked to the same account.

However, if you also come to rely on some third-party apps that can utilize a cloud-based file-sharing service, or you need to share app-specific data, files, and/or documents with other people, for example, you may find that you want or need to use a cloud-based file-sharing service other than iCloud.

 If you opt to use the app-specific iCloud sync features, do not set up the iPhone to sync with your Yahoo!, Google, or Microsoft Exchange–compatible accounts, which are set up from the Mail, Contacts, Calendars screen within Settings. If you try to sync your Contacts, Calendar, Reminders, and Notes data with an online-based account and also with iCloud, you will most likely wind up with duplicate entries.

An ever-growing number of third-party apps designed for the iPhone are compatible with independent, cloud-based file-sharing services such as Dropbox, Box.com, or SkyDrive. Just as with iCloud, setting up an account with many of these cloud-based services is free, and the account comes with a predetermined amount of online storage space.

In some cases, from within the app you're using, you'll need to manually sync your data, documents, or files with your cloud-based account. The process will not always happen automatically and in the background, as it does with iCloud. How the third-party app you're using utilizes a cloud-based files-sharing service will vary.

You'll discover that many of these cloud-based file-sharing services make it easy to share files, data, and documents with other people, and even collaborate on work. You can import, export, or sync files wirelessly from your iPhone as long as you have an Internet connection (Wi-Fi or 3G/4G).

Figure out which third-party apps you'll want to utilize on your iPhone, and then set up a free account with the cloud-based file-sharing service it's compatible with. Note that many third-party apps are compatible with Dropbox.

Sync Other Data and Files Between Your Computer, Network, and iPhone

Depending on the software you use on your computer(s), you may discover that it's possible to sync software-specific data, files, and/or documents between your computer(s) and iPhone via the Internet. When this is possible, you'll typically need to install a proprietary app version of the software onto your iPhone. Then, the Mac or PC version of the software will be able to sync files with its iPhone app counterpart. For example, the FileMaker Pro, Things, and Bento applications for Macs (and in some cases PCs) each has its own iPhone app that allows databases to be synced between a computer and iPhone via the Internet.

If you run Evernote on your iPhone, you can also run the Mac, PC, iPad, or Android version on your other computer(s) or device(s) in order to keep all of your Evernote files and documents synced. Evernote is just one example of a popular and versatile app that has a separate Mac, PC, iPhone, iPad, and Android version available. It's also compatible with Dropbox.

Determine if the specialized software you currently use on your Mac or PC has a proprietary iPhone app available to make syncing data, files, and/or documents related to that software an easy process. The iPhone app that's required to do this will be available from the App Store.

Share Data and Files with Online-Based Applications

Instead of using software installed on your computer to manage a database, your contacts, your schedule, and/or your to-do lists, for example, you may take advantage of online-based apps. For example, Google and Yahoo! both offer robust and popular contact management and scheduling tools that are online based. Facebook also offers a scheduling tool, and many companies utilize Microsoft Exchange for a wide range of data management purposes.

Your iPhone is compatible with many of these online-based applications, and can import, export, and/or sync data between them and the Contacts, Calendar, Notes, and Reminders apps that come preinstalled on the iPhone. Of course, your iPhone will need access to the Internet for this syncing process to work.

To set up your iPhone to sync data with Google, Yahoo!, or Microsoft Exchange, launch Settings and tap the Mail, Contacts, Calendar option. Under the Accounts heading on the Mail, Contacts, Calendar screen, tap the Add Account option. On the Add Account screen, shown in Figure 4-6, select the type of account you want to set

FIGURE 4-6 Choose which type of account you want to be able to sync with your iPhone and then follow the prompts to activate the syncing process. You need to do this only once.

FIGURE 4-7   Choose which app(s) you want to sync online-based data with.

up, such as Google Gmail, Yahoo!, or Microsoft Exchange. When prompted, enter your existing account-related information, including your name, username, and password, along with a description for the account.

When you tap the Next button in the upper-right corner of the screen, your account information will be verified. A menu will then be displayed (shown in Figure 4-7) that allows you to sync your Mail, Contacts, Calendars, Reminders, and/or Notes data with your existing Gmail, Yahoo!, or Microsoft Exchange account. Slide to On the virtual switch associated with each type of data that you want to sync.

From this point on, your mail, contacts, scheduling, to-do lists, and/or notes will remain synced in real time (via the Internet) between your iPhone and your online-based account.

Use the Share Button Incorporated into Many Apps

Beyond automatically syncing data, files, and content with other computers, many apps have a Share button that allows you to share app-specific data or files with

How to...   **Sync Your Facebook Account with Contacts and Calendar**

If you want to sync your Facebook account with the Contacts and Calendar apps on your iPhone, launch Settings and tap the Facebook option. Enter your Facebook username and password, and then turn on the virtual switches associated with Calendar, Contacts, and Facebook on the Facebook screen, as shown here. While friend and event-related data from your Facebook account will now be added to your Contacts and Calendar apps automatically, you'll periodically want to tap the Update All Contacts button as you add new friends to your Facebook account online.

specific individuals via e-mail, text message, Facebook, or Twitter, for example. To share app-specific data with others, simply tap the Share button or option within the app you're using, select your Share method, and then select or enter the contact details for the people with whom you want to share that information.

When you share app-specific data such as a Contacts entry, a photo, or a Pages document from your iPhone with another iPhone, iPad, or iPod touch user, for example, they'll have the option to import that data or content into the compatible app running on their device, or just view the shared content you sent.

PART II

Learn the Basics of iOS 6

5

Discover the Apps That Come Preinstalled with iOS 6

HOW TO...

- Explore the apps that come preinstalled with the iPhone 5
- Integrate Apple's iCloud service and use it with the core preinstalled apps
- Use the Share options that are now built into many apps
- Take advantage of AirPrint and AirPlay
- Utilize other iOS 6 functions you'll find useful

As you've already discovered in previous chapters, your new iPhone 5 comes with a nice selection of preinstalled apps. These apps, in conjunction with the iOS 6 operating system, are designed to handle a wide range of popular tasks and provide the foundation for what makes the iPhone 5 one of the most popular and versatile smartphones ever released.

One thing you're going to notice when you begin using your iPhone 5 with iOS 6, the preinstalled apps, Apple's iCloud service, and the Internet is that Apple has gone to great lengths to offer seamless integration between everything. This integration not only makes it easier to create, access, view, edit, enhance, print, share, sync, and store your data, files, documents, photos, and other content, but also makes this information readily available to you on the iPhone itself and on the Internet (via iCloud), your other iOS mobile devices (such as an iPad), and your primary Mac and/or PC-based computer(s).

As one example of this seamless integration, once you activate iCloud to work with your iPhone (a process that takes about two minutes), data from many of the apps that come preinstalled with the iPhone 5, including Contacts, Calendar, Reminders, Notes, Safari, Photos, and Mail, for example, will automatically sync in real time with your other iOS mobile devices and primary computer(s) that are linked to the same Apple ID account. This means that all of your most important data will be readily accessible and up to date whenever and wherever you need it, regardless of which computer or device you're using. Once you set this up, syncing happens automatically and in the background, as long as your iPhone 5 and your other computers and/or devices have access to the Internet. This same syncing capability can also be set up to work with your documents and other files.

Plus, by visiting Apple's online-based iTunes Store, Newsstand, App Store, and iBookstore, for example, you'll discover the world's largest and most robust selections of digital content that you can purchase (or in some cases acquire for free) and use on your iPhone 5. The content available includes music, TV shows, movies, music videos, audiobooks, e-books, digital publications, podcasts, free educational content and personal enrichment courses and programs for all ages (from iTunes U), ringtones, and more than 700,000 additional third-party apps (many of which can give your iPhone 5 new or enhanced functionality).

This content can all be acquired from, downloaded to, and experienced on your iPhone 5. In fact, any content you've purchased in the past from any of Apple's online business ventures using your older iPhone, or an iPad, iPod touch, or your primary computer(s), is already readily available to you and can be transferred to your iPhone 5 via your free iCloud account, as long as your iPhone 5 is linked to the same Apple ID account as your other device(s) and computer(s).

This chapter will introduce you to a handful of the popular apps that come preinstalled on your iPhone, along with some of the phone's more useful features and functions, like Siri, that can be used in conjunction with the apps. In later chapters, we'll focus on how to use many of the apps introduced here.

Did You Know?

A Vast Selection of Digital Content Is Available Beyond What Apple Offers

Beyond content that's available for purchase from Apple's online business ventures, there is a plethora of third-party apps that give you immediate access to even more online-based digital content. Much of this content can be streamed (or in some cases transferred) to your iPhone via the Internet.

This free and fee-based content includes e-books and digital publications from other online-based bookstores (such as Amazon and Barnes & Noble), movies, TV shows, music videos, audiobooks, streaming audio (live and prerecorded programming from radio stations, for example), and all sorts of other entertaining, educational, or informative videos from services like YouTube, Netflix, and the proprietary apps offered by major television networks, cable TV channels, and cable TV service providers.

Explore the Apps That Come Preinstalled on the iPhone 5

As soon as you activate your iPhone and access its Home screen for the first time, on display will be a selection of preinstalled apps that are ready to use. This section offers an overview of what these apps are and what they do. Subsequent chapters of this book will teach you how to use many of these core apps.

If during the iPhone 5 activation process you restored data from your older-model iPhone, or if you've already activated iCloud functionality on the iPhone and have maintained a contacts database, scheduling info, to-do lists, a collection of photos, Safari bookmarks (and related information), and/or notes on an older iPhone, another iOS mobile device (such as an iPad), or while using the Contacts (Address Book), Calendar (iCal), Reminders, Notes, Mail, Safari, and/or iPhoto apps that now come preinstalled on a Mac running OS X Mountain Lion, your personal data may already be loaded into your iPhone 5 and fully accessible. This also applies to PC users who have downloaded the free iCloud Control Panel for Windows (http://support.apple.com/kb/DL1455) in order to sync compatible files and data between their PC and iPhone.

 Note   If you're a veteran iPhone user, you'll quickly discover that many of the preinstalled iPhone apps you're familiar with have been revamped and enhanced in conjunction with iOS 6, and you'll also discover that the iPhone now comes with a few new apps that you've never seen before.

In earlier chapters, you learned how to use many of the iPhone 5's basic features. Now, you can apply this knowledge when using the core, preinstalled apps that come with your new iPhone. The app icons for the majority of these apps are displayed on your Home screen as soon as you activate the iPhone.

The following sections take a look at the majority of the core, preinstalled apps, in alphabetical order. Unless otherwise noted, simply tap the app's icon on the Home screen to open the app.

 Tip   As you begin using the various preinstalled apps, consider all of the ways they can interact with each other, and consider how you can take advantage of the iPhone's built-in functionality (such as Siri, Dictation, and the Select, Select All, Cut, Copy, and Paste commands), plus services like iCloud, to gain even greater capabilities and versatility.

App Store

Access Apple's App Store (shown in Figure 5-1 with the Featured category displayed) to find, purchase, download, and install additional apps for your iPhone. The App Store app can also be used to acquire free apps and to install updated versions of apps you've previously acquired. You can find additional information about using the App Store in Chapter 20.

FIGURE 5-1   Find, purchase, download, and install optional apps onto your iPhone using the App Store app. A wide range of free apps is also available from Apple's App Store.

  You can also shop for apps from your primary computer using the free iTunes software, and then transfer those apps to your iPhone using the iTunes Sync process or via the Internet using iCloud.

Calculator

This powerful calculator offers you two different screens to choose from depending on the complexity of your calculations. When you hold the iPhone in portrait mode, the Calculator app displays a simple onscreen calculator (shown in Figure 5-2). However, when you rotate the iPhone to landscape mode (shown in Figure 5-3), a more advanced calculator becomes available. Like many apps, Calculator is fully integrated with Siri, so instead of performing mathematical calculations from the iPhone's screen, you can activate Siri and speak math-related questions, like "What is 15 percent of $62.50?" or "What is 17 + 59?"

FIGURE 5-2   The Calculator app's simple calculator mode appears when you hold the iPhone in portrait mode.

FIGURE 5-3   When using the Calculator app, rotate the iPhone to landscape mode to access more advanced functions.

Calendar

This is a powerful scheduling app that allows you to manage and view multiple calendars at the same time. For example, you can keep separate calendars for your work and personal schedule, your kids' schedule, your business trip schedule, and your vacation schedule, but you can view them on the same screen using a color-coded system.

Because Calendar is highly customizable, you can view your scheduling information in a variety of different formats. Figure 5-4 shows the app's Day view, while Figure 5-5 shows the app's Month view. There's also a Week view (see Figure 5-6) and a List view.

 When using the Calendar app, to view the Week view, rotate the iPhone to landscape mode.

Plus, you can sync scheduling data via iCloud with your other iOS mobile devices and Macs that are running Calendar (or iCal on the Mac), as well as with PCs running Outlook, for example. You can also sync your calendars with Yahoo!, Google, Facebook, and other online-based scheduling applications.

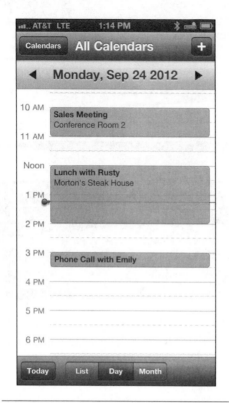

FIGURE 5-4 The Calendar app's Day view

FIGURE 5-5 The Calendar app's Month view

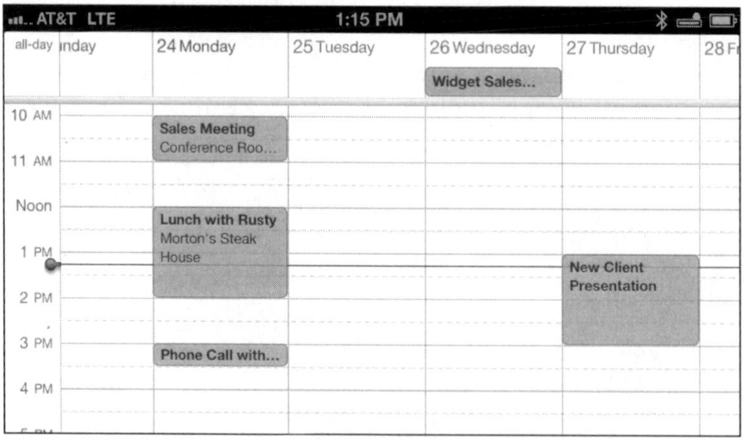

FIGURE 5-6 The Calendar app's Week view (in landscape mode)

You'll learn all about the Calendar, Reminders, and Notes apps and how to use them in Chapter 13. That chapter also covers how to import, export, and sync app-specific data with other computers or devices, plus how to utilize these apps with iCloud.

Camera

The Camera app enables you to control the powerful front- and back-facing cameras that are built into your iPhone 5 and snap digital photos or shoot video. This app works seamlessly with the Photos app, the optional iPhoto app, as well as many third-party photography apps available from the App Store. Using the Camera app to snap pictures (shown in Figure 5-7), you can use the iPhone's built-in flash (rear-facing camera), zoom in or zoom out on your subject(s), and take advantage of the new Panorama shooting mode. The app also offers face recognition and other features to ensure you capture clear, vibrant, in-focus shots in a wide range of situations, even when there's low light.

 You'll discover in Chapter 11 how to shoot amazing photos and entertaining videos with your iPhone using the Camera app. Chapter 11 also covers the Photos app that comes preinstalled with iOS 6, as well as a few of the many third-party photography apps available from the App Store.

Clock

In addition to serving as a world clock capable of displaying the time in any cities around the world that you select (shown in Figure 5-8), this app serves as an alarm (which you can use for reliable wakeup calls) and as a timer and stopwatch.

You can control the Clock app from the iPhone 5's Multi-Touch screen, or use voice commands with Siri. For example, it's possible to activate Siri and say, "Set a

FIGURE 5-7   Your iPhone can serve as a feature-packed, 8-megapixel digital camera that's capable of shooting vibrant, colorful, and clear images in a wide range of conditions. You can also shoot video.

FIGURE 5-8 The Clock app can serve as a world clock and simultaneously display the current time in a handful of cities and/or countries that you select.

wakeup call for 7 A.M. tomorrow" or "Set a 15-minute timer." You can also ask, for example, "What time is it in [insert city]?"

Contacts

This is a feature-packed contact management application that allows you to maintain a highly customizable database of the people you know. The Contacts app works seamlessly with iCloud, so you can keep your contacts database synced with your other iOS mobile devices and the Contacts or Outlook software running on a Mac or PC. Contacts is also fully compatible with Yahoo!, Google, and other contact management applications that are Mac, PC, or online based.

Be sure to read Chapter 8 for complete information about how to use this app, import contact data from your PC or Mac, and sync Contacts data with other mobile devices, computers, and online-based services.

Did You Know?

Your iPhone 5 Can Sync with Macs Running an Older Version of Mac OS X

If you are syncing data between your iPhone and your Mac and your Mac is running Mac OS X Mountain Lion, the Contacts, Calendar, Reminders, Notes, and Safari apps, for example, are all fully compatible. The Photos app is also compatible with the Mac's iPhoto software. However, if you're using a Mac that's running Mac OS X Lion (or an earlier version of the Mac operating system), the Contacts and Calendar apps on the iPhone will sync with Address Book and iCal.

Safari Bookmarks and the Bookmarks Bar data, as well as other app-specific data, can also sync with a Mac running an older version of Mac OS X, but you're better off upgrading to Mac OS X Mountain Lion to ensure full iCloud and app compatibility and seamless integration between your iPhone and your Mac-based data and files.

You'll discover that the information stored within your Contacts app can be accessed and utilized by many other apps and iPhone functions you'll soon be using, including Siri, Maps, Mail, Calendar, FaceTime, and others.

Facebook

Facebook integration is now a part of iOS 6, but if you want to manage all aspects of your Facebook account, you'll need to download the official Facebook app. While this app doesn't come preinstalled on the iPhone 5, you can download and install it for free from within Settings, at the same time you set up Facebook integration to function on your iPhone. Refer to Chapter 2 for more information about setting up and using Facebook on your iPhone.

FaceTime

Use FaceTime to participate in real-time video conferences using your iPhone. While this app works best using a Wi-Fi Internet connection, many wireless service providers also allow it to be used with a 3G/4G Internet connection. With FaceTime, you can communicate with other iPhone, iPad, iPad mini, iPod touch, and Mac users who also set up a FaceTime account. The FaceTime service is free. There is no limit to how many calls you participate in, or how long your calls last. With FaceTime, you can see and hear the people you're communicating with. One focus of Chapter 14 is on how to use the FaceTime app.

To participate in video conferences with non-Apple users (yes, there are still a few of them out there), use the optional Skype or ooVoo Video Chat app, for example.

Find My iPhone

The Find My iPhone app (which also works with other iOS mobile devices and Macs) enables you to locate your lost or stolen iPhone, display its location on a map, and perform several tasks associated with tracking, protecting, or recovering it and its contents. Using the Find My iPhone app, you can activate this feature on your iPhone (which needs to be done in advance, before your iPhone is lost or stolen), plus you can track the whereabouts of your other Macs and iOS devices.

Game Center

The App Store offers thousands of games that have been developed by some of the world's foremost computer, arcade, and video game developers. Game Center is an online-based community operated by Apple that allows you to compete against other players via the Internet when experiencing compatible multiplayer games. Game Center also serves as a forum for posting your high scores and game-related accomplishments. The Game Center app allows you to access the Game Center online service, which is free. You'll learn all about how to use your iPhone as a portable gaming system and how to use Game Center in Chapter 18.

iBooks

While this app doesn't come preinstalled on the iPhone, as soon as you activate the device, you'll be prompted to download and install it. iBooks allows your iPhone to serve as a customizable e-book reader (and also enables you to view PDF files stored on your iPhone). The app also grants you access to Apple's online-based iBookstore, so you can find, purchase, download, and install e-books onto your iPhone. iBookstore also offers thousands of free e-books available for downloading that are formatted for the iPhone. Once you acquire e-books, you can read them easily on your iPhone's screen (as shown in Figure 5-9), and format the content in a variety of customizable ways. Be sure to check out Chapter 17 to learn more about the iBooks app and Apple's iBookstore.

iTunes

Use this app to access Apple's online-based iTunes Store to find, purchase, and download a vast selection of multimedia content, including music, TV show episodes (or entire seasons of TV series), movies, music videos, and ringtones. To make purchases, you'll need to set up or use an Apple ID account that's linked to a credit or debit card. Chapter 16 covers the iTunes app and how to use it.

 You can also acquire content from the iTunes Store using the iTunes software on your primary computer and then transfer that content to your iPhone using the iTunes Sync process or iCloud.

FIGURE 5-9   Using the iBooks app, you can read bestsellers or classic novels directly from your iPhone's screen and store a full library of books on your iPhone. Millions of e-book titles are available from iBookstore.

Mail

You can manage one or more e-mail accounts using the redesigned and highly customizable Mail app. Mail allows you to read, organize, and archive incoming e-mails, plus compose (shown in Figure 5-10) and send outgoing e-mails. Mail is compatible with many types of files that may be included as attachments to incoming e-mails, and it often allows you to access or work with those files using a compatible app on your iPhone.

For example, if someone sends a Word, Pages, or PDF file to you via e-mail, you can open and work with that file from the Mail app and in conjunction with the optional Pages app. If someone sends digital photos to you as an incoming e-mail attachment, you can download them from the Mail app and then view them on your iPhone using the Photos app.

Many apps, such as Photos, Safari, and Contacts, now feature a Share option or button that allows you to compose and send e-mails from within those apps (without first launching the Mail app) and include app-specific content as attachments to those e-mails.

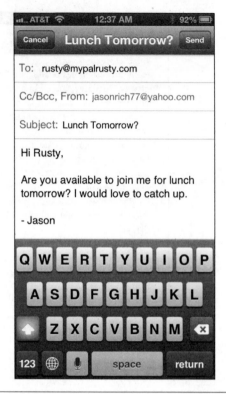

FIGURE 5-10 Compose outgoing e-mails from the Mail app.

Refer to Chapter 9 to learn all about how to manage one or more e-mail accounts, as well as how to send and receive e-mails from your iPhone.

 If you're a veteran iPhone user, you'll discover that when you compose e-mails using the Mail app, you can now attach to outgoing e-mails photos stored within the Photos app on your iPhone. In the past, this had to be done from the Photos app (which is still possible).

Maps

This is one of the apps that Apple has redesigned from scratch in conjunction with iOS 6. In addition to being able to display a map for any location or address, Maps can now provide detailed, real-time, turn-by-turn directions between any two locations (shown in Figure 5-11), plus display interactive, 3D versions of maps. The Maps app fully integrates with Yelp!, for example, so you can access detailed information about millions of businesses, restaurants, landmarks, and other popular locations. Onscreen maps can also be viewed using several different formats. You'll discover how to use all of the latest features built into the Maps app in Chapter 12.

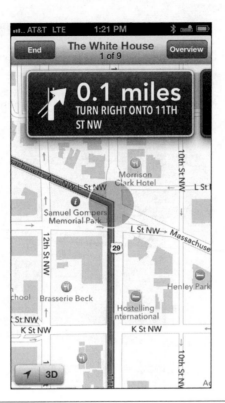

FIGURE 5-11   The Maps app that comes preinstalled with iOS 6 has been redesigned to offer a bunch of new features, like real-time, turn-by-turn directions and live traffic information.

Messages

From one app on your iPhone, Messages, you can exchange text messages and instant messages with any other cell phone user in the world, plus communicate with other iMessage users. One focus of Chapter 14 is on how to use the Messages app.

Music

With the Music app, you can enjoy listening to your personal digital music library one song at a time, select and play an album from start to finish (shown in Figure 5-12), or create personalized Playlists that you can listen to anywhere and anytime. The Music app stores your entire personal digital music library, including songs you acquire from the iTunes Store, "rip" from your own CDs, or transfer into the iPhone from other sources. The app is fully compatible with Apple's premium iTunes Match feature.

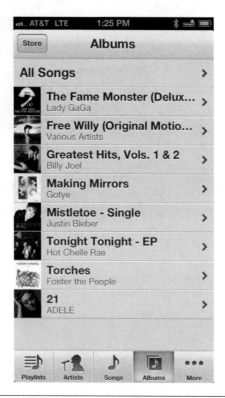

FIGURE 5-12 Your iPhone 5 has all of the functionality of Apple's most powerful iPod digital music players when it comes to enjoying (listening to and managing) digital music.

You can purchase new music with a few taps on the iPhone screen using the iTunes app, which also comes preinstalled on your iPhone, and then listen to that music using the Music app. Chapter 16 covers the Music app.

 When enjoying music, use your iPhone's built-in speaker, connect corded headphones to the iPhone (such as the Apple EarPods that came with your iPhone, or your own headphones or ear buds), or connect your iPhone to external speakers, via either a cable or a wireless Bluetooth or AirPlay connection, and then share the music that's stored on your iPhone with the people around you.

Newsstand

Through Apple, you can purchase (or acquire) digital editions of thousands of different newspapers or magazines and enjoy reading them on your iPhone. If you subscribe to the digital edition of a publication, such as *The New York Times*, for example, the Newsstand app will automatically download the latest edition or issue as soon as it's published, so it'll be ready to read on your iPhone when you wake up each morning. The digital editions of most newspapers and magazines look identical to the printed edition, although in some cases the digital edition that's available for your iPhone offers free bonus content. The Newsstand app allows you to find and read digital publications, plus manage your subscriptions to them. However, in many cases, single issues of a publication can also be purchased and read on your iPhone. Chapter 17 covers how to use the Newsstand app.

Notes

While not a full-featured word processor, the Notes app allows you to create text-based notes on your iPhone and then sync those notes with iCloud so they're readily accessible on your other iOS devices and computers. This app also works nicely with the iPhone's Dictation feature, so you can speak into your iPhone and have what you say transcribed into text and inserted into the Notes app.

 If you want full word processing capabilities on your iPhone so that you'll be able to create, access, view, edit, print, and share Microsoft Word– or Pages-compatible documents, you need an optional app, such as Pages, Documents To Go – Office Suite, or QuickOffice Pro, each of which is available from the App Store.

Passbook

Passbook is new to iOS 6 and is designed to be a centralized place to store, access, and manage tickets, airline boarding passes, store cards, and digital coupons, for example. In the near future, many of the major airlines, as well as retail chain stores, fast food restaurants, movie theater chains, sporting event venues, concert venues, and other businesses, will somehow support this app. How to use this innovative new Passbook app is covered in Chapter 19.

Phone

While your iPhone 5 is capable of doing so many cutting-edge tasks, first and foremost it's a cellular phone that's capable of making and receiving calls. This is all done using the Phone app. If you're a veteran iPhone user, you'll discover some awesome new features built into the latest version of the Phone app, including the ability to manage incoming calls, as shown in Figure 5-13, and better data integration with the Contacts app. Everything you need to know about making, receiving, and managing incoming and outgoing calls from your iPhone is covered within Chapter 7.

Photos

This app works in conjunction with the Camera app and is used to organize, store, display, edit, enhance, print, and share digital photos that are stored on your iPhone 5.

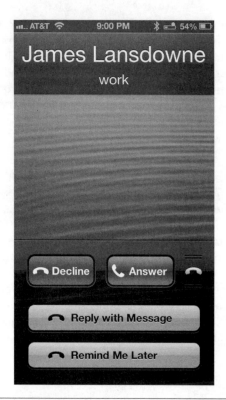

FIGURE 5-13 When an incoming call is received by your iPhone 5, you can answer it, send it to voice mail, or send a prewritten text message to the caller, for example. You can also set a reminder to yourself to call the person back.

Photos also enables you to view and perform minor edits to digital video shot using your iPhone. The Photos app seamlessly integrates with iCloud's Photo Stream feature, plus allows you to create and publish Shared Photo Streams (so you can share multiple images simultaneously with other people).

 For even greater photo editing and sharing capabilities, consider purchasing Apple's iPhoto app and installing it onto your iPhone. Or, if you want enhanced video editing and sharing capabilities, purchase and download Apple's iMovie app.

From the Photos app, you can also share individual images (and in some cases small groups of photos) with other people via e-mail, Twitter, Facebook, or text/instant message. To do this, tap the Share button within the app.

Reminders

Reminders is a highly customizable to-do list manager that allows you to create and manage many separate lists, with each list containing as many individual items as you need. Lists or individual items can each have separate alerts or alarms associated with them (which can be time/date based or location based). Plus, Reminders syncs data seamlessly with iCloud.

Safari

When it comes to surfing the Web from your iPhone, Safari is a full-featured web browser (shown in Figure 5-14) that now offers a handful of new features, like offline Reading Lists. You can also sync your Bookmarks and Bookmarks Bar information with your other computers and iOS mobile devices, plus access from your iPhone tabbed browser windows that are currently open on other computers or devices that are linked to the same iCloud (Apple ID) account. See Chapter 10 to learn how to efficiently surf the Internet and visit your favorite web sites from your iPhone.

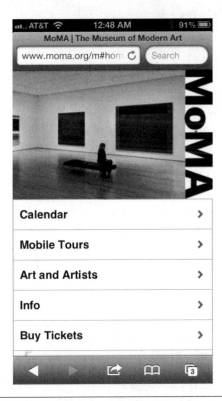

FIGURE 5-14   Web surfing is fun, easy, and efficient when you use the Safari web browser on the iPhone 5.

Stocks

View the status of the stock market as a whole or your individual investments using this easy-to-use and graphically based app. In addition to the stand-alone app, Stocks can also display information using a widget within your iPhone's Notification Center screen. The app is fully integrated with Siri as well. For example, you could ask Siri, "How did the Dow perform today?" and Siri will respond verbally with a summary of the Dow Jones Industrial Average's performance for the day, and display a related graph on the iPhone's screen. You also have the option to ask about individual publicly traded companies. For example, you could ask, "How did Disney perform today?" or "How did Apple perform today?," and Siri will respond with the same types of results.

Twitter

Just like Facebook, Twitter functionality (the ability to compose and send tweets to your followers) is fully integrated into iOS 6 and can be used from a wide selection of apps, as well as from the Notification Center window. However, if you want to manage all aspects of your Twitter account from your iPhone, you'll need to download the free official Twitter app. You can do so from the App Store or from within Settings. Refer to Chapter 2 for more information about setting up and using Twitter on your iPhone.

Videos

Use this app to watch movies, TV show episodes, and music videos that you acquire from the iTunes Store (via the iTunes app) or that you transfer to your iPhone via iTunes Sync or iCloud. This app is also used to view video-based iTunes U content. Chapter 16 covers the Videos app and how to use it.

Voice Memos

This app allows your iPhone to serve as a basic digital audio recorder. You can record conversations, meetings, lectures, concerts, or other audio, and then play back that audio on your iPhone, or sync and share the digital audio files with your primary computer or other users.

Did You Know? **Additional Apps Are Available from the App Store**

In addition to the apps that come preinstalled with iOS 6 on your iPhone, you have access to a vast and ever-growing library of Apple and third-party apps at the App Store. See Chapter 18 to discover more about what's available.

FIGURE 5-15   Access current or extended weather forecasts for your current location or any city in the world using the Weather app.

Weather

Quickly access current or extended weather forecasts for your current location or any city in the world (shown in Figure 5-15) using this powerful yet simple app. The Weather app also works as a widget, and can display weather-related information within the Notification Center screen. The Weather app is fully compatible with Siri as well.

New and Improved iPhone Functions That Work with iOS 6 and Your Favorite Apps

At the beginning of this chapter, the word "integration" was used to describe how your iPhone 5 that's running iOS 6 works with a bunch of preinstalled apps, which in turn can exchange data, files, content, or information with each other to make your experience using the iPhone that much more intuitive and productive.

These preinstalled apps are also fully integrated with the core functionality of the iPhone itself, as well as other services that Apple offers, including iCloud. As you begin using many of the apps mentioned in this chapter, as well as some of Apple's own optional apps (like Pages, Numbers, Keynote, Find My Friends, Cards, iPhoto, iMovie, iTunes U, and Garage Band) and a growing number of third-party apps, you can expect from them some of the functionality and "integration" described in this section.

Siri

Using your voice, issue commands, questions, or requests that Siri can then process by accessing app-specific data, your iPhone's core functionality, as well as information from the Internet. Some of the preinstalled apps can be fully controlled using Siri (and your voice). Be sure to refer to Chapter 3 to learn about the many ways you can use Siri to interact with your iPhone and the apps running on it. While Siri works with many of the apps that come preinstalled with iOS 6, you can also launch any app with a verbal command. The ways in which Siri can be used, and with which apps, are continuously expanding.

Notification Center

Constantly running in the background is the Notification Center app. While you won't see an app icon for Notification Center on your Home screen, this app constantly monitors all of the other compatible apps running on your iPhone, gathers together and organizes the alerts, alarms, and notifications generated by those apps, and displays them in one centralized place—the Notification Center screen (shown in Figure 5-16). This helps you to keep important or timely information easily accessible and nicely organized.

You can access the Notification Center screen on your iPhone at any time by swiping your finger in a downward direction from the very top of the iPhone's Multi-Touch screen. The Notification Center screen, which is fully customizable, displays by default all recent alerts, alarms, and notifications generated by compatible apps. It can also display weather and stock information (using special widgets), and it allows you to compose and send a Twitter tweet or a Facebook status update without first launching the Twitter app or the Facebook app.

The Notification Center also allows you to customize Alerts, Banners, and Badges, as well as audible alarms that various apps running on your iPhone are able to generate.

 As you learned in Chapter 2, the Notification Center integrates with your iPhone's Lock screen and allows various apps to display information that requires your prompt attention. For example, you can immediately be alerted of new incoming e-mails, text messages, voice mail messages, appointment alarms, deadlines associated with to-do list (Reminders) items, and other time-sensitive information.

FIGURE 5-16 The Notification Center screen serves as a central place to view all alerts, alarms, and notifications that have been generated by the apps running on your iPhone.

Location Services

Many of the apps you'll soon be using utilize the Location Services functionality of your iPhone to determine exactly where you are, identify your proximity to other people or places, and help you discover important information about the world around you.

While you can customize which apps have access to location-based information, Siri, Maps, Camera, Photos, Find My Friends, Find My iPhone, Reminders, Passbook, Weather, Phone, Messages, Mail, Facebook, and Twitter are just a sampling of apps that can utilize your location-based information that's gathered, managed, and potentially shared by your iPhone's Location Services functionality.

Facebook and Twitter Integration

While you can manage your Twitter and Facebook accounts using the official Twitter and Facebook apps, respectively, from within many apps you'll be using on your iPhone, you can share information with your Facebook friends or Twitter followers, update your Facebook status, and compose and send tweets that contain app-specific information. For example, you can share photos that you shoot or store on your iPhone with your Facebook friends or Twitter followers from within the Photos app, or compose and send an update or tweet from the Notification Screen. A growing number of apps offer both Facebook and Twitter integration, as well as integration with other online-based social networking services, such as Flickr, Google+, and Instagram.

Share Capabilities

Built into the iOS 6 edition of many preinstalled and optional apps is a new Share button or Share feature. Figure 5-17 shows the Share menu that's associated with the Safari app, for example. By accessing an app's Share menu, you'll be able to send app-specific content or information from various apps using e-mail, text message/instant message, Facebook, Twitter, Photo Stream (if it's a photo), or another compatible service.

FIGURE 5-17 The Share button or Share feature that's now built into many apps allows you to share with other people app-specific content by using e-mail, text message/instant message, Facebook, Twitter, or other compatible services.

iCloud

Throughout this book, you'll be learning about the many different functions that iCloud offers, including capabilities that enable you to maintain a remote backup of your entire iPhone, sync app-specific data with other computers and iOS devices, access content previously purchased from Apple, share your digital photo library, and perform many other cloud-based file-sharing tasks.

Many of the preinstalled apps, like Contacts, Calendar, Reminders, Notes, Safari, Photos, Music, and Mail, fully integrate in various ways with iCloud. For example, if you have iCloud syncing functionality turned on for Contacts, anytime you create or update a contact entry on your iPhone, that update will almost immediately be synced with your other iOS mobile devices and computer(s), so all of your most up-to-date contact information is always accessible.

This data sharing works in both directions. If you purchase a new song on your iPad or primary computer, for example, as long as your iPhone has access to the Internet and shares the same Apple ID account, that song will automatically and almost immediately also be downloaded and become accessible on your iPhone (using the Music app). This also works with e-books, digital publications, and some other purchased content.

What's great about iCloud functionality is that after it's set up once, it works automatically and in the background on an ongoing basis. You never have to think about importing or exporting compatible data, files, photos, or content. Thanks to iCloud, what you need is always available, whenever, wherever, and on whichever device or computer you're using.

For iCloud functionality to work, you need to set up a free iCloud account and then activate it on your iPhone. You also need to turn on and customize app-specific iCloud functions, both on your iPhone and on your other iOS mobile devices, Apple TV, and each of your computers. As you learn about using iCloud with various apps later in this book, you'll learn how to customize the service to fully utilize the functions you want and need.

 While the majority of the core apps (and Apple's other iPhone apps, like Pages, Numbers, and Keynote) sync files and documents using iCloud, many third-party apps are compatible with other cloud-based file-sharing services, such as Dropbox (www.dropbox.com) or Microsoft SkyDrive, as described in Chapter 4. Some third-party apps are also beginning to include iCloud support for backing up and syncing app-specific data.

Dictation

As an alternative to manually entering data or information into the iPhone using the virtual keyboard (or an external keyboard that's connected to or wirelessly linked with your iPhone), you can use the iPhone's Dictation feature with almost any app in order to speak to your iPhone, have it transcribe what you say into text, and then insert that text into the app you're currently using. Refer to Chapter 3 for more information about how to use the iPhone's Dictation feature as a convenient and time-saving data entry tool when using most apps.

AirPrint

Another function built into the iPhone 5 that many apps can take advantage of is AirPrint. It allows you to wirelessly print data, files, documents, photos, or other information directly from the app you're using to an AirPrint-compatible printer. There are more than 200 different AirPrint-compatible printers currently available, from a variety of popular printer manufacturers.

 AirPrint-compatible printers enable you to wirelessly print content directly from your iPhone from any app that includes a Print command. There are, however, options to wirelessly print from your iPhone to printers that do not offer AirPrint functionality. To accomplish this, you will need a third-party app, special software on your computer (such as Printopia 2), or a special device connected to your wireless network (or printer).

AirPlay

Also built into your iPhone is AirPlay functionality, which allows you to stream almost anything that's displayed on your iPhone's screen to an HD television set, a monitor, your home theatre system, or an LCD projector that has an Apple TV device connected to it. For this to work, both your iPhone and the Apple TV device must have access to the same wireless network (Wi-Fi).

AirPlay allows you to display photos and videos you've shot on your iPhone, as well as PowerPoint and Keynote presentations. You can also stream iTunes content, including music, TV show episodes, and movies, in conjunction with an Apple TV device. For example, if you begin watching a TV show episode or movie on your iPhone, when you get home, you can tap the AirPlay icon within the Videos app and begin watching that same TV show or movie (from where you left off) on your television set or home theater system.

AirPlay also allows you to stream audio from your iPhone wirelessly to AirPlay-compatible external speakers connected to the same Wi-Fi network.

 You can connect speakers to your iPhone without using AirPlay by using a cable (that connects to the iPhone's headphones jack) or wirelessly via Bluetooth.

iOS 6's Other Features

Again, regardless of which app(s) you're using, iOS 6 offers a handful of features that you can utilize. For example, the Select, Select All, Copy, Cut, and Paste commands allow you to select content from one app and move it elsewhere within that app or into another app altogether using a series of quick screen taps.

You'll also find that links and content stored within one app can be used to launch and quickly access other apps. For example, if you're looking at someone's entry within the Contacts app (see Figure 5-18), if you tap a listed phone number, the Phone app will launch and a call will be initiated to that number. Similarly, if you tap an e-mail address, the Mail app will launch and you'll be able to quickly compose an e-mail to that person (with the To field automatically filled in for you).

If you tap an address within the Contacts app, the Maps app will launch, display that location, and allow you to obtain detailed directions to it. If you tap a website link that's listed in a Contacts entry, Safari will launch and display that web page. Similar functionality is also offered in many other apps, such as Calendar, Mail, Safari, and Reminders.

Thanks to the iPhone's Multitasking capabilities, you can always quickly switch between apps running on your iPhone. This allows you to handle multiple tasks simultaneously. For example, while participating in a phone conversation (via the Phone app) or listening to music (via the Music app), you can simultaneously access your Contacts database, access your schedule (within Calendar), send a text message,

FIGURE 5-18   Many data fields within apps are active links and can help you launch relevant information within other apps quickly. Shown here is a sample contact entry within the Contacts app.

or surf the Web. You can also cut and paste content more easily between apps using the iPhone's Multitasking feature.

With some wireless service providers, it is not currently possible to talk on the phone and surf the Web at the same time from your iPhone 5 using a 3G/4G data connection. You can, however, talk on the phone and use a Wi-Fi Internet connection at the same time. With AT&T Wireless, you can talk and access the Internet simultaneously, using either a 3G/4G or Wi-Fi connection.

6

Customize Your iPhone

HOW TO...

- Customize the iPhone's Lock screen and Home screen
- Move around app icons and create folders
- Customize iCloud functions related to the iPhone
- Adjust other iPhone settings and options
- Fine tune app-specific settings to customize their functionality

As you've probably discovered by now, iOS 6 allows you to customize your iPhone 5 in many ways to adapt it to your personal work and usage habits. Now that you have your iPhone set up and know the basics about how to navigate the various screens and apps, let's take a closer look at how to customize some of the settings that will help you personalize the appearance and behavior of key iPhone features and functions.

If you upgraded your iPhone 5 from an earlier model, such as the iPhone 4 or iPhone 4S running iOS 5.1, when you set up your iPhone 5 and restored your personal data from an iTunes or iCloud backup (as described in Chapter 2), all of your older iPhone's personal settings and preferences were automatically transferred over to your new iPhone 5. However, as you'll discover, iOS 6 offers additional customization options that were not previously available to you.

Customize Your iPhone's Lock Screen and Home Screen

Anytime you power on your iPhone or wake it up from Sleep mode, one of the first things you'll see is the Lock screen. To unlock the iPhone, slide your finger from left to right along the Slide To Unlock slider near the bottom of the screen (shown in Figure 6-1).

FIGURE 6-1 The iPhone 5's Lock screen

By default, the Lock screen displays the current time and date, as well as a Camera app icon that allows you to quickly launch the Camera app from the Lock screen in order to begin taking photos in seconds.

Turn On the Passcode Lock Feature

To prevent other people from accessing your iPhone, you can turn on the Passcode Lock feature, which requires you to enter either a four-digit numeric code or a longer alphanumeric password in order to unlock the iPhone and gain access to your apps and data.

To turn on the Passcode feature, launch Settings, tap on the General option, and then select the Passcode Lock option. From the Passcode Lock menu screen, tap on the Turn Passcode On button. When prompted, enter your desired four-digit passcode twice. Once activated, for anyone (including yourself) to get past the Lock screen on your iPhone, they'll need to enter your four-digit passcode.

If you don't believe a four-digit passcode is secure enough, you can turn off the Simple Passcode option on the Passcode Lock menu screen. This will allow you to enter and use a custom, alphanumeric password to unlock your iPhone, which can be much longer than four digits or characters.

Keep in mind, even with the Passcode Lock feature turned on, there are a few tasks that can still be handled from the Lock screen while the iPhone is locked. What's possible will be explained later.

Customize the Passcode Lock Feature's Functionality

You can customize the Passcode Lock feature from the Passcode Lock menu screen within Settings when you activate it, or anytime thereafter.

Customize Access to Siri from the Lock Screen

With the Passcode Lock feature turned on, you can decide via Settings whether you (or anyone else) can access Siri from the iPhone's Lock screen or if you must first unlock the iPhone to access Siri. By default, Siri is accessible even with Password Lock turned on, and there are good reasons why you may want to turn this off.

To prevent Siri from being used from the Lock screen, launch Settings from the Home screen, tap the General option, and then tap the Passcode Lock option. Scroll down the Passcode Lock screen. Under the Allow Access When Locked heading, shown in Figure 6-2, turn off the Siri option if you do not want anyone, including yourself, to be able to access Siri from the Lock screen.

When deciding whether or not to make Siri accessible from the Lock screen when the Passcode Lock feature is turned on, keep in mind that, using Siri, it's possible to gain access to data that's stored within many apps on your iPhone. Thus, even if you have the Passcode Lock feature turned on, if you allow access to Siri from the Lock screen, someone could potentially still access data from your iPhone using Siri without knowing the iPhone's passcode.

 Another Siri-related setting you can personalize allows you to automatically activate Siri when you lift up the iPhone and hold it to your ear. By default, to activate Siri, you need to press and hold down the Home button. To turn on the Raise To Speak feature, launch Settings, tap the General option, and then choose the Siri option. On the Siri screen shown in Figure 6-3, turn on the Raise To Speak feature.

Customize Passbook and Incoming Call Lock Features

Also displayed under the Allow Access When Locked heading are two other options, one for accessing Passbook app data and the other for replying to incoming phone calls via text message from the Lock screen. When these features are turned on, you'll be able to access Passbook data (which could give access to prepaid gift cards and personal financial data related to your favorite stores, for example) from an otherwise locked iPhone. Or, if your iPhone receives an incoming call, instead of answering the

FIGURE 6-2 Once Passcode Lock is turned on, the Passcode Lock menu screen within Settings allows you to adjust Siri functionality related to the Lock Screen.

call, you could send the caller a text message directly from the iPhone's Lock screen, again without knowing the iPhone's passcode or password.

As a preventative measure, to keep unauthorized users from accessing any content on your iPhone whatsoever, turn on the iPhone's Passcode feature and then turn off the Siri, Passbook, and Reply With Message options under the Allow Access When Locked heading.

Select a Wallpaper Graphic for Your Lock Screen and Your Home Screen

The iOS operating system allows you to personalize both the wallpaper graphic displayed on the Lock screen and the wallpaper graphic displayed behind the app icons on the Home screen. You can choose from 23 preinstalled wallpaper images or choose any digital photo that's stored within the Photos app of your iPhone.

FIGURE 6-3   When the Raise To Speak feature is turned On, it will activate Siri whenever you pick up the iPhone and hold it up to your ear.

Select a Preinstalled Wallpaper Graphic as Your Lock Screen and/or Home Screen Image

To customize the iPhone's Lock screen and Home screen to display a preinstalled wallpaper graphic, launch Settings and tap the Brightness & Wallpaper option. Under the Wallpaper heading on the Brightness & Wallpaper screen, tap one of the thumbnail images depicting either the Lock screen or the Home screen (shown in Figure 6-4).

Now, tap the Wallpaper option near the top of the screen to see thumbnails for the 23 preinstalled wallpaper images you can choose from to be displayed on your Lock screen and/or Home screen (shown in Figure 6-5). Tap the image of your choice to select it.

The Wallpaper Preview screen appears next (shown in Figure 6-6). This screen shows you what the wallpaper you've selected will look like. Tap the Set button to confirm your decision, or tap the Cancel button to return to the previous screen and choose a different option.

FIGURE 6-4 The Brightness & Wallpaper screen within Settings

Next, a pop-up menu with four command buttons is displayed (shown in Figure 6-7). Tap the Set Lock Screen button to set the wallpaper graphic to be just your Lock screen image. Tap the Set Home Screen button to set the wallpaper graphic to be just your Home screen image. Tap the Set Both button to set the wallpaper graphic to be both your Lock screen image and your Home screen image. You also have the option to tap the Cancel button, which will return you to the previous screen.

Now, when you return to either the Lock screen or the Home screen, the new wallpaper graphic you selected will be displayed. Remember, you can change these images anytime you desire.

Select Your Own Digital Photo as Your Lock Screen and/or Home Screen Image

Instead of using a preinstalled wallpaper graphic to be your Lock screen and/or Home screen image, you have the option to select and display any digital photo that's stored within the Photos app on your iPhone. Many people choose to display an image of their spouse, kids, pet, or favorite vacation getaway, but you can also display your company's logo or any other image.

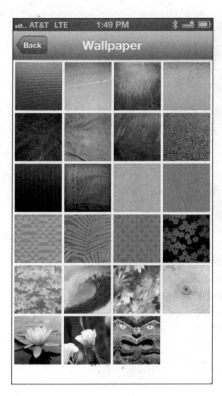

FIGURE 6-5 Tap the Wallpaper option to choose one of these preinstalled wallpaper images for your Lock screen and/or Home screen.

FIGURE 6-6 After tapping the icon of a wallpaper graphic, the Wallpaper Preview screen appears. Tap the Set button to select and save your selection.

To select one of your own digital images to be the Lock screen and/or Home screen wallpaper, launch Settings and select the Brightness & Wallpaper option. Under the Wallpaper heading on the Brightness & Wallpaper screen, tap the thumbnail for the Lock screen or the Home screen.

Displayed below the Wallpaper option will be your various image folders from the Photos app. Tap any of these image folders to display thumbnails of the individual images stored within that folder. Next, tap the image you want to use as your Lock screen and/or Home screen wallpaper.

On the Move And Scale screen (shown in Figure 6-8), determine which area of the selected image will be used, since the Lock screen and Home screen wallpapers must adhere to specific dimensions. Use your finger to move the image around within the frame, or use a reverse-pinch or pinch finger gesture to zoom in or out on the image to make it fill the frame better.

FIGURE 6-7 Decide whether the selected wallpaper will be used on the Lock screen, Home screen, or both.

When the image is repositioned, cropped, or zoomed to your liking, tap the Set button to confirm your decision. When the pop-up menu shown in Figure 6-7 appears, tap the Set Lock Screen, Set Home Screen, or Set Both button, depending on where you want the image displayed, or tap Cancel to return to the previous screen.

 You can use a preinstalled wallpaper for one screen and one of your own digital photos for the other screen if you choose. To do so, repeat the wallpaper selection process twice. The first time, tap the Set Lock Screen button at the end of the process, and the second time, tap the Set Home Screen button.

Rearrange the App Icons on the Home Screen

In addition to customizing the wallpaper that's displayed behind the app icons on your iPhone's Home screen pages, you can reposition any of the app icons on the Home screen or move them to secondary Home screen pages; place in the bottom row of the Home screen whichever four app icons you want docked there; and create and then arrange folders and Safari Home screen shortcuts that appear on the Home screen.

FIGURE 6-8 Choose which portion of a photo you want to use as the wallpaper graphic. You can reposition an image in the frame, zoom in, or zoom out.

The main Home screen displays 20 app icons, along with four additional icons on the bottom row (shown in Figure 6-9). This bottom row of app icons is sometimes referred to as the Dock by Apple. By swiping your finger from right to left when viewing the main Home screen, you can view three additional Home screen pages, each of which also displays up to 20 app icons. You'll notice that the four app icons in the Dock (the bottom row of icons) remain the same on all Home screen pages.

 When viewing the main Home screen, if you swipe your finger from left to right across the screen, you'll gain access to the Spotlight Search screen, which you'll learn more about later in this chapter. Or, from the Home screen, if you tap the Home button twice, you'll access Multitasking mode, which enables you to easily switch between apps that are running on your iPhone.

To rearrange the layout and locations of the app icons on your Home screen pages, begin by pressing and holding your finger down on any one app icon. Within a second or two, all of the app icons will start to shake. Now, place your finger on one app icon that you want to move, and drag it to a new location on the Home screen.

FIGURE 6-9 A fully customized Home screen on the iPhone 5. Up to 24 icons can be displayed.

iOS 6 Offers Several Things You Can Do from the Lock Screen

From the Lock screen, iOS 6 gives you access to several useful features even though the iPhone is technically still locked. For example, if you place your finger on the Camera app icon near the lower-right corner of the screen (see the new custom lock screen here) and flick upward, within a second or two, the Camera app will launch, and you can begin snapping photos using your iPhone. However, you won't be able to do anything with those newly snapped images (except preview a full-screen version of them) until you unlock the iPhone, either by swiping your finger along the Slide To Unlock slider or by entering the passcode or password, depending on how you have your iPhone set up.

Also from the Lock screen, if you quickly press the Home button twice, onscreen controls for the Music app will appear, allowing you to play, pause, rewind, or skip to other tracks in the currently selected music Playlist. You'll learn more about Playlists in Chapter 16.

As you'll learn in Chapter 7, one of the new iOS 6 features is the ability to manage incoming calls from the Lock screen if you opt not to handle them using the traditional method (tapping either Answer or Decline). If you place your finger on the phone handset icon and flick it upward, the Reply With Message and Remind Me Later buttons will appear, shown here.

Tap the Reply With Message button to quickly select a prewritten text message to send to the caller, or tap the Remind Me Later button to set a reminder to call the person back. These features are extremely useful if you're in a meeting or driving, for example, and can't pay attention to the phone or speak with the caller at the moment.

Other information you can opt to display on the Lock screen, even when the iPhone is locked, are Alerts or Banners associated with various apps running on your iPhone. An Alert or Banner can appear on the Lock screen (or on any screen when the iPhone is in use) to indicate an app that's running needs your attention.

For example, the Phone app can display an Alert notifying you of a missed call or unheard voicemail message, while the Messages app can inform you of unread text messages. The Mail app can display Alerts or Banners pertaining to newly received e-mail messages, and the Calendar and Reminders apps can display Alerts or Banners in conjunction with a preset alarm. To customize what types of app-specific Alerts and Banners can be displayed on the Lock screen, launch Settings and tap the Notifications option.

Keep in mind, you can choose to have Alerts and Banners displayed in addition to or instead of having the iPhone play audible alerts or alarms and/or having information displayed on the Notification Center screen. How to set up and customize the Notification Center, along with app-specific Alerts and Banners, is covered in Chapter 2.

Access to certain features of the new Passbook app is also available from the Lock screen. More information about this app can be found in Chapter 19.

Select the four apps you use the most frequently and move their icons to the bottom row, or Dock, of the Home screen. That way, you can quickly access those four apps regardless of which Home screen page you're looking at. For example, you might choose Phone, Mail, Safari, and Messages to be the apps whose icons hold these four easy-to-access icon positions.

If you want to drag an app icon from one Home screen page to another Home screen page, slowly drag that icon to the extreme right or left side of the iPhone's screen. When it reaches the edge, the app icon will automatically jump to the neighboring Home screen page.

You can rearrange as many app icons as you want, as often as you want. When the Home screen looks the way you want it to, press the Home button again once to save your changes. The Home screen will now be fully functional, and you'll once again be able to launch apps from it by tapping on their respective icons.

 If you've created folders or Safari Home screen shortcuts that are now displayed on one or more of your Home screen pages, treat these icons just like app icons in terms of how you move them around and organize them when the app icons are all shaking.

Create Custom App Folders to Organize Your Home Screen

By creating folders on your Home screen, you can group together similar apps and reduce the clutter on your Home screen.

To create a folder, from the Home screen, press and hold down any app icon until all of the icons start to shake. Then, place your finger on one app icon for which you want to create a folder, and when it enlarges, drag it directly on top of another app icon that you also want placed in the folder. Upon doing this, a new folder will be created. Just above the icons you've placed in the newly created folder will be a blank text field. Tap this field to enter a custom name for the folder. If, however, you merge two game apps into the same folder, as shown in Figure 6-10, iOS 6 will recognize this and create a default folder name of Games for you, which you can leave as is or rename.

Once you have created a folder containing two app icons, tap anywhere on the screen to return to the main Home screen. You'll discover that an icon for the new folder now appears on the Home screen. Instead of displaying one app icon, the folder icon will display very tiny thumbnails of each app icon that's stored within it (shown in Figure 6-11).

At this point, while all of the app icons on the Home screen are still shaking, you can add additional app icons to the folder by dragging them, one at a time, from their current location to directly on top of the folder icon. You can add up to 16 app icons into a folder, and you can create multiple folders (grouping different types of apps together) and display those folders on your iPhone's Home screen pages.

 Some people create separate folders named Games, Fitness, Productivity, Photography, and Work, for example, and store related apps in each. You can also create a folder for apps you seldom use, to remove unwanted clutter for your Home screen pages.

FIGURE 6-10   A new folder initially contains two app icons, although you can manually add up to 16 app icons per folder if you choose to. Plus, you can give the folder a custom name.

Remove App Icons from a Folder

After you have created a folder, you can remove an app icon from it and place the icon back on the Home screen. To do so, press and hold your finger on any app or folder icon until all of the icons on the Home screen start to shake. Next, tap the folder icon, which causes all of the app icons within the folder to be displayed (and also shake) at a larger size in a pop-up folder window, as shown in Figure 6-12. Using your finger, drag up and out of the folder window the app icon you want to remove from the folder. (Once you place and hold your finger on a selected icon, it will enlarge while your finger is held on it, at which point you can drag it elsewhere.) The selected app icon reappears on your Home page and is removed from the folder it was previously in.

As indicated by the black and white × icon displayed in the upper-left corner of most of the icons in Figure 6-12, you also have the option to delete an app icon

FIGURE 6-11 A custom folder icon displayed on the Home screen. Shown here is the Games folder, which contains seven game-related apps.

from a folder—which deletes the app itself from the iPhone—as long as it's not one of the core apps that came preinstalled with iOS 6 (such as Game Center). Similar to the directions in the next section for deleting app icons from the Home screen and removing the apps from your iPhone altogether, tap the × icon to delete the app, and then tap the Delete button in the pop-up window to confirm your deletion decision.

Delete Apps from Your iPhone

At any time, you can delete an app from your iPhone altogether (which also makes its app icon disappear). To do this, press and hold down one app icon on the Home screen until all of the icons start to shake. At this point, all of the apps that you've installed on the iPhone (that is, those that did not come preinstalled with iOS 6) will have a small black and white × icon displayed in their upper-left corner as they're shaking (shown in Figure 6-13).

Tap the × icon to delete the app, and then tap the Delete button within the pop-up window to confirm your deletion decision.

FIGURE 6-12 You can drag one icon at a time out of the folder window and back onto the main Home screen.

 When you delete an app from your iPhone, any data stored within that app (or that's associated with the app) is also deleted from your iPhone. This data typically isn't automatically recoverable if you later reinstall the app, unless you've created a remote backup of that app data. How to do this varies based on the app.

Once you delete an app from your iPhone, you can reinstall it anytime in the future by accessing the App Store app, tapping the Updates icon, and then choosing the Purchased option near the top of the screen. A listing of all apps you've ever purchased from the App Store will be displayed. Tap the iCloud icon for the app that you want to reinstall.

 After you acquire an app once, you can reinstall it for free on any compatible iOS device that's linked to the same Apple ID account.

FIGURE 6-13 When the app icons are shaking, tap the × icon to delete the app from your iPhone altogether. You can't, however, delete core apps that come preinstalled with iOS 6.

How to...

Quickly Find Any Information Stored on Your iPhone Using Spotlight Search

Using the Spotlight Search feature is a very quick and efficient way to find information stored within your iPhone, and then access that data or content by automatically launching the appropriate app.

As mentioned earlier, when you're looking at the main Home screen on your iPhone, if you swipe your finger horizontally from *right to left*, you scroll from the main Home screen page to the first of the other three Home screen pages. Each successive swipe from right to left takes you to the next of the Home screen pages. You then swipe from left to right to scroll back through each Home screen page to the main Home screen. However, if you initially swipe your finger horizontally from *left to right* on the main Home screen, you access the Spotlight Search screen. From this screen, you can quickly search for any data that's stored on your iPhone (including app-specific data).

Within the Search iPhone field near the top of the screen, shown here, use the virtual keyboard to enter any keyword or search phrase related to a contact, appointment, to-do list item, date, or other item you want to locate on your iPhone. For example, if you have multiple apps stored in a handful of different folders, and you can't remember where you placed a specific app, enter the app's name into the Search iPhone field to quickly locate it. The search results will be displayed in the main area of the screen. Tap any of the search results to immediately launch the appropriate app and view the data you were searching for.

From Settings, it's easy to customize what content the Spotlight Search feature will access each time you initiate a new search. To adjust this option, launch Settings, tap the General option, and then tap the Spotlight Search option (which you'll find by scrolling down the General screen). On the Spotlight Search screen, shown here, you'll see every type of app on your iPhone that stores data. Tap one app listing at a time to add it to the list of content that will be searched whenever you use the Spotlight Search feature. A check mark appears to the left of the app's listing, indicating that it's been selected. By default all of the major apps and types of content (videos, podcasts, etc.) will be selected. You can unselect or rearrange any item on the list as you deem necessary,

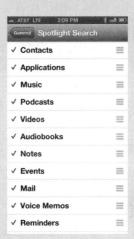

Place your finger on any of the three horizontal line icons associated with a listing to move it up or down the list. Doing this will change the order in which the iPhone's content is searched when you use the Spotlight Search feature. Press the Home button when you're done to save your changes.

You can use Siri as an alternative method for quickly finding and accessing content or information, using voice commands instead of the Spotlight Search feature. For example, if you want to view a particular entry from your Contacts database, activate Siri and say, "Show me [insert name]." Or, if you want to view a listing of your appointments for a particular date, activate Siri and say, "Show me my schedule for [insert date]." Refer to Chapter 3 to learn more about the many ways you can use Siri to access information or content from your iPhone or the Internet.

Customize iCloud Functionality to Sync and Back Up App-Specific Data

Many of the apps that come preinstalled with iOS 6 on the iPhone, including Contacts, Calendar, Safari, Notes, Reminders, and Photos, along with the iWork for iOS apps (and some third-party apps), offer seamless integration with Apple's iCloud file-sharing service.

iCloud can also be used to

- Maintain your own Photo Stream
- Share your digital photos with others by publishing them online using the new Shared Photo Streams feature
- Move documents between iOS devices and Apple computers
- Help to locate your iOS device(s) and/or Mac computers if they're lost or stolen
- Host the online files related to a daily backup of your iPhone (using the iCloud Backup feature)
- Gain access to the iTunes Store, iBookstore, Newsstand, and App Store content you've purchased on any computer or device that's linked to the same Apple ID account
- Manage your entire personal digital music library (using the premium iTunes Match feature)

To utilize iCloud with your iPhone, you first need to set up a free iCloud account if you don't already have one. Then, from the Settings app, you can customize which iCloud features and functions you want to activate on your iPhone.

When you activate your iPhone 5 and set up iOS 6 for the first time, you'll be prompted to set up a free iCloud accout. If you skip this option, you can still do so by launching Settings and tapping on the iCloud button. In the iCloud menu screen, simply enter your Apple ID and related password, and then tap on the Sign In button. If you first need to create an Apple ID account, which is also free, tap on the Get A Free Apple ID button that's displayed near the bottom of the screen.

Remember, you only need one iCloud account that can be shared by all of your Macs, PCs, iPhones, iPads, iPad minis, and/or Apple TV devices. If you already have an iCloud account set up, enter the Apple ID and password that's associated with the account into the appropriate fields on the iCloud menu screen within Settings.

 Note If you already have an iCloud account set up in conjunction with your iMac, MacBook, iPad, iPod touch, or an older model iPhone that you've upgraded from, use that preexisting iCloud account information with your iPhone 5.

At the top of the iCloud screen within Settings (shown in Figure 6-14), enter your iCloud account username and password when prompted. Then, tap the virtual switch associated with each app or iCloud function to turn it on or off. The options include Mail (which pertains only to the free iCloud Mail e-mail account that you're

FIGURE 6-14   From Settings, you can turn on or off various iCloud features on your iPhone and customize how they'll function.

given when you activate an iCloud account), Contacts, Calendars, Reminders, Safari, Notes, Passbook, Photo Stream, Documents & Data, and Find My iPhone. To adjust the iCloud-related settings from Photo Stream and the Documents & Data option, tap on the menu option to reveal a sub-menu that will include a virtual on/off switch.

Turning on the Contacts, Calendars, Reminders, Notes, and Passbook options, for example, will allow your iPhone to automatically sync app-specific data for those apps with your iCloud account, and then sync the data with any other iOS mobile devices or Mac computers that are linked to the same Apple ID and have the same iCloud sync function turned on. So, if you turn on iCloud syncing for Contacts, for example, your iPhone will automatically sync your personal Contacts database with iCloud, as well as with the Contacts app on your iPad, iPad mini, or iPod touch and the Contacts app on your iMac or MacBook.

 If you turn on the iCloud syncing feature for Safari, your Safari bookmarks, Bookmarks Bar, Reading List, and open Safari browser windows will be synced with iCloud, as well as with your other Mac computers and iOS mobile devices.

Purchase Additional iCloud Online Storage Space

Your iCloud account comes with 5GB of free online storage for your personal files. However, any additional storage space that's needed for your Photo Stream, Shared Photo Stream, iTunes Store content purchases (including music, TV show episodes, and movies), App Store purchases, iBookstore purchases, and/or Newsstand purchases is provided for free.

If you need additional iCloud storage space to maintain a daily backup of your iPhone using the iCloud Backup feature, you can purchase it directly from your iPhone. On the iCloud screen within Settings, scroll down to the bottom of the screen and tap the Storage & Backup option. At the top of the Storage & Backup screen, you'll see your total storage, your available storage, and an option that allows you to manage your online storage. To purchase additional online storage, tap the Change Storage Plan button to display the Buy More Storage screen (shown in Figure 6-15).

 The free 5GB of online storage space is adequate for most iPhone users, unless you're also using your iCloud account with multiple Macs and/or other iOS mobile devices.

FIGURE 6-15   If needed, you can purchase additional online storage space for your iCloud account.

You can purchase 10GB of iCloud online storage (giving you 15GB total) for $20 per year. An additional 20GB of iCloud online storage (giving you 25GB total) is available for $40 per year. The third option is to acquire 50GB of online storage (giving you 55GB total) for $100 per year. Tap the option you'd like. When prompted, confirm your decision by entering your Apple ID password. The additional online storage space will be made available to you instantly, and the plan will auto-renew every year until you cancel it.

 If your available online storage space becomes too limited, you can potentially free up online storage space by deleting older archived files you no longer need. To do this, from the Storage & Backup screen within Settings, tap the Manage Storage option. Near the top of the Manage Storage screen is a listing of all backups currently being stored (for all of your iOS mobile devices) within your iCloud account. As you scroll down, you'll see how much storage is being used by other files and data. Tap any listing to delete the listed file and free up online storage space.

Back Up Your iPhone Using iCloud Backup

There are three main methods for maintaining a full backup of your iPhone. You can use the iTunes Sync process or iTunes Wireless Sync process, which involves using the free iTunes software running on your primary computer and linking your iPhone with your computer to create the backup. When you use either iTunes Sync process to back up your iPhone, all of the backup files are stored on your primary computer's hard drive.

The third option is to use the iCloud Backup feature. Once per day, as long as your iPhone has access to the Internet via a Wi-Fi Internet connection and is connected to an external power source, the iPhone will automatically create a backup and store the files online within your iCloud account. Then, if you need to restore your data from iCloud, you can do so from anywhere your iPhone can access the Internet. You don't need to reconnect it to your primary computer, as you do with iTunes Sync.

Keep in mind, all of your app-specific data for the iPhone's core apps (Contacts, Calendar, Reminders, Notes, Safari, Passbook, and so forth) should, theoretically, be continuously synced with iCloud (as long as you have the virtual switch turned on for each app on the iCloud screen). To turn on the iCloud Backup feature (which overrides the iTunes Sync feature), launch Settings, tap the iCloud option, scroll down and tap the Storage & Backup option on the iCloud screen, and then turn on the iCloud Backup virtual switch on the Storage & Backup screen (shown in Figure 6-16).

Once the iCloud Backup feature is turned on, a backup will automatically be created once per day. However, if you tap the Back Up Now button that appears near the bottom of the Storage & Backup menu screen (within Settings), you can create an updated backup at any time, as long as your iPhone has access to the Internet. (The iPhone does not need to be plugged into an external power source to create a manual iCloud Backup.)

FIGURE 6-16 From Settings, you can turn on or off the iCloud Backup option.

Personalize the Sound and Vibration Options of Your iPhone

Like so many other features and functions on your iPhone, you can fully customize anything having to do with sounds, including ringtones, alerts, and alarms. To personalize the sound options on your iPhone, launch Settings and tap the Sounds option.

On the Sounds screen (shown in Figure 6-17), it's possible to turn on or off the vibrate option for when the phone rings and/or when it's already in Silent mode. To turn on the Vibrate feature, tap the virtual switch associated with Vibrate On Ring and/or Vibrate On Silent to set them to the On position.

On the Sounds screen, you can also adjust the volume of the phone's ringer. Use your finger to move the Ringer And Alerts volume slider to the right to make the ringer louder, or to the left to make it softer. You can also adjust the volume using the volume buttons on the side of your iPhone as long as you have the Change With Buttons virtual switch set to On.

FIGURE 6-17   On the Sounds screen within Settings, you can customize all vibrations, ringtones, alerts, and alarms your iPhone generates.

Scroll down the Sounds screen to customize the individual sound effect or ringtone you hear for each type of alert or alarm the iPhone is capable of generating. Under Sounds And Vibration Patterns, you can customize the following options for the sounds you hear:

- **Ringtone**   Heard when you receive an incoming call
- **Text Tone**   Heard when you receive an incoming text message
- **New Voicemail**   Heard when you receive a new voicemail message
- **New Mail**   Heard when you receive an incoming e-mail
- **Sent Mail**   Heard when an e-mail message you've composed has been sent
- **Tweet**   Heard when you receive a new tweet via Twitter
- **Facebook Post**   Heard in relation to new Facebook posts added to your Facebook account
- **Calendar Alerts**   Heard in conjunction with appointment alarms
- **Reminder Alerts**   Heard in conjunction with alarms generated by the Reminders app

For apps that allow you to customize the vibration pattern (if the iPhone is set to vibrate instead of or in addition to generating an audible alarm), you can customize the vibration pattern by launching Settings and tapping on the Notifications option. Select an app, such as Phone, click on the Ringtone option from the Phone menu screen, and then at the top of the Ringtone screen, tap on the Vibration option. The vibration pattern can also be customized for apps like Messages, Reminders, Calendars, and Mail (for each individual e-mail account).

Tap any of the sound options to change the default sound effect or ringtone. A menu that lists dozens of preinstalled sounds and ringtones will be displayed. However, you can also download additional ringtones from iTunes (for a fee) or create your own custom ringtones using the GarageBand app (or another ringtone creator app).

On the Sounds screen, you can also turn on or off keyboard clicks related to the iPhone's virtual keyboard.

Temporarily Turn Off All Sound Generated by Your iPhone

If you're in a meeting, theatre, or house of worship, if you're preparing to go to sleep, or if you just want to be left alone, you can easily and temporarily turn off all audible alerts, alarms, ringtones, and notifications by adjusting the physical Ring/Silent switch on the side of your iPhone.

When you turn on the Ring/Silent switch to mute your iPhone, by default, this will also turn on the vibrate option associated with many apps.

Assign Custom Ringtones to Specific Contacts

As previously mentioned, on the Sounds screen within Settings, you can change the master ringtone that you hear when you receive an incoming call by tapping the Ringtone option and selecting the ringtone of your choice. However, you can also assign unique ringtones to individual contacts within your Contacts database, so you'll be able to tell who is calling you just by hearing which ringtone is played when specific people call.

To assign a custom ringtone to an individual contact that's already stored within your Contacts database, follow these steps:

1. Launch the Contacts app.
2. On the All Contacts screen, locate and tap the contact to which you want to assign a custom ringtone.

3. On the Info screen for that contact (shown in Figure 6-18), tap the Edit button in the upper-right corner of the screen.
4. Scroll down the Info screen for the contact to the Ringtone option (shown in Figure 6-19) and tap it.
5. From the Ringtone menu that appears (which lists all of the ringtones stored on your iPhone), tap your selection for that contact. The ringtone will play.
6. To save that ringtone and associate it with the contact, tap the Save button in the upper-right corner of the screen.

This process only needs to be done once per contact. From this point forward, whenever that person calls you from one of the phone numbers listed within their Contacts entry, the ringtone you selected will be heard. Their Caller ID information will also be displayed on the screen, as usual.

 For more information about using the Phone app to make and receive calls, and to further customize the features of the Phone app, see Chapter 7.

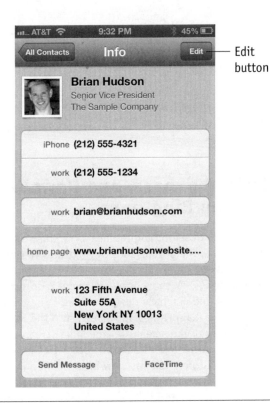

Edit button

FIGURE 6-18   A single entry within the Contacts app

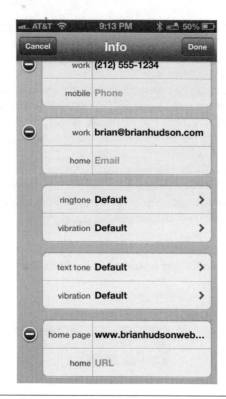

FIGURE 6-19 Tap the Edit icon to edit the entry, and then scroll down and tap the Ringtone option.

How to... Find, Purchase, and Download Custom Ringtones

In addition to selling digital music, TV show episodes, and movies, Apple's iTunes Store offers thousands of ringtones that you can purchase and download onto your iPhone. Many of these ringtones are edited versions of popular songs, TV show or movie themes, or recognizable sound effects.

To find and purchase new ringtones, from your iPhone, launch the iTunes app. On the main iTunes app screen, tap the More (...) icon near the bottom-right corner of the screen. On the More screen that appears, tap the Tones option. (Your iPhone must have access to the Internet so that it can access the iTunes Store.) You can now browse through the vast and ever-growing selection of available ringtones that are custom-formatted for use with the iPhone. Most ringtones from the iTunes Store cost $0.99 each. Once you purchase a Ringtone or Alert sound, it will be added to your Sounds menu and be selectable from within Settings when you tap the Sounds option.

Use Your iPhone with a Wide Range of Bluetooth Accessories

Your iPhone 5 comes fully equipped with the latest Bluetooth technology, which allows the phone to wirelessly communicate with optional accessories, such as Bluetooth-enabled speakers, headphones (for listening to audio), or a headset (for use with the Phone, FaceTime, or Skype app, for example).

 If you plan to use your iPhone while driving, many states require that you use a headset, such as a Bluetooth headset, that offers hands-free phone operation and that only covers one ear.

Before you can use a new Bluetooth device with your iPhone, you need to "pair" it with your iPhone. (Some of the latest Bluetooth accessories will automatically pair with the iPhone.) You need to do this only once for each device.

To pair a new Bluetooth device with your iPhone, first place the device into pairing mode. How to do this should be explained in the owner's manual that came with the device. Then, on your iPhone, launch Settings and tap the Bluetooth option. On the Bluetooth screen, make sure the Bluetooth virtual switch is set to On. When you see the new device listed on the Bluetooth screen, tap its listing to initiate the pairing process (which takes between 5 and 15 seconds).

After a Bluetooth device is paired with your iPhone once, whenever the device and your iPhone are both turned on and in close proximity to each other, they will automatically work together. Your iPhone is capable of managing and working with multiple Bluetooth devices simultaneously.

Adjust iPhone Settings to Help Maintain Your Privacy

As you'll discover, many of the options you can control within Settings relate to specific iPhone features or functions, or how specific apps will work. The Privacy options within Settings, however, are more universal and pertain to what information your iPhone will be able to share with others via the Internet. The Restrictions options available within Settings allow you to determine which iPhone features, functions, and content someone will be able to access if they're using your iPhone (with or without permission).

Configure Privacy Settings

To adjust Privacy settings associated with the overall function of your iPhone, launch Settings and tap the Privacy option. On the Privacy screen, you can determine which apps will be able to share information when your iPhone is connected to the Internet.

To fully utilize all of the features of your iPhone and the new ways various apps interact with each other seamlessly, you'll want to leave the Privacy features at their default settings.

Adjust Location Services Settings

Location Services allows your iPhone to pinpoint your exact location and potentially share it with other people and other apps when you're using, for example, Maps, Photos, Twitter, Facebook, Find Friends, or any of many third-party apps (such as the Starbucks app, to give you the location of the closest Starbucks). To pinpoint your location, your iPhone uses its built-in GPS functionality in addition to crowd-sourced Wi-Fi hotspots and cell phone tower locations. As you'll discover, it's extremely accurate.

To give you a few examples, if you're using the Camera app to take photos and you have Location Services turned on in conjunction with the Camera app, every time you snap a photo, the exact location where the photo was taken will be recorded and saved with that digital photo. You can then use the Places feature within iPhoto, for example, to view a map of where your pictures were shot. This same function also works in conjunction with photos taken and shared using the optional Instagram app. When you compose a tweet to share with your Twitter followers, if Location Services is turned on for the Twitter app, your exact location will be shared in conjunction with that tweet.

If you have privacy concerns about using Location Services with particular apps but don't want to turn off the feature completely, you can turn on Location Services in general but then turn off this feature in conjunction with specific apps. To do this, from the Privacy screen within Settings, tap the Location Services option near the top of the screen. On the Location Services screen (shown in Figure 6-20), turn on the main Location Services option. Then, turn on or off this feature for the various apps listed, such as Camera, Facebook, Find Friends, Find My iPhone, Maps, Photos, Safari, Siri, Twitter, and Weather.

 Siri relies heavily on the Location Services features of your iPhone to respond to many of your requests, such as finding local businesses and restaurants, providing weather forecasts, and so forth.

Decide Which Apps Can Share Data with Each Other... and Other People

From the Privacy screen within Settings, you also have some control over which apps share app-specific data with other apps (and in some cases, share data with other people via those apps). To make these adjustments, launch Settings, tap on the Privacy option, and then, one at a time, tap on the Contacts, Calendars, Reminders, Photos, Bluetooth Sharing, Twitter, and Facebook options to adjust app-specific settings related to the sharing of data with other apps. (Additional apps may also be listed on this Privacy menu screen.)

FIGURE 6-20   The Location Services screen within Settings

For example, if you tap on the Contacts app listing and you have the Find My Friends and Skype apps installed on your iPhone, you'll see separate on/off virtual switches for these two apps. If you turn on the switches, Contacts will be able to share information from your Contacts database with the Find My Friends and/or Skype app.

Configure Restrictions

Yet another way you can control your privacy and keep others from accessing data on your iPhone is to set up the Restrictions features, also from within Settings.

When you enable Restrictions by launching Settings, tapping General, tapping the Restrictions option, and then tapping the Enable Restrictions button on the Restrictions screen, you can allow someone else to use your iPhone but still prevent them from accessing specific apps and/or specific types of content. For example, if your children will occasionally be using your iPhone, you can prevent them from accessing your Contacts database, surfing the Web, or sending/receiving e-mails, but allow them to watch TV show episodes or movies that have a specific rating (such as "G").

Depending on who will be using your iPhone, you can turn on or off specific features, functions, and/or a user's access to various types of content, and you can change these Restrictions.

Adjust App-Specific Settings to Customize Their Functionality

Many apps that allow you to customize their respective settings offer menu options within the apps themselves. However, some apps have customizable features that must be adjusted from within Settings. To make these adjustments, launch Settings and scroll down the main Settings menu.

Below the Privacy option, you'll see listings for many of the iPhone's preinstalled apps, including iCloud, Mail, Contacts, Calendars, Notes, Reminders, Phone, Messages, FaceTime, Maps, and Safari. Tap the app's listing to see which app-specific settings you can adjust.

As you read the various chapters in this book that focus on how to use specific preinstalled apps, you'll learn more about how to customize or personalize the functionality of those apps, in some cases by accessing Settings.

By scrolling down further on the Settings screen, you'll be able to adjust app-specific settings for iTunes & App Stores, Music, Videos, Photos & Camera, and iBooks (see Figure 6-21), as well as Twitter and Facebook.

Just below the Twitter and Facebook options will be a listing of optional Apple apps and third-party apps that have options that are adjustable from within Settings (see Figure 6-22). Tap an app's listing to customize the settings for that particular app. The options available to you will be app-specific. This list will change as you install additional apps onto your iPhone.

As you're becoming acquainted with using your iPhone and various apps, invest some time to explore Settings and its many submenus to discover the hundreds of different settings and options you can adjust so that the iPhone (and its apps) perform in a way that's more personalized and conducive to your work or usage habits.

FIGURE 6-21   From within Settings, you can adjust some app-specific options.

FIGURE 6-22   Some additional, optional Apple apps (Pages, Numbers, and Keynote) and third-party apps with user-adjustable settings are listed toward the bottom of the Settings screen.

PART III

Use Your iPhone's Built-in Apps

7

Make and Receive Calls

HOW TO...

- Answer incoming calls
- Manage incoming calls using new iOS 6 features
- Make calls from your iPhone
- Initiate conference calls
- Customize the Phone app's settings

Your iPhone 5 is first and foremost a cell phone that allows you to make and receive calls. That said, you're probably wondering why information about how to actually use this functionality has been pretty much ignored until Chapter 7. Well, there's a good reason for this.

As you know, your iPhone 5 is capable of handling a wide range of very diverse tasks, and you can interact with your iPhone in a variety of ways—through the Multi-Touch screen, the iPhone's virtual keyboard, a handful of buttons on the phone itself, and Siri. Your iPhone also has the capability to communicate wirelessly with other devices via Bluetooth.

Well, to fully utilize the functions of your iPhone 5 to make, receive, and manage calls, it's important that you first understand how to interact with your phone, because as you're about to discover, much of the knowledge and experience you've acquired thus far that's related to the basic functions of your phone will be needed to use the Phone app.

Yes, first and foremost, your iPhone 5 is, in fact, a cell phone that allows you to make and receive calls. How to fully utilize many of the phone-related features offered by your iPhone is the focus of this chapter.

Launch the Phone App

The Phone app that comes preinstalled on your iPhone provides all of the functionality that you need to make, receive, and manage phone calls. As long as your iPhone

The Phone App Offers Many New or Enhanced Features

Did You Know?

Beyond enabling you to perform the traditional phone tasks of making and receiving calls and managing your voicemails, the Phone app that comes preinstalled on your iPhone 5 now makes it possible to manage incoming calls in a variety of ways, thanks to iOS 6. For example, when you receive an incoming call, if you don't want to answer it, instead of just sending the call directly to voicemail, you can immediately send the caller a prewritten text message and/or set a reminder to yourself to call that person back, as described later in this chapter.

The Phone app also enables you to initiate conference calls with two or more separate parties, and utilize a Bluetooth headset (or hands-free car kit) so that you can talk on the phone hands-free while driving. Both topics are covered in this chapter.

The Phone app continues to be fully integrated with Siri, so you can initiate calls using voice commands, like "Call Rob Martinez at work." It's also possible to customize ringtones for individual people within your Contacts list or Favorites list, so in addition to seeing their caller ID information when you receive an incoming call from them, you'll hear a preselected song or ringtone. How to do this is covered in Chapter 8.

With some wireless service providers, including AT&T Wireless, your iPhone 5 allows you to engage in a phone conversation and access the Internet (using a 3G/4G or Wi-Fi connection) or utilize other apps at the same time. Other service providers allow you to talk on the phone and use other apps, but only allow you to access the Internet via a Wi-Fi connection (if one is available).

Either way, as you're talking on the phone, you can access the Contacts, Calendar, Reminders, and Notes apps, for example, to enter or access and share information related to your phone conversation.

is powered on and not in Airplane mode, the Phone app constantly runs in the background and will launch automatically when you receive an incoming call.

However, to initiate a call or manage your voicemails, for example, you can launch the Phone app manually from the Home screen by tapping the Phone app's icon.

Because you'll be using the Phone app frequently, consider positioning its app icon within one of the four slots at the bottom of your Home screen (referred to as the Dock), as described in Chapter 6. That way, regardless of which Home screen page you're looking at, the Phone app will be readily accessible.

Choose How You'll Speak with Someone on the Phone

The Phone app allows you to interact with the phone itself in several different ways as you engage in phone conversations and manage your voicemails. Which option you use is a matter of personal preference, and based on whether or not you want or need to be doing anything else related to your iPhone while you're participating in a phone call. Here is an overview of your options.

Hold the Phone Up to Your Ear

Once you answer an incoming call or initiate an outgoing call, the iPhone is designed to be held close to your face so that you can hear what the other party is saying (without people around you also hearing that person), and at the same time, you'll be heard by the person you're conversing with.

When using this option, you physically have to hold the phone close to your face (which, in many states, is illegal while driving), meaning you can't see or access the iPhone's screen during a call without interrupting the conversation. Thus, you can't access the iPhone's other apps or features during a call.

 Whenever the iPhone 5 is transmitting, it generates radiation, as do all cell phones and smartphones. Some doctors and scientists believe that this radiation can be harmful to humans over time, and there is some evidence to support this. To protect yourself from some of this radiation, it's recommended that you hold any smartphone at least several inches from your head when engaged in a phone conversation. Thus, using a headset or the iPhone's speakerphone feature is potentially a safer alternative, whether you're driving or not.

Use the Built-In Speakerphone Feature

After you initiate a call or answer an incoming call and establish a connection, you can tap the Speaker option to utilize the Phone app's speakerphone feature. While engaged in a conversation, if you do not have a headset connected to your iPhone, the Speaker option is displayed as one of the six call management options in the center of the call-in-progress screen (shown in Figure 7-1).

However, if you have a corded or Bluetooth headset connected to your iPhone, what you'll see displayed on the iPhone's screen during a call is an Audio Source button (shown in Figure 7-2). To access the speakerphone feature, tap the Audio Source button, and then select the Speaker option to use the speakerphone feature.

When you use the speakerphone feature, everyone around you can hear your conversation, which not only is a privacy issue but also may annoy some people. Plus, the microphones that are built into your iPhone will pick up and transmit any background noise that surrounds you.

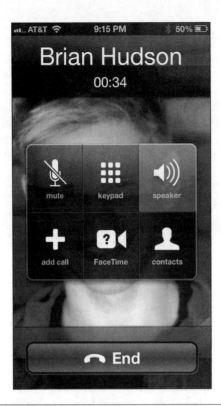

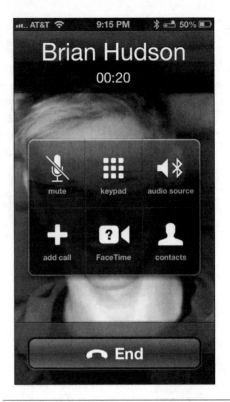

FIGURE 7-1 Tap the Speaker option to switch from holding the iPhone close to your face during a phone conversation to using the speakerphone feature.

FIGURE 7-2 If you have a headset connected to your iPhone, the Speaker button is replaced by an Audio Source button that allows you to switch between the iPhone's built-in speaker, speakerphone feature, or the attached headset speaker during a call.

This feature, however, has certain benefits. For example, if you're driving, the speakerphone feature offers hands-free functionality. In addition, if other people are in the room or car with you and you want them to be able to hear and participate in the phone conversation as well, the speakerphone feature allows them to do so. When you're not driving, being able to look at the screen while talking on the phone allows you to launch and use other apps or look up app-specific data, for example.

 To use the speakerphone feature, you don't need any additional accessories or equipment. However, you can utilize an optional hands-free car kit, which often has its own speaker and microphone or uses the car's stereo system, so that you can engage in hands-free, nonprivate speakerphone calls while driving.

Use a Corded Headset

By connecting a corded headset to your iPhone, you can insert the ear bud speaker(s) into your ear and hear the person you're speaking with on the phone, while the microphone that's built into the headset's cord transmits what you say to the caller.

The benefits of using a corded headset include improved call clarity, privacy, and hands-free functionality. Corded headsets can also be used as headphones (with stereo sound) in conjunction with the Music and Videos apps, for example. When a call comes in, the music or audio you're listening to will pause so you can switch to the incoming call. Headphones (that cover both ears) should not be used when driving, however.

The main drawback of using a corded headset is that there's a cord extending from your iPhone to your ear, so you can't move away from your iPhone during a call (as you can with the speakerphone feature or a wireless Bluetooth headset). The microphone on the corded headset will also pick up ambient noise that surrounds you.

If you choose to use a corded headset, you can purchase one for your iPhone 5 from a variety of companies, but you'll probably find that the Apple EarPods that came with your iPhone offer excellent sound quality and function quite well as a headset.

Use a Wireless Bluetooth Headset

Thanks to the Bluetooth capabilities of your iPhone, you can connect a wireless Bluetooth headset to your iPhone and use it to participate in private, hands-free phone conversations, without a cord bogging you down or getting tangled. You can also walk around and move up to 50 feet away (this varies depending on the headset model) from your iPhone during a conversation.

 The main differences between a headset and headphones are that a headset has a built-in microphone, is small compared to headphones, and is designed to be worn in just one ear. While some headphones have a microphone built in and can also be used as a headset (like Apple's EarPods), they offer stereo sound that's designed to be worn in or over both ears, so you can listen to music or audio associated with video, for example, in stereo sound. This is not conducive to driving. Most traditional headphones have no microphone and are designed solely for listening to audio.

Bluetooth headsets are available from a wide range of manufacturers. They typically consist of a small earpiece that fits into or over your ear and includes a built-in speaker and tiny microphone. Depending on the quality of the Bluetooth headset, the microphone may offer noise-cancellation capabilities, while the speaker may offer noise-reduction technology. This allows you to hear and be heard, regardless of the ambient noise that surrounds you.

For the iPhone 5, the optional Bluetooth headsets from Jawbone (www.jawbone.com), including the Jawbone ICON HD ($99.99) and Jawbone ERA ($129.99), are small, offer state-of-the-art HD sound quality (including noise-reduction and noise-cancellation technology), are programmable, come in a variety of colors, and offer up to four hours of continuous talk time per charge. They're available from the company's website, consumer electronics stores, and online retailers such as Amazon. Figure 7-3 shows a Jawbone ERA headset.

Plan on spending between $39 and $150 for a wireless Bluetooth headset. The best-quality headsets, however, have a suggested retail price of at least $100, but if you spend a lot of time engaged in phone conversations using your iPhone, the additional investment is well worth it. These headsets have their own built-in rechargeable battery that offers several hours of continuous talk time, as well as many more hours of standby time. Choose a headset that offers at least four hours of continuous talk time per charge.

 When you invest in a Bluetooth headset, it will work with any Bluetooth-enabled smartphone or device. Thus, if you upgrade to the iPhone 6 in the future, or want to use Skype on your iPad, for example, the same Bluetooth headset will work.

Once you "pair" the Bluetooth headset to work with your iPhone, anytime the iPhone and headset are both turned on and in close proximity, they'll automatically work together in conjunction with the Phone app (and other apps that generate audio from your iPhone, including the FaceTime and Skype apps, for example). You'll probably discover that using a wireless Bluetooth headset with your iPhone offers convenience, clearer phone conversations, added safety (particularly while driving), privacy during your calls, and greater comfort than a corded headset (with no cord that can get tangled).

FIGURE 7-3   The Jawbone ERA is one of the many optional Bluetooth headsets that work very well with the iPhone 5, especially when you're driving and need hands-free operation. (Image provided courtesy of Jawbone.)

Answer Incoming Calls

As long as your iPhone is turned on and not in Airplane mode, it is capable of receiving calls, assuming that it is within the signal radius of your wireless service provider or is permitted to roam and utilize the signal of another wireless service provider. If your iPhone is in Sleep mode, when an incoming call is received, the Phone app will wake up the iPhone automatically and allow you to answer the call directly from the Lock screen.

 If you allow your iPhone to roam to another wireless service provider, there is often an extra fee associated with this, particularly if you're traveling overseas or you're aboard a cruise ship. Plan on spending between $0.99 and $2.99 per minute (sometimes more) to engage in phone calls on your iPhone while roaming internationally, unless you subscribe to a special calling plan that allows for this.

Answer an Incoming Call While Using the iPhone

Regardless of what you're doing on your iPhone, if you receive an incoming call, the Phone app will launch and the incoming call screen will be displayed. The incoming call screen displays caller ID information from the caller. Just like the caller ID feature you may have on your home or office phone, it typically includes the caller's name, caller's phone number, and/or the city and state the call is originating from.

However, if the caller has an entry within your Contacts database, that caller's photo, full name, and other details about them, including which of their phone numbers they're calling from (home, work, mobile, iPhone, etc.), will be displayed as part of the incoming call screen (shown in Figure 7-4).

 Depending on the resolution of the wallpaper image and how you crop and scale the image when assigning it to a contact entry within the Contacts app, the image you use can be displayed in almost full screen when you receive a call from that person. Otherwise, it will appear as a smaller thumbnail image on the incoming call screen.

If no caller ID information is available (or the caller has blocked this information) and there's no entry within your Contacts database for the caller, the word Private, Blocked, or Unavailable will be displayed on the incoming call screen.

Initially, when the incoming call screen is displayed, in conjunction with the caller's caller ID information or Contacts entry, you'll see a red and white Decline button and a green and white Answer button displayed near the bottom of the screen. Tap the Decline button to ignore the incoming call and immediately send it to voicemail. Instead of tapping the Decline button, you can quickly press the Power (Sleep/Wake) button on the top of your iPhone or either of the volume buttons on the side of your iPhone to silence the ringer and send a call to voicemail.

FIGURE 7-4 The incoming call screen replaces whatever was previously displayed on the iPhone's screen when you receive an incoming call.

 Pressing the Power (Sleep/Wake) button or one of the volume buttons immediately silences the ringer, but you still have between five and ten seconds to answer the call before it goes to voicemail. To send the call to voicemail immediately, tap the onscreen Decline button or double-press the Power (Sleep/Wake) button when an incoming call is received.

To answer the call and begin a conversation, tap the Answer button. A connection with the caller will be established, and the call-in-progress screen (shown in Figure 7-5) will be displayed on your iPhone. At this point, you can tap any of the command buttons displayed in the center of the screen: Mute, Keypad, Speaker/Audio Source, Add Call, FaceTime, or Contacts (all of which are described later in the chapter, in the section "Use Other Options While You're Engaged in a Call"). When you're done with any call, to end it, press the red and white End button at the bottom of the screen (or wait for the other person to hang up, in which case your iPhone will disconnect from the call automatically). If you're using a headset, you can end the call by pressing the Answer button again.

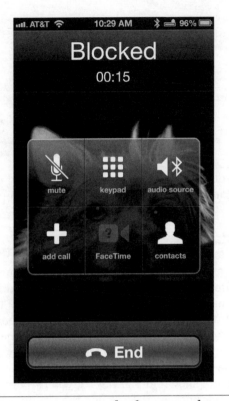

FIGURE 7-5   The call-in-progress screen displays several command icons you can use to manage the call you're engaged in, while you're still talking.

 The FaceTime icon becomes active only when a FaceTime video conference call is possible.

You also have the option of pressing the Home button while engaged in a call in order to access the iPhone's Home screen, so that you can then launch and use another app during the call. Or, you can enter into Multitasking mode and return to using an app that's currently running in the background, also while still engaged in a call. When you do this, a green and white bar is displayed near the top of the iPhone's screen to remind you that you're connected to a call (shown in Figure 7-6). Tap this bar to return to the Phone app and the call-in-progress screen.

 On the incoming call screen, thanks to iOS 6, you now have additional call management features, which will be discussed later in this chapter.

Touch To Return
To Call bar

FIGURE 7-6 You can do other things while engaged in a call, and a green Touch To Return To Call bar will remain displayed at the top of the screen.

Turn On Do Not Disturb to Send Calls to Voicemail

When you turn on the iPhone 5's Do Not Disturb feature, unless you preprogram the phone to act differently, all incoming calls will be sent directly to voicemail. To turn on the Do Not Disturb future, launch Settings and tap the Do Not Disturb virtual switch. You'll know it's turned on because a tiny, crescent moon–shaped icon will be displayed near the top center of the iPhone's screen (to the immediate left of the time display).

To customize the Do Not Disturb feature, launch Settings and tap the Notifications option. Then, on the Notifications screen, tap the Do Not Disturb option. On the Do Not Disturb screen (shown in Figure 7-7), you can turn on the Scheduled option to set predetermined times each day when the iPhone will automatically engage the Do Not Disturb feature. You can also adjust the Allow Calls From option so that all calls (Everyone), nobody (No One), or only people who have been added to your Favorites list (Favorites) will be able to get through with an incoming call while the iPhone is in Do Not Disturb mode. You can also choose specific groups of people from your Contacts database who will be able to get through to you while the iPhone is in Do Not Disturb mode.

 When the Do Not Disturb feature is turned on and active, a tiny, crescent moon–shaped icon is displayed near the very top of the screen, to the left of the current time.

You can also turn on the Repeated Calls option, which allows anyone who calls you, hangs up, and then redials your iPhone's phone number with a three-minute period to override the Do Not Disturb feature and get through to you.

An alternative to sending incoming calls to voicemail automatically by turning on the Do Not Disturb feature is to mute the volume of the iPhone's ringer and turn on Vibrate mode. When you do this, calls will come through, but the phone will not ring. Instead, your iPhone will vibrate to alert you of an incoming call. To turn on the Vibrate mode for your iPhone, launch Settings, tap the Sounds option, and then turn on the Vibrate On Ring and Vibrate On Silent virtual switches (shown in Figure 7-8).

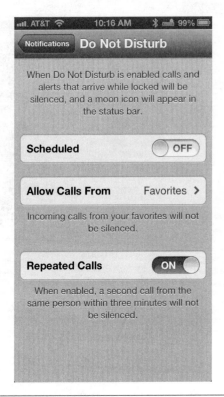

FIGURE 7-7   The Do Not Disturb screen within Settings

Answer an Incoming Call from the Lock Screen

If your iPhone is in Sleep mode when an incoming call arrives, the Phone app will wake up the phone and display the incoming call's caller ID information on the Lock screen (shown in Figure 7-9). In this case, to answer the incoming call, swipe your finger from left to right along the green and white slider near the bottom of the screen. Or, if you have a headset connected to your iPhone, simply tap the Answer button located on your headset.

You also have the option to utilize the new iOS 6 incoming call management features, which will be explained shortly. To do so, place your finger on the phone handset icon and flick in an upward direction.

 To ignore a call from the Lock screen and send it to voicemail, you have the same options outlined earlier: allow the phone to ring for about ten seconds until it automatically goes to voicemail, or quickly press the iPhone's Power (Sleep/Wake) button twice to send the incoming call to voicemail.

FIGURE 7-8 On the Sounds screen, you can mute the iPhone's ringer, plus turn on or off the iPhone's vibrate options.

If you have the Passcode Lock feature activated on your iPhone and you receive an incoming call, the Phone app will override the Passcode feature and allow you to answer the call. However, if you try to do anything else on your iPhone during that call, you will be prompted to manually enter the correct passcode to unlock it.

How to... **Adjust the Volume When Engaged in a Call**

While engaged in a phone call, to adjust the volume of the iPhone's built-in speaker, the speakerphone volume, or the volume of the headset, use the Volume Up and Volume Down buttons located on the left side of the iPhone. If your headset has its own volume control buttons, you can use those as well.

FIGURE 7-9   The Lock screen when it's woken up from Sleep mode by an incoming call

Answer an Incoming Call When Already Engaged in a Call

Just as with a traditional phone, one of the calling features available on your iPhone is call waiting. If you're engaged in a call and someone else tries to call you, the Call Waiting screen is displayed with the new caller's caller ID information. You then have four options:

- **Ignore**   Tap this button to ignore the incoming call and send it to voicemail while you continue with the original call.
- **Hold Call + Answer**   Place the original call on hold and answer the new incoming call that's displayed on the Call Waiting screen.
- **End Call + Answer**   End the original call (hang up) and answer the new incoming call that's displayed on the Call Waiting screen.
- **Use one of the incoming call management options**   Flick phone headset icon upwards and use either the Reply With Message option or Remind Me Later option, discussed in the following section.

If you tap the Hold Call + Answer option, the call-in-progress screen displays command icons that allow you to merge the two calls and create a conference call, as discussed later in the chapter, or switch back and forth between the two calls using the Swap icon.

Manage Incoming Calls Using New iOS 6 Features

Anytime you receive an incoming call, in addition to the Decline and Accept buttons (or the Slide To Answer slider on the Lock Screen), iOS 6 now displays a phone handset icon that gives you access to two new incoming call management features.

To access these features from the incoming call screen, place your finger on the phone headset icon and flick upward. When you do this, on the incoming call screen, two additional command buttons are displayed: Reply With Message and Remind Me Later (shown in Figure 7-10).

Use the Reply With Message Feature

Instead of simply sending to voicemail an incoming call that you choose to not answer, you now have the option to send the caller a brief, prewritten text message. To do this, tap the Reply With Message button while the phone is still ringing.

A pop-up menu will appear that displays several prewritten text messages, such as "I'll Call You Later," "I'm On My Way," "What's Up?" and "Custom." Tap one of these prewritten messages to send it as a text message to the caller, or tap Custom, which allows you to compose and send your own custom text message to the caller.

 When you use the Reply With Message feature, the incoming call is automatically directed to voicemail.

FIGURE 7-10 New incoming call management features added to iOS 6 include Reply With Message and Remind Me Later.

Use the Remind Me Later Feature

On the incoming call screen, if you tap the Remind Me Later option, you can set an alarm to remind you to call that person back in one hour, when you leave your current location, or when you get home. This feature utilizes the iPhone's Location Services option to pinpoint your location and then determine when you move from that location or arrive at your home.

Manage Voicemails

When people leave you voicemail messages after calling your iPhone's phone number, you can access those voicemails directly from your iPhone or from any other phone. To listen to and manage your voicemail messages from your iPhone, launch the Phone app and tap the Voicemail button near the lower-right corner of the screen (shown in Figure 7-11). To access your iPhone's voicemail messages from another phone remotely, follow the directions provided by your wireless service provider.

FIGURE 7-11   The Voicemail screen of the Phone app is used to access and manage your voicemail messages.

If you have new voicemail messages that you have not yet listened to, a Badge icon appears on the Voicemail button to indicate how many voicemail messages you have waiting. At the top of the Voicemail screen, the number of new messages will also be displayed in parentheses.

Displayed along the top of the Voicemail screen within the Phone app, you'll see two buttons, Greeting and Audio. Tap the Greeting button to record and save a new outgoing message for your callers. For example, you could record a message that says, "Hello, this is [insert your name]. I am unable to answer your call right now, but please leave your name and phone number, when you hear the tone, and I will return your call as soon as possible. Thanks for calling."

 If you do not record a custom outgoing voicemail message, your caller will hear a computer voice that instructs them to leave a message.

When you tap the Audio button, choose between holding the iPhone close to your face, using the speakerphone feature, or using a headset to listen to your messages. You're better off using either the speakerphone or headset option, since you'll need to view the iPhone's screen in order to manage your messages as you're listening to them.

Below the Voicemail heading that's displayed near the top center of the screen are your individual message listings. Tap a message listing once to access it. Then, tap the right-pointing arrow icon (the Play/Pause icon) that's displayed to the left of a listing to listen to that message. Or, tap the right-pointing arrow icon that's displayed to the right of the listing to view additional details about the caller (displayed on an Info screen that includes their Contacts entry information, if applicable).

 As you're looking at the Voicemail screen in Figure 7-11, the blue dot displayed to the left of the top voicemail listing indicates it's a new, unheard message. The listing below it that's highlighted in blue is the message currently being listened to. Thus, the Play/Pause icon is displayed to the left of that listing (the Pause option is currently shown).

If you tap the right-pointing arrow icon displayed to the right of a voicemail listing that's related to a message from a caller who does not have an entry within your Contacts database, an Info screen displays command buttons that give you the following options: Call, FaceTime, Send Message, Create New Contact, Add To Existing Contact, or Share Contact. At the top of this screen is information about the incoming call and caller, including the date and time the call was received (shown in Figure 7-12).

If the caller who left a message has an entry within your Contacts database, when you tap the right-pointing arrow icon to the right of the listing, that person's interactive Contacts entry (Info screen) is displayed, at the bottom of which are the Send Message, Share Contact, FaceTime, and Add To Favorites buttons.

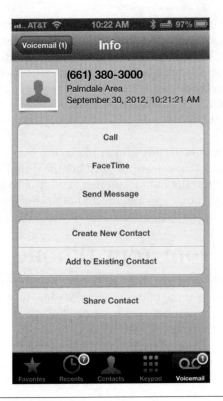

FIGURE 7-12   This detailed call information is what you see if you tap the right-pointing arrow icon to the right of a voicemail listing for a caller who doesn't have a Contacts entry.

As you look at this Info screen, when you tap a listed phone number, the Phone app will initiate a call to that number. Likewise, if you tap an e-mail address, the Mail app will launch and you'll be able to compose and send an e-mail to that person. You can also tap the person's street address to launch the Maps app and see the address displayed on a detailed map or to obtain directions to the caller's location.

Options Available When Listening to Voicemail Messages

As you're listening to a voicemail message, a timer is displayed in the bottom-third of the screen (refer to Figure 7-11) that displays the total duration of the voicemail message and how much of it you've listened to. If you want to rewind or fast-forward within the message, place your finger on the moving dot within the timer and move it either to the left (to rewind) or the right (to fast-forward).

To call back the person who left the voicemail message you're listening to, tap the Call Back button. To delete the voicemail message, tap the Delete button.

If you accidently delete an important voicemail message, near the bottom of the voicemail message listings on the Voicemail screen is an option labeled Deleted Messages. Tap it to view a listing of recently deleted messages. Tap a specific listing, and an Undelete button will become active, which allows you to recover the accidently deleted voicemail message. If you tap the Clear All button displayed at the bottom of this screen, it erases all deleted messages from your iPhone permanently.

When you're done listening to or managing your voicemail messages, tap the Favorites, Recents, Contacts, or Keypad button at the bottom of the screen to access other options within the Phone app that allow you to initiate a call, or press the Home button to exit the Phone app and return to the Home screen.

Make Calls from Your iPhone

There are several ways to initiate calls from the Phone app. After launching the Phone app, the majority of these options are accessible by tapping the Favorites, Recents, Contacts, or Keypad button, which are displayed along the bottom of the Phone app's screen.

However, regardless of what you're doing on your iPhone (or which app is running), you always have the option to press and hold down the Home button for two to three seconds to activate Siri, and then use a voice command to initiate a new call.

Create Favorites and Initiate Calls from Your Favorites List

Displayed in the lower-left corner of the Phone app is the Favorites button. Tap it to display the Favorites screen (shown in Figure 7-13), a customized listing of your favorite contacts, or those whom you deem to be your most frequently called contacts. You can initiate a call to a person or business on the Favorites screen with a single tap on their name.

To add a listing to your Favorites screen, the person or company must already have an entry within your Contacts database. (Chapter 8 covers how to add contacts to your Contacts database.) Launch Contacts, tap the contact's entry in the All Contacts list, and then tap the Add To Favorites button near the bottom of the entry's Info screen. Select one phone number or FaceTime address for that listing that you want to associate with the Favorites listing. This last step is not needed if the contact's entry lists only one phone number or FaceTime address. The entry is now included on the Favorites screen, which you can access by tapping the Favorites icon from any Phone app screen.

As indicated, each listing on the Favorites screen can be associated with one person or company that has an entry in your Contacts database, and each Favorites listing can be associated with only one phone number (or an e-mail address or an Apple ID that's associated with someone's FaceTime account).

FIGURE 7-13   The Favorites screen of the Phone app

You can, however, have multiple Favorites listings for a person, such as one listing for their home phone number, one for their work phone number, one for their mobile (or iPhone) phone number, and one for their FaceTime account (if it differs from their iPhone phone number).

Also, although a Favorites listing can be associated with only one phone number, e-mail address, or Apple ID, you can easily access and view the entire interactive Contacts entry (Info screen) associated with that favorite by tapping the right-pointing arrow to the right of the listing. You can then tap any of the displayed phone numbers to initiate a call to that number, tap an e-mail address to send that person an e-mail message, or tap a listed address to display the location on a map and obtain directions to it. Scroll down to the bottom of the Info screen to access the Send Message, Share Contact, and FaceTime buttons.

Tip   Add as many entries to your Favorites screen as you'd like. You can then scroll up or down the list using your finger if you add more entries than can be displayed on a single screen. Tap any listing to call the person or company that's associated with the listing.

How to... Use Siri with the Phone App

Whether you're viewing the Home screen or running an app on your iPhone, at any time, you can activate Siri and initiate a new call using a voice command, such as "Call [insert name]." As long as that person has an entry within your Contacts database, Siri will look up their phone number, launch the Phone app, and automatically dial the appropriate phone number. If that person's Contacts entry has multiple phone numbers, you can save a step when using Siri by saying "Call [insert name] at home," "Call [insert name] at work," or "Call [insert name]'s mobile."

Also, if you've created a Contacts entry for yourself using the Contacts app, and have included your own home and work phone numbers, you can use Siri and issue a command such as "Call home" or "Call work," and Siri will know which number to dial. This also works if you link your relative's Contacts entries to yours and label them as your mother, father, sister, brother, grandmother, etc. You can then issue a command to Siri such as "Call mom at home."

Instead of manually dialing a phone number for someone who does not have an entry within your Contacts database, you can tell Siri the phone number you want to dial. For example, you could say "Call 508 555 1212."

Finally, because the FaceTime app is fully integrated with the Phone app, you can initiate a FaceTime video call with someone who has a contact within your Contacts entry using a command such as "FaceTime [insert name]."

For complete information on how to perform these and other tasks with Siri, refer to Chapter 3.

If you want to edit your Favorites list by deleting a listing from it or reordering the list, tap the Edit button near the upper-left corner of the Favorites screen. To delete a listing, tap the negative sign icon that appears to the left of the listing.

 As you're viewing the Favorites screen, you can also delete a listing by swiping your finger from left to right across it. Tap the Delete button to confirm your decision.

If you want to reorder your Favorites list, place your finger on one of the Move icons (they look like three horizontal lines, and they're displayed to the right of a listing) and drag it up or down the list. Do this for each listing until they're all displayed in the desired order.

 When you're done editing your Favorites list, tap the Done button near the upper-left corner of the screen.

Call People from Your Recents List

As you make and receive calls using your iPhone, the Phone app maintains a detailed call history. To view this listing, tap the Recents button near the bottom of the Phone app's screen. To place a call to someone listed on the Recents list, simply tap on the call listing. The Badge that's displayed within the Recents button shows the number of missed calls.

Along the top of the Recents screen (shown in Figure 7-14), tap the All tab to view a comprehensive list of all recent incoming calls and outgoing calls made to and from your iPhone. The call listings displayed in black represent outgoing calls you initiated and incoming calls you answered, and the ones displayed in red represent missed incoming calls.

Each listing displays the person's or company's name or phone number, the label associated with that phone number (if they have a listing within your Contacts database), and the time or day of the call. Tap the right-pointing arrow displayed to the right of a listing to view more details about that call, including its exact date, time, and duration and, if applicable, details from the person's Contacts entry.

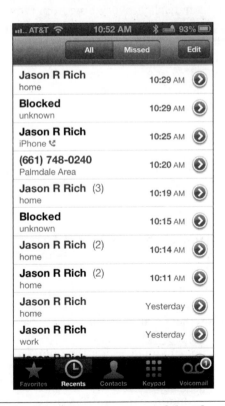

FIGURE 7-14   The All tab of the Recents screen of the Phone app displays a history of all recent calls made to or from your iPhone.

Tap the Missed tab at the top of the Recents screen to display only missed calls. This includes calls that went unanswered by you or that were redirected to voicemail.

To edit the Recents list, tap the Edit button near the top-right corner of the Recents screen.

 As you view the Recents screen, if a number appears in parentheses to the right of a person's name or phone number, that indicates multiple calls in a row to or from that person. For example, if the person called you three times in a row, the number three will be displayed in parentheses.

Find and Call Anyone in Your Contacts Database

You've probably figured out by now that the Contacts app is closely integrated with the Phone app. From the Phone app, tap the Contacts button near the bottom center of the Phone app's screen to display the All Contacts list. The All Contacts list includes all of the contacts from your Contacts database. (Chapter 8 explains how to add contacts to your Contacts database.) When you tap a contact in the list, an interactive Info screen displays everything from their Contacts entry.

Tap any phone number listed in the contact's Info screen to dial that phone number and initiate a new call. As previously mentioned, you can also tap the contact's e-mail address to compose and send an e-mail to them, tap the contact's street address to get directions to or view the location of the address on a map, or tap the Send Message, Share Contact, FaceTime, or Add To Favorites button displayed near the bottom of the listing.

To look up a contact from the All Contacts screen, use the Search field near the top of the screen, or tap one of the letter tabs on the right side of the screen to see listings stored under that letter (based on an alphabetical listing). You can also use your finger to scroll down or up the screen to view the entire All Contacts list and locate the particular listing you're looking for.

Dial Any Phone Number Manually Using the Keypad

To dial any phone number that isn't stored in your Contacts database or that doesn't appear within your Recents list or Favorites list, tap the Keypad button at the bottom of the Phone app's screen. A numeric phone keypad (shown in Figure 7-15) will be displayed.

One digit at a time, manually enter the phone number you want to call, and then tap the green and white Call button to initiate the call. To the right of the Call button is the backspace key, which you can use if you mistype a digit in the phone number. To the left of the Call button is the Add To Contacts button. Once you manually enter a phone number, tap this button to create a new Contacts entry or add the phone number to an existing Contacts entry within your database.

FIGURE 7-15   Use the numeric keypad to manually dial a phone number and initiate an outgoing call.

Initiate FaceTime Calls from the Phone App

FaceTime is a free video conferencing app that is fully integrated within the iPhone's Phone app. When viewing the Info screen associated with any Contacts entry as you're using the Phone app, scroll to the bottom of the screen to find the FaceTime button. Tap the FaceTime button to initiate a FaceTime video conference call with that person, assuming your Contacts database includes the person's FaceTime account information and the person you're contacting is currently active on the FaceTime service. You'll learn much more about how to use FaceTime in Chapter 14.

Use Other Options While You're Engaged in a Call

After you answer an incoming phone call on your iPhone (by tapping the Answer button on the incoming call screen) or initiate a call with someone from the Phone app (by first tapping the Favorites, Recents, Contacts, Keypad, or Voicemail button displayed at the bottom of the screen), you'll be engaged in a phone call and the call-in-progress screen will be displayed (refer to Figure 7-1 or Figure 7-5).

The call-in-progress screen displays the name or phone number of the person you're speaking with, the duration of the call thus far (near the top center of the screen), and seven command icons that you can use while you're engaged in the call. These command icons include the following:

- **Mute** Tap this button during a call to mute the iPhone's microphone (or the microphone on your headset). You will continue to hear the person you're on the phone with, but he or she will not be able to hear you or anything that's happening around you. When the Mute feature is turned on, the Mute button icon is blue.
- **Keypad** If you need to navigate through an automated receptionist or voicemail system, tap the Keypad option to display a phone keypad. You can then enter digits as instructed, such as "Press 1 to speak with sales, 2 for accounts payable, 3 for the shipping department, or 0 to speak with the operator." You can also dial someone's phone extension, for example.
- **Speaker/Audio Source** During a call, switch between using the iPhone's speaker (with the phone held up to your ear) and the speakerphone feature, or switch to a headset if one is connected. The Audio Source button replaces the Speaker button only when a headset is connected or wirelessly linked (via Bluetooth) to the iPhone.
- **Add Call** Use this feature to establish a conference call and bring one or more parties into your current conversation. See the following section.
- **FaceTime** If the person you're speaking with is active on FaceTime and they're currently using an iPhone to speak with you, tap the FaceTime icon to switch to a FaceTime video conference call.
- **Contacts** While you're on the phone, tap this button to look up and use information from your Contacts database.
- **End** Tap the red-and-white End button to terminate a call.

 While you're engaged in a phone call, you can also press the Home button to access the Home screen, and then launch another app or enter into Multitasking mode and reopen an app you were previously using.

Participate in Conference Calls

While you're engaged in a phone conversation and looking at the call-in-progress screen, tap the Add Call button to initiate a call with one or more additional parties (one at a time) and add them to a conference call (or be able to switch between calls with a tap on the screen).

When you tap the Add Call icon, the All Contacts screen is displayed. Find and select the contact you want to add to the current call, or tap the Favorites or Recents list to find the person or company from one of those lists. You can also tap the Keypad button to manually dial a phone number.

After you select the person you want to call, two new command icons are displayed on the call-in-progress screen. The Merge Calls icon replaces the Add Call icon, and the Swap icon replaces the FaceTime icon (shown in Figure 7-16).

When you tap the Merge Calls icon, the original call and the newly established call will be brought into a conference call, and all three parties will be able to converse freely. You can then tap the Add Call icon again and bring yet another party into the call.

You also have the option to tap the Swap icon and manually switch between the two active calls and talk to only one party at a time. You can switch back and forth as often as you'd like. Each time, one of the parties will be placed on hold while you talk to the other party.

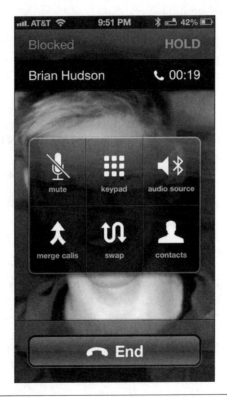

FIGURE 7-16   If you initiate a conference call, two of the command icons displayed on the call-in-progress screen change.

If your cellular calling plan has a predetermined number of talk minutes, participating in a conference call with two parties at once will reduce your available minutes twice as fast. If you participate in a call with three other parties simultaneously, your available minutes will be depleted three times as fast. This is not a concern if you have an unlimited voice/calling plan, however.

Customize the Phone App from Within Settings

Like so many apps you'll be using on your iPhone, the Phone app has a handful of customizable settings that impact how the app performs, and the features and functions you'll have available while using it. To access these customizable functions, launch Settings, scroll down the Settings screen, and tap the Phone option.

On the Phone screen (shown in Figure 7-17), you can view your iPhone's phone number and customize settings associated with a handful of Phone app–related options, including the following:

Depending on which wireless phone carrier your iPhone 5 is designed to work with, the options available to you from within Settings (refer to Figure 7-17) will vary slightly. Not all of these options are available on all iPhone 5 models.

- **Reply With Message** Use this option to compose and save custom messages that will be displayed when you access this new iOS 6 incoming call management feature.
- **Call Forwarding** Set up the Call Forwarding feature with this option. After turning it on, you can forward all incoming calls made to your iPhone to an alternative phone number that you enter into the Forward To field that's displayed. As long as this feature remains on, all incoming calls will be sent to another phone number and your iPhone will not ring.
- **Call Waiting** Tap on the Call Waiting option to access a submenu that's associated with this feature. You can then turn on or off the Call Waiting feature. When turned off, all incoming calls you receive when you're already engaged in a call with someone else will be redirected to voicemail automatically.
- **Show My Caller ID** When you make outgoing calls from your iPhone, if this feature is turned on, your name and phone number will be displayed as part of your caller ID information on the call recipient's phone.
- **TTY** This option enables you to turn on or off TTY (text telephone)/TDD functionality, which is commonly used by people who are hearing impaired. The default setting for this feature is Off.
- **Change Voicemail Password** Tap this option to manually change the password that's associated with your iPhone's voicemail. You will need this password if you try to access your voicemail messages remotely, from any phone other than your iPhone.

FIGURE 7-17   Customize the Phone app from the Phone screen within Settings.

- **Dial Assist (On/Off)**   This feature is used to help you easily make international calls by automatically inserting the correct international access code and country or local prefix, whenever possible, to the number you are calling. This feature is particularly helpful, for example, if you live in the United States but are traveling abroad and calling back to the United States.
- **SIM PIN**   Turn on or off the SIM PIN feature and/or change the SIM PIN with this option. Unless you swap the micro-SIM chip that came preinstalled with your iPhone, this is not a feature you'll be using.
- **Wireless Provider Services**   This feature enables you to make contact with your wireless service provider directly from your iPhone and access the automated services it offers. For example, you can check your bill balance, call directory assistance, pay your bill, and view account-specific information directly from your iPhone. Instead of using this feature, however, you'll find it much easier to use the free iPhone app that's available from your wireless service provider for managing your account (such as the myAT&T app if you're an AT&T Wireless customer). These apps are available from the App Store.

8

Manage Contacts on Your iPhone

HOW TO...

- Create and maintain a contacts database using the Contacts app
- Create, edit, and delete contact entries
- Make Contacts work seamlessly with other apps
- Sync Contacts data with your other iOS devices, computers, and online-based contact management applications

The Contacts app comes preinstalled on your iPhone. While this app is designed to manage your personal contacts database, the data you store within this app is also often accessed by a wide range of other apps as you use your iPhone.

The Contacts database you're about to create and maintain can be highly customized and can include a wide range of different data fields, each designed to handle a particular piece of information related to your various contacts. As you'll soon discover, you can create a fully customized Contacts database by using the labeled data fields that are most important to you.

If you already maintain a contacts database using the Contacts or Address Book software on your Mac, or Microsoft Outlook on a PC (or Mac), or if you use an online-based contact management application from Google or Yahoo!, or that's Microsoft Exchange compatible, you can easily sync your existing contacts database with your iPhone.

The Contacts app is able to import or export data from a wide range of other contact management applications, so chances are, you will not have to re-enter any of your existing contacts data stored on other devices or computers.

If you want to import your existing contacts database from another smartphone (one that is not iOS compatible), export that database into vCard format and then use the iTunes software on your primary computer to transfer the database into Contacts or Outlook on your Mac or PC. You can then sync the database with your iPhone.

Another option is to visit a store operated by your wireless service provider and have an employee perform a data transfer for you, from your old phone to your iPhone 5. This is also a free service offered by the Apple Store.

Create a Customized Contacts Database Using the Contacts App

The Contacts app allows you to create and manage a customizable database of your personal and work-related contacts. The information stored within your Contacts app is also used by a wide range of other apps on your iPhone, so as you're creating each entry within your Contacts database, it's important to include as much information within each entry as possible and to make sure each piece of data is properly labeled.

As discussed in Chapter 7, the Phone app gives you access to your Contacts database. After launching the Phone app, tap the Contacts icon near the bottom center of the screen to access the All Contacts listing. This is a complete and searchable list of the people who have entries stored within your Contacts database.

In the Search field at the top of the All Contacts screen within the Phone app, enter any information pertaining to a contact to quickly find their entry and their phone number(s). You can use the contact's first name, last name, or company name, or any keyword or search phrase that relates to a data field within the Contacts database.

When you're composing a new message in the Mail app, you normally enter in the To field the recipient's e-mail address (such as john@johndoe.com). However, if the intended recipient of your e-mail has an entry in your Contacts database, and that entry includes their e-mail address, instead of entering the recipient's e-mail address into the To field of the Mail app, you can save time by typing the first few letters of that person's first or last name, and the Mail app will access data from your Contacts app, find a match, and give you the option of automatically inserting the recipient's e-mail address into the outgoing message's To field.

If you're using the Maps app, within the Search field, or the Start or End field (when obtaining directions), you can enter the name of a person who has an entry in your Contacts database, and your iPhone will look up and display that person's address.

If a contact has two or more addresses stored in your Contacts database, such as work, home, and vacation home addresses, you'll be given a choice of which address to use when Contacts data is being retrieved by another app, such as Maps.

If you want to send a text message or instant message using the Messages app to someone who has an entry in your Contacts database, after tapping the Compose icon, when the To field appears, enter that person's name, and the Messages app will access your Contacts database to determine their cell phone number or username for a compatible instant messaging or text messaging service.

Siri also has the ability to tap into your Contacts database to access information about you and the people you verbally make reference to as part of your commands, requests, or questions. Once you activate Siri, you can ask questions like, "What's Tristan Mathews' address?", "What is Tristan Mathews' home phone number?", or "When is Tristan Mathews' birthday?", and as long as this information is stored within the proper entries within your Contacts database, Siri will be able to retrieve it. You can also use Siri with commands like," Show me where Tristan Mathews lives." or ask, "How do I get to Tristan Mathews' office?"

If you take advantage of the Related People field within your own Contacts entry, you can associate people with labels, such as "Mother," "Father," "Sister," "Brother," "Aunt," "Uncle," "Grandmother," or "Grandfather," for example, and then when using Siri, refer to those people by their title, as opposed to their name. For example, you can say, "How do I get to my mother's house from here?" or "When is my brother's birthday?"

Again, the more details you incorporate into your Contacts entries, the more helpful Siri can be when retrieving and utilizing information from your Contacts database.

We'll discuss further how many apps and iPhone functions utilize information from your Contacts database that's stored on your iPhone, but know that the more information you initially include within each entry, the more helpful many of your other apps will be in the future when they need details about you and your friends, family, coworkers, customers, clients, and other contacts.

 Depending on which app you're using, there are different ways to manually access information that's part of your Contacts database.

Let's Take a Closer Look at the Contacts App

On your iPhone's Home screen, tap the Contacts app's icon to launch it. From the All Contacts screen that appears, shown in Figure 8-1, you can look up a contact in one of several ways (discussed later in the chapter), or create a new contact entry by tapping the Add Contact icon—the plus sign (+) icon in the upper-right corner of the screen. How to add a new entry to your Contacts database is discussed in the next section.

 When you launch the Contacts app, the Info screen of the last contact entry you viewed may appear instead of the All Contacts screen. In that case, tap the All Contacts button in the upper-left corner of the Info screen to return to the All Contacts screen.

On the All Contacts screen, tap a listing for a contact to view that person's complete contact entry on an Info screen, as shown in Figure 8-2. In addition to being able to view all of the information you've previously included within that entry, you can tap one of the following command buttons displayed at the bottom of the screen

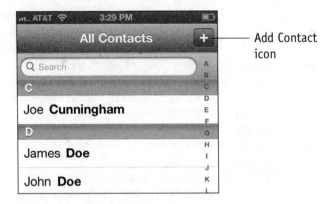

Add Contact icon

FIGURE 8-1 Scroll through your entries, or tap a letter on the right side of the screen to view alphabetized contacts sorted by a particular letter. Tap the Add Contact icon to create a new entry.

FIGURE 8-2 A sample entry within the Contacts app

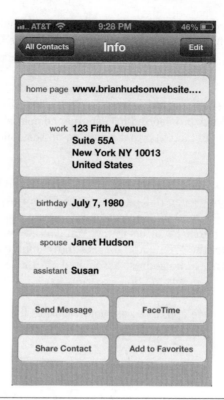

FIGURE 8-3   The four command buttons displayed at the bottom of all Contacts entries.

(shown in Figure 8-3). Up to four buttons appear, depending on which features are currently available to you.

- **Send Message**   Tap this button to send the person whose entry you're looking at a text message or instant message using the Messages app. The Messages app will launch and the New MMS screen will appear. The To field will already be filled in with the intended recipient.
- **FaceTime**   Tap this button to initiate a FaceTime call with the person whose entry you're looking at. (This button only appears if FaceTime is an available option between you and the other party.) For this to work, the person must have a FaceTime account set up, and their entry within your Contacts database must have the FaceTime field filled in. That person must also be currently available to receive a FaceTime call.

Tip   FaceTime functionality (for video conferencing) is built into the Phone app. However, you can initiate a FaceTime call with a contact by looking up their entry in your Contacts database and then tapping the FaceTime button near the bottom of their entry.

- **Share Contact**   Tap this button and then tap Email or Message in the menu that appears if you want to share a particular contact's information with someone else via e-mail or text message. See "Share Your Contacts Data Manually," later in the chapter, for more details.

 When you share a contact, it is sent in the industry-standard .vcf format, so it can be viewed and/or imported into another compatible contact management app, as well as the Contacts app that's running on someone else's iOS device or Mac, for example.

- **Add To Favorites**   Tap this button to quickly add the appropriate information about the contact you're looking at to the Favorites list of the Phone app. When you do this, you will need to select one phone number (or FaceTime address) to associate with that Favorites entry. You can, however, set up several Favorites entries within the Phone app for one individual, each with a separate phone number or FaceTime address associated with it. (See Chapter 7 for more details about adding contacts to your Favorites list.)

 From the Phone app, to access your Favorites list, tap the Favorites icon in the lower-left corner of the screen.

Add New Entries to Your Contacts Database

To add a new entry to your Contacts database, launch the Contacts app and tap the Add Contact icon (the plus sign icon in the upper-right corner of the All Contacts screen). The New Contact screen appears (shown in Figure 8-4). This screen contains a handful of empty data fields pertaining to the new contact entry you're about to create.

Begin by tapping the field labeled First. The iPhone's virtual keyboard will appear, enabling you to enter the contact's first name. When you're finished entering information into a field, simply tap the next field you want to enter information into, in this case the Last field. Enter the contact's last name.

Next, tap the Company field, if applicable, and enter the contact's company name.

 As you're creating a new contact entry, you only need to fill in data fields that apply or that you have information for. You always have the option to leave various fields blank, and you can always return later and edit the entry to fill in additional fields.

The next field is the first Phone field. By default, it's labeled Mobile. Begin by tapping the right side of the Phone field. This time, the virtual keyboard that appears showcases a numeric keypad (shown in Figure 8-5). Enter one of the contact's phone numbers. You do not need to use parentheses or dashes to separate the area code,

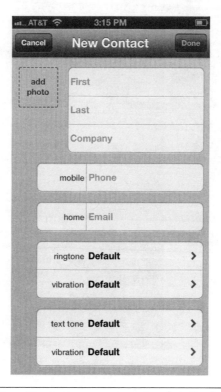

FIGURE 8-4 Use the New Contact screen to enter details about a new contact, one field at a time.

exchange, and last four digits of the phone number (or the country and city code, for international numbers). Just enter the ten-digit phone number for U.S.-based phone numbers. The Contacts app will format the phone numbers automatically.

After you have entered the phone number, tap the blue label (Mobile, by default) that's associated with that Phone field. The Label screen (shown in Figure 8-6) will be displayed. Choose the most appropriate label for that phone number, such as Mobile, iPhone, Home, Work, or Main. After tapping a label, you'll again be returned to the New Contact screen.

Note Any field whose label is blue and has a thin bar between the label and the data field offers the opportunity to change that label by tapping the label and selecting from a variety of options related to that field.

If none of the labels listed fits your needs to describe the content you're including within that field, then scroll down to the bottom of the Label screen and tap the Add Custom Label option. After you create a custom label, it will be displayed as an option every time you access that Label screen. Keep in mind, if you sync your Contacts

FIGURE 8-5 When entering a phone number, the virtual keyboard automatically displays a numeric keypad.

Did You Know? ## Why Using Labels Is Important

As you know, many apps access information from your Contacts database for a wide range of purposes. In many situations, other apps (including Siri) pay careful attention to the label you associate with each field.

For example, if you instruct Siri to "Call Barbara Whitman at home," Siri can only comply with this request if Barbara Whitman has an entry within your Contacts database and his home phone number is properly labeled. This also applies if you ask Siri, for example, "How do I get to Barbara Whitman's office?" Unless you have Barbara Whitman's address labeled as Work, Siri will not be able to comply with your request, launch the Maps app, and then provide directions without first asking you for additional information.

Spending that extra few seconds to properly label each field within a Contacts entry as you're creating it will ultimately save you a lot of time later when various apps need to access information from your database.

FIGURE 8-6   When a field label is displayed in blue and a bar separates the label and the data field, tap the blue label to select an appropriate label from the Label menu. Be sure to differentiate between Home, Work, Mobile, and iPhone phone numbers, for example.

database with certain online-based contact management applications, you may not have the ability to create custom field labels.

When creating or editing contact entries, it's important to differentiate between mobile phone numbers and iPhone phone numbers whenever possible. If you know that a contact uses an iPhone, associate their mobile phone number with the iPhone label, as opposed to the generic Mobile label. Later, this will help the iPhone establish FaceTime calls or send instant messages to that person via Apple's iMessage Service (using the Messages app). This option may not be available if you're syncing your Contacts database with certain online-based applications.

After entering and saving one phone number within a contact entry, a second empty Phone field automatically appears. You can enter as many different phone numbers as apply to that contact, each with its own related label. You need to enter and label each phone number separately. If you don't want or need to add additional phone numbers, tap on a different data field to continue creating the entry or tap on the Done button to save the entry.

Below the Phone field(s), you'll see the Email field. By default, it's labeled Home. Tap the right side of this field to enter the recipient's primary (or only) e-mail address, and then tap the blue Home label associated with that field if you need to change the label to Work or something else that's appropriate.

Just as with phone numbers, after entering and saving one e-mail address within a contact's entry, you'll have the opportunity to add additional e-mail addresses, one at a time, and give each of them a separate label, such as Work, Personal, Home, Private, and so forth.

Scroll further down the New Contact screen and you will see four additional fields, labeled Ringtone, Vibration, Text Tone, and Vibration (a second time). Each has a Default setting in the data field associated with it. This means that when you receive a call from that person, the iPhone will play its default ringtone, or when you receive a text message or instant message from that person, your iPhone will play its default tone. Likewise, if you have your iPhone set up to vibrate, the default vibration will be used.

If you tap the right side of the Ringtone field, you can select a custom ringtone for that person from the Ringtone menu that's displayed. In a same manner, you can also choose a custom text tone for that person, and change how the phone will vibrate in conjunction with an incoming call or text from that person.

 In addition to the options displayed on the menus, you can visit iTunes and purchase new custom ringtones and text tones, or create your own using the GarageBand app, for example.

Next, scroll down further on the New Contact screen to the field labeled Home Page. Here, you can associate a web page with the contact. Tap the right side of the field and enter the URL for that person's website or their company's website. You can use the www.*websitename*.com, http://www.*websitename*.com, or *websitename*.com format. Next, tap the blue Home Page label associated with that URL if you want to change the label to something else, such as Work.

Below the website field is the Add New Address field, shown in Figure 8-7. You can enter multiple addresses for that contact, one at a time, such as their home and work addresses. Be sure, however, to label each address properly.

As soon as you tap the Add New Address field, it expands into multiple fields, allowing you to input the street, city, state, ZIP code, and country associated with the address into separate but related fields. A label will also be displayed on the left side of the expanded address field (shown in Figure 8-8). The default is Home, but you can tap it to change the label to Work or another option from the Label list.

Displayed below the Add New Address field is the Add Field option. It allows you to add custom fields to this particular contact entry. When you tap this field, the Add Field screen is displayed (shown in Figure 8-9). It includes at least 15 optional fields you can add, one at a time.

 Any data field you enter information into within a Contacts entry becomes fully searchable from within the Contacts app, using Siri, when you access Spotlight Search, or from some other apps.

FIGURE 8-7 You can include multiple addresses for each contact, including their home and work addresses. Be sure to properly label each.

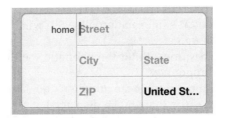

FIGURE 8-8 When you tap the Add New Address field, it expands into several fields in which you can enter and label each address.

These optional fields include

- **Prefix** Add Mr., Mrs., Ms., Dr., or another prefix to the contact's name but keep it as a separate field.
- **Phonetic First Name** Enter the phonetic spelling of the contact's first name if it is difficult to pronounce. This will be useful to you in the future when you

FIGURE 8-9 The Add Field option allows you to select from at least 15 additional data fields to include within a Contacts entry.

look up the contact's information, plus Siri will benefit from this pronunciation information as well.

- **Phonetic Last Name** Enter the phonetic spelling of the contact's last name if it is difficult to pronounce.
- **Middle** Include the contact's middle name, if applicable.
- **Suffix** Add a suffix that will be displayed at the end of the contact's name but stored in a separate, searchable field. You can add Junior (Jr), Senior (Sr), II, III, or another suffix that applies.
- **Nickname** Include the contact's nickname as a separate field in their entry. Their nickname will be displayed in conjunction with their first name and last name.
- **Job Title** Display the contact's job title in conjunction with their company name.
- **Department** Display the specific department in which the contact works within the company.
- **Twitter** Add the contact's Twitter username, using the *@username* format, or use the Update Contacts option found on the Twitter screen within Settings to update

your entire Contacts database with Twitter information pertaining to contacts whose entries represent people who are also your Twitter followers. How Twitter integrates with iOS 6 and the Contacts app is covered in greater detail within Chapter 10.

- **Facebook** Add the contact's Facebook username, or use the Update All Contacts option found on the Facebook screen within Settings to update your entire Contacts database. When you use this command, your iPhone will access your Facebook friends list and automatically compare it to your Contacts database. When it discovers matches, the iPhone will insert the appropriate profile photos and Facebook usernames into your matching Contacts entries.
- **Profile** Add the contact's username for a social networking site, such as Facebook, Twitter, Flickr, LinkedIn, or MySpace. Tap the right side of the field to enter the username, and then tap the blue label on the left to select the service it's for.
- **Instant Message** Add the username for an instant messaging service that the contact uses, such as their AOL or Skype username.
- **Birthday** Add the contact's birthday. Once you enter the contact's birthday into your Contacts database, that information can be displayed within your Calendar app. You can then set the Calendar app to remind you of the birthday in advance. From the Calendar app, tap on the Calendars button that's displayed near the upper-left corner of the screen and then select the Birthdays Calendar and/or the Facebook Birthdays Calendar to display this information as part of your calendar data.
- **Date** Insert another important (and recurring) date that's related to the contact, such as an anniversary. You can select the date and then choose the field label for it. Dates entered into this field will not show up automatically within the Calendar app, however.
- **Related People** Link contact entries of related people together by selecting them from your Contacts database after tapping this option, and then choose a label for each, such as Mother, Father, Parent, Sister, Child, Friend, Spouse, Partner, Assistant, or Manager.
- **Notes** Add text-based notes to the contact's entry. The notes can be any length, and you can update them as needed.

 Link and later display entries together by using the Related People option. Link multiple entries for separate but somehow related people, such as members of a club or organization, members of your extended family, or employees of the same company.

When you're done entering all of the information for a new contact, tap the Done button in the upper-right corner to save the information and view that contact's Info screen.

Add Pictures to Your Contacts Entries

The final piece of information you have the option of adding to a Contacts entry is the contact's photo. Or, if you're creating an entry for a company, you could use its company logo, for example. To associate a digital photo with an entry, tap the Add Photo box to the left of the First and Last fields at the top of the New Contact screen. You'll then be given two options:

- **Take Photo**   If you select this option, the Camera app will launch so that you can snap the contact's photo. You'll then be able to crop and reposition the image before it's added to the contact's entry. To do this, press and hold your finger on the preview image and then move it around with your finger to adjust its position within the frame. You can also use a reverse-pinch finger gesture to zoom in, and then use a finger to reposition the image within the frame. When you're finished, tap the Use Photo button to save the image and link it to the contact's entry.
- **Choose Photo**   This option allows you to select a photo already stored in the Photos app on your iPhone and add it to the contact's entry. To do so, tap Choose Photo, select the album in which the photo is stored, tap the image thumbnail, and then use the Move And Scale screen to zoom in/out or reposition the image so that it nicely fits into the onscreen frame that's displayed (shown in Figure 8-10). Press and hold your finger on the image and then move it around with your finger to adjust its position within the frame. You can also use a reverse-pinch finger gesture to zoom in, and then use a finger to reposition the image within the frame. When you're finished, tap the Choose button to save the image and link it to the contact's entry.

Yet another option for adding photos to your Contacts database is to activate Facebook integration on your iPhone, and then use the Update All Contacts option. While connected to Facebook, your iPhone will find each person's Facebook page, update your Contacts entries with their Facebook username and related information, and add their profile picture to their entry. Then, whenever that person updates their profile photo on Facebook, your iPhone's Contacts database will automatically update the photo as well. Changes to other information in a contact's Facebook profile will also get updated within your Contacts database automatically.

Add Contact Entries from the Maps App

Another way to add a new entry to your Contacts database is from the Maps app. In the main Search field displayed at the top center of the Maps app (shown in Figure 8-11), enter a business name, landmark, or popular destination. Once that business, landmark, or destination is found and displayed on the map, tap the blue and white arrow icon (>) associated with the listing.

A detailed Location screen will be displayed (shown in Figure 8-12). Scroll down to the bottom of this screen and tap the Add To Contacts button. A submenu

FIGURE 8-10 Adjust the photo to fit into the onscreen frame by using the Move and Scale options.

will appear giving you the opportunity to Create A New Contact or Add To Existing Contact.

If you tap the Create A New Contact option, a new contact for that business, landmark, or destination will be added to your Contacts database. You can then edit the listing as you deem appropriate. Or, if you tap the Add To Existing Contact button, you can select a contact entry that's already stored within your Contacts database, and the Maps app information from the displayed listing will automatically be incorporated into that entry.

 Use the Maps app to quickly find businesses you frequent and add them to your Contacts database using the Create A New Contact button, without having to enter any information manually into your iPhone.

Add Contact Entries from the Phone App

When you receive an incoming call, for example, the caller's caller ID information, if available, will be displayed on your iPhone's screen and then stored in the Recents list

FIGURE 8-11 It's possible to find locations using the Search feature of the Maps app, and then add those locations to your Contacts database.

within the Phone app. After the call is over, you can tap the Recents button near the bottom of the Phone app to view the Recents list (shown in Figure 8-13), and then tap the right-pointing arrow icon for the call listing. When the Info screen for that listing is displayed, scroll down and tap the Create New Contact or Add To Existing Contact option (shown in Figure 8-14).

You can then add that person's caller ID information (their name and phone number) to your Contacts database, and edit that entry by adding other information manually, if you desire. This is yet another way to populate your Contacts database without having to do too much manual data entry when using the Contacts app.

 A similar Add Contact button appears at the top of the screen when using the Messages app after you engage in a text message or instant message conversation with someone new. You can create a Contacts entry based on information you receive from the sender that's associated with an incoming text message or instant message.

FIGURE 8-12   After displaying a location in the Maps app, access its Location screen and tap the Add To Contacts button to add it to your Contacts database.

Edit Existing Contact Entries

After you've begun to populate your Contacts database with entries, at any time you can edit individual entries. To do this, launch Contacts and access the All Contacts screen. Select the specific entry you want to edit by tapping it.

As you're looking at the entry you want to edit, tap the Edit button in the upper-right corner of the Info screen. Next, tap any field to add information or change existing information. To delete a field, tap the red and white negative sign (–) icon to the left of the field. To add a new field, tap the Add Field option, select the appropriate field heading, and then enter data and a label, if applicable, into that field.

On the Info screen for a contact, you'll also see the Link Contact option. Tap this to link two or more related contacts together. For example, if you have two separate contacts for two employees within the same company, you can link these two contacts together. This feature can also be used to link separate entries for family members. When you do this, however, the Contacts app then displays the linked entries as a single entry on the screen. As you're creating or editing an entry, you'll find the Link Contacts option at the bottom of a contact's Info screen.

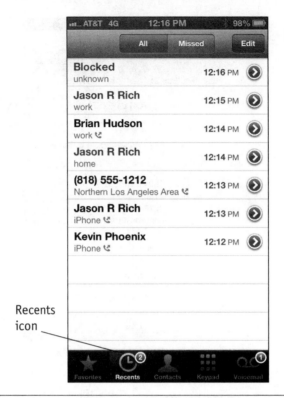

Recents
icon

FIGURE 8-13   In the Phone app, tap the Recents button to view the Recents list.

 Note   Keep in mind, the Link Entry feature is different from grouping Contacts entries together, which can currently only be done using the Contacts app on a Mac. Grouped entries can, however, be synced from a Mac to an iPhone.

When you're done making additions or edits to the Contacts entry, tap the Done button near the top-right corner of the screen (shown in Figure 8-15). If you have iCloud functionality activated on your iPhone, and have chosen to sync your Contacts database with your iCloud account, within seconds after editing an entry, those changes will be uploaded to iCloud and synced with your Contacts database on your computer(s) and other iOS mobile devices (such as your iPad).

 Tip   At any time, if you have iCloud functionality turned on and your Contacts database is synced and stored within your iCloud account, you can visit the iCloud website (www.icloud.com) from any computer or mobile device with Internet access, log in using your iCloud username and password (typically your Apple ID and password), and then access your complete and up-to-date Contacts database using the online-based edition of the Contacts app.

FIGURE 8-14   Select the Create New Contact or Add To Existing Contact option when viewing information about a recent incoming call.

How to...   # Delete Entries from Your Contacts Database

To delete a Contacts entry from your database, view the entry you want to delete, tap the Edit icon near the upper-right corner of the screen, scroll to the bottom of the Info screen for that entry, and tap the red Delete Contact button. When prompted, tap the second Delete Contact button that appears, to confirm your decision. The deletion is not reversible or undoable.

The Contacts entry will then be permanently deleted from your iPhone. Keep in mind, if the Contacts app is set up to sync with iCloud and your other computers or iOS mobile devices, as soon as you delete an entry from your iPhone, that same entry will be deleted within seconds from your iCloud account and your other computers or devices the database is synced with.

FIGURE 8-15 After editing a Contacts entry, tap the Done button to save your changes.

Find and Access Contacts Data

There are several ways to quickly locate and view data from your Contacts database, including:

- From the Home screen, access the Spotlight Search feature (by swiping your finger from left to right), and then enter the contact's name, company name, or any keyword associated with your contact's entry in the database. When the Spotlight Search feature displays a matching result that's accompanied by the Contacts app's icon to the left of it (shown in Figure 8-16), tap that search result to launch Contacts and display that contact's complete entry. All search results will be grouped together by app automatically.
- Launch the Contacts app, enter the contact's name, company name, or any keyword associated with the contact's entry in the Search field of the All Contacts screen, and then tap the search result to display that entry.

FIGURE 8-16   Use the Spotlight Search feature that's accessible from the Home screen to quickly find and display a contact's entry.

- Launch the Contacts app, scroll up or down the All Contacts screen to locate the listing for the contact you want to view, and then tap the listing (refer to Figure 8-1).
- Launch the Contacts app, and tap one of the letter tabs on the right side of the All Contacts screen to view all listings that are sorted based on that letter. Tap the listing for the entry you want to view.
- Use Siri to find and display details about a contact entry. For example, activate Siri and say "Show Me [insert name]" (shown in Figure 8-17). You can also ask specific questions about a contact, such as "Where does Katherine Hamilton live?," "When is Katherine Hamilton's birthday?," "What is Katherine Hamilton's work phone number?," or "What is Katherine Hamilton's e-mail address?" As long as related data is stored in the contact's entry, you can access it using Siri.
- From any app that taps into your Contacts database, such as Phone, FaceTime, Messages, or Mail, tap the Contacts option or To field to access an All Contacts list of all contacts in your Contacts database.

FIGURE 8-17 Use Siri to access and view Contacts-related data using voice commands.

Use the Interactive Fields in a Contact Entry

As you look at the Info screen for an entry in your Contacts database (refer to Figure 8-2), keep in mind that many of the fields are interactive. For example, here's what happens when you tap various information fields:

- Tap a phone number, and the Phone app will launch. The iPhone will automatically dial that phone number and initiate a new call.
- Tap an address, and the Maps app will launch and display that address on a detailed map.
- Tap an e-mail address, and the Mail app will launch, allowing you to compose and send an e-mail to that person. Their e-mail address will automatically be inserted into the To field of the New Message screen.
- Tap the URL field to launch Safari and display the website that's associated with the contact's entry.
- If you have Facebook integration set up on your iPhone, tap the Facebook username within a contact's entry, and the Facebook app will launch and display that person's Facebook Wall.

How to...

Choose How Contacts Are Sorted and Displayed in the Contacts App

When viewing the All Contacts list in the Contacts app, you'll want to choose how the entries are sorted. You do this from within Settings, and you need to do it only once. Launch Settings, tap the Mail, Contacts, Calendar option, and then scroll down to the Sort Order option under the Contacts heading, shown here. Tap the Sort Order option and choose either First, Last or Last, First. This determines if entries will be sorted alphabetically by first name or last name, respectively.

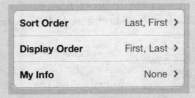

Sort Order	Last, First ›
Display Order	First, Last ›
My Info	None ›

If a particular entry contains only a company name, with no first and/or last name of an individual, that entry will be sorted alphabetically based on the company's name.

Also under the Contacts heading on the Mail, Contacts, Calendar screen is the Display Order option. When looking at the All Contacts list or individual entries within the Contacts app, this option determines whether the first name or last name will be displayed first.

Typically, you'd want to select Last, First for the Sort Order option and First, Last for the Display Order option. Keep in mind, in addition to impacting how entry information is displayed within the Contacts app, these settings also impact other apps that display an All Contacts list based on your Contacts app database (such as Phone, FaceTime, Messages, and Mail).

- If you have Twitter integration set up on your iPhone, tap the Twitter username, and a pop-up menu will allow you to compose and send a tweet to that person or view tweets related to that person.

Share Your Contacts Data Manually

You can share details from one contact entry with someone else via e-mail or text message/instant message (via the Messages app). To do this, select and view a particular entry in the Contacts app. Scroll to the bottom of the Info screen for that entry and tap the Share Contact button (refer to Figure 8-3). Tap either the Email button or Message button, depending on your preferred communication method.

If you tap the Email button, the Mail app will launch and display a blank e-mail form. Fill in the To field with the name or e-mail address of the person with whom you want to share the selected contact's info. By default, the Subject field is filled in with the word "Contact," but you can edit this.

Within the body of the e-mail, the contact's entry will automatically be attached to the outgoing e-mail in the form of a .vcf file (shown in Figure 8-18). If the recipient of the e-mail uses Contacts as their contact management software or app on their Mac, iPhone, iPad, or iPod touch, the recipient can download and automatically import into their Contacts database the contact info you send. This also works with a wide range of other contact management software applications and apps that support the industry-standard .vcf file format.

 If the recipient of the e-mail doesn't want to download and import the contact's info into their own contacts database, they will have the option to simply view the information on their computer's or mobile device's screen.

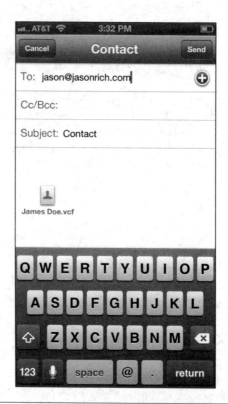

FIGURE 8-18 When you use the Share Contact option, the selected Contacts entry will be sent to the recipient as a .vcf file, which is compatible with many contact management apps running on computers and mobile devices.

If you tap the Message button rather than the Email button, the contact's entry will be sent to the intended recipient in .vcf format via the Messages app as a text message or instant message. Using this Share Contact method, you can share only one contact entry at a time with the person you're sending the e-mail or message to.

 Tip To send a contact's entry via text/instant message, tap on the Share Contact button that's displayed near the bottom of the contact's Info screen. Next, tap on the Message button. Fill in the To field with the person or people you want to send the text/instant message to, and then tap on the Send button. The contact entry will automatically be embedded within the text/instant message in the industry-standard .vcf format.

Sync Your Contacts Database with iCloud

Even if you have an iCloud account and turn on iCloud functionality on your iPhone 5, it's still necessary to turn on the iCloud Sync feature in conjunction with the Contacts app. To set up this feature, launch Settings, tap the iCloud option, and then make sure your iCloud account information is displayed at the top of the iCloud screen (indicating that the iPhone is set up to use iCloud).

Scroll down to the Contacts virtual switch (shown in Figure 8-19) and set it to On. Starting immediately after you do this, your iPhone will automatically upload your entire Contacts database to iCloud, and then keep your database synced on iCloud as long as your iPhone has access to the Internet. This syncing process happens automatically and in the background.

Now, on your Mac(s) running OS X Mountain Lion, launch System Preferences and click the iCloud option. In the iCloud window, make sure your Mac is connected to your iCloud account (and that it's the same account your iPhone is linked to). Add a check mark to the Contacts option (shown in Figure 8-20).

At this point, your Mac will also begin syncing its Contacts app's database with your iCloud account. Now, iCloud will synchronize both databases so that they are identical and update both your Mac and iPhone accordingly so that their Contacts databases remain identical as changes are made to either of them.

If you also have an iPad (and/or iPod touch), launch Settings on it, tap the iCloud option, make sure it's linked to the same iCloud account as your iPhone and/or Mac(s), and then turn on the Contacts virtual switch within the iCloud screen (shown in Figure 8-21). Doing this will also allow your iPad/iPod touch to sync its Contacts app's database with your iCloud account, so all of your Contacts databases on your Mac, iPhone, and iPad/iPod touch will now be synced together and accessible as one identical database on all of your computers and/or iOS mobile devices.

Finally, if you're using a Windows-based PC that also has a compatible contact management application running on it, such as Microsoft Outlook, download the iCloud Control Panel for Windows from the Apple website (http://support.apple. com/kb/DL1455). When you run it, it looks almost identical to the iCloud window

FIGURE 8-19 To activate iCloud functionality to work with the Contacts app, turn on the virtual switch that's associated with this option.

within System Preferences on the Mac (refer to Figure 8-20). Add a check mark to the Mail, Contacts, Calendars, & Tasks with Outlook check box. This will allow your iPhone (and any other devices linked to your iCloud account) to also sync its Contacts database with Microsoft Outlook running on your Windows-based PC.

Sync Your Contacts Database with Other Services

The Contacts database on your iPhone can also sync with your online-based contacts database through Yahoo!, Google, AOL, Microsoft Hotmail, or Microsoft Exchange. To begin this syncing process, on your iPhone, launch Settings, tap the Mail, Contacts, Calendars option, and then tap the Add Account option under the Accounts heading.

On the Add Account screen (shown in Figure 8-22), select Microsoft Exchange, Gmail, or Yahoo!. When prompted, enter your name, e-mail address, password, and a description. See Chapter 9 for more information about how to do this.

FIGURE 8-20   Be sure to turn on iCloud syncing functionality for the Contacts app running on your Mac by accessing the Mac's System Preferences and selecting the iCloud option.

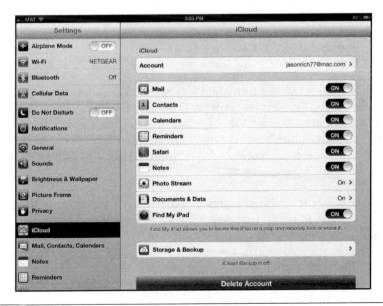

FIGURE 8-21   To sync your Contacts database with your iPhone, iPad mini, or iPod Touch, turn on iCloud functionality and the sync function associated with Contacts from within Settings on the other device.

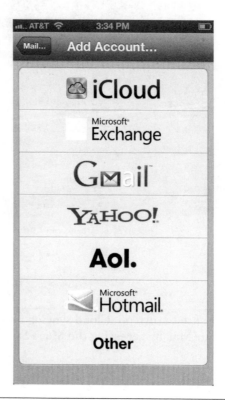

FIGURE 8-22 From Settings, you can set up your Google, Yahoo!, AOL, Microsoft Hotmail, or Microsoft Exchange account to sync with the Contacts database on your iPhone.

After the account information has been verified, when looking at the Yahoo!, Google, AOL, Microsoft Hotmail, or Microsoft Exchange screen within Settings (shown in Figure 8-23 for Yahoo!), turn on the Contacts virtual switch. From this point forward, your online-based contact management application through Yahoo!, Google, AOL, or Microsoft Exchange will sync (and remain synced) with the Contacts app on your iPhone.

 Get into the habit of entering information into your Contacts database about your friends, relatives, coworkers, customers, clients, companies you do business with, professionals whose services you utilize (such as your barber, salon, manicurist, psychologist, dentist, eye doctor, physician, pet groomer, gardener, plumber, electrician, etc.), and other people you interact with. This will ensure you can always access details about these people or companies from your iPhone, whenever and wherever you need to.

FIGURE 8-23   After setting up and verifying the Google, Yahoo!, AOL, Microsoft Hotmail, or Microsoft Exchange account, turn on the Contacts virtual switch.

Keep in mind, you can control which third-party apps can gain access to your Contacts database. To do this, launch Settings and tap the Privacy option. On the Privacy screen, tap the Contacts option. The Contacts screen displays a series of virtual on/off switches representing third-party apps that can access your Contacts database. To block an app from accessing your Contacts database, turn its virtual switch to the Off position. If no compatible third-party apps are currently installed on your iPhone 5, the Contacts screen under the Privacy option will be empty.

9

Send and Receive E-mail Using the Mail App

HOW TO...

- Discover the Mail app's newest features
- Set up your existing e-mail accounts to work with your iPhone 5
- Manage your e-mail accounts and read e-mails
- Compose and send e-mails

Whether you have just one e-mail account or need to manage several different accounts for your personal and work-related needs, the Mail app that comes preinstalled on your iPhone offers the functionality you need to read incoming e-mails, send outgoing e-mails, and manage your e-mail accounts from anywhere your iPhone has a 3G.4G (LTE) or Wi-Fi Internet connection.

If you're a veteran iPhone user, the iOS 6 version of the Mail app offers several new and very useful features, as well as a more streamlined interface that allows you to do more with fewer taps and swipes on the screen. Among the new features of Mail described in this chapter are VIP lists, an option to quickly refresh your Inbox, and the capability to embed a photo or video clip directly into the body of a message.

Set Up Your Existing E-mail Accounts to Work with the Mail App

Before you can begin using the Mail app to manage your existing e-mail accounts, you'll need to set up those accounts to work with your iPhone 5. If you have an iCloud, Microsoft Exchange–compatible, Gmail, Yahoo!, AOL, or Microsoft Hotmail e-mail account, this process is very easy and only needs to be done once. For other types of e-mail accounts, such as corporate e-mail accounts, you may need to enter additional information related to the account, which will be provided by your e-mail account provider or your employer's IT department.

 When you purchase your new iPhone, it includes 90 days of free AppleCare support. If necessary, either call AppleCare's toll-free phone number (800-APL-CARE) or make an appointment at any Apple Store to meet one on one with an Apple Genius who can help you set up your existing e-mail accounts to work with your iPhone.

If you've upgraded from an older iPhone model to the iPhone 5 and have transferred your old iPhone's data to your new iPhone, as described in Chapter 2, your previously saved e-mail account information should have transferred over to the iPhone 5 as well, whether you used the Restore From iTunes Backup option or the Restore From iCloud Backup option. In some cases, it is necessary to re-enter your passwords for your e-mail accounts.

If you're a new iPhone user or want to add more e-mail accounts to work with your iPhone, you'll need to manually set up each of your e-mail accounts to function with the Mail app. To do this, follow these steps:

1. From the Home screen, launch Settings.
2. Tap the Mail, Contacts, Calendars option.
3. Under the Accounts heading on the Mail, Contacts, Calendars screen, tap the Add Account option.
4. On the Add Account screen, select the type of preexisting e-mail account you have. Your options include: iCloud, Microsoft Exchange, Gmail (Google), Yahoo! Mail, AOL Mail, or Microsoft Hotmail. If you have another type of e-mail account, select the Other option from this screen and follow the onscreen prompts.
5. Depending on the type of account you're setting up, you'll be prompted to enter details such as your name, e-mail address, password, and a description for the account. Figure 9-1 shows the setup screen for a Yahoo! Mail account, which will be used in this example. Tap the Name field and enter your full name, or whatever you want to appear within the From field of outgoing e-mails, such as "The Smith Family."
6. Tap the Email field and enter your preexisting e-mail address, using the example@yahoo.com format.
7. Tap the Password field and enter the password associated with your preexisting e-mail account.
8. Tap the Description field and enter a few words that describe the e-mail account, such as Work E-mail, Personal E-mail, Yahoo! Account, or Gmail Account.
9. Tap the Next button in the upper-right corner of the screen. Your iPhone will connect to the e-mail service's server and verify the account. This will take between five and ten seconds. A screen with a handful of virtual switches will be displayed next.

FIGURE 9-1   Depending on the type of e-mail account you're setting up to work on your iPhone, the fields you'll need to fill in may vary. Shown here is the setup screen for a Yahoo! Mail account.

10. On the screen that lists the Mail, Contacts, Calendar, Reminders, and/or Notes app names, turn on the virtual switches associated with the apps that you want to sync with your online-based e-mail account. For example, if you use Yahoo!'s online-based contact management app or scheduling app, in addition to Yahoo! Mail, turn on the virtual switches associated with Contacts and Calendar to automatically sync your app-specific data between your Yahoo! account and your iPhone's apps. (The sync options listed on this screen will vary based on the type of e-mail account you're setting up to work with your iPhone.)

11. Tap the Save button to continue. The Mail, Contacts, Calendars screen within Settings will reappear. Your iPhone is now set up to work with the preexisting e-mail account you just entered.

12. If you have additional preexisting e-mail accounts to set up, repeat Steps 3 through 11 (which might vary) for each account.

Your iPhone's Mail app allows you to manage multiple e-mail accounts simultaneously, but it always keeps e-mails from each account separate, even if information from multiple accounts is displayed on the same screen, such as when you view the All Inboxes screen or the VIP inbox.

Customize the Mail App

To customize the Mail app, launch Settings, tap the Mail, Contacts, Calendar option, and scroll down to the options listed under the Mail heading (shown in Figure 9-2). The following options are displayed that offer customizable settings:

- **Show** This option determines how many individual e-mail messages the iPhone 5 will download from the mail server at any given time. Your options include 50, 100, 200, 500, or 1000 recent message per account.
- **Preview** When viewing the All Inboxes screen or any specific Inbox screen, or Mail-related notifications displayed within the Notification Center screen,

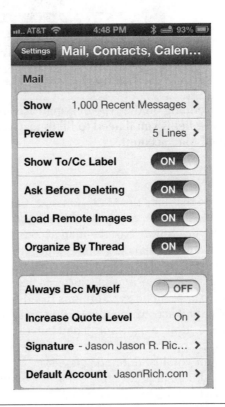

FIGURE 9-2 Customize the Mail app from within Settings from the Mail, Contacts, Calendar screen.

this option determines how many lines of the e-mail's body will be displayed in conjunction with each e-mail preview listing (in addition to the Sender, Date, and Subject fields). Your options include None or between one and five lines.

- **Show To/Cc Label**   For most types of e-mail accounts, turn on this virtual switch to display the To/Cc field as you're looking at or composing e-mails. Keep in mind, this information takes up additional lines on the iPhone's screen, but if you're managing multiple e-mail accounts from your iPhone, the additional detail pertaining to each message could be helpful.

- **Ask Before Deleting**   Turn on this option to be prompted to confirm your e-mail deletion requests. Keep in mind, deleting an e-mail from your iPhone typically does not delete it from the online-based e-mail server.

- **Load Remote Images**   Turn on this option if you want the Mail app to automatically download and display all graphics or photos that are embedded within incoming e-mails. This option allows you to view e-mails as they are intended to be seen by the sender, but using this feature requires a lot of wireless data usage if you frequently receive e-mails with embedded images or graphics. So, if you have a predetermined 3G/4G monthly wireless data allocation, turning off this feature is one way to make your allocation last longer. As you view individual e-mails, you can always tap the placeholder icon for each graphic or photo to download and view it.

- **Organize By Thread**   Instead of sorting e-mails within your various inboxes strictly in reverse-chronological order, you can sort them by subject thread (and in reverse chronological order) by turning on this option. This allows you to more easily read and understand e-mail conversations that transpire over a handful of messages where the sender and you keep hitting the Reply button.

- **Always Bcc Myself**   When turned on, this option will automatically add to your inbox a copy of every e-mail you compose and send. Keep in mind, a saved copy of every outgoing e-mail will also be placed automatically in your Outbox or Sent folder (depending on the type of e-mail account you're using).

- **Increase Quote Level**   This feature automatically indents the body of a message when you forward or reply to it. This makes it easier to read when you add additional text to these messages.

- **Signature**   At the end of every outgoing e-mail, you can automatically add a signature that you create through this option. The Mail app allows you to create multiple signatures, which are then accessible from all of your e-mail accounts, or just from specific e-mail accounts. A signature might include your name, address, phone number, e-mail address, and website URL, all of which get displayed automatically at the end of every e-mail you send. By default, the signature added to your e-mails will be "Sent from my iPhone."

- **Default Account**   If you're managing multiple e-mail accounts from the Mail app, the account you select in conjunction with this option will be the default account used whenever you tap the Compose New Message icon to create and send a new e-mail. From the New Message screen, however, you can always tap the From field and select one of your other e-mail addresses to send that e-mail from.

On the iCloud screen within Settings, you should also turn on the Mail virtual switch. However, this option only turns on iCloud syncing capabilities in conjunction with your iCloud e-mail account.

When you exit Settings, any changes you've made related to the Mail app and its customizable settings will automatically be saved. The settings you adjusted remain in effect until you manually return to the Mail, Contacts, Calendar screen and alter them.

Read and Manage Incoming E-mails Using the Mail App

Once you've set up one or more e-mail accounts to work with your iPhone, launch the Mail app to manage those accounts, read incoming e-mails, and compose outgoing e-mails.

If you have only one e-mail account set up to work with your iPhone, the Mail app opens to the Accounts screen, which displays the default mailboxes/folders associated with that account, such as the Inbox, Drafts, Sent, Deleted, and Junk folders, as well as any custom folders you've created that relate to that individual e-mail account.

If you've set up more than one e-mail account, the Mail app offers a Mailboxes screen (shown in Figure 9-3). This screen lists the inboxes for each account separately, as well as an option to view your VIP or Flagged mailboxes/folders (which are discussed later in this chapter).

 From the Mailboxes screen, you can quickly switch between each of the e-mail accounts the Mail app is set up to manage, and you can access the All Inboxes, VIP, and Flagged inboxes.

View the Contents of One Inbox or All Inboxes

Tap a particular inbox listing (displayed under the Inboxes heading) to view the contents of that inbox. To view a single listing that displays on a single screen all new incoming e-mails from all of your e-mail accounts, tap the All Inboxes option. This makes it easier to quickly sort through and view your new or unfiled e-mails. When you use this feature, however, the Mail app automatically keeps messages related to each account separate, so you won't accidently reply to a work-related e-mail from your personal e-mail account, for example.

Switch Between E-mail Accounts

As you're viewing the Mailboxes screen, scroll down to the Accounts heading if you want to switch between your individual e-mail accounts and then manage them one

FIGURE 9-3   The Mailboxes screen allows you to quickly switch between e-mail accounts and manage them separately, or access the All Inboxes, VIP, or Flagged inbox to see related messages for all of your e-mail accounts.

at a time. When you tap a particular e-mail account, that account's Accounts screen opens, which should include its Inbox, Drafts, Sent, Deleted, and Junk folders, and headings for any other custom folders related to that specific e-mail account. The specific folders (mailboxes) listed when you access an individual e-mail account will be account-specific and will be obtained from your mail server.

Create a Custom Mailbox

For some types of e-mail accounts, from your iPhone, you can create additional, custom folders (mailboxes) that will then sync with your e-mail server. To do this, from the account-specific screen that lists each current folder, tap the Edit button and then tap the New Mailbox button. When prompted, create a name for the new mailbox. Tap the Done button to save your changes.

You Can View a Single Listing of VIP Messages or Flagged Messages

When you tap the VIP option on the Mailboxes screen, a separate inbox is displayed that lists previews for all of the incoming e-mails from senders whom you have designated as a VIP. (See "Add an E-mail's Sender to Your VIP List," later in the chapter.) This single listing will include VIP e-mails from all of your various e-mail accounts. However, the Mail app keeps the accounts separate, so if you reply to a message, for example, that reply will come from the e-mail address the original message was originally sent to.

Similarly, the Flagged option displays a separate inbox that displays previews for all incoming e-mail messages that you've flagged as important. This single listing may include flagged messages from all of your various e-mail accounts, as well as replies or subsequent messages related to an original message that you previously flagged. (See "Flag Incoming E-mails and/or Mark Them As Unread," later in the chapter.)

Tap any e-mail preview listing in either inbox to view and manage, in a separate screen, that entire e-mail message. (An example of this screen is shown later, in Figure 9-5.)

Access E-mail from Your Inboxes

When you click one of your inboxes (or the All Inboxes option), you'll see incoming e-mail messages listed as previews. Depending on how you set up the Mail app from within Settings, each e-mail message preview will display some of the header information, including the Sender, Subject, Time/Date, and between zero and five lines from the body of the e-mail.

Displayed to the left of each e-mail listing may be one or more icons. The Mail app uses a handful of different icons to help you quickly determine the status of each e-mail. The various icons (shown in Figure 9-4) include

- **Blue dot**   Indicates the message is new and unread
- **Star (solid)**   Indicates a new and unread message from someone on your VIP list
- **Star (outline)**   Indicates an already read message from someone on your VIP list
- **Flag**   Indicates the e-mail has been flagged by you as important, or is a reply to or part of a message thread that was originally flagged
- **Left-pointing curved arrow**   Indicates you have read and replied to that message.
- **Right-pointing arrow**   Indicates you've read and forwarded the e-mail to one or more other people

Did You Know?

The Mail App Has a New Quick Refresh Feature

Among the new features added to the iOS 6 edition of the Mail app is the ability to easily refresh your inbox. As you're looking at the All Inboxes screen or a particular e-mail account's mailbox (folder), simply swipe your finger in a downward direction. The Mail app will check to see if you've received any new incoming e-mails and, if so, display them in the appropriate inbox (or on the All Inboxes screen).

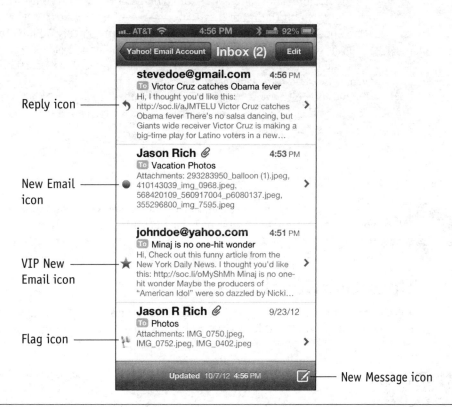

FIGURE 9-4   In conjunction with each e-mail listing displayed in an inbox may be one of several icons.

Set the Mail App to Automatically Retrieve New E-mail Messages

Depending on how you set up your iPhone and the Mail app, you can manually check for new e-mails whenever you wish, or you can have the iPhone automatically log in to your e-mail server and check for new e-mails.

From the Settings app, tap the Mail, Contacts, Calendars option and then tap the Fetch New Data option. On the Fetch New Data screen, turn on the Push feature to have your mail server automatically "push" new e-mails to your iPhone as they're received. Using this feature is the most convenient and ensures your iPhone is always displaying the most recent e-mails received, but it also requires a significant amount of wireless data usage.

Instead of using the Push feature, you have the option to use the Fetch feature (also on the Fetch New Data screen within Settings) and set up the Mail app to check for new e-mails every 15 minutes, every 30 minutes, every hour, or only when you manually tell it to. Choosing the Manually option uses the least amount of wireless data, assuming you don't constantly access your inbox and refresh it manually.

By tapping the Advanced option, you can set up each mailbox separately to utilize the Push, Fetch, or Manual setting for retrieving new e-mails from your e-mail server(s).

Note If no icon is displayed next to an incoming e-mail within an inbox, that indicates you've read the e-mail but haven't done anything with it. (That read message remains in your inbox.)

Read Individual E-mails

To read an individual e-mail, tap its listing within an inbox. The Inbox screen you're looking at will be replaced by a screen that displays the incoming e-mail (shown in Figure 9-5).

Tip To return to the inbox, tap the Inbox button in the upper-left corner of the screen.

At the top center of the screen is the number of the e-mail among the total number of e-mails in that inbox. In Figure 9-5, the e-mail is the first of four e-mails in the inbox. Tap the up arrow button in the upper-right corner of the screen to return to the previous e-mail in your inbox or tap the down arrow button to skip to the next

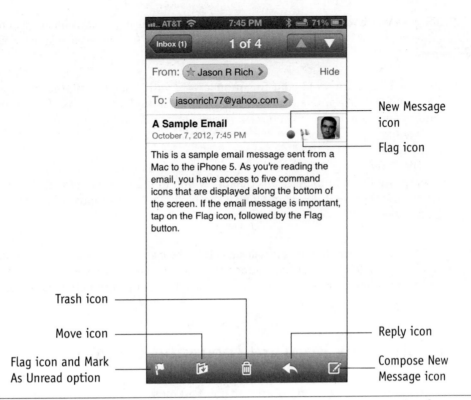

FIGURE 9-5   A sample incoming e-mail, from a VIP sender (star icon). After it was opened, it was flagged as important and marked as unread, so a blue dot icon and a flag icon are displayed in the header.

e-mail in your inbox. The up arrow button is unavailable in Figure 9-5 because the displayed e-mail is the first message.

As you work your way down the screen, you see the message's From and To fields, followed by the Subject field. Below the Subject field is the date and time the message was received.

As you're reading the e-mail, if you tap on the flag icon that's displayed near the lower-left corner of the screen, you can flag the e-mail as important, and/or activate the Mark As Unread option. A blue dot icon will be displayed to the right of the date and time as you're reading the e-mail if you tap on the Mark As Unread option. A tiny orange flag icon will appear to the right of the date and time if you tap on the Flag option. Also, if the Sender of the e-mail has an entry within your Contacts database, and a photo is included within that entry, a thumbnail image of the sender's photo will be displayed to the right of the date and time as you read an e-mail.

The entire body of the e-mail message is displayed next. If the e-mail is longer than the screen, scroll down using your finger to see the complete message.

Tip As you're reading an e-mail, you can zoom in by using a pinch finger gesture or zoom out by using a reverse-pinch finger gesture (a double-tap will not work).

If you place and hold your finger on a word within the e-mail, the Select All, Copy, and Define options will be displayed. You can select sections of the e-mail's content and copy it to your iPhone's virtual clipboard, and then paste that content into another app or another e-mail you're composing, for example. Tap Define to look up the definition of a word.

Displayed along the bottom of the screen as you're reading an incoming e-mail message are five command icons that allow you to manage that e-mail. From left to right, these represent the Flag, Move, Delete, Reply, and Compose commands, which are described in the sections that follow.

Tip If a photo or graphic is displayed within the message, to save that image to the Camera Roll folder of the Photos app, press and hold down your finger on the image and then select the Save To Camera Roll or Open In option associated with a compatible app.

Reply To or Forward Incoming E-mails

When reading an e-mail, tap the curved, left-pointing arrow icon at the bottom of the screen to reply to, forward, or print that e-mail message. A pop-up menu appears that includes Reply, Forward, Print, and Cancel buttons.

Tap the Reply button to compose and send a reply to the incoming e-mail. When you do this, a New Message screen appears, with the To, From, and Subject fields already filled in using information from the message you're replying to. The body of the original message (or the entire message thread) will be displayed at the bottom of the reply message you are about to compose.

Using the virtual keyboard or the iPhone's Dictation feature, compose the reply message and then tap the Send button to send it.

To Forward a message to one or more people, tap on the Forward option. The screen will display an outgoing e-mail screen with the e-mail message you want to forward already embedded near the bottom of the message. Fill in the To field and address the e-mail to the intended recipient(s). You can then modify the Subject (which will be the Subject of the original e-mail), preceded with "Fwd:" to indicate it's a forwarded message. You then have the option to add text to the body of the message, above where the original message has been embedded. When you're ready, tap on the Send button to forward the message.

Tip Tap the Print button to send the message to a printer that's linked wirelessly to your iPhone via the AirPrint feature. If you have a printer that is AirPrint compatible, you can link it wirelessly to your iPhone in order to print emails, documents, files, and photos. To learn more about AirPrint, and the more than 200

AirPrint-compatible printers available from companies like Brother, Canon, Dell, Epson, HP, Lexmark, and Samsung, visit http://support.apple.com/kb/HT4356.

Flag Incoming E-mails and/or Mark Them as Unread

As you're reading an e-mail, tap the flag icon in the lower-left corner of the screen to access a pop-up menu with the three buttons Flag (or Unflag), Mark As Unread, and Cancel.

Tap Flag to mark that incoming e-mail as important. A tiny, orange flag icon will become associated with that e-mail (and all future e-mails in its thread). This flag will be displayed within the inbox and within the header information of the e-mail itself (refer to Figure 9-5).

 Once you flag a message as important, you can tap the flag icon again later as you're reading the e-mail. The Flag button will now be labeled Unflag. When you tap it, the e-mail message will be unflagged.

Tap the Mark As Unread option to leave the message in your inbox with the blue dot (or filled-in star) indicating that it has not yet been read. You can then return to that e-mail later, move it into another folder, reply to it, forward it, or delete it.

Delete Incoming E-mails

There are several ways to delete an incoming e-mail message, including:

 Many of these delete options also work when managing other mailboxes or folders associated with your e-mail account.

- From the All Inboxes screen or a particular inbox screen, as you're looking at the preview listing for an e-mail you want to delete, swipe your finger from left to right across the listing. Tap the Delete button to confirm your decision.
- From the All Inboxes screen or a particular inbox screen, to delete multiple e-mails at once (potentially without reading them first), tap the Edit button in the upper-right corner of the screen. Then, one at a time, tap the e-mail preview listing that you want to delete. A red and white check mark will appear to the left of the listing. Select as many e-mail preview listings from the inbox as you want to delete simultaneously, and then tap the Delete button at the bottom of the screen. (Instead of deleting selected message listings, tap the Move button to move them to another mailbox/folder, or tap the Mark button to flag them or mark them as read).
- As you're actually reading an e-mail message, tap the trashcan icon near the bottom center of the screen, and then tap the Delete Message button to confirm your decision.

One way to delete all of the messages simultaneously from some mailboxes or related folders is to open that folder, tap the Edit button, and then tap the Delete All button that appears in the lower-left corner of the screen. If the Delete All button isn't made available, you can select multiple messages, one at a time, and then tap the Delete button.

Move Incoming E-mails to Another Mailbox or Folder

As you receive incoming e-mails on your iPhone, you can quickly move individual messages or groups of messages into other mailboxes or folders, just as you can when managing your e-mail accounts from your primary computer.

As you're reading an individual e-mail, tap the Move icon at the bottom of the screen, to the immediate right of the Flag icon, and then tap the mailbox or folder you want to move that message to.

Or, from the All Inboxes screen or while viewing any individual e-mail account inbox on your iPhone, tap the Edit button and then tap one message at a time to select it. Once you've selected one or more message preview listings, tap the Move button near the bottom center of the screen, and then select which mailbox or folder you want to move those messages to.

Add an E-mail's Sender to Your VIP List

One new feature the Mail app offers is the capability to create a VIP list. When you receive an incoming e-mail from someone, you can identify that sender as a VIP. Then, from that point forward, any additional e-mails you receive from that sender will be added to a separate VIP list, and the e-mails themselves will display a star icon in the inbox and in the message's header. Thus, you can quickly view e-mails from important people in your life, such as family members, your boss, customers, or clients.

 As you're viewing the All Inboxes screen, new incoming e-mails from VIPs display a star icon instead of a blue dot (which indicates a regular, new, and unread message). However, on the Mailboxes screen, you can tap the new VIP option to see a listing of all incoming e-mails from your VIPs displayed in one place (even if you're managing several separate e-mail accounts on your iPhone).

To add a sender to your VIP list, as you're reading any e-mail from that person, tap the sender's name or e-mail address displayed in the From field of the e-mail. The Sender screen will be displayed, with three command buttons: Add To VIP, Create New Contact, and Add To Existing Contact.

Tap the Add To VIP button. Now, anytime you receive e-mails from that sender, those e-mails will be highlighted with a star and the messages will be included in your VIP mailbox.

To remove someone from your VIP list, open and read any e-mail from that person. When one of their e-mails is displayed on the iPhone's screen, tap on their name or e-mail address that's shown in the From field. When the Sender information window is displayed, instead of a Add To VIP button, you'll see a Remove From VIP button. Tap on it. Keep in mind, if you sync e-mails between other iOS mobile devices and/or a Mac running the Mail app, your VIP list information will sync as well. Thus, if you remove someone from your VIP list on your iPhone, that person will be removed from the VIP list on all devices you sync with your iPhone.

Compose and Send a New Outgoing E-mail

To compose a new message from scratch while using the Mail app, tap the Compose New Message icon that's displayed in the lower-right corner of the screen throughout the Mail app.

The New Message screen will be displayed (shown in Figure 9-6). Fill in the To field with one or more recipients. If the intended recipient already has an entry

FIGURE 9-6 The New Message screen is used to compose and send an e-mail using the Mail app.

in your Contacts database, you can type the person's name. Otherwise, you can manually enter the recipient's e-mail address by using the virtual keyboard.

As you manually type the first or last name of the recipient or an e-mail address, the Mail app will display possible matches from your Contacts database. Tap the appropriate match to add it to the To field. You can then enter additional e-mail addresses or recipients' names into the To field, one at a time. After entering each e-mail address or the recipient's name, tap the Return key on the virtual keyboard.

Tap the plus sign icon to the right of the To field to access an All Contacts list. Here, you'll see listings for all entries from your Contacts database. To find the intended recipient, either use the Search field at the top of the All Contacts screen or use your finger to scroll up or down the list. You can also tap a letter displayed along the right margin of the All Contacts screen to see listings stored under that letter.

When you tap an entry in the All Contacts list, that person's e-mail address is added to the To field and you are returned to the New Message screen.

Initially, the Cc/Bcc, From field is shown as one data field (to save on-screen space) as you're composing an e-mail. When you tap on this field, however, it expands into two or three separate fields, labeled Cc:, Bcc:, and From:. Tap the Cc/Bcc, From field to either add additional recipients who should receive a copy of the e-mail (using the Cc: or Bcc: option), or tap on this field if you want to switch the account from which the outgoing e-mail will be sent from your default e-mail account to another e-mail account that's already been set up to work with your iPhone.

After filling in the To field (and potentially the Cc/Bcc fields) and/or altering the From field, fill in the Subject field with the subject for your e-mail message. If you leave the Subject field blank, the recipient won't know what your e-mail is about and might mistake it for spam, so the Mail app will recommend that you fill in this field before the e-mail is sent.

Once all of the e-mail's header information is complete, tap anywhere in the body of the Message screen (about halfway down). The virtual keyboard will once again appear, and you can compose the body of your e-mail.

 Instead of manually typing the body of your e-mail, remember that the iPhone 5's Dictation feature is also available to you. Tap the Microphone key, and when you hear the tone, begin speaking for up to 30 seconds at a time. Tap the Done button when you're finished speaking. The iPhone will translate what you've said into text, and then insert that text wherever the flashing cursor is located within the New Message screen. Make sure to proofread the result.

As you're composing an outgoing e-mail, with iOS 6, you can now insert a photo or video clip directly into the e-mail, as described in the nearby sidebar. You can also place and hold your finger on a word within the e-mail to use the Select, Select All, Copy, and Paste features of iOS 6 to insert text from another app or move text around within the message. Finally, if you have the Signature feature of the Mail app set up, your default signature will be displayed at the end of the message automatically.

When you're finished writing the e-mail message, proofread it carefully, and then tap the Send button in the upper-right corner of the screen. A copy of the message will be saved in your Sent folder.

How to... E-mail Photos or Video Clips Directly from the Mail App

A useful new feature of the Mail app is that when you're composing a new message, you can now embed a photo or video clip into the body of the message from within the Mail app, as opposed to using the Share option within the Photos app. To do this, press and hold your finger down within the message body section of the New Message screen as you're composing an e-mail (or replying to an e-mail). When you see the Select, Select All, Copy, and/or Paste tabs appear, tap the right-pointing arrow icon.

A new tab that's labeled Insert Photo Or Video will become available (shown in the illustration). Tap it. When the Photos screen appears that displays each of the photo albums stored within the Photos app, open any album by tapping its listing, and then select an image that you want to insert into the outgoing e-mail by tapping its thumbnail.

The image will be added to the body of the outgoing e-mail. To add an additional photo (up to five), repeat this process for each image. Either before or after doing this, you can also add text to the body of the e-mail message.

When the message is composed and contains the text and photo(s) and/or video clip(s) you desire, tap the Send button to send the e-mail to its intended recipient(s).

Remember, if you have your iPhone set up to use the Auto-Capitalization, Auto Correction, and/or Check Spelling features of iOS 6, you may discover that the Mail app has replaced a mistyped word with an incorrect or even inappropriate word, which is why you want to proofread all outgoing e-mails carefully.

To turn on or off the Auto-Capitalization, Auto Correction, and Check Spelling features, launch Settings, tap the General option, and then select the Keyboard option. You'll see virtual On/Off switches associated with each of these features on the Keyboard screen. These are general iPhone-related settings, not Mail app–specific settings that are customizable.

Tip As you're composing an e-mail, at any time, you have the option to tap the Cancel button near the upper-left corner of the screen. When you do this, three command buttons are displayed: Delete Draft, Save Draft, and Cancel. Tap the Delete Draft button to erase the unsent e-mail and return to the Mail app screen you were previously viewing. Tap the Save Draft button to save the unsent e-mail (the draft) in the Drafts folder/mailbox of the e-mail account you originally started to create it from (which is the e-mail address displayed in the From field). You can then return to that message later to finish composing or editing it, and then send it. Tap the Cancel button to continue composing the message from the New Message screen.

Stay Connected via the Mail App, Wherever You Are

Compared to a laptop computer or even an iPad, the four-inch display of the iPhone 5 is relatively small. Yet, the Mail app manages to display and give you easy access to a vast amount of e-mail-related information, while providing all of the functionality you need to efficiently manage one or more e-mail accounts from the iPhone, as long as an Internet connection is available.

Like so many other apps that come preinstalled with iOS 6, the Mail app works seamlessly with the Notification Center and can display details about new incoming messages within the Notification Center screen as they arrive on your iPhone. You also have the option of setting up Alerts or Banners to be displayed on the Lock screen and/or one of the iPhone's other screens whenever new e-mails arrive (regardless of what app is currently running). To set up the Notification Center and various Notification features to work with the Mail app, launch Settings, tap Notifications, and then scroll down to the Mail app listing and tap it.

On the Mail screen, you can set up how each of your individual e-mail accounts will utilize the Notification Center window, Banners, Alerts, and/or Badges. This needs to be set up only once, but you can change the settings at any time. See Chapter 3 for more details about configuring the Notification Center.

10

Surf the Web with Safari

HOW TO...

- Visit your favorite websites from your iPhone
- Use bookmarks and the Bookmarks Bar
- Take advantage of the Reading List feature
- Access iCloud browser tabs
- Manage your Facebook and Twitter accounts from your iPhone

Even with its larger screen than previous iPhone models, you may be thinking that surfing the Internet and visiting websites on your iPhone 5 isn't too practical. Well, think again. Apple has done a remarkable job of fine-tuning its Safari web browser to work extremely well with the iPhone 5's Multi-Touch display, in conjunction with a Wi-Fi or 3G/4G Internet connection.

Thanks to iCloud, all of the bookmarks you have stored on your Mac computer's web browser can automatically remain synced with the bookmarks on your iPhone's Safari web browser. Plus, with the new iCloud Tabs feature, from your iPhone, you can access browser windows that you have open on your primary computer (or another iOS mobile device).

Beyond just surfing the Web, you can manage all aspects of your online social networking accounts directly from your iPhone via specialty apps available from the App Store, so you'll never be more than a few screen taps away from your Facebook, Twitter, Google+, LinkedIn, Instagram, or Pinterest online friends and followers.

Let's take a closer look at how to surf the Web using your iPhone 5.

 The version of Safari that runs on all iOS mobile devices, including your iPhone 5, is not, and probably never will be, compatible with Adobe Flash. Thus, it can't display websites that contain Flash animations. While more and more website designers are turning away from Flash in favor of other techniques for displaying animated graphics within a website (that are also compatible with Safari on your iPhone), if you must visit a Flash-based website from your iPhone 5, you'll need to use an alternative web browser. See "Use Other Web Browsers to Surf the Web," later in this chapter, to discover which apps you can use on your iPhone to view Flash-based websites.

Get Acquainted with the Latest Version of the Safari Web Browser

The main Safari web browser for the iPhone (shown in Figure 10-1) is divided into three main sections. Displayed along the top of the screen are the Address Bar and the Search field. To manually enter a website address (URL), tap the Address Bar and enter the address using the virtual keyboard that appears. Many other ways to access websites are covered in this chapter.

When entering a website URL, you have the option to use one of three formats: http://www.*websitename*.com, www.*websitename*.com, or *websitename*.com. If the website's extension is not ".com," be sure to enter the correct extension so that you'll be directed to the intended website.

Address bar ⟶ www.apple.com/

Search field

Share icon

Forward icon

Back icon

Bookmarks Menu icon

Browser Window icon

FIGURE 10-1 The Safari web browser on the iPhone 5

Enter a keyword or search phrase into the Search field to seek out virtually any information available from the Internet. Based on how you initially set up the Safari app within Settings (see "Customize the Safari App from Settings," later in the chapter), your default search engine that will conduct the search may be Yahoo!, Google, or Bing. To begin a search, tap the Search field and enter a keyword or search phrase for what you're looking for. Next, tap the Search button in the lower-right corner of the virtual keyboard. Within a second or two, your research results will be displayed in the main area of the Safari screen.

Below the Address Bar and Search field is the main viewing area of the Safari screen. It's here that webpage content (or your search results) will be displayed. Depending on the web content you're viewing, you'll be able to scroll up and down the screen, and potentially left and right as well (especially if the website is not formatted for use with a mobile device).

 As you're viewing webpage content, tap any active links using your finger. This serves the same purpose as a mouse click on any computer. To zoom in on a specific area of most webpages, use a reverse-pinch finger gesture.

Displayed along the bottom of the Safari screen are five command icons that allow you to navigate the Internet and perform other actions. In the lower-left corner of the screen is the Back icon (left-pointing arrowhead), and immediately to the right of it is the Forward icon (right-pointing arrowhead). Each is used for the same function as the similar arrow button in any web browser—to move from the current page backward or forward to return to a previously viewed webpage that was open within the same browser window.

Located in the bottom center of the screen is the Share icon, which depicts a box with a curved, right-pointing arrow projecting from it. Tap it to reveal nine additional command icons, which will be explained shortly, in the "Utilize Safari's Share Button" section. Displayed to the right of the Share button is the Bookmarks icon, which resembles an open book. Tap it to access your Reading List, History folder, iCloud Tabs, Bookmarks Menu, and Bookmarks Bar. These options will also be explained in this chapter.

Located in the bottom-right corner of the main Safari screen is the Browser Window icon. Use it to quickly switch between open browser windows, or to close browser windows that are open.

If you rotate the iPhone 5 and view the Safari screen in landscape mode, a sixth command icon appears in the lower-right corner of the screen, as shown in Figure 10-2. This icon with two arrows is the Full Screen icon. Tap it to view the currently open webpage in full-screen mode, without the command icons, Address Bar, or Search field displayed at the bottom and top of the screen. While in full-screen mode, an icon is continuously displayed in the lower-right corner of the screen that allows you to return to Safari's regular viewing mode.

Full Screen
Mode icon

FIGURE 10-2 Tap the Full Screen icon to use Safari in full-screen mode when you hold your iPhone in landscape mode.

<table>
<tr><td>**Did You Know?**</td><td>## The Virtual Keyboard Is Customized for Safari</td></tr>
</table>

Anytime you tap the Address Bar to enter a website URL, the iPhone's virtual keyboard takes on a customized appearance. The bottom row of keys now includes a period key, a backslash key, and a .com key, as well as a Go key. These special keys make it easier to quickly enter and visit website addresses manually.

If you press and hold down the .com key, a menu appears that allows you to select from other popular website extensions, such as .net, .edu, .org, and .us. After you've manually entered a website address, tap the Go key to open a browser window and display that webpage.

Once you visit a webpage, its details will be stored in your History folder. You also have the option to create a bookmark or Home screen shortcut for that webpage, as described later in the chapter, so you can quickly revisit the webpage without having to manually retype its URL. Plus, you always have the option to use Siri to find and launch a particular website or perform web-based searches.

Make Webpages Easier to Read Using the Reader Feature

As you surf the Web, you'll discover every website you visit has its own unique layout and design. However, some websites are designed to be "mobile websites," meaning they are formatted to accommodate the smaller screens found on smartphones and tablets. Viewing mobile websites on an iPhone is typically easier than viewing regular websites that are formatted to be viewed on a full-size monitor.

Many websites can detect that you're visiting them using an iPhone, and will adjust the formatting of each page accordingly. When this doesn't happen automatically, the Safari web browser will take steps to help ensure the site is easy to read on your iPhone's screen.

Regardless of whether a webpage is formatted for a mobile device screen or a full-size screen, it may include excessive "clutter," such as banner ads, graphical eye-candy, or other elements that make reading the actual content of the webpage more difficult. When this occurs, take advantage of Safari's Reader option, when it's available.

Reader automatically removes the onscreen clutter that's associated with a webpage and displays only the relevant text and photos on a well-organized, simply formatted, and easy-to-read screen. When the Reader feature is available, a Reader button appears on the right side of the Address Bar. Figure 10-3 shows what the Reader screen looks like when reading an article without the clutter of a typical webpage.

FIGURE 10-3   You can read clutter-free articles from the Internet using the Reader feature.

Safari's Reader feature should not be confused with Safari's Reading List feature, which is used for an entirely different purpose.

When viewing a compatible webpage in Reader mode, you use a finger to scroll up and down the screen as usual, but you can also tap the aA icon in the upper-left corner of the screen to increase or decrease the size of the text to make the displayed content easier to read.

 Tap the Share button at the top of the Reader screen to send the link to the webpage you're viewing to yourself or someone else via e-mail, Message, Twitter, or Facebook, or to wirelessly print the webpage content using a compatible printer and the iPhone's AirPrint feature.

The Reader feature is just one of several Safari features that make it easier and more efficient to access and read webpages from your iPhone. Keep in mind, Reader is not available when visiting all websites, so look for the Reader button to appear on the right side of the Address Bar as an indication that the feature is available for the webpage you're visiting.

Utilize Safari's Share Button

Like so many of the newest apps being released in conjunction with iOS 6, Safari features an enhanced Share button. Anytime you're viewing a particular webpage, tap this button (which resembles an open book) at the bottom of the Safari screen to reveal the Share screen, which includes the following nine additional command icons (shown in Figure 10-4):

- **Mail** Tap this icon to e-mail a link to the website you're viewing to one or more people. The Mail app will launch, and the Compose Message screen will appear (shown in Figure 10-5). The Subject of the e-mail message will be filled in with the webpage's title. Embedded within the body of the e-mail will be the webpage's URL. Simply fill in the To field and, if you'd like, add more text to the body of the message. Tap the Send button (in the top-right corner of the screen) to send the e-mail message and return to the Safari app.
- **Message** Tap this icon to launch the Message app, and the body of the outgoing message will contain a link to the webpage you're viewing. You can also enter additional text within the body of your message. Fill in the To field, and then tap the Send button (shown in Figure 10-6).

 When you're filling in the To field after choosing the Mail or Message option from the Share menu, if the recipient has an entry in your Contacts database, you can type their name instead of typing their e-mail address, cell phone number (for a text message), or instant message username. Tap the plus sign (+) icon to the

FIGURE 10-4   After tapping the Share button in Safari, the Share screen is displayed.

FIGURE 10-5   You can e-mail details about a website to other people from within the Safari app by tapping the Share button and then tapping Mail.

FIGURE 10-6 Share information about a website with other people via text message or instant message from within the Safari app by tapping the Share button and then tapping Message.

right of the To field to add multiple recipients to the outgoing e-mail or text/instant message.

- **Twitter** If you have Twitter integration set up on your iPhone, tap this icon to compose a tweet that will have the URL for the webpage you're viewing already embedded within it (shown in Figure 10-7). Tap the From field if you're managing multiple Twitter accounts, and then tap the account from which you want to send the tweet. Tap the Add Location option if you want to share your current location within the outgoing tweet. You can also add additional text to the tweet message, but pay attention to the character counter in the lower-right corner of the window. A tweet can only contain 140 characters total, and the website's URL you're sharing will take up some of those characters.
- **Facebook** To share information about the webpage you're viewing with your Facebook friends, tap this icon. You can then enter a text message to accompany the webpage's URL. This information will be displayed as part of your status update as soon as you tap the Post button in the upper-right corner of the Facebook window (shown in Figure 10-8). For this function to work, you must have Facebook integration turned on.

FIGURE 10-7   Compose and send a tweet about the website you're viewing from within the Safari app. In the body of the message, you can add your own text to describe the webpage link you're sending.

FIGURE 10-8   Update your Facebook status to include details about a website you're visiting from within the Safari app.

Tap the globe icon in the lower-right corner of the Facebook window to determine who will see your posting (status update). On the Choose Audience screen that appears, you can select Friends, Only Me, Friends Except Acquaintances, Public, Close Friends, or any of the customized friend groupings you've created as part of your Facebook account.

- **Add To Home Screen** Your iPhone's Home screen can display three types of icons: app icons, folder icons, and Home screen shortcuts. A Home screen shortcut is like a bookmark, but it's displayed on your Home screen. When you tap the Add To Home Screen icon, a special bookmark for the webpage you're viewing will be created and placed in an available slot on your Home screen.

  When you tap the webpage's shortcut on your Home screen, the Safari app launches automatically and immediately accesses and displays that webpage. Figure 10-9 shows a sample Home screen shortcut for the CNN.com website. Once you create a Home screen shortcut, you can treat it like any other app icon on your Home screen in terms of moving it around, deleting it, and so forth.

- **Print** If you have a wireless AirPrint-compatible printer set up in conjunction with your iPhone, tap this icon to send the contents of the webpage you're viewing to the printer to create a hard copy.

CNN icon

FIGURE 10-9 Create webpage shortcuts that can be displayed and accessed from your iPhone's Home screen. Shown here is a shortcut for CNN.com.

- **Copy**   Tap this icon to copy the contents of the webpage you're viewing into your iPhone's virtual clipboard. You can then access another app and use the Paste command to insert the website content into that app.
- **Bookmark**   Tap this icon to create a bookmark for the webpage you're viewing and add the bookmark to Safari's Bookmarks folder. If you have Safari set up to sync data with iCloud, the newly added bookmark will sync with the Bookmarks folder of the version of Safari (or compatible web browser) that's running on your Mac, iPad, or iPod touch, for example.
- **Add To Reading List**   Tap this icon to add the webpage you're viewing to your Reading List. When you do this, its contents are downloaded and stored on your iPhone, so you can return to it anytime later and read it, even if your iPhone is not connected to the Internet. More information about Safari's enhanced Reading List feature is provided later in this chapter.

Access Your Web Surfing History

Like all web browsers, Safari for your iPhone keeps track of all webpages you visit and stores information about them (in reverse chronological order) in the History folder. You can then access your History folder to quickly return to any previously visited website, without having to manually type its URL again.

 To maintain some privacy when surfing the Internet, from Settings, access the Safari screen, turn on the Private Browsing feature, and tap the Clear History button and the Clear Cookies And Data button to prevent Safari from storing your web surfing history and to erase your web browsing history thus far.

To access your History folder, tap the Bookmarks icon at the bottom of the Safari screen, and then tap the History option on the Bookmarks screen. When viewing the Bookmarks screen (shown in Figure 10-10), tap on the History option. You'll then see individual bookmark listings and bookmark folders. In the lower-left corner is a Clear button. Tap it to clear your web surfing history and remove the contents from this folder.

 Tap any listing in your History folder to launch that webpage in a new browser window in Safari.

Manage Safari Bookmarks

Using Safari bookmarks allows you to store your favorite or most frequented websites within one organized list. Doing this allows you to easily revisit webpages without having to remember or retype their URLs each time. And if you have your Bookmarks list set up to sync with iCloud, all of the computers and devices that you have

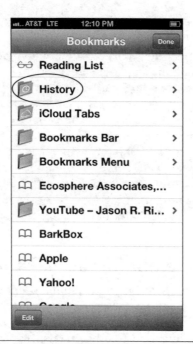

FIGURE 10-10 To access your History folder, tap the History option displayed on the Bookmarks screen within Safari.

linked to the same iCloud (Apple ID) account will maintain the same personalized Bookmarks list, and if you add, edit, or delete a bookmark on one computer or device, that change will almost immediately be reflected on all the other computers and devices linked to the account.

 Most people create an iCloud account using their Apple ID, so this login information is the same. However, you can set up an iCloud account using an alternate e-mail address and password. You might do this if you want to share apps and purchased content acquired from iTunes, iBookstore, the App Store, or Newsstand with your other computers or iOS devices, but you don't want to share/sync iCloud-related data, such as Contacts, Calendar, Reminders, Notes, Safari, and other app-specific data.

When it comes to managing bookmarks on the Safari web browser, you can create, access, edit, and delete bookmarks, organize your Bookmarks list by choosing the order in which the bookmarks appear and creating folders for related bookmarks, and sync your bookmarks with iCloud. The following sections explain how to do each of these tasks.

Create a New Bookmark

As you're surfing the Web, if you come across a webpage you want to create a bookmark for, so that you can easily find it again later and not have to remember or retype its URL, tap the Share button at the bottom center of the Safari screen and then tap the Bookmark button on the Share screen (refer to Figure 10-4).

The Add Bookmark screen will appear (shown in Figure 10-11). Safari automatically fills in the Title field with the Title from the webpage, but you can manually overwrite this with something shorter or more descriptive. Safari also fills in the URL field automatically.

Below the URL field, tap the option that allows you to choose where the bookmark will be saved. The default option is the last location you used. However, if you tap this option, you can choose a folder that's already been created within your Bookmarks list.

Tap the Save button in the upper-right corner of the screen to save each newly created bookmark.

The Mac version of Safari (in addition to many other web browsers for computers) also allows you to create and maintain a Bookmarks Bar. This is a listing of webpages that is displayed across the top of the screen, below the Address Bar. However, to save onscreen real estate, the iPhone version of Safari does not display a Bookmarks Bar. If you're syncing your bookmarks between your Mac (or

FIGURE 10-11   Create a bookmark by filling in the fields within the Add Bookmark screen and then tap the Save button.

PC) and iPhone, one of the folder options you'll see displayed when you save a new bookmark is Bookmarks Bar (which was imported from your other computer or device). You can access it as a separate folder in your master Bookmarks list on your iPhone, but it won't be displayed as a line of tabs across the iPhone's screen when running Safari.

Access Your Saved Bookmarks

To revisit a bookmarked site, open the Bookmarks list by tapping the Bookmarks icon near the bottom of the Safari screen (see Figure 10-12). This icon resembles an open book.

At the top of your master Bookmarks list (refer to Figure 10-10) is an option for viewing your Reading List (a feature that will be explained shortly), followed by options for your History folder and iCloud Tabs (which will also be explained shortly). If you sync your Bookmarks list with other computers or devices, you may also see a Bookmarks Menu folder and a Bookmarks Bar folder. In conjunction with those folders will be individual bookmarks that you've previously saved.

Tap any bookmark listing to open a new web browser window in Safari and visit that website. To access a bookmark that's stored in a folder, tap the folder option to open it, and then tap an individual bookmark to open the current web browser window in Safari and visit that website.

Bookmarks icon

FIGURE 10-12   From the main Safari screen (shown here), view the master Bookmarks list by tapping the Bookmarks icon at the bottom of the screen.

Edit Your Bookmarks

After you've saved a bookmark in Safari, you can always go back and edit its name, its URL, or its saved location. To do this, from within Safari, tap the Bookmarks icon at the bottom of the screen. When the Bookmarks menu appears, tap the Edit button in the bottom-left corner of the screen.

Tap an individual bookmark listing that you want to edit. The Edit Bookmark screen will be displayed, which looks similar to the Add Bookmark screen shown previously in Figure 10-11. Make whatever changes you want to the Title, URL, or location, and then tap the Done button on the virtual keyboard to save your changes. If you have Safari set up to synchronize bookmarks data with iCloud, your changes will also be reflected on your other computers and iOS mobile devices within a few seconds.

Organize Your Bookmarks List

As you're looking at your Bookmarks list (refer to Figure 10-10), you can reorder items on the list manually by tapping the Edit button in the lower-left corner of the screen.

When looking at the Bookmarks lists in Edit mode (see Figure 10-13), choose the individual bookmark that you want to move, and then place and hold your finger on the Move icon, which is displayed to the right of the listing (it looks like three

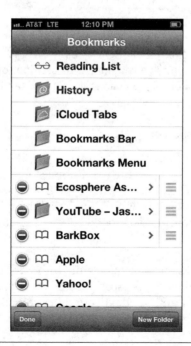

FIGURE 10-13   The Bookmarks screen in Edit mode allows you to edit or move already saved bookmarks within Safari.

horizontal lines). Next, using your finger, drag the listing up or down the screen until it's positioned where you want it to appear in your Bookmarks list. Remove your finger from the bookmark.

To reduce clutter in your Bookmarks list, you can create and maintain customized folders for your bookmarks. This means you can group together bookmarks anyway you see fit, store them in folders, and then add a custom name to each folder, such as Personal, Work, Favorites, Banking, Entertainment, News, and so forth. If you want to create a new bookmark folder, tap the New Folder button in the lower-right corner of the Bookmarks screen. Then, while in Edit mode, tap on the New Folder button that's displayed near the lower-right corner of the screen. When prompted, enter the Title for the bookmark, and then tap on the Bookmarks option to select where in your bookmarks folder hierarchy the folder will be placed. Then, after you've made your changes, tap the Done button to save them.

Delete Bookmarks

To delete bookmark listings (or folders) from your Bookmarks list, access the Bookmarks screen by tapping the Bookmarks icon at the bottom of the Safari screen, and then tap the Edit button in the lower-left corner of the screen. Displayed to the left of each listing that can be deleted will be a Delete icon (which looks like a red and white negative sign icon; refer to Figure 10-13). Tap this icon to delete the URL or a folder from the list. Tap the Delete button that appears to confirm your deletion decision.

 You can also delete a bookmark by navigating to the proper folder and then swiping your finger from right to left or left to right over the bookmark's name. The red Delete button will appear to the right of the name. Tap Delete to remove the bookmark or, if you change your mind, tap the Done button to cancel the deletion.

Sync Bookmarks via iCloud

After you turn on iCloud functionality on your iPhone (and have set up a free iCloud account), you'll also need to turn on iCloud syncing functionality for Safari. When you do this, Safari will automatically sync your bookmarks, Bookmarks Bar, Reading List, and open browser tabs with iCloud, making this information accessible from your other computers and iOS mobile devices. Likewise, Safari-related information from your other computers and iOS mobile devices will also become available on your iPhone.

To turn on the iCloud syncing feature for Safari, launch Settings, tap the iCloud option, make sure the iCloud Account name displayed at the top of the screen is the same account used with iCloud on your other computers and/or iOS mobile devices, and then scroll down to the Safari virtual switch and turn it to On (shown in Figure 10-14).

FIGURE 10-14 Turn on iCloud syncing for Safari from within Settings.

 Turning on the iCloud syncing feature for Safari only needs to be done once. From that point forward, your Safari-related information will continue to be synced with iCloud automatically and in the background.

Read Webpage Content Offline Using the Reading List Feature

While the Bookmarks feature of Safari allows you to store URLs for webpages that you'd like to easily revisit later, the Reading List feature allows you to store entire webpages on your iPhone, enabling you to go back and read articles or review content later—even when you aren't connected to the Internet. The content of the page is actually downloaded and stored on your iPhone.

To add to your Reading List a webpage or article that you're viewing in Safari, tap the Share button and then tap the Add To Reading List button (refer to Figure 10-4).

 Any movies or audio files that are associated with a webpage you store in your Reading List will not be downloaded and stored. This feature is most useful for saving articles, for example. The content can, however, contain still images, graphics, or photos.

When you access content stored on your Reading List, it is based on what appeared on the webpage at the time you saved the content to your Reading List. So, if that content has since been updated, you'll need to revisit the webpage itself, not rely on your Reading List file, if you want to read the latest version of the content.

Once you've populated your Reading List with webpages or content, you can access that saved information by tapping the Bookmarks icon in Safari and then tapping the Reading List option near the top of the Bookmarks screen (refer to Figure 10-13).

Upon tapping the Reading List option, the Reading List screen (shown in Figure 10-15) will be displayed. This screen includes a listing for each article or webpage you've saved within your Reading List. At the top of the screen are two command tabs, labeled All and Unread. Tap the All tab to view all of the articles and webpages stored within your Reading List, or tap the Unread tab to display only those articles you haven't yet read. Tap any item in the list to read the content.

 If you see the word "Waiting..." displayed in conjunction with a listing, this means your iPhone is downloading the related web pages and storing them so that they will later be accessible for offline viewing. This process should take between 10 seconds and one minute, depending on how much content needs to be transferred and saved.

FIGURE 10-15 The Reading List screen within Safari

To delete an item from your Reading List, as you're looking at the Reading List screen (refer to Figure 10-15), swipe your finger from left to right across the listing, and then tap the Delete button that appears. As with other Safari content, if your iPhone is set up to sync with iCloud, your Reading List will remain synced between your iPhone, Mac(s), iPad, and other iOS mobile devices, and any changes you make on your iPhone will be reflected on each device or computer (and vice versa).

Switch Between Open Browser Screens

Just as with any web browser, with Safari on your iPhone, you can have multiple browser windows open simultaneously. Of course, you can view only one browser window at a time on the iPhone's limited size screen. However, by tapping the Browser Window icon in the lower-right corner of the Safari screen (refer to Figure 10-12), you can easily switch between open browser windows.

If applicable, the number displayed within the Browser Window icon located near the bottom-right corner of the main Safari screen indicates how many browser windows are currently open and accessible.

Tap the Browser Window icon. As soon as you do this, the browser window that was active on the screen will shrink in size and be displayed as a thumbnail. You can now swipe your finger from left to right (or right to left) to scroll between open browser window thumbnails, each representing a separate open browser window.

To select which browser window you want to view, tap the thumbnail for it. Or, to close an open browser window, tap the red and white × icon in the upper-left corner of the browser window thumbnail (shown in Figure 10-16).

On your iPhone, you can have up to eight browser windows open simultaneously.

Discover the New iCloud Tabs Feature

Once you have iCloud functionality turned on and have your iPhone set up to sync Safari information between your iPhone, Mac(s), and other iOS mobile devices, you can sync your open browser windows in real time using the iCloud Tabs feature, thanks to iOS 6. This means that when you use tabbed browsing on your Mac, PC, iPad, or other device connected to your iCloud/Apple ID account, any open browser windows will be synced with your iPhone, so you can instantly switch from surfing the Web on your primary computer, for example, and continue surfing on your iPhone, and the same browser windows will be accessible.

To access this feature from your iPhone, tap the Bookmarks icon at the bottom of the Safari screen, and then tap the iCloud Tabs option on the Bookmarks screen (refer to Figure 10-10). You'll see a listing of the open browser windows on your other

FIGURE 10-16 Tap the × icon as you're looking at a thumbnail for a browser window to close that window.

computers and/or iOS mobile devices that are linked to the same iCloud/Apple ID account. You can then open any of those browser windows in Safari on your iPhone.

At the same time, any browser windows you have open on your iPhone will be accessible by tapping the iCloud Tabs icon found in Safari running on a Mac or iPad, for example.

 Use Siri to Help Find Information on the Web

Regardless of which apps are running on your iPhone, at any time, you can activate Siri and perform a search on the Web for information. For example, you could activate Siri and say "Search the Web for [insert topic or keyword]." You can also use the command "Google [insert topic or keyword]" (Siri understands the use of "Google" as a verb) or say "Search Wikipedia for...".

Another option is to tell Siri exactly which website you want to visit. For example, you could activate Siri and say "Visit w w w dot jasonrich dot com" to access www.JasonRich.com.

Using any of these commands will cause Siri to launch the Safari app and display related search results on the iPhone's screen. Refer to Chapter 3 for more information about using Siri.

Customize the Safari App from Settings

Like many apps on your iPhone, Safari has a handful of customizable features that impact how the app performs. To customize the Safari app, launch Settings, scroll down to the Safari setting, and tap it.

On the Safari screen within Settings (shown in Figure 10-17), you have the following options under the General, Privacy, Reading List, and Security headings. Tap one option at a time to adjust its settings.

- **Search Engine**   Select either Google, Yahoo!, or Bing to be your iPhone's default search engine when you enter a keyword or search phrase into the Search field of Safari. If at any time you want to use a search engine other than your default, you can always visit www.google.com, www.yahoo.com, or www.bing.com (or the website of another search engine of your choice) by entering the URL into the Address Bar or accessing it as a saved bookmark.

- **AutoFill**   When turned on, this feature allows Safari to access your own Contacts entry and pull information from it in order to automatically fill in online forms you encounter as you're surfing the Internet. For example, if you opt to order something online, you can use AutoFill to fill in the name, address, and phone number fields so that you don't have to manually enter this information. On the AutoFill screen (shown in Figure 10-18), set the Use Contact Info virtual switch to

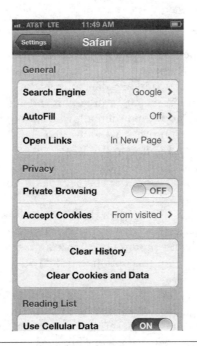

FIGURE 10-17   The Safari screen within Settings

FIGURE 10-18 You can turn on or off the AutoFill option and customize how this feature works on the AutoFill screen.

On. On the same screen, you can also turn on the Names & Passwords switch so that Safari remembers the usernames and passwords for websites you visit.

- **Open Links**   When you tap a link within a webpage that you're viewing, this setting determine whether Safari follows the link and displays the webpage information within the currently open and active browser window or opens a new browser window and then allows you to switch back and forth, as needed, between the open browser windows. The latter option is the most popular. Select the In Background option to use it.
- **Private Browsing**   If you turn on this feature, Safari will not keep track of the websites you visit within the History folder, nor release information about you to the websites you visit.
- **Accept Cookies**   Turning on this feature allows Safari to store cookies associated with the webpages you visit. A cookie allows that webpage to remember details about you and your preferences, for example.
- **Clear History**   Tap this option to quickly delete the entire History folder that's stored in Safari.
- **Clear Cookies And Data**   Tap this option to delete any cookie or website data that Safari has stored on your iPhone that pertains to websites you've visited.
- **Use Cellular Data**   As describer earlier, the Reading List feature allows you to download and save articles and webpages to your iPhone's internal storage and later view that content even if your iPhone isn't connected to the Internet. When

this virtual switch is set to On, Safari will use your 3G/4G Internet connection to download and save articles or webpages you add to your Reading List. If this switch is set to Off, webpage data will be added to your Reading List only if a Wi-Fi connection is available.

- **Fraud Warning**   Leave this featured turned on. It helps to prevent you from visiting fraudulent or counterfeit websites that are designed to look like legitimate websites but actually steal personal information or serve other sinister purposes.
- **JavaScript**   Leave this feature turned on if you want to access webpages that utilize JavaScript, a popular website programming language.
- **Block Pop-Ups**   Leave this feature turned on to prevent websites you visit from opening pop-up windows that often display ads or other distracting content.
- **Advanced**   The features offered after tapping the Advanced option typically aren't used by everyday iPhone users and thus can be ignored.

Use Other Web Browsers to Surf the Web

As you begin surfing the Web using Safari, you'll discover that it's a versatile and easy-to-use web browser that makes excellent use of your iPhone 5's display size and Multi-Touch screen capabilities. However, as you read earlier in this chapter, Safari is not compatible with Adobe Flash.

In the App Store, you'll discover a handful of alternate web browsers, some of which are Flash compatible, such as Photon Flash Video Player & Private Web Browser for Flash Video ($3.99). When you access the App Store, enter in the Search field the keyword "Web Browser" to find and be able to download and install alternate web browsers, such as Mercury Web Browser (Free), Opera Mini Web Browser (Free), or Atomic Web Browser (Free).

To find specialty apps that make surfing the Web or handling specific Internet-related tasks easier or more efficient, launch the App Store app and tap the Featured icon at the bottom of the screen. Then, tap the Categories button in the upper-left corner of the screen. From the Categories menu, select Social Networking. You can also tap the Search field in the App Store and enter the name of the online social networking service you want to access from your iPhone, or use the keyword "Web Browser" or "Internet" to find related apps.

Stay Active on the Online Social Networking Services

For every popular online social networking service or instant messaging service, there's a special app that's available from the App Store to access it. For example, you'll find specialty apps for managing your Facebook, Twitter, Google+, LinkedIn, Instagram, Flickr, or Tumblr account. Using a specialized app to manage one or more of your online social networking accounts (as opposed to accessing them from Safari) provides a more streamlined user interface, makes better use of the iPhone's screen, and offers specialized functionality that fully utilizes the phone's Multi-Touch display.

If you're active on Facebook or Twitter, you already know that iOS 6 offers Facebook and Twitter integration that allows you to compose and send Facebook status updates or tweets from within many different apps, as well as directly from the Notification Center screen. However, to fully manage your Facebook or Twitter account, you'll need to download and install the official Facebook or Twitter app, or a third-party app designed to offer similar functionality, as described in the following sections.

 From your iPhone, to watch YouTube videos that are streamed directly from the Internet, download and use the official YouTube app, as opposed to visiting www.youtube.com using Safari. This free app is available from the App Store. The YouTube app no longer comes preinstalled on your iPhone, like it did with iOS 5.1 (and earlier iOS versions).

Use the Official Facebook App

If you're already active on Facebook, you'll need to turn on Facebook integration on your iPhone (which allows you to send Facebook status updates from many different apps, as well as from the Notification Center screen). To do this, launch Settings, scroll down, and then tap the Facebook option.

On the Facebook screen within Settings (shown in Figure 10-19), enter your Facebook username and password in the appropriate fields and tap the Sign In button. This turns on Facebook integration on your iPhone (you need to do this only once).

Next, tap the Install button to download and install the official Facebook app. You can use this app, the icon for which will appear on your Home screen, to manage all aspects of your Facebook account as long as your iPhone has access to the Internet. Once the iPhone app is installed, you'll need to enter your Facebook username and password into the app itself.

 If you don't have a Facebook account, but you want to set one up for free, tap the Create New Account button.

Also from the Facebook screen within Setting, you can set up your iPhone to share Calendar-, Contacts-, and Facebook-related data between your Facebook account and the Contacts, Calendar, and Facebook apps. By doing this, the birthdays of your Facebook friends, for example, will be displayed in your Calendar app, and the usernames and profile photos of each of your Facebook friends, for example, will be added to your Contacts database (when there's already a Contacts entry set up for that Facebook friend). Plus, events you're invited to (and RSVP to) on Facebook will automatically appear within the Calendar app on the iPhone.

To adjust these options, launch Settings and tap on the Facebook option. From the Facebook menu screen within Settings, turn on the virtual switch that's associated

FIGURE 10-19   The Facebook screen within Settings

with the Calendar, Contacts, and/or Facebook option displayed below the Allow These Apps To Use Your Account. When you turn on the Calendar option, your iPhone will automatically access your Facebook events and online-based calendar, download, and then display that content within the Calendar app. From the Calendar app, if you then select to view the Facebook Birthdays Calendar, the birthdays of your Facebook friends will be displayed within the Calendar app.

When you turn on the Contacts option, your iPhone will compare your online Facebook friends listing with the entries within your Contacts database. When matches are found, the Facebook username and profile pictures associated with those matches will be downloaded and displayed within the appropriate entries of the Contacts app on your iPhone. As you add new Facebook friends in the future, you'll need to periodically tap on the Update All Contacts button to automatically update applicable entries within your Contacts database.

Use the Official Twitter App

Twitter integration on your iPhone also needs to be turned on. To do this, launch Settings and tap the Twitter option. On the Twitter screen (shown in Figure 10-20), enter your username (*@username*) and your password in the appropriate fields, and then tap the Sign In button. You need to do this only once per Twitter account, but you can enter multiple Twitter accounts into your iPhone, one at a time.

FIGURE 10-20 The Twitter screen within Settings

 If you don't have a Twitter account, but you want to set one up for free, tap the Create New Account button.

Also from the Twitter screen within Settings, it's possible to download and install the official Twitter app, so that you can manage all aspects of your Twitter account(s) on your iPhone. To do this, tap the Install button near the top of the screen. You'll then need to enter your Twitter username and password directly into the app.

Use an Unofficial Facebook or Twitter App

Beyond the official Facebook and Twitter apps, you'll discover in the App Store many third-party apps that offer specialized functionality for managing one or more Facebook or Twitter accounts from your iPhone. To find these apps and discover what each can do (compared to the official Facebook and/or Twitter app), enter the keyword Facebook or Twitter in the Search field at the App Store. Alternatively, launch the App Store app on your iPhone and tap the Featured icon at the bottom of the screen. Then, tap the Categories button in the upper-left corner of the screen. From the Categories menu, select Social Networking.

For example, beyond the official Twitter app, from the App Store, you'll find many third-party apps, like Twitterific and TweetCaster, that can be used for managing your Twitter account(s) from your iPhone. These apps offer a different user interface and, in some cases, additional or slightly different features.

Use Optional Apps for Google+, Instagram, LinkedIn, and More

Beyond Facebook and Twitter, there are dozens of other online social networking services you can access from your iPhone either with Safari or using a specialized app from the App Store. For example, you'll find specialized apps for Google+, Instagram, LinkedIn, MySpace, Pinterest, Flickr, Grindr, and eHarmony (as well as third-party apps that allow you to manage accounts from other services using a single app, for example).

 To find these apps, launch the App Store app on your iPhone, tap on the featured icon, tap on the Categories button, and then choose Social Networking from the Categories menu. You'll then be able to browse through the related apps. If you're looking for an app that works with a specific online social networking service, such as LinkedIn, use the Search option within the App Store.

The Instagram app allows you to take photos on your iPhone, edit the images by adding effects and filters to them, and then share them on the Instagram service (shown in Figure 10-21). Now that Instagram is owned by Facebook, certain functionality related to the Instagram app works seamlessly with the Facebook app and the Facebook online service.

FIGURE 10-21 The optional Instagram app allows you to manage your Instagram account from your iPhone and share photos shot using your iPhone.

11

Shoot, Edit, and Share Photos and Videos

HOW TO...

- Use the Camera app to shoot digital photos and video
- Use the Photos app to view, edit, print, and share photos and videos
- Create prints from photos shot on your iPhone 5
- Use Shared Photo Streams

Taking great pictures and shooting entertaining videos is both a skill and an art form. The skill involves knowing how to use your iPhone and the photography apps available for it. The art involves tapping your own creativity to determine what, when, and how to frame and shoot thought-provoking and visually interesting images that people will enjoy.

The artistic aspect also come into play when editing your photos or videos, as well as in how you showcase and share them. Digital photography using an iPhone 5 is definitely something just about anyone can do...and do well. Plus, it's fun!

Thanks to the two cameras built into your iPhone 5, the enhanced capabilities of the Camera and Photos apps that come preinstalled with iOS 6, and the literally hundreds of other photography apps available for the iPhone 5, it's never been easier to shoot, edit, and share clear, vibrant, and visually impressive digital photos and video.

 The iPhone 5's Retina display makes digital photos and HD movies look amazing when viewed on the screen.

You're about to discover that the newly improved Camera app allows you to take digital images that are as good as those produced by many of the stand-alone, point-and-shoot digital cameras currently on the market. Your iPhone can also be used to shoot, edit, view, and share 1080p HD-quality videos.

However, unlike stand-alone digital cameras (which typically cost $100 to $500 or more), your iPhone enables you to view, edit, and enhance the images you shoot right there on your iPhone, and then share them in a variety of ways.

This chapter provides an introduction to using the Camera and Photos apps and offers a preview of other photography-related apps. You'll also discover some of the many ways you can share your photos and videos, such as by creating prints, by uploading your photos or videos to Facebook, Twitter, or Instagram, or by creating online photo Albums using iCloud's new Shared Photo Streams feature.

In order to shoot awesome photos or amazing videos using your iPhone, you'll need to take full advantage of one or both of the iPhone's built-in cameras; use the Camera app (or another app) to actually shoot the photos and/or videos; and then use another app (such as Photos, iPhoto, or iMovie) to edit, enhance, view, and share your photos and videos. However, thanks to iOS 6, the iPhone 5, its built-in cameras, and the various photography/video-related apps all work seamlessly together, plus they're surprisingly easy to use—even for novice photographers.

Become Familiar with Your iPhone's Built-In Cameras

As you begin taking photos (or shooting video) with your iPhone, you should be aware of a few things. First, while the iPhone 5 has both front- and rear-facing cameras, the rear-facing camera allows you to snap photos or shoot video at a much higher resolution than the front-facing camera.

The front-facing camera, which Apple refers to as a FaceTime HD camera, offers 1.2MP resolution and can capture HD video at 720p (up to 30 frames per second with audio). Most people use the front-facing camera to participate in FaceTime video calls, as well as to shoot photos or video that include themselves. However, if you want to capture photos or video at significantly higher resolution, you'll definitely want to use the iPhone 5's rear-facing camera.

The rear-facing camera is an 8MP camera. It offers a new panoramic shooting mode and allows you to shoot HD video at 1080p resolution (up to 30 frames per second with audio).

 The resolution of any digital camera (for taking still images) is measured in megapixels (MP). One megapixel is equal to one million pixels or colored dots that comprise the image. So, the higher the number of pixels, the higher the resolution, and the more detailed and vibrant the photos you take will appear. Similarly, when it comes to shooting HD-quality video, the two popular resolutions for high-definition television sets or monitors are 720p and 1080p. A video with 1080p resolution means that each frame is displayed at a resolution of 1,920 x 1,080 pixels (up to 30 frames per second). Anytime you shoot video using your iPhone, audio will simultaneously be recorded using the phone's three built-in microphones.

Shoot Photos Using the Camera App

The Camera app that comes preinstalled on your iPhone 5 is used for taking photos or shooting video. While there are many other apps that can also be used for this purpose, the Camera app is easy to use and nicely integrates with the Photos app, as well as other features and functions that are built into your iPhone.

Launch the Camera App and Locate Its Controls

You can launch the Camera app in one of two ways:

- **From the Lock screen**   Displayed next to the Slide To Unlock slider on your iPhone's Lock screen is a camera icon. Place your finger on this icon and flick upward to immediately launch the Camera app to take digital photos or shoot videos. You can do this even if the Password Lock feature is active. However, you won't be able to do anything but snap photos or videos, and then view the most recently shot images or video clips, until you unlock the iPhone using the proper passcode.
- **From the Home screen**   Tap the Camera app icon on the iPhone's Home screen to launch the app.

 If you are snapping photos using the Camera app, you can activate the shutter button either by tapping the onscreen shutter button or pressing the Volume Up or Volume Down button on the side of the iPhone.

Once the Camera app is launched, you can begin snapping photos or shooting videos right away, or you can adjust several different settings within the app. The main Camera app screen (shown in Figure 11-1) serves as your viewfinder and gives you access to the Camera app's adjustable settings.

 You can hold the iPhone in portrait mode or landscape mode to shoot photos or video.

Displayed near the bottom center of the Camera app's main screen is the shutter button. When the Camera app is set to take digital photos, a camera icon appears within the shutter button. When the app is set to shoot video, a red dot appears within the shutter button.

To switch between photo mode and video mode, tap the virtual switch in the lower-right corner of the screen. When the switch is positioned to the left, the Camera app is in photo mode, as indicated by the still camera icon above the left side of the switch. Move the switch to the right to shoot video, as indicated by the video camera–shaped icon.

The thumbnail icon in the bottom-left corner of the Camera app's screen represents the last image or video clip you shot. Tap this thumbnail to quickly switch from the

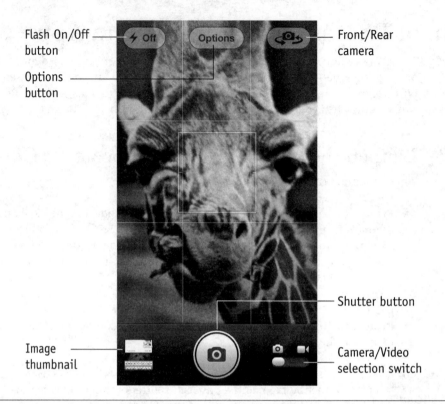

Flash On/Off button

Options button

Front/Rear camera

Shutter button

Image thumbnail

Camera/Video selection switch

FIGURE 11-1 The Camera app's screen allows you to adjust camera settings and serves as your viewfinder when taking pictures or shooting video.

Camera app to the Photos app, which also comes preinstalled on the iPhone 5 (and is discussed later in this chapter).

To quickly switch between the front- and rear-facing cameras that are built into your iPhone, tap the Camera Selection icon in the top-right corner of the Camera app's screen. Displayed in the top-left corner of the screen are the flash controls. See "Use Your iPhone's Built-in Flash When Taking Photos," later in the chapter, for details about using the flash controls.

Also, when using the rear-facing camera to shoot photos, an Options button appears in the top center of the Camera app screen, as shown in Figure 11-1. Tap it to reveal an onscreen menu that allows you to turn on or off the Grid feature, turn on or off the HDR shooting mode, or activate the Camera app's new and extremely impressive Panorama shooting mode.

When turned on, the Grid feature superimposes a nine-panel grid over the viewfinder (see Figure 11-1), which you can use to help frame your shots. You can also use it to help ensure that you're holding the camera (your iPhone) level when taking a photo or shooting video. This grid does not actually appear in your photos or videos, however. The Panorama shooting mode will be explained later in this chapter.

To enable you to easily take pictures or shoot video on your iPhone, the Camera app automatically focuses on your subject(s). By tapping the viewfinder where your subject appears, you can select the subject of your photos as you're taking pictures. When taking photos of groups, the Camera app has a built-in face-detection feature that helps to ensure everyone's face in your photos comes out crystal clear.

Snap Clear, Vibrant Photos Using Your iPhone 5

To begin snapping photos, launch the Camera app, choose between the front- and rear-facing cameras (while making a point to use the rear-facing camera whenever possible for the best results), activate or deactivate any of the other available options if you wish, and then point your iPhone at your subject(s) and frame your shot within the viewfinder.

Once you position your subject(s) on the screen, if the Camera app doesn't focus in by itself on your intended subject(s), tap the screen where they appear, which activates the Camera app's auto-focus sensor, and then tap the shutter button (or press the Volume Up or Volume Down button) to snap a photo.

When framing your subject(s) within the viewfinder, to use the Camera app's zoom feature, use a reverse-pinch finger motion on the viewfinder screen. The Zoom Slider will be displayed along the bottom of the screen. Place your finger on the Zoom Slider and move it right or left to adjust the zoom. You can also use the reverse-pinch or pinch finger gesture to adjust the zoom intensity.

Each image you take using the Camera app is automatically placed in the Camera Roll Album of the Photos app. From there, you can view, edit, enhance, crop, rotate, print, or share your photos. If you have the iCloud Photo Stream feature set up, your images will be uploaded to your Photo Stream as you take them, assuming your iPhone is connected to the Internet via a Wi-Fi connection. Both the Camera Roll Album and the iCloud Photo Stream feature are discussed later in this chapter.

 To quickly see the image you just shot, tap the image thumbnail in the lower-left corner of the screen. If you do not choose to immediately view an image, the Camera app will be ready for you to take an additional shot.

Take Stunning Panoramic Photos

To take visually stunning panoramic shots of vast landscapes, a city skyline, or a large group of people, for example, use the new Panorama shooting mode that's built into the Camera app. Here's how to use this feature, which works exclusively with the rear-facing camera when you hold your iPhone in portrait mode:

1. Launch the Camera app.
2. Select the rear-facing camera.
3. Tap the Options button, and when the menu of options appears, tap the Panorama button. The iPhone will then launch the Camera app's panoramic

How to...

Take Better Photos and Videos Using Your iPhone

Regardless of which app you use to take pictures or shoot video, the following tips will help you take better, more artistic, and more creative shots using your iPhone.

- Hold your iPhone extremely still when taking a photo or shooting video. (If you're shooting video that requires you to move the camera, use slow, steady movements.)
- Choose your primary subject, and then figure out how to take advantage of what's in the background, foreground, or to the sides of your subject to make the image more visually interesting. Perhaps you can frame your subject, or add a sense of depth to the image by taking advantage of what surrounds your subject.
- Pay attention to your primary light source and beware of unwanted shadows. As a general rule, your light source (such as the sun, if you're shooting outside) should be behind you, the photographer, and shining onto your subject. Ideally, you want the light source to shed an even light on your subject that isn't too intense. If the light source is facing you, you will see glares in your images, plus they'll often turn out overexposed. Even in low-light situations, you can use the existing light to capture the ambience of the setting, instead of using the harsh white light generated by the flash. When shooting in low light, however, it's even more important to hold the iPhone very still when pressing the shutter button, to avoid blurry images.
- If you're using the flash, to avoid red-eye, hard shadows, and overexposed images, don't get too close to your subject. You're better off walking a few steps back from your subject and then taking advantage of the Camera app's zoom feature to get a close-up of your subject while standing farther away. However, if you're too far away from your subject when using the flash, the light from the flash won't reach your subject, and the photo will turn out underexposed (too dark).
- Be creative when framing your shots. Instead of positioning your subject in the center of the frame and shooting head-on, consider moving your subject off-center (along one of the Grid feature's grid line interception points, or along one of the grid's horizontal or vertical lines). You can also position the camera (your iPhone) above, below, or to the left or right of your subject, and then shoot the subject from an angle in order to create a more visually interesting shot.

FIGURE 11-2   Take panoramic photos using the Camera app's new Panorama shooting mode.

shooting mode (shown in Figure 11-2). The Panoramic image viewfinder is displayed in the center of the screen.

4. Hold the iPhone so the viewfinder is to the extreme left of your subject, and tap the shutter button.

 If you tap the large arrow icon within the onscreen Panorama viewfinder, you can shoot the panoramic image from right to left instead of from left to right.

5. Slowly move the iPhone from left to right, keeping it as level as possible, and using a steady motion. If you go too fast or don't hold the iPhone steady enough, a warning message will appear on the screen.

6. As you move the iPhone from left to right, the arrow icon that's displayed in the Panorama viewfinder will slowly move to the right, indicating that you're capturing the image. When the arrow reaches the right side of the viewfinder window, the image has been fully captured. There is no need to tap the shutter

FIGURE 11-3 This panoramic photo of Gillette Stadium (home of the New England Patriots) was taken on the iPhone 5.

button a second time. However, at any point during this process, you can manually finish the shot by tapping the shutter button again.

7. Just like when taking a regular shot, tap the preview thumbnail in the lower-left corner of the screen to look at the image. When you do this, hold your iPhone in landscape mode. Figure 11-3 is a sample panoramic photo shot using the iPhone 5's Camera app.

Take Advantage of the Photo App's HDR Shooting Mode

HDR stands for *high dynamic range*. The HDR shooting mode uses the iPhone's built-in camera and photo-taking abilities slightly differently to capture ambient light and create more vibrant photos. The HDR mode actually captures three different images simultaneously each time you tap the shutter button (each capturing and utilizing the light differently), and then merges the pictures together automatically to create one image. The result is often a more detailed image that better utilizes the light. However, this process slows down the Camera app a bit, so you'll experience a longer gap (just a few extra seconds) in between being able to take shots.

To take photos using HDR shooting mode, launch the Camera app and do everything as you normally would, but before you tap the shutter button to actually snap the photo, tap the Options button and then tap the HDR virtual switch to turn on this feature (as shown in Figure 11-4). It will remain on until you manually turn it off.

Note HDR shooting mode works only with the rear-facing camera, and only when shooting digital photos (not video). Also, the flash can't be used when shooting with the HDR mode.

Use Your iPhone's Built-in Flash When Taking Photos

After launching the Camera app and preparing to snap photos using the rear-facing camera, tap the flash icon in the upper-left corner of the screen. Tap the On button to use the iPhone's LED flash with every shot. Turn on the Auto Flash feature to use the

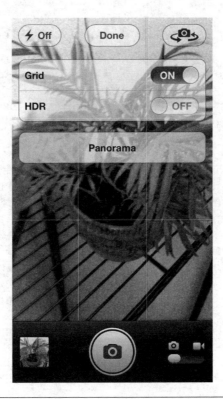

FIGURE 11-4   From the Options menu, turn on the rear-facing camera's HDR shooting mode.

flash only when it's needed. When you press the shutter button to snap a photo, if the iPhone determines additional light is needed, the LED flash will activate. You can also turn off the flash so it will not be used at all, regardless of the lighting situation.

   When holding your iPhone and taking pictures, make sure your finger does not cover the rear-facing camera lens or flash if you're using the rear-facing camera. You may need to reposition your hand(s) to keep this from happening.

If you want to shoot photos using only existing light mode, or if you're in an area or at an event where it's not permissible to use a flash, turn off the Flash option. The Camera app will still work using whatever existing light is available. However, to avoid blurry images, you'll need to hold your iPhone extremely still when taking a photo.

   In low-light situations, if you do not want to use a flash, you'll typically get better results if you turn on HDR shooting mode.

Shoot Videos Using the Camera App

Instead of shooting still images (digital photos) using the Camera app on your iPhone, it's just as easy to shoot videos. Keep in mind, however, that the video feature requires a lot of internal storage space and battery power, so this feature is best for shooting short video clips, as opposed to long-length home movies.

To begin shooting video using the Camera app, follow these steps:

1. Launch the Camera app.
2. Tap the switch in the lower-right corner of the screen to place the Camera app into video mode. (The switch should be positioned to the right.)
3. Select the front- or rear-facing camera, keeping in mind the rear-facing camera offers better resolution. Using the front-facing camera allows you to easily incorporate yourself into the video.
4. If you're using the rear-facing camera, tap the Flash button in the upper-right corner of the screen to turn on or off the flash, or to activate the Auto Flash mode so that the flash will go on automatically when the Camera app deems it necessary. When shooting video, when you turn on the flash, it remains on and serves as a continuous light source.
5. Notice that the shutter button displays a small and dim red dot. To begin shooting video, tap the shutter button once. The red dot turns bright red and flashes, indicating that you're recording. Also while recording, a timer display appears in the lower-left corner of the viewfinder window (your iPhone's screen).
6. As you're recording video (shown in Figure 11-5), anything that you can see within the viewfinder (your iPhone's screen) will be recorded. To record the best-quality video, avoid shaking the iPhone or making quick movements.

 As you're recording video, the iPhone automatically activates one or more of its three built-in microphones to record the audio in the surrounding area. If you fumble with the iPhone a lot while recording, the sounds of your fingers or clothing brushing against the iPhone may be picked up by the microphones and recorded.

Once your video clips are recorded, they automatically get saved in the Camera Roll Album in the Photos app. As you'll see when you launch Photos, the video thumbnails displayed in the app have a small video camera icon displayed within them, as well as a time icon (indicating the length of the video), which differentiates them from the thumbnail images that represent photos.

Using the Photos app, you can trim your video clips by editing out the beginning or end. However, to access more advanced editing tools, you'll need to use an optional video editing app, such as Apple's own iMovie ($4.99), which is available from the App Store.

FIGURE 11-5 As you're shooting video, a timer is displayed near the lower-left corner of the screen. The dot in the shutter button icon will also turn bright red to indicate you're recording.

Use the Photos App to View, Edit, and Enhance Your Photos

After you've taken photos or shot video using the Camera app, one of your options is to use the Photos app (that comes preinstalled with iOS 6) to view, edit, enhance, print, share (discussed later), and organize your images and videos.

 As you're viewing an image in full-screen mode, after a few seconds, the command icons disappear so that you can get a better look at your photo. To make the icons reappear, tap the middle of the screen.

Navigate the Albums Screen of the Photos App

Launch the Photos app from the iPhone's Home screen, or by tapping the image thumbnail near the lower-left corner of the screen when using the Camera app. When

Did You Know?

The Optional iMovie App Greatly Enhances the iPhone's Video Editing and Sharing Capabilities

Just like its Mac counterpart, the optional iMovie app for the iPhone/iPad ($4.99) offers advanced video editing and sharing tools, and you can the app right on the iPhone. The features built into the app enable you to do such things as produce Hollywood-style movie trailers using templates and your own video footage; choose a theme for your video that gives you access to special effects and transitions that fit the theme and that can be dragged and dropped into your video; manually add special video effects, animated titles, and/or sound effects into your videos; and fine-tune and edit your video's content.

After you edit your video using iMovie, you can upload it directly from the app onto an Internet service such as YouTube, Facebook, or Vimeo, or you can showcase your production on your HD television set (by connecting your iPhone to a TV or monitor using an optional HDMI cable or using the AirPlay feature in conjunction with Apple TV). You can also use iCloud to sync your productions with your other computers or iOS mobile devices that are linked to the same iCloud account.

The iMovie app is extremely powerful and offers a lot of advanced editing and video sharing features. To get the most out of using this app, take advantage of the built-in tutorials. Extensive online help for using this app is also available from Apple by visiting http://help.apple.com/imovie/iphone/1.4/index.html.

you launch Photos, one of the main screens of this app is the Albums screen (shown in Figure 11-6). This screen displays listings for all of the separate Albums you have stored on your iPhone, including the Camera Roll Album, which is where photos and videos shot using the Camera app are stored by default.

Displayed along the bottom of the Albums screen are the following three command icons:

- **Albums** Tap this icon to display the listing of Albums stored on your iPhone.
- **Photo Stream** Tap this icon to view and manage your iCloud Photo Stream and/or Shared Photo Streams (which will be explained shortly).
- **Places** Tap this icon to view a map that showcases where your images that utilize geo-tagging were shot (also explained shortly). If you have Location Services turned off on your iPhone, the Places option will not be displayed because it won't be active.

FIGURE 11-6   The Albums screen in the Photos app lists each Album that contains your images and videos.

As you're viewing the Albums screen with the Albums icon selected, tap the plus sign icon in the upper-left corner of the screen to create a new Album, into which you can move and save one or more of your images or videos. Tap the Edit button (in the upper-right corner of the Albums screen) to delete Albums from your iPhone and/or change the order in which the Albums are displayed.

View and Edit the Contents of an Album

Tap an Album listing in the Albums screen, and the screen will be replaced with thumbnails that represent each photo or video clip that's stored in that Album (as shown in Figure 11-7). The title of the Album is displayed at the top center of the screen. Tap an image's thumbnail to view that image in full-screen mode.

If an Album has more thumbnail images than can be shown on one screen, use your finger to scroll up or down to see all of the thumbnail images in the Album. The number of photos and videos stored in that Album is displayed near the bottom center of the screen. If you want to return to the Albums screen at any time, tap the Albums button in the top-left corner of the screen.

FIGURE 11-7 Tap an Album listing to view thumbnail images representing each photo or video stored in that Album. Tap a thumbnail to view that image in full-screen mode.

To edit the contents of an Album, or to move, delete, or share one or more images from the Album, tap the Album's listing in the Albums screen and then tap the Edit button in the top-right corner of the thumbnails screen. Once you're in Edit mode, tap one or more images stored in the Album to select them. When a thumbnail is selected, a check mark appears in the thumbnail image.

After you've selected images, tap either the Share, Add To, or Delete button displayed along the bottom of the screen, or tap the Cancel button to exit Edit mode without doing anything. See the "Share Your Photos and Videos" section later in this chapter for more information about sharing.

View Individual Photos Stored in an Album

When viewing the thumbnail images within any Album, tap any thumbnail to view that image in full-screen mode. When you do this, tap anywhere on the screen to make a handful of onscreen command icons and buttons appear (shown in Figure 11-8).

Slideshow Play icon

AirPlay icon

Share icon

Trash icon

FIGURE 11-8   Tap an image in full-screen mode to access options related to that image.

The left-pointing arrow button in the upper-left corner of the screen displays the name of the Album that contains the photo you're currently viewing. Tap it to return to the previous Album thumbnail screen. Tap the Edit button in the upper-right corner of the screen to access a handful of photo editing and enhancement tools, which will be explained shortly.

Along the bottom of the screen, you'll see up to four command icons, which, from left to right, include the Share icon, Slideshow Play icon, AirPlay icon (if AirPlay is active), and trashcan icon. We will discuss sharing in the "Share Your Photos and Videos" section later in this chapter.

Tap the Slideshow Play icon to create an animated slideshow that will be displayed on your iPhone's screen, complete with slide transitions and background music of your choice. The images from the selected Album will be featured in the slideshow.

If you have the AirPlay option active, and your iPhone is connected to the same wireless network as your computer(s) and/or Apple TV, you can wirelessly stream your photos and/or videos to view them on your television or computer screen.

To delete the image you're currently viewing from your iPhone, tap the trashcan icon, and then confirm your decision by tapping the Delete Photo button.

Edit and Enhance Individual Photos

As you're viewing an individual image in full-screen mode using the Photos app, tap the Edit button in the upper-right corner of the screen to access the app's four editing and photo enhancement tools, shown along the bottom of the screen in Figure 11-9. From left to right, these tools include the following:

- **Rotate**   Tap this icon to rotate the image 90 degrees at a time.
- **Auto-Enhance**   Tap this icon to adjust the lighting, colors, contrast, and other elements of a photo automatically, with a single tap. This one feature can often dramatically enhance the look of an image.
- **Red-Eye Reduction**   If you used a flash to take photos of people and the resulting images show an unwanted red-eye effect, tap this icon to remove the red

FIGURE 11-9   The Photos app offers four tools for editing and enhancing photos.

Apple's iPhoto App Dramatically Enhances Your iPhone's Photo Editing Capabilities

While the Photos app offers basic photo editing and enhancement capabilities, Apple's optional iPhoto app ($4.99) offers a vast toolbox of advanced capabilities for editing, enhancing, organizing, and sharing digital images. This is one of many optional photo editing apps available from the App Store. It allows you to better manage all of your digital images, plus create Journals, which are customizable collages that feature your images and that can easily be shared.

The iPhoto app for iPhone/iPad offers much of the same functionality as iPhoto '11 for the Mac and is compatible with this software. Thus, you can organize your images into Albums or Events, flag images, create tags for images, auto-enhance images, or use any of the individual photo editing tools that are built into the app.

Individual photos, groups of photos, Events, or Albums can then be shared, printed, or used to create professional-quality slide shows. In addition to working seamlessly with Facebook and Twitter, iPhoto also works with Flickr.com.

eye from each subject's eyes. You'll be prompted to tap a subject's eyes that have unwanted red eye, and the Photos app will fix it.

- **Crop**   Use this editing tool to crop and/or reposition an image within the frame. You can adjust any side of the image frame or drag one of the corners in or out to crop the image.

When you're done using one or more of the editing and enhancement tools, tap the Save button (in the upper-right corner of the screen) to save your changes to that image. The editing tool icons will be replaced by the image view icons, allowing you to then share, copy, move, or delete the image, for example.

Geo-Tag Your Photos and Video

If you have the iPhone's Location Services option turned on (it is by default) in conjunction with the Camera app, anytime you shoot a photo or video using your iPhone, the exact location where it was taken will be recorded as part of the image/video file. This is called *geo-tagging*.

Then later, when you're using the Photos app, you can tap on the Places option that's displayed near the bottom-right corner of the screen when viewing any Album, and display a detailed map that shows the exact location where your photos were taken. On the map that's displayed, each red pushpin represents a location. Tap on a pushpin to see how many photos were taken at that location. Then, tap on the right-pointing arrow next to the number of images listed to view thumbnails of those images.

Using the Places feature is one way your digital photos (and videos) are organized and sorted. The geo-tagging information that becomes part of each image's digital file can also be utilized by many photo apps and software applications running on a Mac or PC, such as Cards or iPhoto.

Share Your Photos and Videos

Some of the ways you can share photos or videos you shoot using your iPhone 5 include

- E-mail one or more people up to five images at a time directly from the Photos app.
- Send images as part of text/instant messages using the Messages app.
- Sync your digital photos (and videos) with your computer(s) and your other iOS mobile devices via iCloud Photo Stream (as long as the other computers and devices are linked to the same iCloud account).
- Wirelessly print images using an AirPrint-compatible photo printer.
- E-mail or transfer images stored on your iPhone 5 to a photo lab to have traditional prints and/or photo gifts created.
- Share photos online using iCloud's new Shared Photo Streams feature.
- Share photos online via a social networking service such as Facebook, Twitter, Instagram, or Google+, or via a photo sharing service such as Flickr.com.
- Transfer images and videos from your iPhone to your Mac or PC using the iTunes Sync process. (You can also transfer images and videos from your Mac or PC to your iPhone to store and view them on your iPhone.)

 After you transfer photos to your desktop or laptop computer, you can view, edit, enhance, print, archive, and/or share them using photography software such as iPhoto '11 (Mac), Photoshop Elements (PC/Mac), Aperture 3 (Mac), or a vast selection of other photography-related applications available for your computer. There are also many different online-based photo services, like Google's Picasa and Flickr.com, that allow you to store, edit, showcase, and otherwise manage your digital photo collection.

Share Your Contents of an Album

You can share the contents of an Album by opening one of your photo Albums and tapping on the Share button displayed along the bottom of the screen (as discussed

FIGURE 11-10   The Share menu offered in the Photos app includes a handful of options for sharing your photos with other people.

in the "View and Edit the Contents of an Album" section). Then a Share menu will appear (shown in Figure 11-10). From this menu, you can share the selected images via e-mail or text/instant message, create and/or add them to a Shared Photo Stream, publish them on Facebook, print them wirelessly using AirPrint, or copy the images to your iPhone's virtual clipboard (so you can paste them into another compatible app). If only one image is selected, you can share it via Twitter as well. Only the Share options that are available to you, based on how your iPhone is set up, will be displayed. For example, if you select to share more than five images, the Mail option is no longer an option and it will not be displayed.

If you opt to share photos via e-mail, you can include up to five photos within an outgoing e-mail message. Tap the Mail button, and when the New Message screen appears, fill in the To and Subject fields, add text to the body of the e-mail, and then tap the Send button. The photos or video clips you selected will already be embedded into the outgoing e-mail message.

Share Individual Photos Stored in an Album

While viewing an individual photo within an album (as discussed in the "View Individual Photos Stored in an Album" section), tap the Share button in the bottom-left corner to access the Share menu, which enables you to send the single image via e-mail or a text/instant message, add it to a Shared Photo Stream (or your personal Photo Stream), publish it online via Twitter, post it on Facebook, assign it to a specific entry within the Contacts app, print it using an AirPrint-compatible printer, copy it to your iPhone's virtual clipboard, or use it as your iPhone's Lock screen or Home screen wallpaper.

Use Other Options to Share Your Photos Online

By tapping the Share button, you can share one or more images with other people in a variety of ways. For example, you can publish photos on your Facebook Wall (as shown in Figure 11-11) or publish one photo at a time on your Twitter feed. You can do this directly from within the Photos app.

FIGURE 11-11 From the Share menu in Photos, tap the Facebook option to publish a photo on your Facebook Wall (as part of a status update).

You also have the option to use the official Facebook and/or Twitter apps, which give you added control and features for uploading and sharing photos with your online friends, assuming you have a Facebook or Twitter account set up and you're active on these services.

From the App Store, you'll also discover a wide range of other apps that allow you to share photos online via other online social networking services, such as Google+, Tumblr, Pinterest, and Instagram. Using these apps, you can select photos (and often video clips) stored in the Photos app and share them with your online followers and friends, and sometimes the general public.

There are also specialized iPhone apps available from online photography services, such as Bump, Dropbox, Flickr, LiveShare, Shutterfly, SkyDrive, SmugMug, and Snapfish, for example, that allow you to upload, create, and share individual photos or entire photo galleries online with other people. You can also find these apps by looking in the Photo & Video category of the App Store or by using the search phrase "Photo Sharing" within the App Store's Search field.

Sync Your Photos Using iCloud's Photo Stream

If you have your iPhone set up to work with iCloud to sync app-specific data and files, and/or to back up your iPhone using the iCloud Backup feature, you can also turn on the Photo Stream feature (launch Settings, tap the Photos & Camera option, and then turn on the My Photo Stream virtual switch). Photo Stream enables you to maintain an online gallery that contains up to 1000 of your most recent images, and then automatically sync that gallery (your Photo Stream) between your iPhone, other iOS mobile devices, and/or your Mac or PC computers that are linked to the same iCloud account.

Once you set up iCloud's Photo Stream feature, it works automatically and in the background, as long as your iPhone has Wi-Fi Internet access. As a result, when you snap a new photo using the Camera app, in addition to being saved in the Camera Roll Album in the Photos app, that image will be uploaded automatically to your Photo Stream, and almost instantly be viewable on your other iCloud-connected computers and/or devices.

When viewing Photo Stream images on those other devices (or viewing images on your iPhone that were not shot using the iPhone), you'll need to save the images on that computer or device before you can edit them. As you're viewing a Photo Stream, you can also select and delete specific images. However, when you delete an image, it will be deleted from your Photo Stream and all devices and computers you have synced with Photo Stream.

New images added to your Photo Stream, whether they're added from your iPhone, iPad, iPod touch, Mac, or PC, will remain part of your Photo Stream for up to 30 days or until you reach 1000 images, at which time older images are automatically replaced by newer images.

After you activate the Photo Stream feature, you can view your Photo Stream from your iPhone by launching the Photos app and tapping the Photo Stream button at the bottom of the main Albums screen or at the bottom of the screen when viewing thumbnail images from any individual Album.

On your iPhone, your primary Photo Stream is labeled My Photo Stream, and it's listed near the top of the Photo Stream screen within Photos. It's also accessible using the optional iPhoto app.

When viewing the thumbnail images in your Photo Stream, tap the Edit button to select one or more of the images, and then tap the Share, Save, or Delete button to manage those images. The Share button allows you to share the selected images using the same Share options that are available elsewhere in the app. The Save button, however, is used to transfer the images from your Photo Stream and store them permanently on your iPhone within either an existing Album or a new Album that you create. This prevents those photos from expiring from your Photo Stream after 30 days or being replaced once you reach 1000 images. Tap the Delete button to remove one or more images from your main Photo Stream. This will almost instantly impact the Photo Stream that's accessible from all of your computers and iOS mobile devices.

The main iCloud Photo Stream feature stores your (up to) 1000 images online (via your iCloud account) and makes them available only to your other computers and devices that are linked to the same iCloud account. If you want to share images with other people, or access them from other computers (not linked to your iCloud account), use the new Shared Photo Streams feature instead, which is discussed in the following section.

Use Shared Photo Streams to Showcase Your Photos

The iCloud Shared Photo Streams feature is a new addition to iOS 6. It allows you to create individual Photo Streams (online galleries) comprising one or more images that you publish online via iCloud, and then share those Photo Streams with specific people. This allows you to create an Album with 5, 10, 20, or 100 images (or more) and then decide who will be able to view the Album online.

To use Shared Photo Streams, you must first turn on this feature from within Settings. To do this, launch Settings, tap the Photos & Camera option, and then turn on the Shared Photo Streams virtual switch. This feature is separate from the My Photo Stream option previously discussed (which allows you to sync your 1000 most recent images with computers and iOS mobile devices linked to the same iCloud account).

To create a Shared Photo Stream, launch the Photos app and open the Album that contains the images you want to share, such as your Camera Roll Album. Tap the Edit button. One at a time, tap the image thumbnails for the photos you want to select and add to a Shared Photo Stream. Next, tap the Share button and select the Photo Stream

How to... Create Prints from Photos Taken Using Your iPhone

After you've shot lots of photos using your iPhone, you'll probably want to make traditional prints from some of them. To do this, you have several options.

You can use the AirPrint feature built into iOS 6, connect your iPhone to an AirPrint-compatible photo printer, and then print your images on special photo paper to create good quality prints yourself.

You also have the option to e-mail or transfer images stored on your iPhone to a photo lab, and then have that lab create professional-quality prints of almost any size for you. From images taken on your iPhone, you can easily order wallet size, 4×6", 5×7", or 8×10" prints, for example, that will be excellent quality.

Many one-hour photo labs in pharmacies or stores (like Target or Wal-Mart) allow you to e-mail or upload images directly from your iPhone to a special website (using an optional app). You can then pick up your prints within an hour or so.

There are also a handful of photo labs that have proprietary apps that allow you to upload images from your iPhone to the photo lab, order prints, and then have those prints mailed to you within a few business days. The cost for this service is typically on a per-print basis, and is often comparable to what one-hour photo labs charge.

If you're interested in ordering prints from images stored on your iPhone and having a lab create those prints (for pick-up or to be mailed to you), visit the App Store and download a free print-ordering app, or acquire the free app available from your local photo lab. Some of your app options include Free Prints, Kodak Kiosk Connect App, MoPho: Prints and Photo Gifts, MotoPhoto, PostalPix, RitzPix, Snapfish, and Walgreens.

option. From the Add To A Photo Stream screen, a list of your existing Shared Photo Streams will be displayed. Either select one of these Photo Streams to add the selected images to it, or tap the New Photo Stream option.

If you tap the New Photo Stream option, at the top of the Photo Stream screen that appears, you'll see an empty To field (see Figure 11-12). Fill in the names or e-mail addresses of the people you want to share your Photo Stream with. If the people have existing entries within your Contacts database, type their names, one at a time. If no preexisting Contacts entry exists for a person, manually enter that person's e-mail address.

FIGURE 11-12 Create a Shared Photo Stream from your iPhone and decide with whom you'll share those images with via iCloud.

Then, in the Name field, enter a title for your Shared Photo Stream. Below the Name field, if you turn on the Public Website virtual switch, anyone who visits www. iCloud.com and accesses your Shared Photo Streams will be able to view your images. When this switch is turned off, only the people you invite to see your images will be able to access your online-based Shared Photo Streams. The Photos app will send those people an e-mail that includes a special website address (URL) they can use to access the images online once they're published. If someone is using a Mac or iOS mobile device, they'll have the option to download the photos to their computer or device from your Shared Photo Stream. Otherwise, they can just view the photos online.

Tap the Next button that's displayed near the top-right corner of the screen to continue. You can now add a text-based caption to your Shared Photo Stream, which will also be included in the e-mail sent to the people who you invite to view your photos. Tap the Post button to publish your photos online and send the invitation e-mails to the desired recipients.

To edit your Shared Photo Stream after it's created, tap the Photo Stream icon near the bottom of the screen in the Photos app and select the Shared Photo Stream you want to alter. Next, tap the Edit button. You can then add more photos to that Shared Photo Stream or select and delete images from it, plus share individual images with others using the same Share options that are available elsewhere in the Photos app.

Discover the Hundreds of Other Photography-Related Apps Available from the App Store

Beyond the many photography-related apps for the iPhone that can be used to order prints or share photos online, there are also literally hundreds of third-party apps available from the App Store that are designed for photo editing and enhancement. These apps typically offer photo editing tools, visual effects, image filters, and sharing options, for example, that are different from what the Photos and iPhoto apps offer.

How to...

Find Optional Photography Accessories That'll Help You Improve Your Photos and Videos

In addition to photography apps you can install on your iPhone, there are a growing number of optional iPhone 5 photography accessories available that also enhance your picture taking (and video shooting) capabilities. For example, you can purchase a tripod for your iPhone, such the iStabilizer Flex tripod for the iPhone ($29.95, www.istabilizer.com) or the Joby GorillaMobile Tripod for the iPhone ($39.95, www.joby.com).

The OlloClip ($69.95, www.olloclip.com) is an attachable external lens system for the iPhone 5 that clips onto the edge of the iPhone and gives you access to wide-angle, fisheye, and macro lenses. The OlloClip works flawlessly with any photography apps you're already using with your iPhone 5. The OlloClip is small enough to store in a pocket when not in use, enabling you to attach it to the iPhone in seconds when you're ready to take pictures.

For shooting 360-degree videos that are stunning and that can be shared instantly online (and via Facebook), you'll want to attach a Kogeto Dot lens accessory to your iPhone 5 ($49.00, www.kogeto.com) and then use the free app that comes with it.

These are just a sampling of the photography accessories available for the iPhone 5. To find more, use any Internet search engine, such as Yahoo! or Google, and enter the search phrase "iPhone 5 Photo Accessories."

To find apps like Adobe Photoshop Express, Color Splash, FX Photo Studio, Retouch, Clone Camera, InstaPicFrame, Photo Editor by Aviary, Photo Slash Pro, Photo Wizard, Photogene 2 for iPhone, PicShop, and countless others, launch the App Store app and use the search phrase "Photo Editing" to browse through the Photo & Video category.

Between using the Camera, Photos, iPhoto, and other optional apps, you'll discover your iPhone can be used as an incredibly powerful digital camera that allows you to take, edit, organize, and share visually stunning digital photos or videos.

 Using Apple's optional Cards app, you can create photo greeting cards suitable for many different occasions, and Apple will professionally print and send those cards to your desired recipients. These cards look as nice as anything you'd buy at a greeting card store, but they are fully customized with your personal message and custom photo(s). Although the Cards app is free, a per-card fee of $2.99 applies if you have Apple print and mail your card to a recipient (within the United States) via first-class mail.

12

Use the New Maps App to Navigate Your World

HOW TO...

- Get acquainted with the newly revamped Maps app
- Get turn-by-turn navigation directions
- Look up addresses or locations using Maps
- Discover Maps app alternatives

Through the use of the iPhone 5's built-in GPS technology combined with crowd-sourced Wi-Fi hotspots and cell towers, anytime your iPhone is not in Airplane mode or turned off, it can figure out exactly where you are, tell you what's around you, and help you easily get to wherever it is you're going. Depending on the app you're using, your iPhone can also share your location with others, or help you pinpoint the whereabouts of friends, family members, or coworkers who also have an iOS mobile device (using the optional Find My Friends app or official Facebook apps, for example).

The newly revamped Maps app makes full use of the iPhone 5's Location Services features and offers a handful of useful functions that make navigating through your world a much more exciting endeavor. Maps not only will help you get to where you're going by providing detailed, turn-by-turn directions, but will also help you find businesses, restaurants, landmarks, and popular destinations (such as airports) with ease.

 As you'll discover, the Maps app works seamlessly with Siri, as well as with the Contacts app. This integration reduces the amount of manual data entry that's necessary, yet expands the information that your iPhone can provide to you.

The Maps App Is a Work in Progress...

Shortly after Apple released iOS 6 and the revamped Maps app, iPhone and iPad users began experiencing glitches with the app. In an open letter to its customers, Apple CEO Tim Cook acknowledged these problems and vowed they'd be promptly fixed.

Chances are, by the time you read this, the features and functions of the Maps app will be working flawlessly. However, in the words of Mr. Cook, "While we're improving Maps, you can try alternatives by downloading map apps from the App Store like Bing, MapQuest, and Waze, or use Google or Nokia maps by going to their websites and creating an icon on your home screen to their web app." Information about some of the alternate navigation-related apps available for the iPhone is provided at the end of this chapter.

Turn On Location Services and Siri Before Using Maps

To utilize the Maps app, your iPhone needs to be able to access the Internet using a 3G/4G or Wi-Fi connection, but it also needs to have the Location Services feature turned on. To do this, launch Settings, tap Privacy, and then tap the Location Services option.

Near the top of the Location Services screen, make sure the Location Services virtual switch is set to On. Then, scroll down the Location Services screen and turn on the Maps virtual switch as well (shown in Figure 12-1). To return to the Settings screen, tap the Privacy button in the upper-left corner, followed by the Settings button in the same location.

Next, if you haven't already done so, turn on Siri. While Siri isn't required to use the Maps app, this feature adds a lot more functionality to the app. To do this, from the main Settings screen, tap the General option, and then tap the Siri option. Near the top of the Siri screen, turn on the Siri virtual switch.

Finally, make sure your iPhone is not in Airplane mode (discussed in Chapter 2) and that it has access to the Internet. While the Maps app works fine with a Wi-Fi Internet connection, you'll need to use it with a 3G/4G Internet connection if you plan to take advantage of the app's navigation features. Otherwise, as soon as you leave a Wi-Fi hotspot's signal radius, your Internet connection will be lost and the Maps app will stop functioning properly.

If you begin relying heavily on the Maps app for real-time navigation and turn-by-turn directions, this will deplete your monthly wireless data allocation from your 3G/4G wireless service provider faster. Plus, it will drain the iPhone's battery faster. Consider investing in a car charger that will keep the iPhone running while in your vehicle, while simultaneously charging the battery.

FIGURE 12-1   Turn on both the main Location Services virtual switch and the Maps virtual switch located further down the Location Services screen.

Get Acquainted with the Newly Revamped Maps App

The Maps app's icon that appears on your iPhone 5's Home screen may look familiar (if you're a veteran iPhone user), but from the moment you launch the iOS 6 edition of this app, you'll discover many changes. For starters, Maps no longer relies on Google Maps to help you get to where you're going. Instead, Apple has developed its own proprietary mapping system that offers vector-based maps, flyover views, and visual and spoken turn-by-turn directions between locations that you select.

Obtain Turn-by-Turn Directions Between Start and End Locations

When you launch the Maps app directly from the Home screen, the app's main screen is displayed (shown in Figure 12-2). Tap the Directions icon (the bent, right-pointing

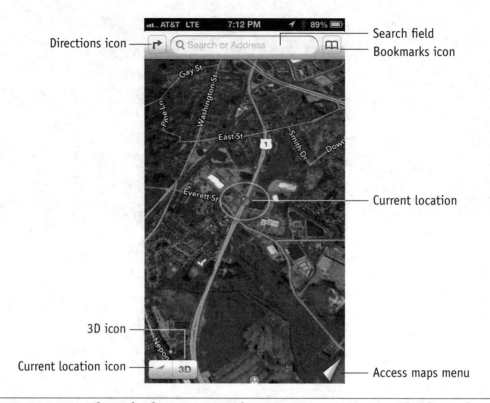

Directions icon

Search field

Bookmarks icon

Current location

3D icon

Current location icon

Access maps menu

FIGURE 12-2 The Hybrid map view on the main Maps app screen. The dot in the center with a circle around it is the iPhone's current location.

arrow) in the upper-left corner of the screen to enter or select a Start location and an End location in order to obtain directions between those points.

Note By default, the Start location will be your Current Location. However, you can enter any address into this field or tap the Reverse Directions icon (shaped like a sideways *S*) displayed to the immediate left of the Start and End fields to make your End location your Current Location.

Enter a Start location and an End location in the empty data fields associated with the Directions feature of Maps (shown in Figure 12-3). You can type a full address, such as 230 Park Avenue, New York, NY 10169 (entering a ZIP code is always optional), or, depending on your needs, you can simply enter a city and state, just a state, or just a country. For example, to view a map showing a driving route between New York City and Boston, Massachusetts, you could simply enter New York, NY in the Start field and Boston, MA in the End field.

Next, tap either the car icon, pedestrian icon, or bus icon near the top center of the screen. When you tap the car icon, Maps provides you with driving directions

FIGURE 12-3   Tap the Directions icon to display the Start and End fields and the Reverse Directions icon. You'll also see the car, pedestrian, and bus icons and the Route button.

between the Start and End locations. Tap the pedestrian icon to obtain walking directions between those locations, or tap the bus icon to access directions using public transportation (if applicable).

In some cases, walking or public transportation options will not be available from the Maps app.

Next, tap the Route button in the top-right corner of the screen. Your iPhone will determine up to three routes between the Start and End locations, allow you to pick one, and then provide detailed, turn-by-turn directions.

If you enter just the name of a business or business type, Maps will assume you want results for the last area you searched (unless you tap the arrow icon in the lower-left corner of the screen first to pinpoint your location). However, if you enter a major landmark, even if it's not close to you, such as the White House, maps can often figure out what you're referring to and pinpoint it on a map without your including the city and state.

Keep in mind, because the Maps app integrates with the Contacts app, you can enter the name of someone who has an entry within your Contacts database to display their address. As you type information into the Start and End fields, the iPhone will automatically offer suggestions from your Contacts entry listings, as well as from the Internet. For example, in the Start field, you can leave the default Current Location as is, and in the End field, enter the name of someone from your Contacts database (or vice versa). Matches from your Contacts database will be displayed below the End field. Tap a match to insert it into the Start or End field, whichever has the active cursor within it.

Choose Between Up to Three Potential Routes

After you tap the Route button, a Route Overview screen is displayed (shown in Figure 12-4). This zoomed-out map will show your starting point (with a green virtual pushpin) and destination (with a red virtual pushpin). The dark blue line outlines the suggested route to follow. It is accompanied by a flag that says Route 1.

Up to two alternate routes display light blue lines for the portions of the routes that differ from Route 1, and the routes are accompanied by a Route 2 flag and

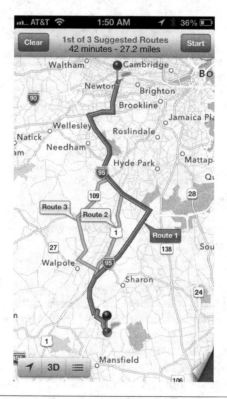

FIGURE 12-4 The main route between the Start and End locations is displayed as a dark blue line. Up to two alternate routes are also displayed and labeled on the map.

(potentially) a Route 3 flag. To follow either Route 2 or Route 3 instead of Route 1, tap the appropriate Route flag.

One reason to choose an alternate route would be based on current traffic conditions. The Maps app can overlay real-time traffic conditions on any map. To view this information, tap the lower-right corner of the Maps app's screen. When the Maps menu appears (shown in Figure 12-5), tap the Show Traffic button. If heavy traffic or construction is taking place along any of the outlined routes, red lines and/or warning icons will be displayed on the map.

After selecting the route you want to follow, tap the Start button in the upper-right corner of the screen. Siri will speak each turn you need to make, while the Maps app displays a close-up map and detailed, turn-by-turn directions on the iPhone's screen, offering functionality just like a stand-alone GPS unit. Follow the directions until you reach your destination. As you move toward your destination, the information on the screen constantly updates in real time.

Tip If you're not driving the vehicle, as the Maps app is providing turn-by-turn directions, you can trace the highlighted route with your finger on the screen to see a preview of where you'll be going.

FIGURE 12-5 The Maps menu appears when you tap the lower-right corner of the main Maps app's screen.

Figure 12-6 shows what a sample navigation screen looks like when using the Maps app for turn-by-turn directions to a location. Notice that certain businesses (including gas stations and restaurants), street names, and landmarks are also displayed on the map using text and graphic icons. In conjunction with each turn, Siri will offer verbal directions in addition to what's actually shown on the map.

 As you're following the turn-by-turn directions, tap anywhere on the iPhone's screen to reveal two command icons, End and Overview. Tap End to return to the main Maps screen (and exit the turn-by-turn directions feature), or tap Overview to view the zoomed-out Route Overview map, with your current location, your estimated time to arrival (ETA) to your destination, and the current distance to your destination displayed near the top center of the screen.

Pinpoint Your Current Location

While the Maps app is helping you navigate between locations, or anytime you're looking at a map using this app, tap the northeast-pointing arrow icon in the lower-left corner of the screen to recalculate and pinpoint your exact current location on the map. This will be showcased on the map with a blue dot that pulsates.

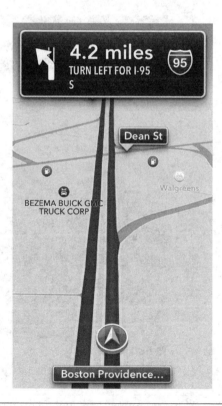

FIGURE 12-6 When using Maps for turn-by-turn directions, each upcoming turn is highlighted on the map.

Switch to a 3D Map View

As you're looking at any map on the iPhone's screen generated by the Maps app, tap the 3D button in the bottom-left corner of the screen to switch to a more visually interesting 3D viewing perspective. This feature works with the Standard, Hybrid, and Satellite map views, discussed a bit later in the chapter.

View Text-Based Directions

While Maps is helping you navigate between two locations using the Directions functionality of the app, tap the Directions List icon (near the lower-left corner of the screen, to the immediate right of the 3D button) to view a text-based listing of turn-by-turn directions (shown in Figure 12-7). To exit this screen and return to the map, tap the Done button in the top-right corner of the screen.

Change Your Map View

When you access the Maps menu (refer to Figure 12-5), which you can access at any time by tapping the lower-right corner of the screen while using the app, you'll see a

FIGURE 12-7   From the Maps app, you can view complete text-based directions between two locations.

handful of additional command buttons displayed, including three buttons that allow you to choose your map view. These command buttons include

- **Drop Pin**   Tap this button to add a virtual pushpin to any location on the map you're currently viewing.
- **Print**   If your iPhone has access to an AirPrint-compatible printer, you can print out directions or any Maps-related information by tapping this command button.
- **Show/Hide Traffic**   For many metropolitan areas, when you tap the Show Traffic button, the Maps app will superimpose real-time traffic conditions over the map you're viewing. This can help you select an alternate route *before* you get stuck in traffic.
- **List Results**   If you perform a location search using the Maps app, red virtual pushpins for each search result will be displayed on a map, and you can tap a pushpin to reveal more information about that location. However, when you tap the List Results button, a text-based listing of these results is displayed (shown in Figure 12-8). You can then tap the blue-and-white right-pointing arrow icon (>) associated with a listing to view detailed information about that location.

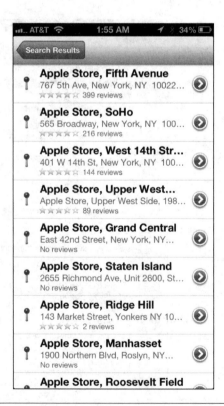

FIGURE 12-8   View a text-based but interactive listing of location search results. Tap any listing to view more information or see that particular address on a map.

Access the Three Main Map View Options, Plus 3D and Flyover

Displayed along the bottom of the Maps menu are the following three Map View command buttons:

- **Standard**   Displays a traditional, multicolored, and detailed map on the screen. This is the default view.
- **Hybrid**   Displays road names and other information superimposed over an overhead satellite photo view. A sample Hybrid map of Manhattan is shown in Figure 12-9.
- **Satellite**   Displays an area using a photorealistic, highly detailed overhead view that showcases clear images taken from a satellite. (While these images are detailed and accurate, they are not real-time satellite photos, so you can't use them for spying, for example.)

When Flyover view is available, as you're viewing a map of a metropolitan area, the Flyover icon (which looks like three tall buildings) is displayed instead of the 3D button. Tap this icon to display a three-dimensional Flyover view of the region, which is shown from the perspective of an airplane cockpit (shown in Figure 12-10). Use your finger to navigate your way around on the map. You can also zoom in or out.

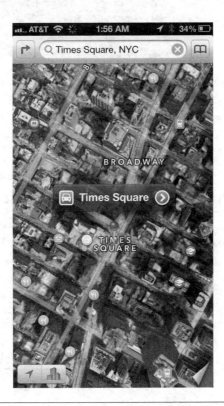

FIGURE 12-9   The Hybrid map view uses satellite imagery combined with street names and other details overlaid on the map image.

FIGURE 12-10 When available, the Flyover view in Maps is one of the coolest features this app offers. Navigate the map using your finger. Plus, you can zoom in or out.

How to... Zoom In or Out When Viewing a Map

When viewing a map within the Maps app, you can zoom in or out. To do this, use a reverse-pinch finger motion on the iPhone's Multi-Touch display to zoom in, or use a pinch finger motion to zoom out. You also have the option of double-tapping the specific location on a map that you want to zoom in on. Each time you double-tap the same location on a map, you'll zoom in a bit closer.

Meanwhile, you can keep zooming out on a map until you're viewing the entire planet Earth from space. Regardless of how much you zoom in or out on a map, the pulsating blue dot always represents your current location.

View a Map of Any Location

On the main Maps app screen, instead of tapping the Directions button to enter a Start and End location to obtain turn-by-turn directions between two locations, you can enter any location into the Search field in the top center of the screen to view a map of that location. You can enter the name of a country, state, or city to see a general map, or enter a detailed address (street number, street name, city, state/country) to see a specific location on a map. For example, if you simply type Boston, MA, an overview map of the city of Boston will be displayed. You can then zoom in to view areas of the city in much greater detail.

A new feature in the iOS 6 version of the Maps app is integration with Yelp!. Thus, you can now enter in the Search field the name of any business, restaurant, business type (such as "bank," "post office," "gas station," "hospital," or "salon"), landmark (such as the White House or the Grand Canyon), tourist attraction, or airport, followed by a city and state, in order to find and view your search result on a map. For example, in the Search field, type "Apple Store, New York, NY" to view the locations of the Apple Stores in the New York City area (shown in Figure 12-11). Or, if you're looking for a gas

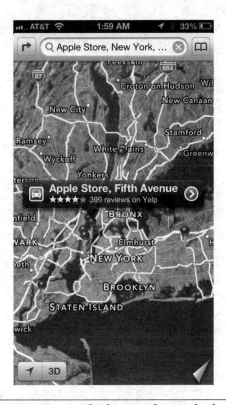

FIGURE 12-11 Using Maps, you can look up and map the location of a business, restaurant, landmark, or a popular destination. Shown here are the locations of Apple Stores in New York, New York.

station, type "gas station, Newton, MA" to view the locations of all gas stations in the Newton, Massachusetts area. For whatever it is you're looking for, follow the request with a comma and then the city and state you want to search in.

 If you enter a business name or business type into the Search field without including a city and state, the Maps app will assume you want listings based on your last search location, unless you tap the arrow icon near the lower-left corner of the screen first to pinpoint your current location.

As shown in Figure 12-11, the results of your search are displayed on the map using red virtual pushpins. Tap any pushpin to review a banner that displays the name and location of what the pushpin represents. On the right side of that banner, you'll see a right-pointing arrow icon. Tap it to display a detailed Location information screen for that business, restaurant, or location.

Interact with the Location Screens

The Location screen for a business, restaurant, or location incorporates information from Yelp!. On the screen, you'll see Info, Reviews, and Photos tabs (shown in Figure 12-12). Tap the Info tab (the default selection) to view the phone number, home page (if applicable), address, and a handful of command buttons, which include the following:

- **Directions To Here**   Based on your current location, tap this button to have the Maps app provide detailed directions to the location of the search result.
- **Directions From Here**   Based on your current location, tap this button to have the Maps app provide detailed directions from the search result's location to your current location.
- **More Info On Yelp**   Tap this button to access Yelp!'s website and access more information about that location, business, restaurant, or destination. If you have the optional Yelp! iPhone app (free) installed, which is recommended, the app will launch and display detailed information about the research result.
- **Add To Contacts**   Add the business, restaurant, or location to your Contacts database with the tap of this button. You can then edit the entry as you see fit, and refer to it anytime later from within the Contacts app or using Siri.
- **Add To Bookmarks**   Like Safari, the Maps app allows you to maintain a customized bookmark list of locations you've looked up or accessed from the app. When you save a bookmark, you can quickly re-access that location on a map again later, without having to re-enter the address manually. At the bottom of the Bookmarks screen are two other tabs, Recents and Contacts. Recents allows you to revisit recently searched-for locations, while Contacts give you access to your All Contacts list to find an address for one of your Contacts entries.

 To access your personalized Maps bookmark list, tap the Bookmark icon near the top-right corner of the Maps app's main screen. On the Bookmarks screen, you can then edit your bookmarks or access a previously viewed and saved location on a map by tapping a bookmark listing.

FIGURE 12-12   The Location screen for a particular location (the Apple Store on Fifth Avenue in New York City) that was found using the Maps app

- **Share Location**   Tap this button to share details about the search result with other people via e-mail, text/instant message, Twitter, or Facebook.
- **Report A Problem**   If you discover a listing or search result is inaccurate, tap this button to report the error to Apple.

If you're looking at a listing for a business, restaurant, or tourist attraction, for example, the Information screen for it will often display hours of operation, the distance from your current location, and other useful information. For a restaurant listing, the Information screen might also display its average star-based rating (from Yelp!), its menu price range, its food delivery information, whether the restaurant takes reservations, and/or whether it is suitable for kids.

Keep in mind, most of the data fields displayed on a Location screen are interactive. So, if you tap a listing's phone number, your iPhone will automatically launch the Phone app and initiate a call to that number. Likewise, if you tap an address, it will promptly be displayed on a map. If a website URL is displayed as part of a listing on the Location screen, when you tap it, Safari will launch and display that website.

When you tap the Reviews tab displayed on a Location screen, you'll be able to view Yelp!-related star-based ratings and detailed reviews from other people. Or, if you tap the Photos tab, digital photos that have been taken and uploaded by Yelp! users will be displayed in the form of thumbnails. Tap an image thumbnail to view a larger version of the image on the iPhone's screen. You can then zoom in on the photo to see more detail.

Access the Maps App from the Contacts App

As you're using the Contacts app (discussed in Chapter 8) and viewing any individual entry, simply tap an address within that entry and the Maps app will launch and display that address. You can then obtain detailed directions to that location from your current location (or any other address) by tapping the right-pointing arrow icon above the red virtual pushpin on the map and then tapping the Directions To Here button.

Use the Maps App with Siri

So far, you've read about many of the different ways you can manually interact with the Maps app by entering information into the Directions Start and End fields or into the Search field. However, one of the easiest ways to interact with the Maps app is using Siri.

Regardless of what you're doing on your iPhone, at any time, you can activate Siri by pressing and holding down the Home button for two to three seconds, and then speak your request. In regard to using Siri with the Maps app, here are some examples of what you could say:

- "How do I get home from here?" (From your current location.)
- "How do I get to work from here? (From your current location.)
- "Get me directions to [insert a location, Contacts entry, business name, tourist attraction, etc.]."
- "Find the closest gas station."
- "Where is the closest post office?"
- "Find me Chinese restaurants in Boston, Massachusetts."
- "Show me [insert address]." (This will display the desired address on a map.)
- "How do I get to [insert location, such as an airport]?"
- "Show me where [insert contact's name] lives."
- "Find [insert landmark, such as the White House in Washington, DC]."

If you say, "Find the Cheesecake Factory in Braintree, Massachusetts," for example, Siri will display a detailed information screen for that restaurant (shown in Figure 12-13). Part of this information screen (if you scroll down) will include a map thumbnail. Tap that map thumbnail to launch the Maps app and view that location on an interactive map.

FIGURE 12-13 On the information screen displayed by Siri, you can launch the Maps app for that location with a single tap.

 If the restaurant whose information screen you're viewing accepts phone reservations, active Siri once again and say something like, "Make a reservation for two for tonight at 8 P.M." By integrating with the Open Table online service, Siri will make a reservation for you, if possible, and then confirm that reservation.

Find Third-Party Maps Apps

While the Maps app offers a handful of extremely useful features and works seamlessly with other apps and with Siri, if you visit the App Store, you'll discover other maps and navigational apps that offer similar functionality or, in some cases, other features you may find useful.

To find these apps, launch the App Store app and tap the Featured button or Charts button. Then, tap the Categories button in the upper-left corner of the screen. Select the Navigation option. If you first tapped the Featured button, once you select the Navigation category, you'll see third-party apps listed under the New, What's Hot, Paid, and Free headings.

Use your finger to scroll horizontally through the app listings under each heading, or tap the View All option to the right of each heading. Or, if you tapped the Charts button and then selected Navigation, you can view the current most popular apps listed within the Paid, Free, and/or Top Grossing charts.

Some of the alternative apps to the Maps app that you'll discover within the App Store include: Garmin U.S.A. ($49.99), MotionX GPS Drive ($0.99), MapQuest (Free), Waze Social GPS Traffic & Gas (Free), and Bing Get Me There (Free).

Based on the city you're in, you'll also discover apps that can help you utilize mass transit systems and public transportation, such as busses, trains, and subways. These apps can be particularly useful if you're planning a trip to an unfamiliar city, such as New York City, Washington DC, or London, and want to utilize the public transportation system instead of renting a car.

 If you're traveling overseas and using international data roaming, you could be charged up to $20 per megabyte (not gigabyte) for wireless data sent or received. Thus, using the Maps app could become extremely expensive. To save money, consider prepaying for international wireless data service from your current service provider, or purchasing and inserting a local, prepaid micro-SIM chip into your iPhone that works in whatever country you're visiting (and with the model iPhone 5 you own).

13

Organize Your Life with the Calendar, Reminders, and Notes Apps

HOW TO...

- Manage your schedule using the Calendar app
- Keep track of your to-do lists using the Reminders app
- Use Notes to store text-based information

Three apps that come preinstalled on the iPhone 5 are Calendar, Reminders, and Notes. While each of these apps allows you to manage a different type of information, each can be used to help you keep your life organized. Calendar is a scheduling app that allows you to create, manage, and then view multiple calendars on a single screen. This allows you to keep your personal life and work-related appointments separate, yet view them in one place using a single app.

The Reminders app allows you to create and manage multiple to-do lists. Each list you create can include as many separate items as you'd like, and each item can have a separate alarm/deadline associated with it. Thus, you can use this app to create a grocery list, for example, or use it to manage a multiphase project that involves a variety of different tasks and deadlines.

The Notes app is a free-form text editor. Use it to type notes on the iPhone's screen with the virtual keyboard, or dictate your notes using the iPhone's Dictation feature. This app serves as a virtual notepad, and is a viable alternative to writing down memos and reminders to yourself on random scrap paper.

One of the main reasons to use the Calendar, Reminders, and Notes apps is that they all work seamlessly with iCloud and allow you to automatically sync your app-specific data with your computer(s) and/or other iOS mobile devices that are linked to the same iCloud account.

The App Store Offers Many Alternative Scheduling, List Management, and Note Taking Apps

As you browse the App Store and look in the Business and/or Productivity categories, you'll discover many third-party apps that allow you to manage a schedule, create and manage lists, and/or take notes on a virtual notepad. If you discover that the Calendar, Reminders, and/or Notes apps do not fully address your needs, access the App Store and enter in the Search field the phrase "scheduling," "list management," or "note taking" to find similar apps that offer a different set of features or a user interface that's more to your liking.

For example, instead of using the Notes app, which is basically a text editor, the optional Evernote and Microsoft OneNote apps both offer a more robust set of note taking tools, while the MyScript Memo, Sketch Pad 3, and Jot! Whiteboard apps, for example, allow you to use your finger or an optional stylus to write on the iPhone's screen in order to record handwritten notes. The SoundNote app is one of many apps that allow you to either type or handwrite notes (or draw on the iPhone's screen and save the drawings as notes). The optional Pages app, for example, allows your iPhone to work as a full-featured word processor that's compatible with Pages for Mac and Microsoft Word (for PC and Mac).

As part of this iCloud integration, from any computer or Internet-enabled device, you can visit www.iCloud.com, log in using your iCloud username and password, and then utilize online-based versions of these apps that will automatically be populated with your data. So, if you accidently leave your iPhone at home, you can still securely access your schedule while on the go by using any computer.

The Calendar app is also designed to integrate and share data with other apps, including the official Facebook app, while the Calendar and Reminders apps both work seamlessly with the Notification Center and Siri. In addition, these apps can sync data with online-based scheduling apps offered by Google and Yahoo! and apps that are Microsoft Exchange–compatible.

Note See Chapter 4 for more information about syncing Calendar-, Reminders-, and Notes-specific data with iCloud, your other computer(s), other iOS mobile devices, and/or online-based applications.

Manage Your Schedule Using the Calendar App

Calendar can be used as a powerful, stand-alone app to help you keep track of your appointments and manage your time using the iPhone. Using color-coded calendars, it's possible to manage your work and personal schedule, schedules related to different projects, and a schedule to keep track of where your kids need to be and when—all in separate calendars that can be viewed simultaneously.

 The Calendar app refers to all appointments, meetings, and other obligations as "events."

What you'll probably find the most useful about this app is that it can sync your scheduling information with the Calendar app running on your Mac (or with Microsoft Outlook on a PC or a Mac) and the Calendar app on your iPad. Or, if you already use an online-based scheduling tool from Google or Yahoo! or one that is Microsoft Exchange compatible, the Calendar app on your iPhone can easily sync with that as well.

As you'll discover, using this app, you can also share event-specific information with other people, invite others to an event via e-mail, and then have the Calendar app keep track of who will be attending based on RSVPs.

Another useful aspect of the Calendar app is that it's highly customizable. With the tap of a button, you can quickly switch between a List, Day, or Month view of your schedule, or rotate the iPhone into landscape mode to see what Apple calls a Week view (though you can view only five days' worth of appointments, not seven).

 When using the List, Day, or Month view, tap the Today button to instantly jump back to the current date. Use finger swipes or the directional arrows displayed on the screen to scroll between dates.

The List view (shown in Figure 13-1) displays your day-by-day appointments in chronological order in a vertical list format. Scroll up or down within this display to view all of your past or upcoming appointments, and then tap any event listing to view all of the details about it on a separate Event Details screen.

The Day view (shown in Figure 13-2) showcases your schedule for one day at a time. The date is displayed near the top center of the screen, and an hour-by-hour layout of your schedule is displayed in the main area of the screen. Scroll up or down to see the entire day, and scroll left or right to view other days, one at a time.

The Month view (shown in Figure 13-3) displays a month-at-a-glance calendar in the top section of the screen, and lists the events scheduled for the selected day in chronological order in the lower half of the screen. By default, the current day (Today)

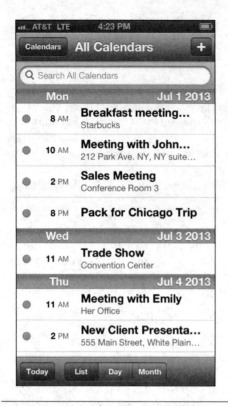

FIGURE 13-1 The List view of the Calendar app

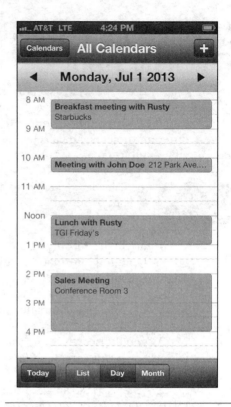

FIGURE 13-2 The Day view of the Calendar app

is the date selected, but you can tap any day within that month's calendar to jump to an alternate day, or you can change the month you're viewing using the directional arrows displayed to the right and left of the month and year heading near the top center of the screen.

Note The dots below dates in Month view indicate that those particular days have one or more events associated with them. The dots to the left of the listings in the bottom half of the screen (refer to Figure 13-3, for example) are color-coded based on which calendar each event is associated with. If you are managing only one calendar using the Calendar app, all the dots will be the same color.

The Week view (shown in Figure 13-4) shows five days at a time, but allows you to scroll horizontally to additional days prior to or after the period you're currently viewing. You can then scroll up or down to view hour-by-hour time increments. To access the Week view, turn your iPhone to landscape mode (sideways). Turn it back to portrait mode to return to the app's other views.

FIGURE 13-3   The Month view of the Calendar app

FIGURE 13-4   Rotate the iPhone into landscape mode to see the Week view of the Calendar app.

Import Events from Facebook into the Calendar App

Before using Facebook integration in conjunction with the Calendar app (or any app for that matter), you must be logged into Facebook and supply your Facebook account information from within Settings. Launch Settings and tap the Facebook option. Enter your username and password, and then turn on the Calendar virtual switch on the Facebook screen.

After turning on Facebook integration on your iPhone, you can automatically import all Facebook events into the Calendar app. To do this, tap the Calendars button and scroll down to the Facebook heading. Tap the Facebook Events option to add a check mark to it. You can also display the birthdays of your Facebook friends. Tap the Birthdays option under the Facebook heading to add a check mark next to it.

Note The Week view is a display-only view of your schedule. You can't enter new information into the app when using this view.

View One Calendar at a Time, or View Multiple Calendars Simultaneously

If you opt to manage multiple calendars separately using the Calendar app, you can switch between calendars by tapping the Calendars button in the top-left corner of the screen and then choosing one or more color-coded calendars that you want to view. To view all of your calendars simultaneously, tap the Show All Calendars button.

Add a New Calendar or Edit or Delete an Existing Calendar

To create a new calendar in the Calendar app, tap the Calendars button in the upper-left corner of the screen, and then tap the Edit button (in the same location) on the Calendars screen (shown in Figure 13-5). Then tap on the Add Calendar... button. You'll be prompted to enter a name for the Calendar and select a color to associate with it. Tap the Done button to save your changes.

 You can only create new calendars that are associated with the Calendar app. If you're syncing Calendar data with Google or Yahoo!, for example, you can't create new calendars from the iPhone.

FIGURE 13-5   View and select one or more separate calendars to view simultaneously by tapping the Calendars button.

To change the name or color associated with an existing calendar, tap its listing. On the Edit Calendar screen, you can also opt to share that specific calendar with another person by tapping the Shared With option, or make it "Public" so you can share it with multiple people. After you turn on the Public Calendar virtual switch, tap the Share Link option to decide with whom you'll share that specific calendar's data.

 You can make a calendar Public only if you are syncing your Calendar app data with iCloud. This feature does not work if you're syncing your Calendar data with Google or Yahoo!, for example.

To delete an existing calendar from your iPhone, on the Edit Calendar screen, tap the red and white Delete Calendar option. This also erases the calendar from other computers or devices the Calendar app is syncing data with, so proceed with caution. Only calendars created using the Calendar app (on your iPhone or a Mac, for example) can be deleted from the Calendar app on your iPhone. Google or Yahoo! calendars can't be deleted from the iPhone.

Manually Enter New Events into the Calendar App

To enter a new event into the Calendar app using your iPhone, tap the plus sign icon in the top-right corner of the screen when viewing the List, Day, or Month view. At the top of the Add Event screen that's displayed (shown in Figure 13-6), start by entering the title for the event using the iPhone's virtual keyboard. Then, if applicable, enter the event's location. As you work your way down the Add Event screen, the Starts and Ends fields are next. Tap this field to access the separate Start & End screen (shown in Figure 13-7).

 As you create a new event, you can enter as much or as little information about that event as you desire. Keep in mind, however, that the more information you include within each event listing, the more helpful your iPhone will be later when you look up event-related information using Siri, or when accessing event locations using the Maps app, for example.

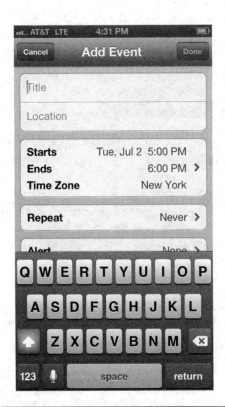

FIGURE 13-6 Enter new event (appointment) information, one event at a time, in the Add Event screen.

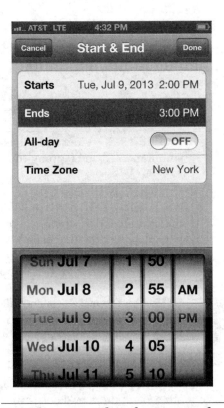

FIGURE 13-7 Select the Starts and Ends dates and times for each event. Don't forget to tap the Done button once you've entered this information.

To enter a Start date and time for an event, tap the Starts field, and then use the Date, Hour, Minutes, and AM/PM dials near the bottom of the screen to enter the appropriate information. Next, tap the Ends field. Again, use the Date, Hour, Minutes, and AM/PM dials to select when the event ends. An event can last for five minutes, an entire day, several days, or even several weeks or months. If an event will last an entire day, turn on the All-Day virtual switch on the Start & End screen. When you do this, you only need to enter a Starts date and an Ends date.

 You can easily display in the Calendar app the birthdays of people who have entries in your Contacts database. As you're creating or editing each Contacts entry, tap the Add Field option, choose Birthday, and add the contact's birthday to their entry. Then, in the Calendar app, tap the Calendars button and scroll down to the Other heading. Tap the Birthdays listing and add a check mark next to it. The birthdays of people who have entries in your Contacts database will now be displayed in the Calendar app.

For example, if you wanted to block out one week on your calendar for a vacation, in the Title field, enter the word Vacation. In the Location field, you can enter where you'll be vacationing, such as Hawaii. Then, when you tap the Starts/Ends field, turn on the All-Day option, and then choose the start and end date of your vacation, such as July 7 to July 14.

When you're done entering the Starts and Ends date and time, tap the Done button in the top-right corner of the screen. Now, you can further customize the newly created event listing by tapping any of the following fields:

- **Repeat**   Tap this field to set up a recurring event. The default for this option is Never, meaning it does not repeat. However, you can tap the Every Day, Every Week, Every 2 Weeks, Every Month, or Every Year option to set up the frequency of a recurring event. That event will then be displayed within your calendar at the selected frequency.

- **Invitees**   Tap this option and then fill in the To field with the names or e-mail addresses of people you'd like to invite to the event via e-mail. If the invitees have entries in your Contacts database, type their names. Otherwise, manually enter each person's e-mail address. Tap the Done button after you've entered the desired invitees. The Calendar app will then send to those people an e-mail that includes all of the event details you're currently entering into the Calendar app. The invitees will have the option to RSVP, plus import the event information into the Calendar app they have running on their Mac or iOS mobile device (or compatible scheduling software/app).

- **Alert**   For each event, you can create up to two audible alarms for it by tapping the Alert option. In the Event Alert menu (shown in Figure 13-8) that's displayed, you can set an alarm for one of these time periods: At Time Of Event, 5 Minutes Before, 15 Minutes Before, 30 Minutes Before, 1 Hour Before, 2 Hours Before, 1 Day Before, or 2 Days Before. The default selection is None, meaning that

FIGURE 13-8 You can associate one or two alarms with each event from the Event Alert menu.

no alarm will be associated with the event. Tap the Done button to save this information and return to the Add Event screen.

To create a second audible alarm, tap on the Second Alert button after the first alarm is created. Next, from the Event Alert menu, follow the same steps as used to create the first alarm. Be sure to tap the Done button to save your changes.

- **Calendar**   If you're managing multiple calendars using the Calendar app, such as a Personal calendar and a Work calendar, tap the Calendar option to determine which calendar the event you're creating will be associated with. Each calendar you manage using the Calendar app is automatically color-coded.
- **Availability**   Tap this option to choose how you'll be listed during the blocked-out time period for the event. The options are Busy or Free.
- **URL**   If there's a webpage associated with the event, enter it in the URL field. Then, when you view the event, you can tap the URL to launch Safari and view the webpage.
- **Notes**   Tap the Notes field to enter text-based notes associated with the event. You can include as many notes for each event as you desire.

As soon as you're done entering all of the relevant event information, you must tap the Done button in the top-right corner of the screen to save the event information and incorporate it into your schedule.

Once you tap the Done button after entering all of the relevant information for an event, the event is stored in the Calendar app and becomes visible when using any of the various calendar views. If you have Calendar set up to sync with iCloud, as soon as you tap the Done button (assuming your iPhone has access to the Internet), the newly created event is uploaded to iCloud and synced with your scheduling data "in the cloud," meaning it is also synced with your primary computer(s) and other iOS mobile devices connected to the same iCloud account.

 As you're viewing the List, Day, or Month calendar view, tap the Invitations icon near the bottom-right corner of the screen to see if you've been invited to participate in other people's events; if you have, you can RSVP and add those events to your calendar. The option only appears if you have your iPhone set up to share Calendar app–related information with iCloud, Microsoft Exchange, or a CalDAV-compatible scheduling application (from Google or Yahoo!, or example).

View, Edit, and Delete Events

From the List, Day, or Month calendar view, tap any event listing to view the Event Details screen for that event (shown in Figure 13-9). As you're viewing an Event Details screen, tap the Edit button in the upper-right corner to edit that event, to add information to or delete information from each field, or to change the date/times and/or alerts associated with it.

To delete an event, on the Event Details screen, tap the Edit button, scroll down to the bottom of the Edit screen, and then tap the Delete Event button. This will delete the event information from your iPhone and from all of the computers and devices the Calendar app syncs data with, so proceed with caution.

Access Calendar Information Using Siri

The iPhone's Siri feature is fully integrated with the Calendar app. For example, using Siri, you can create new events or look up existing events through your voice commands. To schedule a new event, activate Siri and say one of the following:

- "Set up a meeting today at [insert time] with [insert name] at [insert location]."
- "New appointment with [insert name] at [insert time] on [insert day or date]."
- "Schedule a meeting for [insert day and time] with [insert name] at [insert location]."

Using Siri, you can also look up Calendar-related information. For example, you can active Siri and say something like the following:

FIGURE 13-9 Tap any event listing to view the Event Details screen for that event.

- "When is my next meeting?"
- "Where is my next meeting?"
- "When is my meeting with [insert name]?"
- "What does the rest of my day look like?"
- "What's on my calendar for [insert day or date]?"

 Using Siri, you can also cancel or reschedule meetings.

Set Up the Calendar App to Work with the Notification Center

As you begin using the Calendar app, you can set it up to work with the Notification Center so that upcoming appointments appear in the Notification Center screen.

You can also set up separate Banners or Alerts to be displayed on the iPhone's screen in conjunction with each event, plus set up custom alarms in conjunction with the Calendar app.

 Setting up the Reminders app to work with the Notification Center is done using the same steps discussed here in reference to the Calendar app.

Setting up the Calendar app to work with the Notification Center only needs to be done once. To do this, launch Settings and tap the Notifications option. Scroll down to the Calendar listing and tap it.

On the Calendar screen (shown in Figure 13-10), if you want information about events to be displayed in the Notification Center screen, turn on the Notification Center virtual switch, and then tap the Show option to determine how many Calendar app events should be listed in the Notification Center screen at any given time. (Your options include 1, 5, or 10 items.)

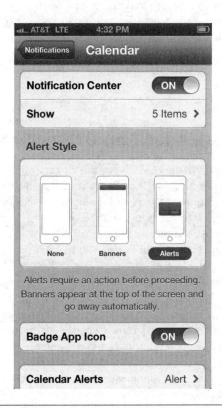

FIGURE 13-10   Decide how the Calendar app will interact with the Notification Center from within Settings.

Next, if you also want each event to be displayed in the form of a Banner or Alert, tap the appropriate option under the Alert Style heading. This can be done in addition to or instead of having events listed in the Notification Center screen.

 To have just a Banner or Alert displayed on the screen, without having Calendar-related information displayed in the Notification Center screen, turn off the Notification Center virtual switch and then adjust the Alert Style option.

Also on the Calendar screen, you can tap the Badge App Icon virtual switch to adjust whether or not Badge app icons appear on the Calendar app icon that's displayed on the iPhone's Home screen in conjunction with upcoming events.

It's also possible to set up a custom sound for alarms generated by the Calendar app. Do this by tapping the Calendar Alerts option and selecting an audible alarm from the menu. Next, decide if you want Calendar-related information (Banners, Alerts, and/or Alarms) to be displayed on the Lock screen by turning on or off the View In Lock Screen virtual switch.

 In addition to custom configuring how the Notification Center works with the Calendar app, from Settings, you can also adjust other Calendar app–specific settings. To do this, launch Settings, tap the Mail, Contacts, Calendars option, and then scroll down to the Calendars heading. Adjust any of the options listed on the Mail, Contacts, Calendars screen.

Did You Know?

The Calendar App Offers Time Zone Support

If you travel frequently, one of the customizable settings related to the Calendar app that you'll probably want to adjust is Time Zone Support, which you access from Settings by tapping the Mail, Contacts, Calendar option. When Time Zone Support is turned off, your events are always displayed based on the time zone of your current location. When Time Zone Support is turned on, however, all of your events will be displayed based on the time zone you manually select.

For example, if you're in New York City and you create an appointment for 3 P.M. (EST) and associate an alarm with it, but then travel to Los Angeles, which is in a time zone that's three hours earlier, when the Time Zone Support feature is turned off, the alarm for that appointment will be generated at noon (California time), which is 3 P.M. (East Coast time). If you turn on Time Zone Support and manually set the iPhone's Time Zone for Los Angeles, that same alarm will be generated at 3 P.M. California time (6 P.M. New York Time).

Create and Manage To-Do Lists Using the Reminders App

The Reminders app that comes preinstalled on the iPhone 5 works in much the same way as the Calendar app in terms of how it syncs app-specific data with iCloud, works with Siri, and also works seamlessly with the Notification Center. This app, however, is designed to help you manage one or more detailed to-do lists.

What's nice about this app is that you can create and manage multiple to-do lists, each with its own name. Each list can have as many individual to-do items as you deem necessary, and if you wish, each item can have a date and time alarm and/or a location-based alarm associated with it. This gives you a tremendous amount of flexibility to use this app for a variety of purposes that are conducive to maintaining lists.

 The Reminders app on the iPhone can sync with the Reminders app on your Mac (running OS X Mountain Lion), the Reminders app on your iPad, and/or the online-based Reminders app you can access by visiting www.iCloud.com (and logging in using your iCloud/Apple ID username and password). The app is also compatible with other list management software and online-based applications that you may be running on your primary computer or other mobile devices.

On the iPhone 5, the Reminders app utilizes three main screens:

- **Lists screen**   This screen (shown in Figure 13-11) allows you to create, edit, delete, and organize separate to-do lists within the app.
- **Named List screen**   When you tap any listing for a list in the Lists screen, you can view that specific list on a separate screen (shown in Figure 13-12). The name of the specific list, such as Reminders or Grocery List, will be displayed at the top of the screen.

 As you're looking at a list in the List screen, to return to the Lists screen, tap the List icon in the upper-left corner of the screen. It looks like three horizontal lines.

- **Details screen**   Each to-do list is composed of separate to-do list items. When you tap a specific item within a list, all the details pertaining to that item are displayed on the Details screen (shown in Figure 13-13). It's from here you can set up a date/time alarm or a location-based alarm for that item, set a priority level for the item, select which list an item will be included in, and add text-based notes to an item.

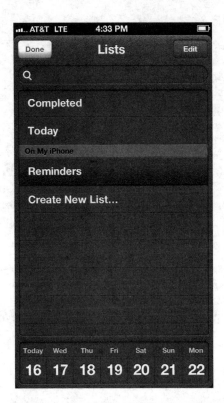

FIGURE 13-11 The Lists screen of the Reminders app shows each individual list you've created.

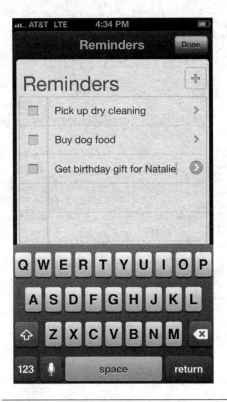

FIGURE 13-12 The Named List screen allows you to display the contents of one list.

View, Search, Create, Edit, or Delete a List

The Lists screen (refer to Figure 13-11) in the Reminders app displays a list of all your lists and enables you to view, search, edit, and delete those lists and create new lists.

Under the title of the Lists screen is a Search field. Use it to search the contents of your lists to find specific information quickly.

Below the Search field is the Completed list. Whenever you add a check mark to a check box that's associated with any item within a list, that item will be added to the master Completed list. To view your Completed list, tap this option.

Displayed below the Completed list option is the Today option. Use this to create and view a separate list that's associated with a specific day or date. When you tap the Today option, you'll be able to create or view a list associated with the current day. However, at the bottom of the Lists screen, you can scroll horizontally through the date listings to switch to a different date and view, or create a list that's associated with a selected date.

FIGURE 13-13   View and edit details pertaining to a specific item within a list by viewing that item's Details screen.

Any other lists you create (either on the iPhone or on a computer or device you're syncing Reminders data with) will be listed below the Today option on the Lists screen. Tap one of these listings, if applicable, to view the items that make up that list.

To create a new list from scratch, tap the Create New List option. The virtual keyboard will be displayed, and you'll be prompted to enter a custom title for the list (shown in Figure 13-14). Input the title, and then tap the Done button. When you're ready to begin populating the list with items, tap the list name.

To delete a list from the Lists screen, swipe your finger from left to right across its listing, and then tap the Delete button. Or, tap the Edit button, and then tap the negative sign icon displayed to the left of the name of the list that you want to delete (shown in Figure 13-15).

When you delete a list, all reminders and alerts that are associated with specific items within that list also get deleted.

FIGURE 13-14 When you create a new list, you'll need to give it a title. Here, the new list called Grocery List is being created.

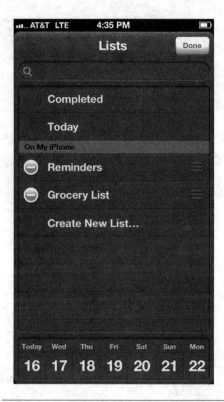

FIGURE 13-15 When viewing the Lists screen, tap the Edit button to edit or rearrange the list, or delete entire lists from the Reminders app.

To rearrange the order in which the lists are displayed on the Lists screen, tap the Edit button, place your finger on the Move icon (three horizontal lines, as shown in Figure 13-15) to the right of a list name, and drag the list up or down to the desired position within the list of lists.

Remember, anytime you make changes to a list within Reminders, if you have the app set up to sync with iCloud, those changes almost immediately impact the data stored in all versions of the Reminders app that are linked to the same iCloud account.

Manage and View a Specific List

After you have created a list from the Lists screen, tap the list to view it, edit it, or populate it with items. The List screen will be displayed. It looks like a lined virtual notepad. At the top of the screen, the title of the list is displayed.

To add the first item to a list, tap the plus sign icon near the top-right corner of the screen (refer to Figure 13-12), or tap the first line at the top of the virtual notepad. An empty check box appears in the left margin, and the iPhone's virtual keyboard is displayed. Create the item to be added to the list. For example, if you're creating a grocery list, you might type "Milk." Or, if you're creating the day's To-Do list, you could type, for example, "Pick up dry cleaning."

Once the item is entered, you have two options. You can tap the Return button, which moves the cursor to a new line on your list and allows you to add another item. Your other option is to tap the right-pointing arrow icon to the right of the item you just created in order to access the Details screen for that item.

 To erase one item at a time from your list (without completing it), swipe your finger from left to right across the item and then tap the Delete button to confirm your decision.

As you're looking at your to-do list, as you complete an item, tap the empty check box icon. A check mark will appear in the check box and, at the same time, the item will be added to your master Completed list.

 When viewing a List screen, to return to the Lists screen, tap the icon in the upper-left corner that looks like three horizontal lines.

If you tap the Edit button while you're looking at a List screen, you can delete items from the list by tapping the negative sign icon to the left of each item. You can also rearrange your list by holding your finger on the Move icon to the right of one item at a time and moving it up or down the list. Tap the Done button when you're finished editing your list.

Did You Know?

Reminders Works with Siri

Keep in mind, one of the easiest ways to add new items to a list is to use Siri. To do this, activate Siri and begin your command by saying "Remind me..." or "Add..." Here are a few examples:

- "Remind me to pick up my dry cleaning today at 2 P.M."
- "Remind me to feed the dog when I get home."
- "Add [insert item] to my [insert list title] list." (For example, say, "Add milk to my Grocery list.")

For more information about how to use Siri with the Reminders app (or in conjunction with any compatible app), refer to Chapter 2.

Customize Each To-Do Item in a List from Its Details Screen

As you're viewing a list in the List screen, tap the right-pointing arrow icon to the right of any item to view the Details screen for that item. On the Details screen, you can set a date/time alarm or a location-based alarm, set a priority for the item, associate the item with a specific list, and add notes to an item.

 On the Details screen, you can delete the item by tapping the Delete button near the bottom of the screen.

Create a Date/Time Alarm for a List Item

To set a date/time alarm for an item, on the Details screen, turn on the Remind Me On A Day virtual switch. Two additional fields will appear on the Details screen. The first lists a date and time. Tap this field to set the date and time you want to associate with the item (shown in Figure 13-16). Use the Date, Hour, Minute, and AM/PM dials to set the alert time for this item.

FIGURE 13-16 Set a date/time alarm for a list item in the Details screen.

Then, if you want the item to have a recurring alarm associated with it, tap the Repeat option and select Everyday, Every Week, Every 2 Weeks, Every Month, or Every Year. The default selection for the Repeat option is Never, meaning that it is nonrecurring.

Once an alarm has been associated with the item, tap the Done button to save your changes. At the appropriate time, an alarm will be generated in conjunction with that item. Based on how you've set up the Reminders app to work with the Notification Center, an alarm will sound, plus details about that item will appear within the Notification Center screen and/or be displayed on the iPhone's screen in the form of a Banner or Alert. Details about the alert you set will be displayed just below the item on the List screen.

See the section "Set Up the Calendar App to Work with the Notification Center," earlier in the chapter, for more information about adjusting how the Reminders app can work with the Notification Center on your iPhone. You can also refer to Chapter 3.

Create a Location-Based Alarm for a List Item

One feature that's offered in the iPhone edition of the Reminders app that's not available in the iPad version, for example, is the ability to create location-based alerts for individual list items. Using the Location Services feature of your iPhone, the Reminders app keeps tabs on where you are geographically. This enables Reminders to alert you when you arrive at or depart from a particular location when you set up location-based alerts and associate them with particular items on a list.

For example, if you have a list of phone calls you need to make today, you can set up Reminders to display that list when you arrive at your office. To do this, you only need to associate the first item on your Today's Calls list with a location-based alert. Similarly, if you've created a grocery list with the Reminders app, you can set it up so the list appears when you arrive at your favorite supermarket.

To set up a location-based alert for a specific list item, launch the Reminders app, select a list, and then tap the right-arrow icon to the right of a specific list item to view that item's Details screen. On the item's Details screen, turn on the Remind Me At A Location virtual switch (refer to Figure 13-16). Three new fields will be displayed.

In the first field, select or enter the location you want to associate with that alarm, such as your Home or Work address, or the location of your supermarket. Next, tap either the When I Leave or When I Arrive field to select one of them. This will determine whether the alarm will be generated when you first get to the selected location or when you leave that location. Tap the Done button to save your changes. Details about the alert you set will be displayed just below the item on the List screen.

For this feature to work, you must turn on both the master Location Services option for your iPhone and the Location Services option for the Reminders app. To do this, launch Settings, tap the Privacy option, and select the Location Services option. Turn on the master Location Services virtual switch, and then scroll down on the Location Services screen and turn on the Reminders virtual switch.

Set a Priority for an Item

In addition to setting an alarm in conjunction with an item, you can associate a priority with it. To do this, tap the Show More option on an item's Details screen. Tap the Priority option, and select between the None, Low, Medium, and High options. Tap the Done button once you've made your selection.

Now, when you look at that item on your list, it will have between zero and three red exclamation points associated with it. If applicable, they're displayed to the immediate left of the item (shown in Figure 13-17). One exclamation point (!) means Low priority, two exclamation points (!!) means Medium priority, and three exclamation points (!!!) means High priority.

Add an Item to a Specific List (or Move an Item Between Lists)

As you're looking at the Details screen for a particular item, you can reassign that item to a different list by tapping the Show More option and then tapping the List option. Each of the lists currently stored in the Reminders app will be displayed. Select the one you want to assign this particular item to, and then tap the Done button.

FIGURE 13-17 When you give a list item a Low, Medium, or High priority, it's displayed with one, two, or three exclamation points as you view a list.

If you don't assign an item to a list, it will be placed into the default list you associate with the Reminders app. To set the default list once, launch Settings, tap the Reminders option, tap the Default List option on the Reminder screen, and then make your selection.

Add Notes to an Item

Also from the Details screen for an item, if you tap the Show More option and then tap the Notes field, you can attach text-based notes to that item. Your notes can be as long and as detailed as you deem appropriate. You can enter your notes using the virtual keyboard, or you can tap the Dictation key to dictate your notes into the app. When you're done adding notes to an item, tap the Done button to save your changes.

Compose, View, Organize, and Share Text-Based Memos Using the Notes App

If you want or need a full-featured word processor on your iPhone 5 that allows you to access or create Microsoft Word–compatible documents, sync those documents with your primary computer and/or other iOS devices, and/or share those documents with other people (via e-mail, for example), you'll want to download and install the optional Pages app ($9.99) or one of the other full-featured word processors for the iPhone that are available from the App Store, such as Documents To Go Premium – Office Suite ($16.99) or QuickOffice Pro ($14.99).

Depending on your note taking needs, you may find the extremely popular Evernote app (free) to be a worthwhile edition to your app library. You'll learn more about Evernote in Chapter 20.

Useful Features of the Notes App

The Notes app that comes bundled with your iPhone 5 is a basic text editor. It allows you to compose, organize, and share notes. It serves as a virtual notepad. Some of the useful features of this app are:

- When you create a note, you can give it a custom name, plus the date and time it was created is automatically associated with it.
- You can use the virtual keyboard to type your note, or use the iPhone's Dictation feature to speak your notes and have the app translate what you say into text.
- The Notes app can store as many separate notes as you need, each of which becomes searchable using the Spotlight Search feature or using the Search field within the Notes app.
- You can set up the Notes app to automatically sync with iCloud. A fully compatible version of the Notes app comes on the Mac (running OS X Mountain Lion), plus you can access the online edition of Notes by visiting www.iCloud.

com. Your app-specific data can also sync with your other iOS mobile devices (via iCloud) or with your online-based Google, Yahoo!, or Microsoft Exchange accounts. How to set up this feature is covered in Chapter 4.

- Using the Share feature built into the app, you can share individual notes with specific people via e-mail or text/instant message.
- If you have an AirPrint-compatible printer linked to your iPhone, you can use the Print command to print individual notes.
- The Notes app works with the Select, Select All, Cut, Copy, and Paste features built into iOS 6, so you can move text around within the Notes app, or between two apps. For example, you can copy a paragraph of text from a webpage and paste it into a note.

When you launch the Notes app for the first time, what you'll see is a blank, yellow-lined virtual notepad displayed on the screen, with the heading Notes at the top (shown in Figure 13-18). Once you begin to populate the Notes app with notes, the Search field is displayed near the top center of the screen. You can then use this Search field as one way to locate and view specific content stored within the app.

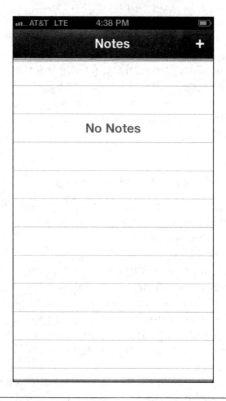

FIGURE 13-18 The Notes app starts off as an empty virtual notepad that you can then populate by composing separate notes.

If you have iCloud functionality turned on for this app, tap the Accounts button to view all accounts or specific accounts that are set up in conjunction with the Notes app through iCloud, or one or more of the compatible online-based services you use for e-mail, contact management, and scheduling (such as AOL, Google, Yahoo!, or Microsoft Exchange).

Create a New Note from Scratch

To create a new note from scratch, tap the plus sign icon in the top-right corner of the screen. The New Note heading will appear, along with the date and time. Use the virtual keyboard (or the Dictation feature) to compose your text-based note. The first line you type into the Note becomes its title/heading. (In Figure 13-19, the first line of the note says Sample, so that becomes the note's title/heading.) So, to create a unique heading or title for a note, enter it into the first line of the note and tap the Return key.

When you're done composing your note, tap the Done button (in the upper-right corner) to save that note.

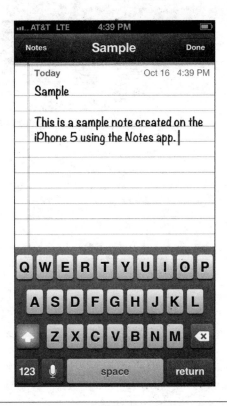

FIGURE 13-19 Compose a new note on the New Note screen. Tap the Done button when you're done entering text into that note.

The Notes app works on the iPhone in portrait or landscape mode. When it comes to typing on the virtual keyboard, you may find it easier to use landscape mode, because the onscreen keys are slightly larger. You also have the option of using an optional, external keyboard with your iPhone to help improve your typing speed and accuracy.

Once you tap the Done button, the virtual keyboard will disappear and four command icons will be displayed at the bottom of the Notes screen (as you're viewing the note you just created). These buttons are shown in Figure 13-20. Tap the left- or right-pointing arrow icon to move back or forward by one page in your virtual notebook.

Tap the Share button to share that specific note with one or more other people via e-mail or text/instant message (using the Messages app). From the Share menu, you can also print the note or copy the contents of the note into your iPhone's virtual clipboard. To delete the note, tap the trashcan icon.

After you have created one or more separate notes, tap the Notes icon in the upper-left corner of the screen to return to the main Notes screen, which displays

FIGURE 13-20   After tapping the Done button when editing a note, four command icons are displayed near the bottom of the screen.

a list of all your notes. From this list, you can tap any note to view it, or swipe your finger from left to right across a note's listing to delete it.

As soon as you tap the Done button after creating a new note, or once you delete a note from the Notes list, that change is reflected almost immediately on any computer(s) or devices that your Notes app is syncing data with.

Managing Your Notes

As you'll discover, the Notes app offers an easy and quick solution for composing text-based notes that you can then view, edit, print, organize, archive, and/or share with other people. From within Settings, you can switch between three default fonts that your notes will be displayed using. You can't switch between fonts within individual notes or from within the Notes app itself.

To change the default font, which impacts all notes created using the Notes app, launch Settings and tap the Notes option. Under the Font heading, choose between the Noteworthy, Helvetica, or Marker Felt font.

Anytime you're viewing a note in the Notes app, if you place your finger on a word and hold it there for a second or two, a menu will appear above that word, giving you access to the Select, Select All, Copy, Cut, and Paste options. Tap the right-pointing arrow icon to the right of this menu to reveal additional options, including Suggest and Define. Suggest will recommend the correct spelling for an incorrectly spelled word, while the Define option will allow you to look up the definition of that word using the iPhone's built-in dictionary.

Another option for correcting a misspelled word is to tap a word that is underlined with a red-dotted line (meaning the word is not in the iPhone's built-in dictionary). You will be shown potential, correctly spelled replacements.

The right-pointing arrow that gives you access to the Suggest and Define options is only available if you have the Auto-Correction and/or Spell Check feature turned on from within Settings. To do this, launch Settings, tap the General option, and then select the Keyboard option. Turn on the virtual switch that's associated with Auto-Capitalization, Auto-Correction, Spell Checking, and/or Enable Caps Lock. You can also set up keyboard shortcuts, which can be a handy feature when composing notes in which you often use the same phrases, sentences, or even paragraphs of text.

As with most apps that utilize the virtual keyboard, if you place and hold your finger on specific keys, alternate letters or symbols for that key are made available to you.

14

Communicate Using Video Conferencing and Text Messaging

HOW TO...

- Use FaceTime for video conferencing
- Use iMessage to send and receive text and instant messages
- Use other text/instant messaging and video conferencing options using your iPhone

A few years back, Apple's decision to add a front-facing camera to the iPhone made it possible for the device to be used for video conferencing. So, instead of just talking to someone using your smartphone, you could see and hear them, in full color, using the FaceTime app in conjunction with Apple's FaceTime service and the Internet.

Using Apple's FaceTime service, you can participate in a real-time video conference with anyone who is using a Mac, iPhone, iPad, iPad mini, or iPod touch, who is also a FaceTime user, and who has their computer or device connected to the Internet. As an iPhone user, your phone number serves as your unique FaceTime identifier (username). However, as you'll learn shortly, you can also set up an e-mail address or your Apple ID to be your FaceTime identifier.

Prior to the release of iOS 6, using FaceTime required a Wi-Fi Internet connection. Now, some wireless service providers allow FaceTime to be used with a 3G/4G Internet connection. Keep in mind, though, that using your iPhone for video conferencing via 3G/4G requires a tremendous amount of wireless data usage, so if you have a monthly wireless data allocation, you're better off using FaceTime with Wi-Fi, or else you could see your wireless phone bill increase significantly due to usage overages.

What's great about using FaceTime is that this app comes preinstalled with iOS 6 and is fully integrated into the Phone and Contacts apps. Participating in FaceTime video conferences via Wi-Fi is also free (unless you have an unlimited 3G/4G wireless data plan). There are no restrictions as to how often you can use the FaceTime service, nor are there limits as to how long each call can be. The service is even free if you're video conferencing from the United States with people outside the country, or if you're traveling abroad, connect to a Wi-Fi hotspot, and choose to call back to the United States.

Beyond using FaceTime on your iPhone 5 to participate in real-time video conferences, you can also use other free and fee-based apps and services, like Skype, ooVoo, FriendCaller, GoToMeeting, and many others, for video conferencing via the Internet.

In addition to using your iPhone 5 for video conferencing, as an actual phone to make and receive calls (see Chapter 7), and to send and receive e-mail (see Chapter 9), another way you can efficiently communicate with other people with your iPhone is to use text messaging or instant messaging. For this, you can use the Messages app with Apple's own iMessage service. Or, you can use Messages with the text messaging service that's part of your wireless service plan (from AT&T Wireless, Verizon Wireless, or Sprint PCS, for example).

As you'll discover shortly, when it comes to instant messaging, you have a wide range of options in terms of services you can use, such as iMessage, AIM, Facebook Chat, Yahoo! Messenger, Google Chat, Skype, and Microsoft Messenger, to name just a few. From the App Store, you'll discover proprietary apps for each of these services, plus third-party apps that allow you to connect and interact on several of these services at once.

 Even if you're using Siri in conjunction with the Messages app, do not even consider texting or instant messaging while driving! Not only is this against the law in many states, it's also extremely dangerous, and could result in a potentially fatal accident. Likewise, refrain from sending or reading text/instant messages while walking across a street, or when engaging in other activities that require your total attention.

Use FaceTime for Video Conferencing

While FaceTime on the Mac or iPad requires a stand-alone app, on the iPhone 5, FaceTime functionality is built into the Phone app. So, once you set up your free FaceTime account, as long as your iPhone is turned on and able to connect to the Internet via Wi-Fi (or, in some cases, using a 3G/4G connection, depending on your wireless service provider), you can make and receive FaceTime calls (and participate in real-time video conferences).

To activate FaceTime on your iPhone, launch Settings and tap the FaceTime option. On the FaceTime screen, turn on the FaceTime virtual switch (as shown in Figure 14-1). Then, set up a free FaceTime account using your Apple ID. To do this, tap the Use Your Apple ID For FaceTime button.

You'll then be prompted to enter your existing Apple ID username and password. However, you can also create a new Apple ID by tapping the Create New Apple ID

FIGURE 14-1   Turn on the main FaceTime app using the FaceTime virtual switch. You can then customize a handful of settings on this screen.

option. Once you've entered your username and password, tap the Sign In button to continue.

A screen that lists your iPhone's phone number and Apple ID/iCloud-related e-mail address is displayed. Currently, you can use either of these as your unique FaceTime identifier, which is basically your phone number for using the FaceTime service. Your identifier is also how other people can find and contact you on the FaceTime service.

 At this point, you can associate one or more additional, preexisting e-mail addresses to work as your FaceTime identifier. To do this from the FaceTime screen, tap the Add An Email option and follow the onscreen prompts.

FaceTime is now ready to be used on your iPhone 5 via the Phone app. So, to begin using it, first launch the Phone app from the Home screen. In order to connect with another FaceTime user, you need to know either their iPhone phone number or their unique FaceTime identifier (the Apple ID or e-mail address that person used to set up and log in to the FaceTime service). If you don't have this information, you'll need to obtain it from the person you want to participate in a FaceTime call with. Once you know their FaceTime username (or phone number), making a FaceTime connection is easy.

Tip As you're creating or updating your individual entries in the Contacts app, be sure to properly label each person's iPhone phone number, if you know they use an iPhone. As you enter their mobile number, tap the blue label associated with that field. Instead of choosing the Mobile label, choose the iPhone label.

Accept FaceTime Calls

At this point, you can receive and accept a FaceTime call from another FaceTime user who knows your iPhone's phone number, your Apple ID, or the e-mail address that's linked to your FaceTime account. When someone else initiates a FaceTime call to you, an Incoming Call screen is displayed on your iPhone. This is very similar to what happens when you receive a regular phone call on your iPhone.

Answer a FaceTime Call While Your iPhone Is Active

When you receive an incoming FaceTime call, if you're using your iPhone for something else, or it's turned on and the Home screen is displayed, whatever was displayed on the iPhone's screen will be replaced by FaceTime's Incoming Call screen (shown in Figure 14-2). It displays the caller's name, phone number, or FaceTime e-mail address, along with a message that says, "[Insert name/phone number] would like FaceTime..."

Note In some of the figures in this chapter, "stock photos" are used for demonstration purposes. When you actually use FaceTime on your iPhone, what you'll see is live video of yourself (in the small video window) and the person you're communicating with (in the main area of the screen).

You see at the bottom of the screen the familiar red and white Decline button and green and white Accept button that are displayed when you receive an incoming telephone call, but the icon on the buttons now shows a video camera instead of a telephone, indicating that you're receiving a FaceTime call rather than a traditional phone call. A separate video camera icon (this one with a line through it) also appears to the right of these buttons.

Tap the Decline button to reject the incoming FaceTime call. A listing for that call will appear in the Recents list of the Phone app, and the caller will receive a message stating you're unavailable. Tap the Accept button to launch FaceTime and initiate a video conference with the caller.

If you flick the video camera icon (to the right of the Accept button) upward with your finger, the Reply With Message and Remind Me Later buttons are displayed (shown in Figure 14-3). These work exactly how they do when using the Phone app (refer to "Manage Incoming Calls Using New iOS 6 Features" in Chapter 7).

Incoming caller name

Call recipient

FIGURE 14-2   The Incoming Call screen for a FaceTime call from someone who has an entry in the iPhone's Contacts database (Rusty Rich). This is what you see if the call is received while your iPhone is in use (not in Sleep mode).

Answer a FaceTime Call While Your iPhone Is Locked and in Sleep Mode

If your iPhone is locked and in Sleep mode when you receive a FaceTime call, the iPhone will wake up automatically. To answer the call and activate FaceTime, swipe your finger from left to right along the Slide To Answer slider. To access the Decline, Accept, Reply With Message, or Remind Me Later buttons, flick your finger upward on the video camera icon next to the slider. As you can see in Figure 14-4, the Lock screen for an incoming FaceTime call looks a bit different from the Lock screen for an incoming telephone call (see Figure 7-9, for example).

Initiate a FaceTime Call

If you want to have a video conference with someone via FaceTime, it's as easy as making a regular phone call if you know their iPhone phone number or Apple ID/e-mail address (whichever they used to set up their FaceTime account).

FIGURE 14-3   Instead of answering a call, you can send the caller a text message using the Reply With Message feature, or tap the Remind Me Later button to set a reminder for yourself to call the person back.

The easiest thing to do is to create a Contacts entry for the person you want to FaceTime with, and include in their entry their properly labeled iPhone phone number or FaceTime e-mail address. Then, from the Phone app, tap the Contacts option, locate that person's Contacts entry in the All Contacts screen, and take a look at the FaceTime button that appears near the bottom of their entry (Info screen). If the person is currently able to receive FaceTime calls, a tiny video camera icon appears in the FaceTime button. Tap the FaceTime button, and FaceTime will launch and attempt to initiate a call with that person.

 If you attempt to initiate a FaceTime call with someone who can't receive FaceTime calls, you'll receive an error message on your iPhone's screen.

Initiate a FaceTime Call via Your Favorites List

Here's just one of the ways to set up a Favorites listing. Begin by launching the Phone app and tapping the Contacts option. On the All Contacts screen, locate and tap the

FIGURE 14-4   If someone calls you via FaceTime while your iPhone is in Sleep mode, the phone will wake up and display this incoming FaceTime call information on the Lock screen.

Did You Know?

On Your iPhone, Your FaceTime and Phone App Favorites and Recents Lists Are the Same

On the Mac or iPad, the FaceTime app has its own Favorites list and Recents list. On the iPhone, however, your Favorites and Recents lists that are associated with the Phone app also work with FaceTime.

Thus, from within the Phone app, you can set up a Favorites listing for a contact and associate their FaceTime number, Apple ID, or e-mail address with that listing. Then, in the future, when you access your personalized Favorites list, you can initiate a FaceTime call to that person with a single tap on their Favorites listing.

person's entry. Scroll down to the bottom of that entry (Info screen) and tap the Add To Favorites button. When the Add To Favorites menu appears, tap the displayed iPhone phone number or e-mail address that the person has associated with their FaceTime account. (You'll need to obtain this information directly from the contact if you don't already have it.) Tap that listing.

 Note Keep in mind, each listing within your Favorites list can be associated with only one phone number, e-mail address, or Apple ID. But, you can have two or more listings within your Favorites list for the same person/contact (i.e., one for their home, work, mobile, and/or FaceTime phone number and/or address).

That person, along with their FaceTime contact details, will be added to your Favorites list. Tap the Favorites option at the bottom of the Phone app's screen to view it. Unlike your other Phone app Favorites listings, a tiny video camera icon appears to the right of the newly created Favorites listing, indicating it's for FaceTime. Now, anytime you and the other person are both active on the FaceTime service, you can initiate a FaceTime call to that person with a single tap.

A third way to initiate a FaceTime call is via the Recents list. When you access the Recents list in the Phone app, you'll notice that all FaceTime calls made and received (as well as missed FaceTime calls) are also listed, with a tiny video camera icon displayed below the person's name or phone number. To reconnect with that person via FaceTime, tap their Recents listing. FaceTime will launch and attempt to initiate a FaceTime call with that person.

Yet another way to initiate a FaceTime call to someone is from the Messages app. If a person you've corresponded with in the past has an active FaceTime account, you can launch Messages, tap their previous text/instant message conversation, scroll to the top of the screen, and then tap the FaceTime button that's displayed.

Using Siri, you can initiate a FaceTime call with someone in your Contacts database, if the other person is available, by activating Siri and saying, "FaceTime with [insert name]."

Participate in a FaceTime Call

Once a FaceTime call is established, your iPhone's screen shows a video window of the person you're video conferencing with. In the upper-right corner of the display, you'll see a thumbnail video window that displays your video feed (shown in Figure 14-5), which is captured by the front-facing camera on your iPhone. If you're looking into your iPhone's camera, you should see your face in this thumbnail video window. This is what the other person is seeing in their primary video window.

 Tip Use your finger to drag your video thumbnail window to any corner of the iPhone's screen.

FIGURE 14-5   A FaceTime call in progress. Your image appears in the small thumbnail video window, and the person you're talking to appears in the main area of the screen.

Displayed along the bottom of the FaceTime screen are three command icons. On the bottom left is the Mute icon. Tap it if you want to continue the video conference but temporarily turn off your iPhone's microphones. Thus, the person you're speaking with will be able to see you but not hear you. When the Mute button is active, it turns blue.

Displayed near the lower-right corner of the FaceTime screen is the camera selection button. Use it to instantly switch between the iPhone's front- and rear-facing cameras during a FaceTime conversation. Remember, whatever you see in the tiny video thumbnail window is the video feed you're transmitting, and it's what the other person is seeing, in real time.

 While engaged in a FaceTime call, you may want to switch from the rear-facing camera so the person you're chatting with can see whatever you're looking out at, such as your surroundings or the people you're with.

To end a FaceTime call, tap the End button near the bottom center of the FaceTime screen.

 When participating in a FaceTime call, you can hold the iPhone in portrait or landscape mode. In landscape mode, the command icons that are normally displayed along the bottom of the screen are relocated to the right margin of the screen.

While you're engaged in a FaceTime call, it's possible to use your iPhone 5's Multitasking capabilities to simultaneously use another app (see Chapter 3 for details about Multitasking mode). When you do this, you will continue broadcasting, but the person you're speaking with will only hear you, not see you, and you will only be

How to... **Experience the Best-Quality FaceTime Calls**

First and foremost, the quality of each FaceTime call you experience will be related directly to the speed and quality of the Internet connection you are sharing with the other person. However, there are a few things you can do to improve the picture and sound quality when participating in FaceTime calls:

- Position the primary light source in the room in front of you, so it lights up or shines on your face. Avoid having a bright light (such as window during daylight) directly behind you.
- Use a stand or tripod to position the iPhone on a table or flat surface so that it's eye level with you. (See the end of Chapter 11 for suggestions on shopping for a tripod.)
- If you opt to hold your iPhone during a FaceTime call, try to hold it as still as possible. Excessive movement or shaking will create a blurry image. Also, do not cover up the iPhone's built-in microphones with your fingers, or the person you're communicating with will hear muffled sounds.
- Try to be in a quiet room with little or no ambient noise. Turn off the television or radio. Your iPhone's microphone will pick up any noise in the area and transmit that along with your voice, making it difficult for others to hear you. Likewise, if you're outside, avoid wind noises.
- Consider using a wireless Bluetooth headset or the Apple EarPods that came with your iPhone 5. This can dramatically improve the audio quality of the conversation and remove some of the background noise in the room. Many Bluetooth headsets have noise-reduction built into the microphone and speaker.
- Use the Volume Up and Volume Down buttons on the side of your iPhone, or the volume controls on your EarPods, to adjust the volume of the person you're speaking with.

able to hear them. To return to the FaceTime app, tap the green bar that says "Touch To Resume FaceTime," displayed along the top of the screen. The two-way video conference will be reestablished.

 During a regular phone conversation using the Phone app, you can switch to a FaceTime call by tapping the FaceTime icon displayed on the Call In Progress screen, assuming the other party is using an iPhone and you're both able to connect to a Wi-Fi hotspot (or use FaceTime with your 3G/4G plan).

Use FaceTime Alternatives for Video Conferencing

The benefits to using FaceTime are that the app comes preinstalled on your iPhone, it's integrated with the Phone and Contacts apps, and it's always free to use. The main drawbacks to FaceTime are that you can participate in video conferences only with other Apple Mac, iPhone, iPad, or iPod touch users and, in many cases, a Wi-Fi Internet connection is required.

If you want to video conference with any other computer or mobile device users, consider installing the free Skype app onto your iPhone. This service allows for free Skype-to-Skype voice-over-IP or video conference calls using a Wi-Fi or 3G/4G connection. In addition to the Skype app for iOS mobile devices, there are also Skype apps for Android and other popular smartphones and tablets, as well as for the PC and Mac. Thus, you can freely communicate and video conference with just about anyone, not just Apple computer or device users.

Also available from the App Store are a handful of other apps that work with competing Internet-based video conferencing services, some of which are free, while others are fee based. GoToMeeting, for example, offers video conferencing features more suitable for business users, while ooVoo allows you to video conference with multiple people simultaneously. (By comparison, FaceTime allows you to video conference with only one person at a time.)

Many of the online social networks, like Facebook and Google+, and popular instant messaging services also offer video conferencing capabilities that can be used in conjunction with special apps running on your iPhone.

Use the Messages App for Text Messaging and Instant Messaging

Text messaging and instant messaging both allow you to communicate with other people using text-based messages. You type a message, tap Send, the messages appears on the other person's screen, and the recipient can reply immediately. This communication occurs in almost real time if both parties are actively participating; otherwise, after you send a message to someone, it will be waiting for them when they return to their phone, tablet, or computer (and vice versa).

Originally, instant messaging was an Internet-based technology that allowed people connected to the same instant messaging service to communicate using text-based messages in real time from their computers. Meanwhile, text messaging offered similar functionality, but was created to allow cell phone and smartphone users to communicate using text-based messages sent and received over a wireless service provider's cellular network.

While instant messaging via the Internet, through a service like AIM (AOL Instant Message), Facebook Chat, Yahoo! Messenger, Microsoft Messenger, or Google Talk, is free and unlimited, text messaging services (from a wireless service provider) are typically fee based. Your wireless service plan either includes a predetermined number of text messages that can be sent/received per month or charges you a small fee per message.

When you use instant messaging, you can typically only communicate with other people who use that service. However, when using text messaging, you can exchange messages with any other smartphone or cell phone, regardless of the phone's make and model or wireless service provider.

In recent years, text messaging and instant messaging capabilities have merged in many ways. From your iPhone, you can send and receive instant messages using an app for almost any popular instant messaging service, plus you can send and receive text messages through your wireless service provider.

Apple has blurred the text messaging and instant messaging line even more with the introduction of its Messages app and its own online-based iMessage service. Using iMessage, it's possible to send an unlimited number of instant messages to any other iMessage user via your iPhone. When your iPhone has access to the Internet via Wi-Fi, messages are sent and received via instant messaging automatically. However, if an online connection can't be established, iMessage defaults to using your wireless service provider's text messaging service.

iMessage allows you to communicate, for free, with other Mac, iPhone, iPad, or iPod touch users via a Wi-Fi Internet connection or a 3G/4G connection. This will not impact your text messaging allocation from your wireless service provider. However, if an Internet connection can't be established by iMessage, traditional cellular-based text messaging will be used to ensure your messages get sent and/or received.

When you use iMessage, you can send and receive photos, video clips, Contact entries, and other app-specific information when you use a compatible app's Share button and then choose the Message option. It's even possible to use the Messages app in conjunction with Siri to dictate your messages, or have Siri read your incoming messages. (See Chapter 3 for more information about using Siri.)

Using iMessage with the Messages app is always free, as long as you're using a Wi-Fi Internet connection with your iPhone. If you're using a 3G/4G Internet connection, this will utilize some of your monthly wireless data allocation.

As you're communicating using the Messages app, messages sent and received for free via Apple's iMessage network are always displayed within blue text bubbles. Meanwhile, messages sent and received using your wireless service provider's text messaging service are displayed within green text bubbles in the Message app.

Set Up the Messages App to Work with Apple's iMessage Service

Right out of the box, your iPhone's preinstalled Messages app is set up to work with your wireless service provider's text messaging service. If someone sends a text message to your iPhone by using your iPhone's phone number, it will be received and displayed using the Messages app. When this occurs, it will be counted as one message in your monthly text messaging allocation, which is part of your wireless service plan (through AT&T Wireless, Verizon Wireless, Sprint PCS, etc.).

 The Messages app can be fully integrated with the Notification Center. You can set it up so that incoming text messages are displayed as Banners or Alerts and/or within the Notification Center screen. You can also set up Messages to display a Badge on its Home screen app icon. To set this up, launch Settings, tap Notifications, and then tap the Messages option. Refer to Chapter 2 for more information about customizing the Notification Center to work with the Messages app.

Also right out of the box, you can send text messages to any other iPhone, cell phone, or smartphone in the world, regardless of the other phone's make or model or which wireless service provider it's connected to. To do this, launch the Messages app, tap the Compose Message icon in the upper-right corner of the Messages screen, fill in the To field with the intended recipient's mobile phone number, type the body of your text message (shown in Figure 14-6), and then tap the Send button. Within a few seconds, that message will be received by the recipient, as long as their phone is turned on. Otherwise, it will be displayed as soon as their phone reestablishes a connection with is its cellular network.

If you want to use Apple's free iMessage service with your iPhone (as well as your Mac and/or iPad), you first need to set up a free iMessage account, and then link the account to the Messages app on your iPhone. To do this, launch Settings and tap the Messages option. Turn on the iMessage virtual switch near the top of the screen. Then, tap the Use Your Apple ID For iMessage button. When prompted, enter your Apple ID and/or related password, and then tap the Sign In button. iMessage will link your iPhone's phone number and your Apple ID/iCloud-related e-mail address to your free iMessage account automatically.

At this point, anyone who also uses the iMessage service can enter your iPhone's phone number or Apple ID/iCloud e-mail address into the To field, type their message, and tap/click the Send button, and you will receive that message via iMessage on your iPhone through the Messages app.

FIGURE 14-6   This is what the Messages app screen looks like when you begin a
new text message or iMessage conversation.

From the Messages screen within Settings, you can set up additional e-mail
addresses from which you can send and receive instant messages via iMessage
(using the Messages app). To do this, tap the Send & Receive button. When the
iMessage screen is displayed, tap the Add Another Email option, and then enter
your preexisting e-mail address.

If you're sending a message via iMessage to another iPhone user, your iPhone's
phone number will be used as your identifier. Otherwise, if you're communicating
with a Mac, iPad, or iPod touch user, your iMessage-related e-mail address will be used
as your identifier.

Send and Receive Text/Instant Messages Using the Messages App

To start a new text/instant message conversation with someone, launch Messages and
tap the Compose Message button near the top-right corner of the screen. Fill in the To

field with one or more recipients, enter your message in the message field, and then tap the Send button to send your message. To add multiple people to the To field and send the same message to a group of people simultaneously, after you enter the first name, phone number, or e-mail address into the To field, tap the plus sign icon and enter an additional person's contact information. Repeat this process for each person you want to add. As you're filling in the To field, if the iPhone finds and displays a match to what you're entering from your Contacts database, you can tap that match. You can then immediately enter an additional recipient into the To field without tapping the plus sign icon.

If you want to send a photo or video clip with your message, tap the camera icon displayed to the left of the message field (refer to Figure 14-6). You are given two options. Tap the Take Photo Or Video option if you want to use one of the iPhone's built-in cameras to take a photo or video and then include it in your message. Tap the Choose Existing button to select a photo that's already stored on your iPhone (within the Photos app). You can send one photo or video at a time. After a small version of the image is loaded into the Messages screen, tap the Send button. You can include text with the photo or video clip. If someone sends you a photo, or you want to view a photo you sent in full-screen mode, tap the image thumbnail. You can then tap the Share button to share the photo using any of the Share options available.

Tip Many other iPhone core apps include a Share option that enables you to send app-specific content via text/instant message.

Once you're engaged in a conversation, the messages you send are displayed in text bubbles along the right margin of the screen. Whatever the other person types is displayed in separate text bubbles along the left margin of the screen (shown in Figure 14-7). If you're using iMessage to communicate via the Message app, you will be notified each time a message's recipient receives your latest message. Look for the word "Delivered" to be displayed below each outgoing message. This is shown in Figure 14-7, below the message "Hey, what's up?".

Displayed along the very top of each conversation dialog screen are several buttons, some of which vary depending on which options are available:

- **Messages**   Tap to return to the list of all message conversations you've participated in.
- **Edit**   Tap to delete or forward specific parts of your text-based exchange.
- **Call**   Tap to initiate a call to that person.
- **Email**   Tap to send an e-mail message to that person.
- **FaceTime**   Tap to initiate a FaceTime video conference with that person (if applicable).
- **Contact**   Tap to view that person's entry in your Contacts database (if applicable).
- **Add Contact**   Tap to add an entry for the person you're communicating with to your Contacts database.

FIGURE 14-7 A text/instant message conversation using the Messages app. The color of the text bubbles indicates whether you're using text messaging or iMessage, although they work seamlessly with each other.

As soon as you initiate a new conversation, the back-and-forth dialog that ensues will be stored in the Messages app until you delete it. Thus, you can return to a text-based conversation later, review what was discussed, and pick up where you left off, or forward parts of the message conversation to someone else by tapping the Edit button. A list of each conversation you've engaged in is displayed in a listing format in the Messages app. Tap a listing to reopen that conversation. Depending on how information is saved on your iPhone, each conversation listing will display either the person's name, phone number, or iMessage user name.

To forward parts of a text-based conversation to someone else, when viewing the conversation screen, tap on the Edit button that's displayed near the top-right corner. Tap on the elements of the conversation you want to select and forward. Then, tap on the Forward button that's displayed near the bottom-right corner of the screen. In the To field, enter the iMessage username(s), cell phone number(s), or names of the people you want to forward the message to and tap the Send button.

How to... **Communicate Using Abbreviations and Emoticons When Using Text/Instant Messaging**

With the fast-growing popularity of text/instant messaging, a new language has been devised that involves using abbreviations and emoticons to communicate. For example, instead of typing "Are you okay?" when sending a text message, it's perfectly acceptable to type "R U OK?"

There are many common text-based acronyms that are part of the text/instant message vernacular, such as BRB (Be Right Back), TTYL (Talk To You Later), and LOL (Laugh Out Loud). You can also use emoticons to convey emotions, such as:

- Smiley face   :)
- Frown face   :(
- Wink   ;)

To learn more about commonly used acronyms and emoticons, visit www.webopedia.com/quick_ref/textmessageabbreviations.asp.

One way to easily add emoticons and symbols to your text/instant messages is to use an alternate virtual keyboard layout. This feature must be turned on from within Settings. To do this, launch Settings, tap the General option, followed by the Keyboard option. On the Keyboard screen, tap the Keyboards option. Tap the Add New Keyboard option and then select the Emoji keyboard layout. Exit from Settings.

Now, when you access the Messages app (or any other app that uses the virtual keyboard, including Mail), a new key will be displayed between the "123" key and Dictation key. It will look like a globe.

Tap this new globe-shaped key to access an alternate keyboard layout that displays hundreds of different emoticons and symbols that can be incorporated into text messages, e-mail messages, documents, and so forth. Tap the appropriate virtual keys to include specific emoticons or symbols in your text, and then tap the globe-shaped key again to return to the regular virtual keyboard layout.

As you're looking at the list of conversations, if you decide to delete one or more of the conversations, tap the Edit button and then tap the negative sign icon next to the conversation(s) you want to delete. To delete a single conversation, as you're looking at its listing, swipe your finger from left to right, and then tap the Delete button to confirm your decision.

Using the Messages app, you can participate in multiple and separate text-based conversations simultaneously, and you can switch between them, in real time, as needed. To switch between conversations, tap on the Messages button that's displayed in the upper-left corner of the screen to switch from the conversation you're currently in (refer to Figure 14-7) back to the Messages screen that displays all of your conversations. Then, tap on another conversation listing to switch to that one. Or, from the Messages screen, tap on the Compose icon (in the upper-right corner of the screen) to start a new message.

If you also use an iPad or Mac, you can use the same iMessage account on all of your devices. Thus, you can begin an instant message conversation using your iPhone and then continue it from your Mac (or vice versa), as long as all versions of the Messages app are logged in using the same account information.

Use Alternative Options to iMessage and the Messages App

While the Messages app can be used to send and receive text messages via your wireless service provider over its cellular network, and to communicate via iMessage with other iMessage users via the Internet, you'll need to use other, third-party apps to send and receive text/instant messages using other services.

For example, if you want to communicate via AIM (AOL Instant Messenger), you'll need the AIM app for the iPhone. This will allow you to communicate with other AIM and AOL users via instant messaging. To communicate with your Facebook friends using Facebook Chat, you can use the official Facebook app or the separate Facebook Messenger app.

There are also separate apps for Google +, Yahoo! Messenger, Microsoft Messenger, and virtually all the other instant messaging services. If you have an account on multiple instant messaging services, you may want to use one of the many third-party iPhone apps that work with multiple services simultaneously, such as textPlus Gold, TextNow, Textie Messaging, Text Me!, Kik Messenger, and Infinite SMS.

To find apps that work with multiple instant messaging services, visit the App Store and enter in the Search field the phrase "Instant Messaging," or enter the name of the instant messaging service you want to use from your iPhone.

PART IV

Your iPhone Is a Portable Entertainment System

15

Use Your iPhone to Experience Multimedia Entertainment

HOW TO...

- Use the iTunes app to find, purchase, and download multimedia content
- Use the Music app to listen to digital music
- Use the Video app to watch purchased TV shows and movies
- Discover the new Passbook app

Beyond helping you to communicate efficiently, helping you to manage your information, and working for you as a powerful productivity tool, your iPhone 5 can also help you to relax and can even entertain you. For example, from the iTunes Store, you can acquire digital music, TV show episodes, movies, and other multimedia content. You can do so directly from your iPhone by using the iTunes app.

To find, purchase, and acquire digital music, you can use a 3G/4G connection or a Wi-Fi Internet connection. However, due to their large file sizes, to download TV show episodes, movies, and audiobooks, for example, you'll need to use a Wi-Fi connection from your iPhone, or download the content to your primary computer and then use the iTunes Sync process to transfer the multimedia files to your iPhone.

 Note Apple's online-based iTunes Store's selection of music, TV shows, and movies is one of the largest in the world. Using your Apple ID, you can purchase and download content with a few taps on the screen, plus enjoy an ever-changing and ever-growing selection of free content that the iTunes Store offers.

After you have transferred iTunes Store content to your iPhone, use the Music and Videos apps that come preinstalled with iOS 6 to enjoy that content, on demand, wherever you happen to be. When you connect the Apple EarPods that came with your iPhone 5 (or use other headphones), your iPhone becomes a feature-packed handheld entertainment system with a ten-hour battery life that allows you to

Did You Know?

You Can Transform Your iPhone into a Portable Home Theater System

Using Apple's optional Lightning Digital AV Adapter, it's possible to connect your iPhone to any HD television or monitor. Or, using the iPhone's AirPlay feature in conjunction with an Apple TV device that's connected to a TV (or home theater system), you can wirelessly stream audio or video content from your iPhone to your TV or monitor and share that content with others.

So, with the AirPlay feature, if you begin watching your favorite TV show on your iPhone while you're on the road, you can continue watching that show uninterrupted on your home theater system by tapping the AirPlay button on the iPhone's screen (displayed in the Videos app). To do this, an optional Apple TV device ($99) is required. To learn more about Apple TV, visit www.apple.com/appletv.

Using other optional accessories, such as wireless stereo speakers and/ or Brookstone's HDMI Pocket Projector ($299.99, www.brookstone.com), for example, you can create a home stereo or home theater experience just about anywhere, and share music, audio, and video content stored on your iPhone with others. The Brookstone HDMI Pocket Projector is a pocket-sized, battery-powered projector that projects whatever is displayed on your iPhone's screen onto any blank wall, creating a virtual screen that's up to 60 inches (diagonal). When you also connect battery-powered speakers to your iPhone (via an audio cable, Bluetooth, or Airplay), you can create a truly portable and battery-powered home theater system almost anywhere. (To use the Brookstone device, you'll also need Apple's Lightning Digital AV Adapter, which is sold separately.)

privately enjoy your favorite music, TV shows, and movies at home, aboard an airplane, at the gym, or just about anywhere.

To enjoy music, TV shows, and movies with other people, you can use your iPhone 5's internal speaker or connect your iPhone to external speakers by using an optional audio cable, the Lightning port on the bottom of your iPhone, a wireless Bluetooth connection, or a wireless AirPlay connection, depending on the speakers you want to connect.

Because the iTunes, Music, and Videos apps all offer many useful features, it would take an entire book to cover them all. Instead, this chapter highlights important things you need to know in order to use each of these apps efficiently. This chapter's focus is on how to enjoy music, audiobooks, and video content (TV shows, movies, etc.) on your iPhone.

As you'll discover shortly, beyond downloading and storing music, TV show episodes, movies, and other multimedia content on your iPhone, you can also stream similar content directly from the Internet using various specialized apps that allow you to access streaming TV and movie services.

Remember, when you purchase and download multimedia content from the iTunes Store (or other sources), once those files are stored on your iPhone, an Internet connection is no longer needed to listen to or watch the music, audiobooks, TV shows, or movies you've downloaded. Streaming content, however, requires a constant Internet connection (as you're actually enjoying the content), and depending on the app, a Wi-Fi connection and a paid subscription to a service (such as Netflix, Hulu Plus, or Sirius XM) may be required.

Apple has been a pioneer both in distributing digital music and in developing and offering cutting-edge digital music and video players—Apple iPods—that allow you to experience digital music and video content while on the go. All of the features and functionality of Apple's most advanced iPod models are built into the iPhone 5 and are readily accessible via the Music and Videos apps. These versatile apps allow you to organize and play your library of songs (and other audio files, such as audiobooks), TV shows, music videos, and movies on your iPhone, so they're always readily accessible to you.

Gather Entertaining Content Using the iTunes App

If you use the iTunes software on a Mac or PC, you probably know it's used for a variety of purposes, such as managing your digital music library, accessing the iTunes Store, and/or syncing data with your iPhone.

On the iPhone, however, the iTunes app that comes preinstalled on the device is used for one primary purpose—to access the iTunes Store in order to acquire music, TV show episodes, movies, audiobooks, ringtones, and music videos. (You can also rent movies from the iTunes Store.) Much of this content must be purchased, although some of it's offered for free. Once the content is stored on your iPhone, you use another app, such as Music or Videos, to enjoy that content.

The iTunes app is also used to access your online-based iCloud account in order to download content you've already purchased from iTunes. This includes all past purchases made from other computers, Apple TV, or iOS mobile devices (such as your iPad or iPod touch).

Using the iTunes app requires an Internet connection. For acquiring music, ringtones, and music videos, a 3G/4G connection works fine. However, for TV shows, movies, and audiobooks, a Wi-Fi connection is needed, due to the large files sizes of this content.

When you launch the iTunes app from the Home screen, you'll discover that its user interface is very similar to the App Store app. Along the bottom of the iTunes app's screen are five icons: Music, Movies, TV Shows, Search, and More. The command buttons and tabs displayed along the top of the screen will help you to browse through whichever type of content you've selected (the default option is Music).

The following sections provide a quick summary of how to use the icons displayed along the bottom of the iTunes app's screen.

Shop for Music Using the iTunes App

Tap the Music icon near the bottom-left corner of the screen to browse Apple's vast selection of digital music (shown in Figure 15-1). You can purchase and download one song at a time or an entire album with a few taps on the screen.

 In mid-October 2012, Apple redesigned the iTunes Store. While much of the functionality is the same as it's always been, command icons and the look of the online-based store have changed.

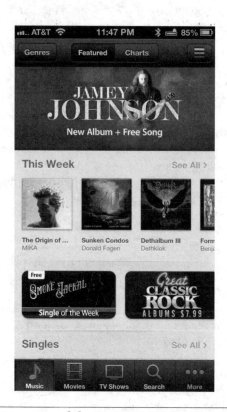

FIGURE 15-1   The main screen of the iTunes app when it's connected to the online-based iTunes Store and the Music option is selected

Find Free Music

The iTunes Store also offers a selection of free music you can download each week, often from new or up-and-coming artists, or in some cases, from artists looking to promote a new album or tour. Look for graphic banners and other mentions about free music as you browse the iTunes Store. If you refer to Figure 15-1, for example, the graphic banner at the top of the screen promotes a new album by Jamey Johnson and indicates a free song is available for download.

Find Featured Music

At the top of the screen when the Music option is selected, tap the Featured tab to display a handful of headings, such as This Week, Singles, and What's Hot, along with a handful of music selections (displayed using album cover icons) below each. Swipe your finger from left to right (or right to left) to scroll through the selections under each heading, or tap the See All option related to a heading to see all of the offerings displayed on a single screen.

Find Currently Popular Music

Tap the Charts tab to view Songs, Albums, and Music Videos charts. These are listings of what's currently the most popular based on sales and/or downloads. You can view individual charts that are compiled from all music categories, or tap the Genres button (in the top-left corner of the screen) to narrow down your selection to a specific type of music, such as Alternative, Children's Music, Classical, Country, Electronic, Hip-Hop, Pop, Rock, or Reggae. There are 21 music categories to choose from.

Find Music Details on an Info Screen

When browsing the iTunes Store using the iTunes app, each single or album offering is displayed using a basic listing. A listing includes an album cover, title, and artist. Tap a listing to view a detailed Info screen for each song or album.

The Info screen for a single song often displays album- or song-related artwork along the top of the screen, as well as the album cover artwork near the top-left corner of the screen (shown in Figure 15-2). Near the top center of the screen, you'll see the name of the song, the name of the artist, and summary information about the song (including its music genre and release date). On the right side of the screen is the Price button (which shows the actual price, not the word "Price").

Tap the Price button (or Free button) to purchase that song and immediately download it to your iPhone. When you tap the Price button, it transforms to say "Buy Single" (or "Get Song" if it's a free song). Tap this button to confirm your decision. Enter your Apple ID password when prompted. The music file will be downloaded to your iPhone within 10 to 30 seconds, depending on the size of the file and the speed of your Internet connection. You can then listen to that music using the Music app on your iPhone.

FIGURE 15-2 The Info screen for a single song available from the iTunes Store

 Some songs that are available when you purchase an entire album are not sold separately as singles. This is a decision made by the record label or recording artist, not Apple.

Displayed below the song information and the Price button are three command tabs, labeled Songs, Reviews, and Related. Tap the Songs tab to view the song(s) being offered. If you're looking at the listing for a single, as shown in Figure 15-2, only one song and a corresponding Price button are displayed. If you're looking at an album listing (shown in Figure 15-3) and you want to purchase the entire album, you would tap the Price button located above the three tabs. However, you'll also see each song from that album listed separately under the Songs tab, each with a separate Price button (usually), allowing you to purchase individual songs from the album, one at a time. By tapping a song title in this listing, you can also preview individual songs.

 If you tap the song's title listed under the Songs tab, a preview of that song will be streamed to your iPhone and start playing. Tap the song title again to make the song preview stop playing before it finishes on its own.

FIGURE 15-3   A sample Info screen for an album that's available from the iTunes Store

Tap the Reviews tab to view the star-based ratings chart for the song or album. Scroll down this screen to read detailed, text-based reviews from other iTunes Store customers. You can also tap the Write A Review button and add your own star-based rating or review, or tap to "Like" the song on Facebook.

Tap the Related tab to view other music from that artist, or other music from the same genre that you might be interested in.

Tip   As you're looking at an Info screen in any category of iTunes content, to return to the iTunes Store screen that you were previously looking at, tap the left-pointing arrow icon in the top-left corner of the screen (labeled "Music" in Figures 15-2 and 15-3).

You'll also discover a Share button (a box icon with a right-pointing curved arrow coming out of it) near the top-right corner of the screen. Tap it to share information about the iTunes content you're looking at via e-mail, text/instant message, Twitter, or Facebook. This menu also enables you to copy the link to the current iTunes Store page to your iPhone's virtual clipboard, and then paste that link into another app.

How to... Pay for Content from the iTunes Store

In order to use the iTunes Store to make purchases, you first need to set up an Apple ID account and link a credit card or debit card to that account in order to pay for your online purchases. Then, just like when visiting the App Store or iBookstore, you'll be able to make purchases with a few taps on the screen, without having to constantly re-enter your billing information. To create or manage an Apple ID account, or to retrieve a forgotten username or password, visit https://appleid.apple.com.

If you don't want to link a credit/debit card to your Apple ID, you can pre-purchase iTunes Gift Cards and then redeem them in the iTunes Store to pay for your content purchases. To learn more about how iTunes Gift Cards work, visit www.apple.com/gift-cards. As soon as you make a purchase from the iTunes Store, the purchase price will be billed to the credit/debit card linked to your account, or deducted from an iTunes Gift Card balance.

As a parent, if you want to limit a child's spending on iTunes, you can set up an iTunes Allowance. This allows you to automatically deposit a predetermined amount of money into your child's iTunes account each month. To set up this feature, or learn more about it, visit www.apple.com/itunes/gifts.

Tap the History icon in the upper-right corner of the screen (which looks like three horizontal lines) to view a history of the iTunes content you've previewed in the past. To clear this history as you're viewing it, tap the Clear button (near the top-left corner of the screen).

If you've already purchased a particular song or album from iTunes, when you return to its Info screen within the iTunes Store, instead of a Price button, you'll see a Play button if it's already loaded on your iPhone. Or, you can download that content again to your iPhone from your iCloud account, regardless of where it was originally purchased, as long as your iPhone is linked to the same Apple ID as your other computer(s), Apple TV, and/or iOS mobile devices.

Once you purchase a song or album from the iTunes Store, you own that content. It becomes part of your personal digital music library, and you can listen to it as often as you want and/or download it onto your other computer(s) and iOS mobile devices that are linked to the same Apple ID. That music content is also stored, for free, online in your iCloud account and is accessible from there.

Purchase or Rent Movies from Your iPhone

If you're interested in purchasing (or renting) a movie and downloading it directly to your iPhone so that you can watch it anytime later, tap the Movies icon at the bottom of the iTunes app's screen.

The layout of the Movies section of the iTunes Store, shown in Figure 15-4, is almost identical to the layout of the Music section (refer to Figure 15-1). When you tap the Featured tab near the top center of the screen, you'll see New & Noteworthy movies listed, as well as several other categories (by scrolling down the screen). Tap the Charts tab to view the most popular movies on iTunes.

Tap the Genres button in the upper-left corner to narrow down your search for a movie by selecting a genre, such as Action & Adventure, Comedy, Kids & Family, Classics, Drama, Horror, or Romance. There are 14 movie genres to choose from.

When you tap a movie listing, a detailed Info screen for that movie is displayed. Again, the layout of this screen is very similar to the Info screen for music. Starting at the top of the Info screen, the information that's displayed includes the movie's title and movie artwork, its rating (G, PG, PG-13, R, etc.), its Rotten Tomatoes (a movie review website) average rating, its iTunes average star-based rating, and its Price button.

 Some movies listed on iTunes are only available for purchase. In this case, a Price icon with the price and the word "Buy" is displayed. Some movies can also be rented. In this case, a second Price icon with the rental price and the word "Rent" is displayed. The difference between buying or renting a movie from iTunes versus streaming a movie from another service, such as Netflix, is explained shortly.

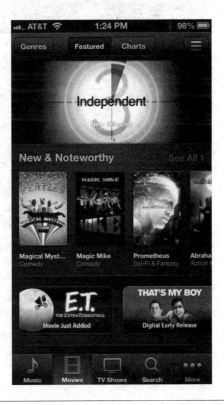

FIGURE 15-4   Find movies to rent or purchase from the iTunes Store, which you can then view on your iPhone using the Videos app.

Tap the Details tab to view a short trailer for the movie and to read a plot summary, information about the cast and crew, and other details about the movie (shown in Figure 15-5). By default, movies displayed in the iTunes Store when accessed from your iPhone are offered in high definition (HD). These HD movies cost a bit more than standard-definition (SD) movies. Watching an HD movie on your iPhone takes full advantage of the iPhone 5's Retina display.

At the bottom of the Info screen (when the Details tab is selected), if the movie is also available in SD, a button that says Also Available In SD is displayed. When you tap this button, the purchase and rental price for that movie will decrease, usually by one or two dollars, sometimes more. You'll then be able to purchase or rent the movie in SD. The difference between watching an HD movie versus an SD movie on your iPhone is similar to the difference between watching a movie on an HD flat-screen TV versus watching it on an SD TV. When you watch the HD version of a movie, the picture appears more detailed and vibrant.

Tap the Reviews tab to "Like" the movie on Facebook, view Rotten Tomatoes review information, and see the Ratings and Reviews published on iTunes, including the movie's star-based ratings chart.

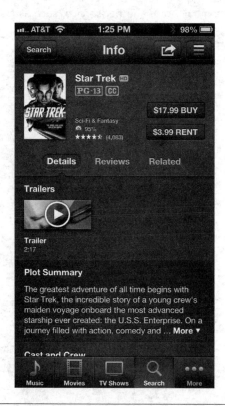

FIGURE 15-5 The Info screen for a movie you can purchase or rent from the iTunes Store

Did You Know?

There's a Difference Between Buying, Renting, and Streaming a Movie on Your iPhone

When you purchase a movie from the iTunes Store, you own it, just as if you purchased a DVD to play on your DVD player, except the digital file for that movie is stored on your iPhone and within your iCloud account.

You can watch a purchased movie as often as you want, on any computer or device that's linked to the same Apple ID account that it was originally purchased using, without having to pay for it again. When you purchase a movie from iTunes using your iPhone, or download it from your iCloud account, it gets stored within the iPhone's internal storage, enabling you to view it later, even if no Internet connection is available.

When you rent a movie from iTunes directly from your iPhone, the file gets downloaded to your iPhone. It will not, however, also be stored within your iCloud account. A rented movie file can be stored on only one computer or device at a time. You can, however, transfer the rented movie from your iPhone to your primary computer (or vice versa) using the iTunes Sync process.

It's important to understand that when you rent a movie, it remains saved on your iPhone for up to 30 days, after which time it is automatically deleted, regardless of whether or not you've watched it. In addition, once you start watching a rented movie, you can watch it from start to finish as often as you'd like within a 24-hour period, but after that time is up, the movie file automatically deletes itself from your iPhone (or whichever computer or device you were watching it on). The movie file will erase itself even if you have not finished watching it yet. However, if you're literally in the middle of watching the movie at the 24-hour point, you will be allowed to finish watching it, as long as you don't stop or pause the movie. Like a purchased movie, once a rented movie is stored on your iPhone, you can watch it without an Internet connection.

Another option for watching movies on your iPhone is to stream movies directly from the Internet. You can do so by using a specialized app from a specific movie streaming service, cable TV provider (such as Infinity), TV network (ABC, CBS, or NBC), or cable TV channel (Lifetime, Syfy, HBO, Showtime, etc.). For example, if you're a paid cable TV subscriber at your home, you can install the app for that cable TV provider onto your iPhone and then stream on-demand content to your iPhone, including movies.

Or, if part of your cable TV subscription includes HBO, Showtime, or Cinemax, for example, you can install the HBO GO, Showtime Anytime, or MAX GO app (or more than one of these) onto your iPhone and then

(Continued)

stream on-demand movies from that premium cable TV network anytime and anywhere (within the United States), as long as a constant Internet connection is available.

Yet another option for streaming movies is to subscribe to the Netflix service or Hulu Plus service, and then use the Netflix or Hulu Plus app on your iPhone to stream movies from that service and watch them on your iPhone's screen. For a flat monthly fee of $7.99 (for each service), you can watch an unlimited number of movies.

When you stream movies, TV shows, or audio content from the Internet, that content is sent to your iPhone, where you view or hear it using a specialized app. However, the content is not saved on your iPhone. As a result, to stream content, you must have a constant Internet connection established. In most cases, a Wi-Fi connection is required. You can typically stream content as often as you'd like, with no per-view charges.

When you tap the Related tab, you'll see similar movies that customers also bought or rented on iTunes. As you're looking at the Info screen for a movie, you also have the option to Share details about that movie with others via e-mail, text/instant message, Twitter, or Facebook. To access these options, tap on the Share icon that's displayed near the top-right corner of the screen. Also displayed near the top-right corner of the Info screen is the History icon. Tap on it to see a listing of movies you've recently viewed the Info screens for (and quickly return to any of those listings).

In addition to Hollywood blockbusters that have been released through iTunes, from the iTunes Store, you can also choose from a vast and ever-growing selection of independent films, foreign films, documentaries, and special-interest films, some of which have been released only through iTunes. There's also a Still In Theaters section that allows you to rent movies that are still playing in theaters. The fee for this is typically higher than renting a regular movie from iTunes.

Purchase Single Episodes or Entire Seasons of Your Favorite TV Shows

The iTunes Store also offers a vast selection of current and classic TV shows for purchase and download. You can purchase one episode of a TV series at a time, or download an entire season of a TV series at once.

 If you purchase the current season of a TV series, as each new episode airs on TV, that same episode will be made available on iTunes (and can be downloaded to your iPhone and made available via your iCloud account) within 24 hours. Apple sends you an e-mail each time a new episode from that season is available for download from the iTunes Store. If you purchase a past season, all episodes from that season are available for immediate download.

To browse through the ever-growing selection of TV shows, TV movies, and other programming, launch the iTunes app and tap the TV Shows icon at the bottom of the screen. Tap the Featured tab to see what's new, or browse through the various categories and genres to find your favorite shows.

Just as with music and movies, when you tap a TV series listing, an Info screen for it is displayed (shown in Figure 15-6). You can then choose to purchase and download one episode or an entire past season of that series. Some long-running shows offer multiple seasons, each of which can be purchased separately. Again, when you purchase a season pass for the current season of a TV series, each new episode will be made available about 24 hours after it airs on television.

To purchase one episode of a TV series at a time, from the Info screen for that series, tap on the " > " icon that's associated with an episode's listing. Then tap on the Details button and look near the lower-half of the Info screen.

If you tap on the Reviews button, you'll be given the option to "Like" the TV show on Facebook, view the star-based ratings associated with that TV show, and read the text-based reviews published by other Apple iTunes customers. If you tap on the Write A Review button, you also have the option of writing and publishing your own review.

Meanwhile, to share information about the TV show you're viewing with other people via e-mail, text/instant message, Twitter, or Facebook, tap on the Share icon.

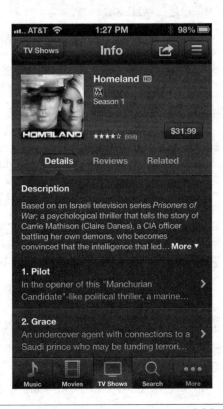

FIGURE 15-6   The Info screen for a TV series that's available from the iTunes Store

Or to view TV show listings you've previously viewed while browsing the iTunes Store, tap on the History icon that's displayed near the top-right corner of the screen.

 If you're looking for the most recent episode of your favorite current show, when viewing that show's Info screen, make sure you select the current season. Pay attention to the air date and episode number of each episode before making your purchase.

The benefit to purchasing TV show episodes on iTunes is that you can watch them on your iPhone or any computer, Apple TV, or iOS mobile device that's linked to the same Apple ID account. Plus, you can watch the episode over and over again. In addition, TV show episodes or seasons acquired from iTunes are always commercial free. (Unlike movies, TV show episodes can't be rented from the iTunes Store.)

If you use a TV network's app to stream on-demand TV shows to your iPhone, that content will typically include commercials (unless you're watching programming from a commercial-free premium network, such as HBO or Showtime).

Search the iTunes Store for Whatever You're Looking For

Between music, TV shows, movies, ringtones, and music videos, the iTunes Store offers an incredible amount of content that you can acquire directly from your iPhone. To make finding exactly what you're looking for much faster, tap the Search icon at the bottom of the iTunes app's screen. In the Search field, enter the title of a song, album, TV show, or movie, the name of an actor, director, recording artist, or band, or any keyword or search phrase that's related to any content that's available from the iTunes Store. Tap the Search button on the virtual keyboard to initiate the search.

Your search results are displayed on the screen below the Search field, sorted by content type. Your search results may fall within more than one category. For example, if you do a search for the TV show *Glee*, because music from the show is also available for purchase, you'll see search results under the Songs, Albums, TV Seasons, and TV Episodes headings (shown in Figure 15-7). You'll also discover free podcasts, ringtones, books, and audiobooks related to the *Glee* TV series, plus see a search result for the *Glee* motion picture.

Tap any of the search result listings to access the related Info screen, from which you can acquire that content.

Discover What Else You Can Access from the iTunes App

Beyond browsing for, purchasing, and downloading music, TV shows, and movies using the iTunes app, when you tap the More icon in the bottom-right corner of the

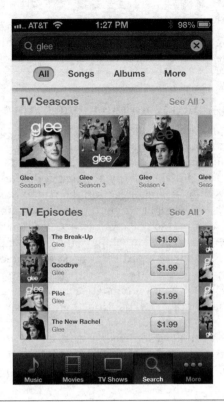

FIGURE 15-7 Quickly find any iTunes Store content using the Search feature. Your search results will be sorted based on the type of content that's available.

iTunes app's screen, you'll find several additional types of content that are available, including audiobooks and ringtones. You'll also be able to gain access to your past iTunes Store purchases.

 From the More screen, you can also access the iTunes Genius feature. Once activated, this feature will evaluate all of your past iTunes purchases and make educated recommendations for similar content you might enjoy.

Acquire Audiobooks from the iTunes Store

To shop for and download audiobooks from the iTunes Store, tap on the More button that's displayed near the bottom of the iTunes screen and select the Audiobooks option. You can then browse through the ever-growing selection of audiobooks available, including audiobook adaptations of current bestsellers. Purchasing and downloading audiobooks works the same way as acquiring TV shows or movies from the iTunes Store. However, to listen to audiobooks, you'll ultimately use the Music app.

Instead of shopping for audiobooks from the iTunes Store, you can access Audible.com (www.audible.com) and then use the free Audible app (available from the App Store) to enjoy your audiobook library.

Acquire Ringtones from the iTunes Store

In addition to music, music videos, TV shows, and movies, Apple's iTunes Store also offers an ever-growing selection of downloadable ringtones you can purchase and use with your iPhone. Ringtones can be used in conjunction with the Phone app, or can be assigned for use with almost any app that generates audible alerts or alarms.

To purchase optional ringtones from the iTunes Store, tap on the More option that's displayed near the lower-right corner of the iTunes app. Then select the Tones option. Each ringtone you purchase will cost $1.29. Once downloaded, you can determine how that ringtone will be used by launching Settings and tapping on the Sounds option. Or to associate a ringtone with a particular person (Contacts entry), launch the Contacts app, select the appropriate entry, tap on the Edit button, and then tap on the Ringtone and/or Text Tone field. When prompted, select the custom ringtone you want to associate with that contact. Tap the Done button to save your changes.

If you don't get along with your mother-in-law, you can download the music from the shower scene in the movie *Psycho*, for example, and associate that with her ringtone or text tone, so that's what you'll hear anytime she calls or texts.

Download Your Past iTunes Store Purchases from iCloud

All of your iTunes Store purchases (as well as apps, eBooks, and digital publications) are automatically downloaded to whichever computer or device the content is originally purchased on. That same content is instantly stored within your free iCloud account. It then becomes accessible to all of your other computers, Apple TV, or iOS mobile devices that are linked to the same Apple ID account.

Thus, if you purchase a song from iTunes on your Mac, within seconds, you can also download and install (for no additional charge) that same song on your iPhone. Your iCloud account remembers and stores all of your past iTunes purchases, starting from when you first opened your Apple ID account, which might have been several years ago when you acquired your first Apple iPod, for example.

From your iPhone, to access your past iTunes purchases, launch the iTunes app, tap the More icon, and then tap the Purchased option on the More screen. Next, select the type of content you want to access—Music, Movies, or TV Shows. (Depending on your past purchase history, Audiobooks and/or Ringtones might also be listed here.)

If you tap the Music option on the Purchased menu, for example, all of your past music purchases are displayed on the iPhone's screen alphabetically, sorted by artist. Near the top of the screen, tap the All tab to view all of your purchases, or tap the Not On This iPhone tab to view only past iTunes purchases not currently stored on your iPhone.

Did You Know?

The Podcast and iTunes U Apps Also Offer Free iTunes Content

Every week, the iTunes Store offers a new selection of music, TV show episodes, TV show featurettes/previews, music videos, and other content that you can acquire for free. In addition to this content, you can also access thousands of free podcasts, plus free educational and personal enrichment programming available from iTunes U. However, you'll now need to use separate apps to access Podcasts and iTunes U content from the iTunes Store.

To access free podcasts through the iTunes Store, download and install Apple's free Podcasts app. You'll need to install the free iTunes U app to access the vast selection of content available from Apple's iTunes U service. The Podcast and iTunes U apps are both available from the App Store.

When you tap an artist's name, a listing of content you've purchased that's related to the selected artist is displayed. In conjunction with each listing is an iCloud icon, instead of a Price button. Tap the iCloud icon to download that content to your iPhone.

Whenever you purchase new music on your computer, Apple TV, or another iOS mobile device in the future, you can set up your iPhone to automatically (and almost immediately) download those new music purchases (at no additional charge). To set up the Automatic Downloads option, launch Settings, select the iTunes & App Stores option, and then turn on the Music virtual switch, located under the Automatic Downloads heading.

If your iPhone has access to the Internet via a Wi-Fi connection, the newly purchased music (acquired from another device or computer) will be downloaded to your iPhone automatically. Also on the iTunes & App Stores screen, if you have the Use Cellular Data virtual switch turned on, the iPhone will use a 3G/4G connection to automatically download and install new music purchased onto your iPhone, if Wi-Fi is not available.

Discover the Cost of Purchasing, Renting, or Streaming Content

While some content available from the iTunes Store is offered for free, in most cases, you'll need to purchase (or in the case of movies, purchase or rent) this content. The following table lists the prices related to acquiring music, TV shows, movies, music videos, audiobooks, and ringtones from the iTunes Store. The prices for streaming similar content from the Internet are discussed after the table.

In some cases, prices may be higher or lower. All prices are subject to change.

	Content Type	Price
Music	Single (one song)	$0.69 to $1.29 each
	Entire album	$7.99 to $15.99
TV Shows/Movies	Single episode (SD)	$1.99
	Single episode (HD)	$2.99
	Entire TV season for a series (in SD or HD)	Varies
	Made-for-TV movie (SD)	$3.99
	Made-for-TV movie (HD)	$4.99
Movies	Movie rental (SD)	$0.99 to $3.99
	Movie rental (HD)	$1.99 to $4.99
	Movie purchase (SD or HD)	$0.99 to $19.99
Music Videos	Music video (available in HD only)	$1.49 to $1.99
Ringtones	Ringtone	$1.29 each
Audiobooks	Audiobook	$0.99 to $41.95

If you subscribe to a streaming service, such as Netflix or Hulu Plus, expect to pay a flat monthly fee of $7.99 for unlimited access to the service's library of TV shows, movies, and other video content. Streaming programming from network or basic cable TV channels via their respective apps is free but often includes commercials.

If you're a paid subscriber to a cable TV or satellite TV service, on-demand TV episodes and movies are offered for free but often include commercials. (Download the proprietary app offered by your cable TV provider, such as Xfinity TV for Comcast or TWC TV for Time Warner Cable. Some restrictions apply regarding what programming is offered and how you can access it. This varies greatly between cable and satellite TV providers.) To access streamed programming from a premium cable TV channel, such as HBO, Showtime, or Cinemax, you need to be a paid subscriber to that network, but using the respective iPhone app (HBO GO, Showtime Anytime, or MAX GO) to stream programming (within the United States) is free.

Streaming audio programming from a local radio station, radio network, or music service is typically free (using a specialized app). However, a monthly subscription is required to access streaming content from Sirius XM Satellite Radio on your iPhone using the Sirius/XM Internet Radio app.

Experience Your Digital Music Library with the Music App

There are several ways to load digital music onto your iPhone. You can purchase and download music directly from the iTunes Store using the iTunes app; you can transfer previously purchased digital music from the iTunes Store to your iPhone using iCloud; you can purchase digital music from another online source; or you can "rip" your own audio CDs, convert them into digital music files, and then transfer those files to your iPhone using the iTunes Sync process. Use the iTunes software on your computer (or other, third-party software on your Mac or PC) to convert your audio CDs into digital music files that the Music app on your iPhone will recognize.

 Using the optional iTunes Match service ($24.99 per year), you can use iCloud to sync your entire digital music collection with all of your computers and devices, regardless of where or how that music was acquired. To learn more about the iTunes Match service, visit www.apple.com/itunes/itunes-match.

Whichever method(s) you use to load and store music on your iPhone, once those digital music files are saved within your iPhone's internal storage, you can access and enjoy your music using the Music app. The Music app offers all of the features and functionality of an Apple iPod digital music player. Thus, you can play individual songs, play entire albums (from start to finish, or in a random song order), manage your digital music library, and create personalized Playlists.

To gain full control over your digital music and the Music app, launch the app from the iPhone's Home screen. You can, however, access the Music app's music controls from the iPhone's Lock screen or while in Multitasking mode. This enables you to play and pause music and skip between tracks included in a preselected Playlist. More information on how to do this will be given shortly.

Enjoy Your Digital Music on Your iPhone

When you launch the Music app, displayed at the bottom of the screen are five command icons, labeled Playlists, Artists, Songs, Albums, and More (shown in Figure 15-8). Using these command icons, you can access, enjoy, and manage your personal digital music library. Here's a summary of what these command icons are used for:

- **Playlists**   Create, manage, and play custom Playlists, which can be made up of two or more songs stored on your iPhone. You can have as many different Playlists stored on your iPhone as you'd like, and then switch between them based on your mood or what activity you're engaged in. For example, many people create special Playlists to enjoy during workouts, while running, when driving, while at work, while meditating (or doing yoga), or when getting ready for bed. Figure 15-9 shows the Playlists screen in the Music app. (How to create Playlists

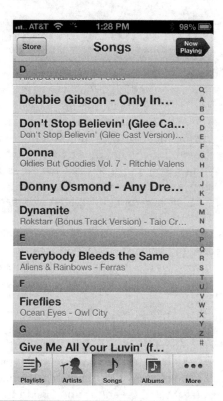

FIGURE 15-8 The main command icons for controlling the Music app are displayed along the bottom of the screen. The Songs icon is currently selected, displaying a list of songs stored on the iPhone.

is covered a bit later, in the sidebar "Create and Enjoy Custom Playlists Using the Music App.")

- **Artists**   View an alphabetized list of recording artists, bands, and music groups whose music you own as part of your digital music collection. This includes both individual songs (singles) from artists and entire albums.
- **Songs**   View an alphabetized list of song titles for all songs stored on your iPhone. (The name of the artist is displayed below each song listing.)
- **Albums**   View an alphabetized list of album titles for all albums stored on your iPhone. This list includes individual songs from specific albums. So, if you tap the title of an album for which you own only one or two songs, only those songs you own will be playable.
- **More**   Sort and display the music stored on your iPhone from compilation albums, or based on the music's composer or genre.

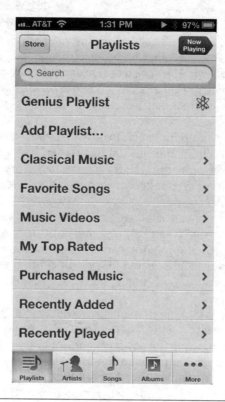

FIGURE 15-9   You can use the Music app to create as many personalized Playlists as you'd like.

How to... Customize the Controls for the Music App

By default, the five command icons at the bottom of the Music screen are labeled Playlists, Artists, Songs, Albums, and More (refer to Figure 15-8). However, you can select different icons to appear in place of these icons (except More, which stays constant). To do this, launch the Music app, tap the More icon, and then tap the Edit button near the upper-left corner of the screen. The Configure screen that appears displays eight command icons, any of which you can move into one of the four available positions at the bottom of the Music app's screen

To replace one of the command icons, place and hold your finger on the Playlists, Artists, Songs, Albums, Audiobooks, Compilations, Composers, or Genres option near the top of the screen and drag it over the icon that you want to replace at the bottom of the screen. Tap the Done button when you're finished, to save your changes.

Using the iTunes Complete My Album feature, after you purchase one or more songs from a particular album, you can go back and purchase the rest of that album at a prorated price from iTunes, based on how many songs from that album you already own. The Complete My Season feature allows you to purchase the rest of a TV series' season at a prorated price, if you have already purchased one or more episodes from that season.

Tap any song or album listing to begin playing that music. While music is playing, the Now Playing screen appears. On this screen, you can play or pause the music, fast-forward or rewind within the track, skip to the previous or next track, adjust the volume, put the song in Repeat mode, or handle a few other tasks related to the playback of that song.

However, once music is playing, you can leave the Now Playing screen and access other areas of the Music app, or press the Home button to access the Home screen and begin using other apps. (You can also switch to another app using the iPhone's Multitasking mode.) The selected music will continue playing in the background. The music will also continue playing if you place your iPhone into Sleep mode (without pausing the music first).

When music is playing in the background (as you're using other apps), you can control it using the control buttons on your Apple EarPods (or other corded headphones you're using, if they have control buttons built into the cord). Or, you can access the Music app's controls from the Lock screen or while in Multitasking mode. (How to do this is explained shortly.) If an incoming call is received, the music that's playing will automatically pause when you answer the phone or FaceTime call.

The onscreen controls for playing your music are pretty self-explanatory. However, you should spend a few minutes exploring the Music app so you become acquainted with how to select music and then play, pause, fast-forward, rewind, and skip between tracks.

To adjust the volume of the music that's playing using the Music app, use your finger to move the Volume slider on the Now Playing screen to the left to lower the volume or to the right to increase the volume. You can also use the Volume Up and Volume Down buttons on the side of your iPhone, or use the volume controls on your headphones. The Volume Up and Volume Down buttons on the iPhone and the controls on the EarPods cord work while music is playing, even if the iPhone is in Sleep mode.

Control the Music App from the Lock Screen and While in Multitasking Mode

As music is playing on your iPhone, you can exit the Music app and use your iPhone for other purposes, while the music continues to play in the background. When the music is playing in the background, you can always relaunch the Music app to control your music. However, you can also access the Music app's controls from the Lock screen or while in Multitasking mode.

When viewing the Lock screen, press the Home button twice (quickly) to make the Music app's music controls appear (shown in Figure 15-10). You can then play/pause the music, switch between tracks in the preselected Playlist, and/or switch between the iPhone's speakers and external speakers or headphones. To handle any other tasks, you'll need to unlock the iPhone.

While you're using the iPhone, to access the Music app's controls from Multitasking mode, press the Home button twice (quickly). Swipe your finger from left to right across the Multitasking mode's lineup of app icons displayed along the bottom of the screen. The Music app's music controls will be displayed at the bottom of the screen. See Chapter 3 for more details about Multitasking mode.

 As you're looking at the music controls when in Multitasking mode, tap the Music app icon to relaunch the Music app.

Use the Music App with External Speakers

If you have your iPhone set up to work with AirPlay in conjunction with your Apple TV or AirPlay-compatible speakers, the Airplay icon is displayed in the lower-right corner of the Now Playing screen. Tap the AirPlay icon to access a pop-up menu that

FIGURE 15-10   You can control the Music app from the Lock screen of your iPhone.

How to... Create and Enjoy Custom Playlists Using the Music App

In addition to selecting and playing individual songs or albums from the Music app, you can create custom Playlists. To do this, from the main Music app's screen, tap the Playlists icon in the lower-left corner of the screen. When the Playlists screen is displayed (shown earlier, in Figure 15-9), you'll see a handful of pre-created Playlists, such as My Top Rated, Recently Added, Top 25 Most Played, and Purchased Music, that you can listen to right away or edit to your liking. If you choose the Genius Playlist option, you can select one song stored on your iPhone, and the Music app will then select similar songs from your digital music library and create a personalized Playlist for you.

To create a custom Playlist from scratch, tap the Add Playlist option (near the top of the Playlists screen). First, create a title for your new playlist, such as Workout Music or Driving Music, using the virtual keyboard. Tap the Save button to continue. Next, a complete listing of all songs available to you (stored on your iPhone or in your iCloud account) is displayed. Choose one song at a time to add to your Playlist by tapping the plus sign icon to the right of the song's listing. Select as many songs as you'd like, but you must select at least two.

Once you've selected songs for your Playlist, tap the Done button. Your Playlist selections are displayed on a separate screen, near the top center of which are three command buttons, Edit, Clear, and Delete. Tap the Edit button to either delete songs from the playlist (by tapping the negative sign icon next to each) or rearrange the order of the songs (by placing your finger on the Move icon—three horizontal lines—to the right of a song listing and dragging it up or down within the list). Tap the Done button when you're finished editing the Playlist.

Tap the Clear button to keep the Playlist name you created but erase all of the selected songs. You can then return to your master song list and choose which new songs to add to the Playlist. Tap the Delete button to delete the entire Playlist.

If songs you've selected are stored in your iCloud account but not on your iPhone, tap the iCloud icon on the Playlist screen to download the missing songs. Tap the Playlists button in the top-left corner of the screen to return to the list of Playlists. From any Playlist screen, tap any song listed to begin playing your Playlist, starting from the song you tap.

Your newly created custom Playlist appears on the Playlists screen when you tap the Playlists icon on the Music app's screen. Tap your Playlist to begin playing it in a preset or random (shuffled) order. As your Playlist is playing, tap the Shuffle button to randomize the order in which songs are played. Thanks to iCloud, all of your Playlists can be synced automatically between your iPhone, computer(s), Apple TV, and other iOS devices that are linked to the same Apple ID account.

allows you to select between using your iPhone's internal speaker or streaming the music from your iPhone to your Apple TV or external speakers.

If you have wireless Bluetooth speakers connected to your iPhone, those speakers are used automatically instead of the iPhone's built-in speaker. However, if you tap the AirPlay icon, you can switch from the external Bluetooth speakers to your iPhone's internal speaker (or wireless headphones), and then later switch back to the Bluetooth speakers, if you desire, using the same menu. You will continue to control the music's playback and volume from your iPhone.

If you have AirPlay-compatible wireless speakers linked to your iPhone, tap the AirPlay icon to switch between those speakers, the iPhone's internal speaker, and optional wireless headphones, if applicable.

Using the Home Sharing feature that's built into the Mac (in conjunction with a wireless network), you can stream music from your iPhone to your Mac and play that music through your Mac's speakers, for example. To turn on this feature from your iPhone, launch Settings, tap the Music option, and then scroll down to the Home Sharing option. Then, turn on this feature on your Mac as well from within the iTunes software running on the computer. From the iTunes pull-down menu on your computer, select Preferences and then click the Sharing option.

 To learn more about the Home Sharing feature that's built into your iPhone and Mac, visit http://support.apple.com/kb/HT3819.

While music is playing and the Music app is running, rotate the iPhone to landscape mode to view and manage your music using what Apple calls its Cover Flow display, which is shown in Figure 15-11.

Anytime music is playing, press or tap the Pause button to stop the music. You can do so from the Music app or the Music app's controls on the Lock screen, while in Multitasking mode, or from the controls on your corded headphones (such as your Apple EarPods).

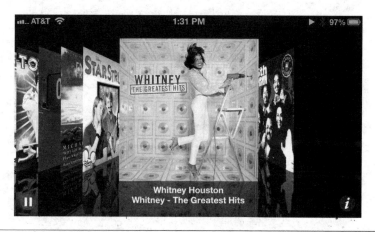

FIGURE 15-11   The Cover Flow display of the Music app allows you to scroll through your music by viewing album covers as opposed to text-based lists.

Watch Video Content Acquired from the iTunes Store Using the Videos App

Once you've purchased and downloaded video content (TV shows, movies, or music videos) from the iTunes Store, you can watch that content using the Videos app that came preinstalled on your iPhone 5.

As you're using the Videos app, if you want to access the iTunes Store to shop for additional video content to purchase or rent, tap the Store icon. This will cause the iTunes app to launch, and you'll be connected to the online-based iTunes Store.

 The Videos app is used to watch video content acquired from the iTunes Store. If you want to watch videos you've shot yourself, use the Photos app or iMovie app. Or, if you've acquired or plan to stream movies from another source, use the proprietary app that's associated with that movie source, such as the Netflix app or HBO GO app.

When you launch the Videos app, a listing of all compatible video content stored on your iPhone is displayed under specific headings, such as TV Shows, Movies, and Music Videos (shown in Figure 15-12). Tap a listing to view more information about

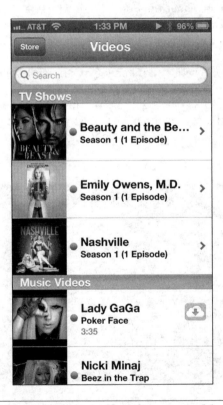

FIGURE 15-12 The Videos screen lists all of the compatible video content stored on your iPhone. Tap a listing to watch the video. Tap the Store button to launch the iTunes app and visit the iTunes Store to acquire more content.

that content and begin playing it on your iPhone's screen. A blue dot displayed to the left of a listing indicates the video content is newly added and has not yet been viewed.

As previously mentioned, you can visit the iTunes Store to acquire new video content by tapping the Store button near the top-left corner of the Videos screen.

As you begin playing video content, hold your iPhone in landscape mode. The video will start playing once you tap the Play button. At any time, tap anywhere on the screen to make the onscreen controls appear (shown in Figure 15-13).

Displayed along the top of the screen is a slider that shows how far along you are within that video. On the left of the slider, a timer shows how much of the video you've already watched. On the right side of the slider, a separate timer shows how much of the video remains.

 To make the onscreen controls disappear, tap anywhere on the screen that's not on a control icon.

Tap the Done button in the upper-left corner of the screen to exit the Play Video mode and return to the Video app's screen. Displayed near the bottom center of the screen is a control panel that displays video playback control icons. Here, you'll find the Play/Pause button, the Rewind and Fast Forward icons, the AirPlay icon, and the volume slider. If you tap the Rewind icon or Fast Forward icon, you will jump to the previous chapter or next chapter, respectively, within that video (if applicable). However, if you press and hold down the Rewind icon or Fast Forward icon, you will quickly rewind or advance the video as you're viewing the content on the screen.

Tap the AirPlay button to stream the video content to your Apple TV or Mac (when Home Sharing is active) or stream the audio from the video to external speakers, if you have speakers linked to your iPhone using AirPlay or Bluetooth.

As you're viewing video content, if applicable, a full-screen/widescreen icon will be displayed near the top-right corner of the screen. This allows you to

FIGURE 15-13   You can control video playback using the onscreen controls of the Video app, or the controls built into your corded headphones.

switch between full-screen mode and widescreen mode. This icon often becomes available when watching standard-definition videos or other video content that's not preformatted to be viewed on a widescreen TV or monitor (or in this case, your iPhone's HD display).

 As you're viewing some movies or TV shows using the Videos app, you may discover a text bubble icon displayed to the left of the Rewind, Play/Pause, and Face Forward icons when the on-screen controls are displayed. Tap on this text bubble icon to access options for turning on/off captions or alternate languages. This is only available in some purchased video content, so the icon will typically not appear.

Discover the New Passbook App

While the new Passbook app that comes preinstalled on your iPhone isn't used to watch multimedia content, you can use it when you venture out into the real world to go see a movie, sporting event, show, or concert in person.

The Passbook app works with a handful of other iPhone apps from specific companies and allows you to manage, among other things, electronically purchased tickets, retail coupons, loyalty cards, and airline boarding passes, all from a centralized place.

For example, if you purchase movie, concert, or sporting event tickets online using your iPhone, when you arrive at the theater or venue, the Passbook app will launch and display the digital admission ticket, which the box office or ticket taker at that venue can scan right from your iPhone's screen.

At the time the iPhone 5 launched and the Passbook app was added to iOS 6, this app was more of a concept than an app you could begin using in your day-to-day life. However, as time has gone by, more and more companies and retailers have begun supporting the Passbook app in many different and innovative ways.

When you launch the Passbook app, a menu screen is displayed that explains some of the potential uses for this app, such as to manage airline boarding passes, tickets, store cards, and coupons (shown in Figure 15-14). From this screen, tap the App Store button to visit the App Store and see which specific companies and retailers currently support the Passbook app through their own proprietary iPhone apps.

As of November 2012, the proprietary apps that support the Passbook app include Airbnb, Air Canada, American Airlines, Amtrak, Apple Store, Eventbrite, Live Nation, Living Social, Lufthansa, MBL.com At Bat, MLB.com At The Ballpark, Sephora to Go, Starbucks, Target, Ticketmaster, United Airlines, and Walgreens. Additional apps are being added weekly as companies discover new and innovative ways to use the Passbook app's functionality.

Once you install a Passbook-compatible app on your iPhone and begin using it, you'll be prompted to link that app with the Passbook app. This only needs to be done once per app. Then, how a particular app utilizes Passbook functionality, and how

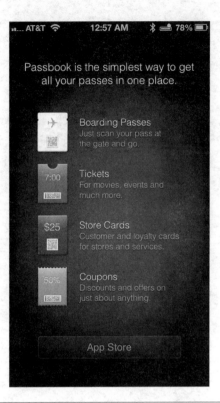

FIGURE 15-14   To begin using the Passbook app, tap the App Store button (at the bottom of the screen) to access, download, and install Passbook-compatible apps from airlines, retail stores, entertainment companies, and so forth.

you can take advantage of that functionality, will vary greatly, so follow the directions provided by the app.

When you use Passbook in conjunction with the Live Nation app, for example, you can find and purchase a concert or event ticket online, store the digital ticket on your iPhone, and then have the ticket taker/box office scan your iPhone screen when you arrive at the venue. The Passbook app will detect where you are and automatically display the ticket details. Thus, the Passbook app can store all of your concert and show tickets purchased through Live Nation in one convenient place. The Fandango app works in much the same way as the Live Nation app, but it's used for purchasing movie tickets.

In the months and years ahead, you'll be seeing many different companies offering Passbook-compatible apps that allow you to save time and money when working with that company as a ticket buyer, consumer, or retail consumer.

16

Use Your iPhone as an E-book Reader

HOW TO...

- Use the iBooks app to access iBookstore
- Read e-books and PDF files using iBooks
- Make your iPhone compatible with Kindle or Nook e-books
- Read newspapers and magazines using the Newsstand app

While the relatively small screen of the iPhone 5 may not seem suitable for reading an e-book or perusing through the pages of a newspaper or magazine, thanks to the latest version of the iBooks and Newsstand apps (as well as proprietary apps for specific publications), not only is reading e-books, PDF files, and the digital editions of newspapers and magazines possible on the iPhone 5, it's also convenient and practical.

The latest version of the iBooks app (version 3.0) was released on October 23, 2012. So, if you purchased an iPhone 5 early in its release and immediately downloaded the iBooks app, be sure to install the free update from the App Store.

Although Apple's iBooks app does not come preinstalled on your iPhone 5 in conjunction with iOS 6, it is readily available from the App Store for free. The purpose of iBooks is to provide seamless access to Apple's iBookstore, which is an online-based e-book store that offers one of the largest selections of free and paid e-books in the world. The iBooks app is also used to read specially formatted e-books and PDF files on the iPhone's screen.

As of October 2012, iBookstore offered more than 1.5 million different e-book titles, including digital editions of current and out-of-print books, books by self-published authors, and books from small and large publishing companies. In fact, you can find this book in e-book form at iBookstore and read it directly from your iPhone 5.

Did You Know?

You Can Make Your iPhone Compatible with Kindle or Nook E-books, Plus Access Free eBooks

If you already have an Amazon Kindle or Barnes & Noble Nook e-book reader and have acquired a personal library of e-books, you'll discover that these e-books are not compatible with the iBooks app on your iPhone. However, from the App Store, you can download and use the free Kindle app or Nook app for the iPhone, each of which enables you to access and read, respectively, the Kindle- or Nook-formatted e-books you already own.

Also, if you opt to use the iBooks app to read e-books, there are a few other options for acquiring free and paid e-book titles beyond accessing Apple's iBookstore. You can find these options by using any Internet search engine. However, the process for purchasing, downloading, and installing those e-books into your e-book reader app will not be as straightforward or seamless as shopping within iBookstore for e-books to read using the iBooks app.

Meanwhile, the Newsstand app does come preinstalled on your iPhone in conjunction with iOS 6. This app is used to access the Newsstand area of the App Store, help you manage subscriptions to digital publications, and, in some cases, read those publications. More often than not, however, each digital newspaper or magazine requires its own proprietary app, available for free from the App Store (accessible via the Newsstand app). Through in-app purchases, you can then acquire single issues or ongoing subscriptions to a publication.

Note While Apple has gone to great lengths to make e-books as readable as possible on the iPhone 5's screen, realistically, if you do have access to an iPad or iPad mini tablet, a Kindle, or a Nook, you will definitely find it easier on your eyes to read e-books on those devices that have larger screens.

Customize the iBooks App from Settings

Before you begin using the iBooks app (or anytime later, for that matter), you can customize some important options from within Settings. To do this, launch Settings and tap the iBooks option. On the iBooks screen (shown in Figure 16-1), you'll see the following options:

- **Full Justification** Turn this feature on or off to right/left justify text that's displayed on the screen as you view each page of an e-book. When turned on, the text on each page will be lined up with both the left and right margins, so it will look even on both sides of the page. Some people find this format easier to read.

FIGURE 16-1 The iBooks screen, accessible from Settings

- **Auto-Hyphenation** If you turn on this feature, at the end of a line of text, iBooks breaks and hyphenates words that don't fit fully within the right margin. With the feature turned off, any word that doesn't fit moves to the beginning of the next line.
- **Both Margins Advance** When turned on, this feature allows you to turn the page of an e-book by tapping either the left or right margin to advance one page. This is an alternative to using a horizontal finger swipe.
- **Sync Bookmarks** When turned on, all of your automatically and manually saved bookmarks are synced with your iCloud account immediately (assuming your iPhone has access to the Internet). Thus, you'll be able to pick up your iPad, for example, and continue reading that same e-book from exactly where you left off on your iPhone (or vice versa).
- **Sync Collections** When turned on, your iPhone automatically downloads all of the e-books you currently own from your iCloud account, and keeps your entire e-book library synced and stored on your iPhone.
- **Show All Purchases** When turned on, all e-books you've acquired from iBookstore are displayed as you look at the Library screen (explained in the next section) with either the Books or Purchased Books Collections page selected. Books that you own but that are not currently installed on your iPhone display a tiny iCloud icon in the upper-right corner of the e-book's cover. Tap the cover

to download that e-book from your iCloud account to your iPhone (if the Sync Collections option is turned off).

- **Online Content** iBooks now allows e-book publishers to update content within their publications. When this feature is turned on, any content updates related to e-books you've acquired from iBookstore will automatically be updated and made available on your iPhone.

Once you've adjusted the customizable options for iBooks within Settings, tap the Home button to exit Settings. You can then launch the iBooks app from the Home screen.

Explore the iBooks Library Screen

Once you've installed the iBooks app onto your iPhone, launch it by tapping its app icon on your Home screen. The first thing you'll see is the Library screen, which resembles a virtual bookshelf. It's the central hub of the iBooks app, from which you can access iBookstore, open an e-book to begin reading, access already purchased e-books stored in your iCloud account, or access and view PDF files stored on your iPhone.

If this is your first time using iBooks, the virtual bookshelf will be empty, unless Apple opts to include a sample from a book that iBookstore is promoting. However, once you've acquired and downloaded e-books from iBookstore, the Library screen will become populated with book covers that represent the books you own.

Displayed just below the Store button on the Library screen are two Library screen viewing icons. The icon on the left is the default Library bookshelf view (shown in Figure 16-2). Tap the icon to the right (it looks like three horizontal lines) to view an alternative Library screen that uses a listing format. The benefit to using this listing view (which was previously only available on the iPad) is that you can sort your e-book library using the Bookshelf tab, Titles tab, Authors tab, or Categories tab at the bottom of the screen.

 If you download a free sample of an e-book, a red "Sample" banner is displayed on the book's cover when viewed on the Library screen. In Figure 16-2, this is shown for *How To Do Everything: MacBook Air* (in the top-left corner). When you open the book to read the sample text, a special Buy icon is displayed near the top center of the screen. Tap it to purchase the entire e-book. You'll also discover a Buy page when you're done reading the free sample.

Among the e-books displayed on the Library screen in Figure 16-2 is a custom photo book (in the middle of the top shelf) created using the Blurb.com service. When you create and publish a custom photo book using Blurb, for a small additional fee, the service will create an iPhone- and iPad-compatible e-book version that you can store and view on your iOS mobile device. For more information about Blurb photo books and how to create them, visit www.blurb.com.

Displayed along the top of the Library screen are three buttons, labeled Edit, Books, and Store. (The Books button might be labeled Purchased Books, PDFs, or the

FIGURE 16-2   The Library screen of the iBooks app, populated with a handful of e-book titles

name of whichever Collections page you last viewed.) Tap the Edit button to select and delete or select and move e-books that are displayed on the main Library screen. After tapping the Edit button, tap your book selection(s) and then tap the Move button or Delete button in the upper-right corner of the screen (shown in Figure 16-3). When you move an e-book, you can transfer it to another Collections screen, which allows you to manually sort your e-books based on subject, content, author, or another personal preference. You can then quickly access the various Collections from the Collections screen in iBooks. To access the Collections screen, tap the Books button.

Tap the Store button to access iBookstore to acquire free e-books from Apple or shop for paid e-books. iBookstore offers one of the largest e-book selections in the world, and as you'll discover in the next section, finding what you're looking for is a quick and easy process.

 To visit iBookstore, your iPhone must have access to the Internet via a 3G/4G or Wi-Fi connection, so if you're about to board an airplane or will be in an area with no Internet connection, be sure to download e-books onto your iPhone beforehand. Once e-books are loaded into the iBooks app, you don't need an Internet connection to read them.

FIGURE 16-3 You can move e-books from the main Library screen to custom-created Collections pages (selectable from the Collections screen) to organize your personal e-book library however you'd like.

Tap the Books button near the top center of the Library screen to create new and custom Collections pages and then manually sort your personal e-book library. When you tap the Books button, by default, you see a Collections screen with Collections labeled Books, Purchased Books, PDFs, and Favorites already set up.

To edit these pages, tap the Edit button in the bottom-right corner of the screen. To create an additional, custom Collections page (which you can name yourself), tap the New button at the bottom of the screen (shown in Figure 16-4).

To view books you own that are stored in your iCloud account but have not been transferred to (synced with) your iPhone, tap the Purchased Books option. When you return to the Library screen, the books you own that aren't installed on the iPhone display a tiny iCloud icon in the upper-right corner of the book's cover. Tap the book cover to download the book from your iCloud account.

 If you have the Sync Collections feature turned on within Settings (refer to Figure 16-1), all of the e-books you own will automatically be downloaded to your iPhone and displayed on both the Books and Purchased Books Collections pages. For this to work automatically, you also need to initially launch Settings, select iTunes

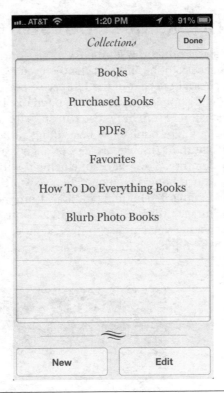

FIGURE 16-4   From the Collections screen in iBooks, you can create custom Collections pages (folders). Here, custom Collection folders named How To Do Everything Books and Blurb Photo Books have been created.

& App Stores, and then turn on the Books virtual switch under the Automatic Downloads heading.

The iBooks app can be used to view PDF files or PDF-formatted e-books that are transferred to and stored on your iPhone (via iTunes Sync, iCloud, or e-mail, for example). When a PDF file is accessible from iBooks, it will be stored in and accessible from the PDFs Collections page. See "View PDF Files Using iBooks," later in the chapter, for more details.

iBooks allows you to view PDF files, but not annotate or edit them. A wide range of powerful PDF viewers that also allow you to annotate and edit PDF files are available from the App Store, such as PDFpen. To find them, enter the search phrase "PDF" into the Search field of the App Store.

Tap the Done button to exit the Collections screen and return to the main Library screen.

Shop for E-books at iBookstore

You'll be able to access and browse Apple's iBookstore via the iBooks app anytime your iPhone has access to the Internet. Launch the iBooks app and tap the Store button in the upper-right corner of the Library screen (refer to Figure 16-2).

Your iPhone will connect to the Internet and display the main page of Apple's online-based iBookstore. From here, you can shop for any of the millions of e-book titles available from major publishers, bestselling authors, independent publishers, and self-published authors. iBookstore also offers a vast selection of free e-books that you can download and read on the iPhone using the iBooks app.

When using your iPhone, you'll quickly discover that shopping for e-books from iBookstore is very similar to shopping for apps from the App Store or iTunes content from the iTunes Store. At the bottom of the iBookstore screen (shown in Figure 16-5), you'll see five icons that you can use to navigate the online-based store and quickly find the e-books you're looking for.

FIGURE 16-5 The main page of Apple's online-based iBookstore with the Books icon selected

You can also shop from iBookstore using the iTunes software on your primary computer, and then transfer your e-book purchases to your iPhone via the iTunes Sync process or from iCloud. It's also possible to e-mail yourself an e-book (ePub file) or PDF document as an attachment, which you can open on your iPhone using the Open In iBooks option from the Mail app.

These command icons include

- **Books** Tap to browse through iBookstore's offerings, starting with the New In Fiction and New In Nonfiction categories. Additional categories (which are constantly changed by Apple) may also be displayed, such as Buzz Books or Popular Pre-Orders. Use your finger to scroll horizontally through listings, or tap the See All option to the right of a category heading on the main Books screen. You can also view books by category by tapping the Categories button near the top-left corner of the Books screen. (The Categories button is available on several screens in the iBooks app as you're browsing iBookstore.) Scroll down to the bottom of the Books screen to find options to Redeem iTunes Gift Cards and manage your Apple ID account from within iBookstore.
- **Top Charts** Tap to view listings for the most popular or bestselling books in iBookstore. By tapping the Books tab at the top of the screen (below the Top Charts heading), you can display charts of bestselling paid and free books. To narrow these charts down by a category, tap the Categories button and choose a category. Once again, you can scroll through e-book listings within each section by scrolling horizontally, or tap the See All option displayed next to a section heading, such as Paid Books or Free Books.

 Instead of viewing bestselling or popular e-books from iBookstore, you can view bestseller lists from the *New York Times* by tapping the Top Charts icon at the bottom of the iBookstore screen and then tapping the NYTimes tab near the top of the screen. A separate Bestsellers list for Fiction and Nonfiction are displayed.

- **Top Authors** Tap to view an alphabetized list of popular authors who have e-books available from iBookstore. You can scroll down and view each name, or tap a letter tab on the right side of the screen to jump to a particular letter in the alphabetized listing. Near the top of the screen, tap the Top Paid or Top Free tab to narrow down your search and locate free versus paid e-books (sorted by authors' names).

 Tap any author's name to view a listing of e-books written by that author which are available for free or for purchase from iBookstore. You can then read each book's description and/or purchase/download the book by tapping its Price icon.

- **Search** Use this feature to quickly find any e-book by typing its title, author, subject, or any keyword associated with the book into the Search field at the top of the screen. A listing of search results will be displayed. Tap any result to view more details about that e-book and/or to purchase/download it.

- **Purchased**   Tap to view a comprehensive listing of all e-books you've previously purchased from iBookstore, including books acquired from your other computers or iOS mobile devices that are linked to the same iCloud/Apple ID account. Once you make a purchase, it gets stored automatically within your iCloud account and can be downloaded to any of your other compatible devices (or re-downloaded to your iPhone) for free. Tap the iCloud icon associated with an e-book listing to download the already purchased e-book to your iPhone (shown in Figure 16-6).

An alternate way to view a list of already purchased e-books (if you have the Sync Collections option turned off in Settings; refer to Figure 16-1) is to access the Library screen and tap the Books button (the label of which may be whatever Collections page you previously selected). On the Collections screen, select the Purchased Books option. When you return to the Library screen, the e-books you own that are not installed on your iPhone display an iCloud icon. Tap the book covers, one at a time, to download the e-books onto your iPhone.

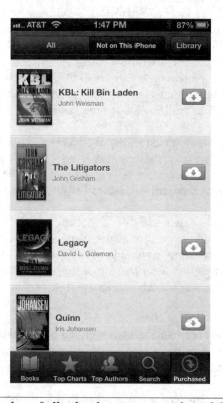

FIGURE 16-6   Display a list of all e-books you've purchased from iBookstore, regardless of from which computer or device each was purchased. Notice the iCloud icon instead of a Price icon associated with each listing.

How to... **Quickly Return to iBooks' Library Screen**

While exploring iBookstore via the iBooks app, to return to the app's main Library screen (or the last Collections page you viewed), tap the Library button in the upper-right corner of the iBookstore screen. As soon as you purchase and download an e-book, it is displayed in your main Books Collection page, available for you to open and read it on the iPhone's screen using the iBooks app.

Displayed in the top-left corner of most iBookstore screens is the Categories button. Tap this button to browse iBookstore based on a particular book category or subject, such as Arts & Entertainment, Business & Personal Finance, Computers & Internet, Fiction & Literature, Health, Mind & Body, Nonfiction, Reference, Romance, or Sports & Outdoors. Just like a traditional bookstore, iBookstore categorizes its offerings into 24 different categories to help you quickly find what you're looking for when browsing by subject matter or topic.

Find Details on an E-book's Info Screen

Regardless of how you locate e-books in iBookstore, what you'll see displayed initially are condensed listings for each e-book title. A listing typically includes the book's cover, its title, and its author. To view a more detailed description of the e-book and acquire it, tap the listing.

Just like in the App Store, for example, when you tap an individual e-book listing in iBookstore, an Info screen for that e-book title is displayed (shown in Figure 16-7). At the top of an Info screen is the book's cover, title, author, printed page length, average star-based rating, and overall number of ratings received (if applicable). To the right of this information, you'll see a Price button (which shows the actual price, not the word "Price") and a Sample button.

Tap the Price button to purchase and download the e-book. You will be prompted to confirm your decision by entering the password associated with your Apple ID. If you're acquiring a free e-book, instead of a Price icon, a Free button will be displayed. Tap it to download the e-book, for free. However, you will still need to enter your Apple ID password.

Note Within 15 to 45 seconds after you acquire an e-book, it will be downloaded to your iPhone and available to read from the Library screen in the iBooks app. Return to the Library screen and tap the e-book's cover to open the book and start reading.

Almost all e-books offered from iBookstore allow you to download a free sample of the book. This might include the first few pages or a sample chapter. What's included in the sample is determined by the book's publisher. Tap the Sample button

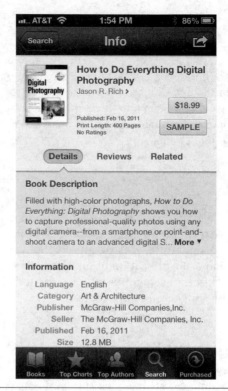

FIGURE 16-7 A sample Info screen from an e-book available from iBookstore

to download a free sample. Within a few seconds, it will be available to read from the Library screen in the iBooks app.

As you scroll down an e-book's Info screen, you'll see three command tabs, labeled Details, Reviews, and Related. Tap the Details tab to view a description of the book as well as an Information section.

 The e-book's description is a summary of the book that's supplied by the publisher.

The Information section includes details about the book, such as what language it's published in and its category, publisher, seller, publication date, file size (which determines how much internal storage space it'll utilize when stored on your iPhone), and printed page length.

Tap the Reviews tab to view the star-based ratings chart and text-based reviews that your fellow iBookstore customers have posted about the e-book title. Keep in mind, not all e-books have reviews or star-based ratings associated with them. These star-based ratings and reviews, however, are typically unbiased opinions from people who have read the book. You can also choose to "Like" the e-book on your Facebook page if you enjoy it.

As an iBookstore customer, you can also create your own star-based ratings and written reviews for a book. To do this, tap the Write A Review button.

Tap the Related tab to view listings for other books by the same author, as well as other books available from iBookstore that are similar in terms of subject matter or content.

As you're viewing any e-book's Info screen, tap the left-pointing arrow icon in the upper-left corner of the screen to return to the previous screen within iBookstore (labeled Search in Figure 16-7), or tap the Share button in the upper-right corner of the screen to share details about the book with other people via e-mail, text/instant message, Facebook, or Twitter. You can also copy the link for the e-book to your iPhone's virtual clipboard and then paste the link into another app.

Read an E-book Using iBooks

On the Library screen in iBooks, tap the book cover for the book you want to read. The book will "open" virtually on your iPhone's screen, and you can begin reading (or continue reading, as shown in the example in Figure 16-8, in which the book *Micro*, by Michael Crichton and Richard Preston, is open to page 480). Swipe your finger from right to left to turn to the next page, or swipe your finger from left to right to move back one page. (If you have the Both Margins Advance option turned on within Settings, shown earlier in Figure 16-1, instead of swiping your finger, you can tap either the left or right margin to advance one page.)

Displayed along the top of the screen are several icons and buttons. If they are not initially visible, tap anywhere on the screen (except the left or right margin if you have the Both Margins Advance option turned on) to make them appear.

Tap the Library button at any time to return to the Library screen of the iBooks app. To exit the app altogether and return to the iPhone's Home screen, press the Home button. Either way, iBooks keeps track of (bookmarks) the page number at which you stopped reading the book. So, when you reopen that same e-book later, it opens to the exact page where you left off.

If you have iBooks set up to sync with iCloud (and have the Sync Bookmarks virtual switch turned on within Settings; refer to Figure 16-1), your automatic and manually saved bookmarks are automatically synced. Thus, for example, you can begin reading an e-book on your iPhone, exit the e-book, and then pick up where you left off using the iBooks app on your iPad. Keep in mind, if you share your iCloud/Apple ID account with other family members, and two or more people are reading the same e-book at the same time, that will mess up the bookmark syncing process.

When the onscreen command icons for iBooks are visible as you're reading, the bottom of the screen indicates how far along in the book you are. The page number you're on, the total number of pages in the e-book, and the number of pages remaining in the chapter are displayed (refer to Figure 16-8). The graphic displayed

Table of Contents icon

Screen Formatting icon

Search icon

Manual Bookmark icon

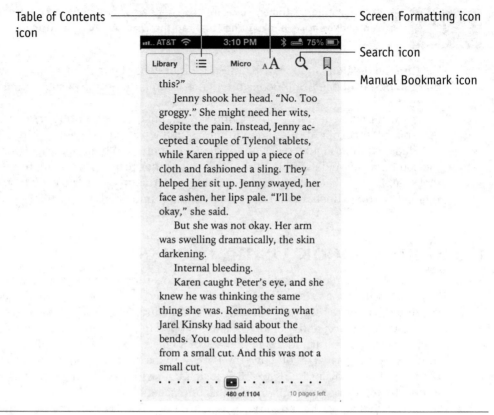

FIGURE 16-8 A sample page in an e-book being read using iBooks

immediately above the page number is actually a slider. Place your finger on the square within the slider, which looks like a line of dots (refer to Figure 16-8), and move it left or right to quickly move back or forward within the e-book.

Manually Set Bookmarks as You Read

As previously mentioned, anytime you exit an e-book you're reading using the iBooks app, iBooks automatically bookmarks the page you're on. However, at any time, you can create your own manual bookmark by tapping the Bookmark icon in the upper-right corner of the screen while you're reading. A red ribbon icon will appear in the top-right corner of the page.

When you manually create a bookmark, it gets saved in the iBooks app. You can create as many manual bookmarks as you'd like, and then refer to those bookmarked pages anytime later. To access a manually saved bookmarked page, tap the Table of Contents icon near the top-left corner of the screen and then tap the Bookmarks tab near the top center of the Table of Contents screen (which is described a bit later in the chapter). A listing of your manually saved bookmarks will be displayed. Tap any bookmark listing to return to that page within the book.

How to...

Annotate Text with Notes as You Read

As you're reading an e-book in the iBooks app, you can annotate it and create a text-based note that can be "attached" to any page in the e-book. To create a note, hold your finger on any word and then expand the selected text, if you'd like, to include a sentence, a paragraph, or all text on that page. A pop-up menu appears with several options, including Copy, Define, and Highlight. Tap the right-pointing arrow icon to the right of the Highlight option to reveal additional options, labeled Note, Search, and Share. The options are described here:

- **Copy**   Tap to copy the selected text to iOS 6's virtual clipboard. You can then paste that text into a note within iBooks or into another app.
- **Define**   Tap to look up the definition of the selected word.
- **Highlight**   Tap to use a virtual highlighter and then highlight the word, sentence, or paragraph in the color of your choice. You can also underline text or access other options from the Highlight menu that appears above the selected text.
- **Note**   Tap to create a note on the page using a virtual sticky note. The iPhone's virtual keyboard appears, enabling you to compose a text-based note of any length that will then be attached to the highlighted word, sentence, paragraph, or page within the e-book. When you're finished typing your note, tap the Done button. In the right margin of the page will be a sticky note icon indicating that you've added an annotation. (You can choose the color of the sticky note using the Highlight option.) Tap the highlighted text or sticky note icon to reopen and read the note. Later, you can tap the Table of Contents icon and then tap the Notes tab to view a listing of all notes you've added to a particular e-book, as discussed in the next section.
- **Search**   Tap to find recurrences of that word within the e-book.
- **Share**   Tap to display a Share menu that allows you to share the selected text with other people via e-mail, text/instant message, Facebook, or Twitter.

Interact with the Book Through the Table of Contents

Displayed to the immediate right of the Library button is the Table of Contents icon. Tap this icon, followed by the Contents tab on the Table of Contents screen, to view the interactive table of contents associated with the book you're reading (shown in Figure 16-9). When you tap any listing in the Table of Contents screen, the e-book reopens to the appropriate chapter, section, or page.

Tap the Bookmarks tab near the top center of the Table of Contents page to access your list of manually saved bookmarks that are associated with the book you're

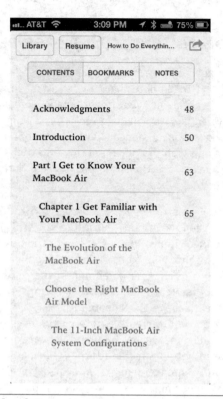

FIGURE 16-9 The Table of Contents screen for a sample e-book being read using iBooks

reading, or tap the Notes tab to view the notes you've composed and saved related to that e-book. On the Bookmarks screen, you can also delete saved bookmarks or notes. One way to do this is from the bookmarks or notes listing. Swipe your finger across the listing, from left to right, and then tap the Delete button.

To return to the book and continue reading, tap the Resume button, or to return to the Library screen in the iBooks app, tap the Library button.

If you've created and saved notes related to the e-book, tap the Share icon in the upper-right corner of the Table of Contents screen to access the Email and Print buttons. Tap the Email button to e-mail your notes to yourself or to someone else from the iBooks app. Tap the Print button to print your notes if you have an AirPrint-compatible printer wirelessly linked to your iPhone.

Adjust the Look of an E-book's Text on the iPhone's Screen

As you're reading any e-book using the iBooks app, tap the AA icon near the top-right corner of the screen to customize the appearance of the text on the virtual page. The pop-up menu window shown in Figure 16-10 is displayed. At the top of this window, use the Brightness slider to adjust the screen brightness. Move it to the right to increase the brightness or to the left to decrease it.

Tap the smaller A button on the left to shrink the size of the e-book's text on the screen, or tap the larger A button on the right to increase the size of the text. To change the font that's used to display the text, tap the Fonts button. A handful of different font choices will be displayed. Tap your selection.

When you tap the Theme button, the menu window changes to include additional options (shown in Figure 16-11). In addition to the screen brightness slider, you can now alter the color scheme of the e-book's pages. Your choices are White, Sepia, or Night. Tap one of the circular icons to make your selection.

FIGURE 16-10 Adjust the appearance of onscreen text in an e-book you're currently reading by tapping the AA icon near the top-right corner of the iBooks app's screen.

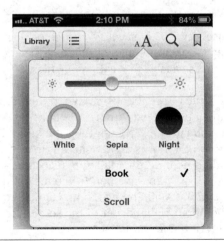

FIGURE 16-11 Change the theme of the e-book you're reading or turn on the new Scroll option from this menu.

New to iBooks version 3 is the Scroll option. When you select Book, you can turn pages in the e-book horizontally only. However, when you select the Scroll option, the entire e-book is displayed using a continuous vertical scrolling feature. You can now use a finger to scroll up or down to move throughout the e-book.

When you make any changes using the tools available in the AA menu window, the entire e-book will reformat itself automatically to reflect those changes on the iPhone's screen. You can modify the appearance of the text in an e-book as often as you'd like, based on your own personal preferences.

Perform a Keyword Search Within an E-book

As you're reading an e-book, tap the Search icon (which looks like a magnifying glass) to perform a keyword search within the entire text of the e-book. Enter a word or phrase in the Search field and then tap the Search button. Your search results will be displayed on the screen. These results will represent all occurrences of that word or phrase within the e-book you're reading. Tap any listed result to jump to that page within the e-book.

 Within the Search field, you can also enter a page number, enabling you to jump right to that page within the e-book.

View PDF Files Using iBooks

If you have PDF files stored on your iPhone, such as PDF files transferred from your primary computer via iTunes Sync (or iCloud) to your iPhone, or PDF files received as attachments to incoming e-mails, you can open and view those files in the iBooks app.

 You can also view PDF files you've created on your iPhone using the Pages app, Numbers app, or Keynote app, or that have been created using any other third-party app that's capable of creating PDF files.

To access PDF files from iBooks, return to the Library screen and tap the Books button (which might be labeled Purchased Books, PDFs, or the name of whichever Collections page you last viewed). On the Collections screen, tap the PDFs option.

If you receive a PDF file as an attachment to an incoming e-mail, press and hold down the attachment icon in the Mail app to access a menu with several options (shown in Figure 16-12). Tap the Open In iBooks option. You also have the option to view the PDF file in the Mail app by tapping Quick Look. After you do this, tap the Share icon (in the upper-right corner of the screen) to access the Share menu, and then tap the Open In iBooks button.

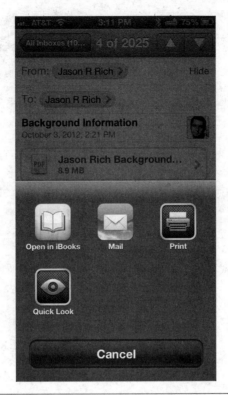

FIGURE 16-12   Load a PDF file from an incoming e-mail directly into iBooks by holding your finger on the PDF file's icon in the e-mail and then selecting the Open In iBooks option.

Read Newspapers and Magazines Using the Newsstand App

Just as the iBooks app is used to access iBookstore and acquire e-books, and then read those e-books on your iPhone's screen, the Newsstand app is used to access the Newsstand section of the App Store and acquire digital editions of newspapers and magazines (as well as graphic novels/comic books), and then read those publications on your iPhone.

Each digital publication has its own app you'll use to read that newspaper or magazine. However, the Newsstand app is used to manage details about your digital subscriptions and help you find publications to read, as well as to access and launch the individual publication-related apps.

A Library screen that's somewhat similar to the Library screen in iBooks will be displayed (shown in Figure 16-13). Tap the Store button to access the Newsstand section of the online-based App Store and then shop for publications to read.

FIGURE 16-13 The main screen of the Newsstand app. Tap the Store button to shop for new publications.

Once in Newsstand, seek out the publication(s) you want to read, and then acquire the publication's app. From that publication-specific app, you can purchase either a single issue or a subscription. If you purchase a subscription, as new issues of the publication are released, they are automatically downloaded to your iPhone (if it's connected to the Internet) and displayed in the Newsstand app on its Library screen. So, if you subscribe to the *New York Times* or the *Wall Street Journal*, for example, every morning when you wake up, the latest edition of the newspaper is loaded into your iPhone and ready for you to read. This also applies to magazines.

Digital newspapers and magazines (as well as graphic novels) each require their own proprietary app, which is available free from the App Store. When you tap a newspaper's or magazine's cover graphic in Newsstand, the appropriate app will launch so you can read that publication and/or purchase additional single issues of that publication.

When using iOS 6, the proprietary app needed to read a digital newspaper or magazine often doesn't appear on your iPhone's Home screen and is accessible only through the Newsstand app.

How to...

Manage Your Digital Newspaper and Magazine Subscriptions

Once you've acquired publication-specific apps for newspapers and magazines and have subscribed to those digital publications, you'll be able to manage your subscriptions directly from your iPhone (as long as an Internet connection is available). To do this, launch Newsstand and tap the Store button. From the main Newsstand section in the App Store, scroll to the bottom of the screen and tap the Apple ID [Your Username] button. When the pop-up window appears, tap the View Apple ID button. Enter your Apple ID password when prompted.

On the Account Settings screen, tap the Manage button under the Subscriptions heading (shown here). A listing of all current and expired subscriptions will be displayed. Details about each subscription, when it expires, and its price are also displayed. Tap one listing at a time to manage it.

For some magazines, if you already subscribe to the printed edition, the digital edition is offered to you for free. However, for other magazines, you have to pay extra to access the digital edition via your iOS mobile device. If you're not already a subscriber to a publication, you'll be able to purchase single issues (often for the same price as the printed edition) or purchase a subscription at a deeply discounted rate when compared to the single issue price.

Also on the Account Settings screen, you have the option to update your payment information. However, if you'll be redeeming an iTunes Gift Card to pay for your Newsstand purchases, from the main Newsstand screen within the App Store, instead of tapping the Apple ID [Your Username] button, tap the Redeem button, and then enter the iTunes Gift Card's redemption code when promoted.

Note If you use both an iPhone and an iPad, you'll discover that most, but not all, digital publications and e-books can be read on either iOS mobile device. However, some digital publications and "enhanced" e-books are iPad-specific, and will not be accessible from the iPhone. When a publication can be read on either device, you can access your purchases on either or both devices via iCloud, but you won't have to pay for the same publication twice. If multiple family members use computers or iOS mobile devices that are linked to the sample Apple ID, they too will be able to access all book and magazine purchases linked to that Apple ID account.

17

Play Games on Your iPhone

HOW TO...

- Discover the different game play experiences that await
- Distinguish between single-player and multiplayer games
- Find games in the App Store
- Experience Game Center on the iPhone

Thanks to its ultra-fast A6 microprocessor, vivid Retina display, built-in speaker, three-axis gyro, accelerometer, and the other technology packed into it, the iPhone 5 can serve as a powerful handheld gaming system that offers an ever-growing library of optional game apps. Regardless of your age or the type of game(s) you enjoy, you'll find a vast selection available from the App Store.

 One of the great things about playing games on the iPhone is that, using the Internet (with a 3G/4G or Wi-Fi connection), many of the games enable you to compete anytime and anywhere with other human players (also using iOS devices or Macs), including friends, family members, and even total strangers (safely). So, if it's 3:00 A.M. and you can't sleep, or you're riding the bus to work and want a distraction, you can log in to Apple's Game Center (which you'll learn more about shortly) and challenge other players to your favorite multiplayer games.

No matter what types of games you enjoy, you'll find a fast-growing and extremely diverse selection of challenging apps for the iPhone available from the App Store. Some of these games are designed specifically to challenge or entertain you for just a few minutes at a time (as you take short breaks throughout your day or need a quick escape from real life). Many other iPhone games, however, will immerse you in an imaginary world and keep you engrossed in it for hours on end.

The iPhone's built-in three-axis gyro and accelerometer allow gamers to interact with their iPhone using motion to add realism and greater control over onscreen action. In addition to tapping the screen to interact with a game, you can physically tilt, turn, and rotate the iPhone itself to control what happens within some action-

The World's Leading Game Developers Now Support the iPhone

Due to the unprecedented global popularity of the iPhone, some of the world's foremost computer and video game designers and developers have adapted existing games or created new games to work flawlessly on the iPhone. As a result, many of the most popular PC and Mac computers games, arcade games, and games for the Nintendo Wii, Sony PlayStation, Sega Genesis, and Microsoft Xbox 360 console systems have been faithfully adapted for the iPhone. Plus, you'll discover a growing number of new and original games designed from the ground up to be experienced exclusively on the iPhone that take full advantage of its Multi-Touch display, built-in speakers, three-axis gyro, and Internet connectivity, for example, to help immerse you in the gaming action.

In fact, out of the more than 20 app categories offered in the App Store, the Games category is the most diverse and offers the greatest selection, as indicated by the number of subcategories it requires. When you tap the Featured icon and then select the Games category in the App Store, you'll be prompted to select a subcategory, such as Action, Adventure, Arcade, Board, Card, Casio, Dice, Educational, Family, Kids, Music, Puzzle, Racing, Role Playing, Simulation, Sports, Strategy, Trivia, or Word.

The Games category also includes many of the most popular apps available in the App Store. When you tap the Charts option in the App Store and look at the comprehensive listing of popular Free, Paid, or Top Grossing apps from all categories (shown here), a disproportionate number of apps listed are games.

oriented games. For example, in the Spinning Top Adventure game (shown in Figure 17-1), the goal is to tilt the iPhone in order to move the constantly spinning top through a series of complex mazes.

Instead of relying on the iPhone 5's built-in speaker, consider playing your favorite games using your Apple EarPods or an optional headset. This will allow you to experience the stereo sound and realistic digital sound effects that are important elements of many games.

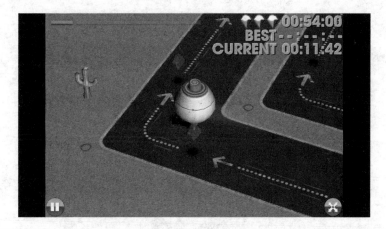

FIGURE 17-1   The Spinning Top Adventure game is just one of the many games that utilize the iPhone's three-axis gyro and allow you to control onscreen action by physically moving around or tilting the iPhone itself.

Discover iPhone 5 Games Suitable for People of All Ages

It's important to understand that not all games are suitable for people of all ages. While there are educational and fun games designed for preschool and elementary school age children, there are also many games that offer high-intensity action that sometimes includes graphically depicted violence, blood, and other themes more suited to older gamers.

To help you select games that are most suitable for yourself or your kids, when you visit the App Store and look at the detailed descriptions of specific game apps, tap the Details tab of the Info screen and then scroll down to the Information section (shown in Figure 17-2 for the popular Angry Birds game). Here, you'll see a heading labeled Rating.

 In the case of the popular action/puzzle game Angry Birds, the app has received a 4+ rating, meaning it's suitable for all ages.

Apple has devised a rating system that will help you quickly determine the age appropriateness of a game or app. Apple assigns an age appropriateness rating to an app based on ten questions an app's developer must answer about the app when submitting it to Apple for distribution through the App Store.

Here's an overview of what the various ratings mean:

FIGURE 17-2   To choose games that are suitable for yourself or your kids, pay attention to each game's Rating in the Information section of the Info screen's Details tab.

- **4+**   These apps are suitable for all ages and contain no objectionable content.
- **9+**   These apps may be too complicated for young kids or contain themes that are not suitable for younger people. For example, the game might contain mild violence or "horror-themed" content.
- **12+**   These apps are suitable for preteens through adults. They may contain some mild violence or other themes you might not want a young child exposed to, or the apps may be too complicated for young people. They're ideal for people over the age of 12. For example, these games might showcase realistic or intense cartoon-like violence, involve real or pretend gambling, or include mature or suggestive themes.
- **17+**   These apps are designed specifically for older teens and adults. They might contain graphic and/or realistic violence, simulated gambling, sexual content, mature or suggestive themes, or other content deemed inappropriate for young people. For example, a multiplayer poker game may receive a 17+ rating because it simulates gambling, while a first-person shooter might receive this rating due to the killing and blood depicted within the game.

The game's Rating (which deals with the age appropriateness of an app and is provided by Apple) is different from the star-based ratings and reviews an app receives from other App Store customers. These star-based ratings and reviews are based on the overall quality of the app, based on the experiences of other people using them. Apple's game ratings are different from the Entertainment Software Rating Board (ESRB) rating system that the video and computer gaming industries have adopted.

Distinguish Between Single-Player and Multiplayer Games

Some games are single-player games, meaning you play alone. In some cases, single-player games allow you to compete against computer-controlled opponents that simulate human players. Computer-controlled opponents allow you to compete in multiplayer games, for example, like checkers, chess, or Monopoly, or card games, like poker and blackjack, when human players are not available.

There are also many multiplayer games that require just one iPhone but require two or more players to experience. These are often turn-based games that involve passing the iPhone around between players.

Yet another type of game allows two or more players to compete head-on, in real time, via the Internet. These games require each player to have their own copy of the game installed on their iPhone (or compatible device), which must be connected to the Internet. These games allow people to compete against each other regardless of whether they are in close proximity or located across town or on opposite sides of the planet.

If you know the title of a game you want to play, launch the App Store and enter the name of a game in the Search field. You can also use the Search field to find a specific type of game, by entering a search phrase like "poker," "crossword puzzles," "golf," or "Sudoku."

Discover Games You'll Love

Now that you know your iPhone is capable of playing incredibly entertaining, often challenging, and sometimes addicting games, you need to figure out what type of gaming experience you want to have, and decide whether you want to play alone or against other people.

To browse through the most popular games currently available for the iPhone, launch the App Store app to visit the App Store, tap the Charts icon, choose the Games category, and then select a Games subcategory. A listing of Paid, Free, and Top Grossing games for that Games subcategory will be displayed. Next to each of these headings, tap the See All option to view all game selections that are applicable.

As you browse the App Store looking for great games, look for games that have been designed specifically for the iPhone 5 to take full advantage of its larger screen and other advanced capabilities. Any iPhone-specific or hybrid game app will, however, work on the iPhone 5. A hybrid app works with any iPhone or iPad, and automatically adapts to the screen size of the device you're using, while an iPad-specific game will not run on an iPhone 5.

Sample 12 Awesome Games Worth Playing

The following is just a small sampling of popular games available for the iPhone that are suitable for all ages. The selection of iPhone games being optimized or enhanced specifically for the iPhone 5 is ever growing. Games that have not yet been optimized for the iPhone 5's larger screen automatically display black bars on the left and right sides of the screen. This does not in any way impact game play. Over time, most popular iPhone games will be optimized and enhanced for the iPhone 5.

Many parents and grandparents enjoy finding games, like Words With Friends or an adaptation of a popular board game (such as Monopoly), that they can experience with their children or grandchildren via the Internet. You can experience multiplayer games on your iPhone 5 with other people who are using any model of iPhone, iPad, or iPod touch, or who have the same game as you loaded on their Mac (when you connect and interact through Apple's Game Center).

Angry Birds

For reasons you'll find very obvious once you start playing one of the games in this series, Angry Birds has become wildly popular around the world; in fact, it has become a global gaming phenomenon. While the premise may sound ridiculous, in reality, all of the Angry Birds games (one of which is shown in Figure 17-3) are fun, funny, challenging, entertaining, and somewhat addicting. You can play for just a few minutes at a time, or spend hour after hour trying to get through all of the increasingly more difficult levels.

So here's the premise: There are many different species of cartoon-like birds that are in an ongoing battle against the greedy pigs, who have stolen the birds' eggs. Now, the birds are angry and want revenge. Each species of bird has a unique power or capability that can be used to destroy the various fortresses and structures constructed by the pigs.

As you encounter each new structure (all of which are built virtually using real, physics-based models), you use a giant slingshot to catapult one bird at a time at each structure. Then, using each bird's unique power, your goal is to demolish each structure and crush all of the pigs.

Progressing through the game requires strategy, perfect timing, and a bit of creativity, and each level gets increasingly more difficult as you work with different types of birds and encounter countless obstacles and challenges.

FIGURE 17-3   The original (paid version) of Angry Birds for the iPhone

The games in the Angry Birds series have captured the attention of gamers of all ages and from all over the world, making these among the most popular apps ever created for the iOS mobile devices. If you haven't yet experienced Angry Birds, start by installing the free version of the original Angry Birds game to experience firsthand what all of the excitement is about. The free versions of the Angry Birds games offer just a handful of "sample" levels. If you like the game, you can then upgrade to the paid version of the original Angry Birds game or to Angry Birds Space, Angry Birds Seasons, or Angry Birds Rio. The paid version of each game offers dozens of levels each, and new levels are continuously being added as the developer (Rovio Entertainment) releases app updates for each version of the game.

Call of Duty: Black Ops Zombies

Designed for more mature gamers, Call of Duty: Black Ops Zombies (by Activision Publishing, Inc.) is a violent shooting game that offers fast-paced game play, superior graphics, realistic sound effects, and high-intensity action. It's an original game that's based on the popular Call of Duty games for the Nintendo, Sony, and Microsoft gaming consoles. This iPhone/iPad adaptation features an arsenal of new, never-before-seen weapons, plus more than 50 levels of nonstop, zombie-killing action.

You can experience Call of Duty: Back Ops Zombies (the App Store Info screen for which is shown in Figure 17-4) as a one-player game, or you can play it with up to three other people simultaneously via the Internet. In multiplayer mode, voice chat is available, so you can freely converse with the people you're playing with...or against. The game itself is priced at $6.99, but you'll discover a variety of optional in-app purchases available, ranging in price from $0.99 to $49.99, that greatly enhance the game play by providing you with more powerful weapons, defenses, and other power-ups.

FIGURE 17-4 The Info screen for Call of Duty: Black Ops Zombies in the App Store

Chess Free

If you enter the keyword "chess" into the Search field of the App Store, you'll receive more than 1,300 search results. There are many different free and paid chess games available for the iPhone. Some are single-player games (where you compete against a computer-controlled opponent), while others are multiplayer games.

Some of the chess games offer highly advanced tutorial features, while others are compatible with online-based gaming services that allow you to compete against PC and Mac users and other mobile device and tablet device users.

Chess Free (from Optime Software, LLC) is a basic chess game that's free of charge (shown in Figure 17-5). This game offers excellent graphics, a one- or two-player game play mode, plus a variety of other features a serious chess player will appreciate. The free version of the game is advertiser supported, which means banner ads are displayed on the screen as you play. You can, however, upgrade to the premium (ad-free) version for $1.99.

FIGURE 17-5 Chess Free is one of many chess games available for the iPhone. This free version displays ads at the bottom of the screen.

Doodle Jump

Doodle Jump (shown in Figure 17-6) is a light-hearted, action-based puzzle game that's both fun and addicting. The premise is simple. You control a cartoon-like character who is constantly jumping. Your goal is to guide this character as he moves upward on the screen. To stay in the game, with each jump, the character must land on a stable or moving platform. If he misses his target, he falls to the ground and the game ends.

As you help the character continuously jump and move upward, he'll encounter a wide range of power-ups and obstacles, which makes the game more challenging. You'll need to think fast and react faster to be successful.

To make the game more interesting, a variety of different themes are available. You'll discover both a free version and a premium version of this incredibly popular and rather adorable game. The paid version offers nine unique themes. You can play it for just a few minutes at a time, or it can keep you entertained for hours on end. The graphics are cute but simplistic, which adds to the game's charm. Doodle Jump is suitable for all ages.

FIGURE 17-6 Doodle Jump, by Lima Sky, is an action-based puzzle and strategy game that requires quick reflexes.

Flight Control

If you grew up playing action/puzzle games, like Tetris, you know that these games are fun and addicting because they're very easy to learn, but they are very difficult to ultimately master. While Tetris and many other games like it are available from the App Store, another game that offers similar qualities, but a totally different game play experience, is Flight Control, by Firemint Pty Ltd.

In this game, you take on the role of an air traffic controller at a somewhat busy airport. Your goal is to line up approaching airplanes, provide them with a landing trajectory, and ensure they arrive safely. However, as you experience this game, you'll need to oversee multiple runways and manage different types of incoming aircraft that travel at different speeds, and that approach from all directions. Your primary objective is to prevent midair crashes. If two airplanes crash, the game ends.

The paid version of Flight Control (shown in Figure 17-7) offers a handful of different airport layouts, plus a selection of different aircraft. The graphics are simple and the game play is straightforward, but overall, this is a challenging and rather addicting game.

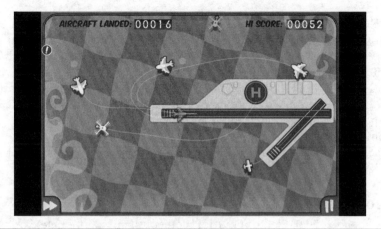

FIGURE 17-7   Flight Control is a action-based puzzle game that starts off easy but gets progressively more challenging as you advance within the game.

Fruit Ninja

The premise behind this upbeat and very colorful game (shown in Figure 17-8) is rather simple, which is what makes it so much fun to play. When you swipe one or more fingers across the iPhone's Multi-Touch screen, it simulates sharp knives being thrust through the air. Your goal is to chop up an ever-expanding assortment of flying fruits. Each time your knives make contact with a fruit, it'll be sliced, diced, and destroyed—which earns you points and creates a rather huge onscreen mess. This game is suitable for all ages. Free and paid versions of the game are available.

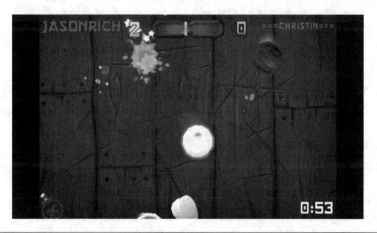

FIGURE 17-8   Fruit Ninja, by Halfbrick Studios, is a fun and challenging action-based game that's suitable for all ages.

Infinity Blade II

This award-winning game by Chair Entertainment Group, priced at $2.99, is designed for teen and adult gamers. It's a somewhat violent but extremely challenging and entertaining action game in which the main character (Siris) must engage in combat with a variety of different enemies using an arsenal of knives, swords, spells, and other weapons. In addition to providing nonstop action, Infinity Blade II offers superior 3D-like graphics and realistic sound, which provide for a truly immersive game play experience.

Optional in-app purchases are available within Infinity Blade II, which range in price from $0.99 to $49.99.

Monopoly

Monopoly ($0.99; Electronic Arts) is one of many traditional board games that have been faithfully adapted for play on the iPhone. What's great about these iPhone editions is that you can play alone (against computer-controlled opponents) or challenge one or more friends. This game is suitable for all ages.

Other popular board game adaptations available from the App Store include: The Game of Life, Battleship, Boggle, Scrabble, Yahtzee, Hungry Hungry Hippos, Risk, Clue, Trivial Pursuit, Connect Four, and Uno. You'll also discover many traditional board game re-creations, including checkers, chess, Reversi, Backgammon, and Mahjong.

NYTimes Crosswords

If you enjoy solving crossword puzzles, you probably look forward to the new puzzle that's published daily in the *New York Times* newspaper. Well, you can now enjoy an interactive edition of the daily *New York Times Crosswords*, which can be downloaded to your iPhone daily. Plus, with a paid subscription, you get access to more than 6,000 previously published crossword puzzles from the *New York Times* archives.

The NYTimes Crosswords app is offered for free on the App Store (by Magmic Inc.), but you have to pay a subscription to download the daily puzzles as an in-app purchase. The subscription fee is $2.99 per month, $9.99 for six months, or $16.99 per year.

The app is very easy to use and provides a faithful adaptation of the appearance of each crossword puzzle that appears in the newspaper. You can even opt to write your answers in the puzzle using a virtual pen or erasable pencil.

Pac-Man

Before the advent of 3D and photorealistic computer graphics, there were classic coin-operated arcade games, like Pac-Man, that offered hours of fun and challenging game play with only the most basic of graphics and sound effects. In Pac-Man, you control the Pac-Man character as he moves around within a maze gobbling up dots and power-ups, while avoiding the ghosts (Blinky, Pinky, Inky, and Clyde).

Well, Namco's classic arcade game has been faithfully adapted for the iPhone (shown in Figure 17-9). It features graphics and sound effects that are almost identical

FIGURE 17-9   Pac-Man will transport you to the early days of coin-op arcade games.

to the coin-op arcade version. From the App Store, you'll also find faithful adaptations of many other classic arcade games, including Ms. Pac-Man, Space Invaders, NBA Jam, Midway Arcade (which features ten classic arcade games), Breakout, Atari's Greatest Hits (which offers paid access to more than 100 games), Frogger, and Paperboy.

VIP Poker

Whether you're an avid card player or you simply enjoy the occasional challenge offered by experiencing a few hands of poker, blackjack, solitaire, Spades, gin rummy, bridge, Hearts, cribbage, or even Go Fish, you'll find a wide range of iPhone games that allow you to experience these and other popular card games, alone or against other people.

Tip   The best way to find an iPhone version of a card game you love is to access the App Store and type the name of the game in the Search field. Then, browse through the search results, read the game descriptions, pay attention to the reviews, and look at the sample screenshots to find the game app you think you'll enjoy the most based on the features, graphics quality, and level of realism it offers.

VIP Poker, by TinyCo Inc., is one of many poker simulations for the iPhone that allow you to compete online against other players in real time. This particular app offers Texas Hold'em and other poker variations that follow casino rules. For this particular version of poker, your iPhone must have an Internet connection (via 3G/4G or Wi-Fi).

Words With Friends

If you enjoy word games, like Scrabble, you'll love playing Words With Friends (shown in Figure 17-10). As its title suggests, this game is designed to be played online against other people...and it's both challenging and addicting. (An Internet connection is required to play.)

Words With Friends offers both a free version, which shows ads, and an ad-free paid version ($2.99). It's become one of the most popular iPhone games ever created. To date, more than 20 million people have played Words With Friends on the iPhone, iPad, or another mobile device.

Because it's a turn-based game, you can compete against up to 20 different people at the same time (in 20 different games), and continuously switch between games.

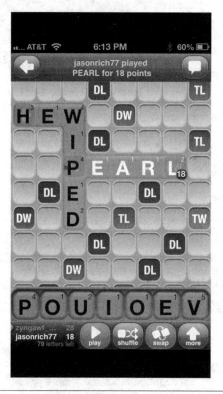

FIGURE 17-10   Similar to Scrabble, Words With Friends (by Zynga) is one of the most popular iPhone games ever created.

You can play against friends or family members, or get safely matched up with total strangers. As you play, you can participate in text-based chats with your competitors.

The rules for Words With Friends are very similar to Scrabble. You're given a handful of letter tiles and must create words by placing them on a game board in order to earn points. This is a great vocabulary-building game to play with your kids or grandchildren, or against other adults.

Experience Multiplayer Games on Game Center

In addition to offering an ever-growing selection of stand-alone game apps, Apple has created Game Center—an online-based gaming service that allows you to find opponents to play your favorite games against, plus publish your gaming high scores and achievements for all to see.

Game Center is a free service that you access using the Game Center app that comes preinstalled with iOS 6. The first time you launch the app, you'll be instructed to create a free account. You can use your existing Apple ID and password, or create an account using an alternate e-mail address and a password you create.

Once you're logged in to Game Center, you'll discover that it's compatible with many of the multiplayer games that are available for the iPhone (and that are available from the App Store). To find Game Center–compatible games, tap the Games button at the bottom of the Game Center screen (shown in Figure 17-11). A list of the games currently installed on your iPhone that are Game Center compatible will be displayed. Scroll down and tap the Find Game Center Games banner to launch the App Store and browse a special section of the App Store that's dedicated to Game Center–compatible games that fall into all game categories and genres (shown in Figure 17-12).

 Note While some of these game apps may be paid apps, once you purchase them, you can play them as often as you'd like through Game Center for free.

By tapping the Me icon at the bottom of the Game Center screen, you can create a mini public profile for yourself that other Game Center members will be able to view. You can include your photo, but this is optional. Your profile will also contain details about which games you play, as well as your high scores and gaming achievements (which are compiled by Game Center). As part of your profile, you can edit your online status to say anything you want.

Like any online community, Game Center is also about making friends online. Tap the Friends icon near the bottom of the Game Center screen to view your current online friends or find new ones. To find new friends, tap the Add Friends banner and follow the onscreen prompts. Game Center will help you locate your real-life friends, as well as your online friends from other services who are also active on Game Center.

FIGURE 17-11 Navigate Game Center by tapping the command icons at the bottom of the screen: Me, Friends, Games, Challenges, and Requests.

FIGURE 17-12 The App Store offers a separate section dedicated to helping you find, purchase (if applicable), download, and install Game Center–compatible multiplayer games.

Once you have online friends, you can receive challenges from them and send challenges to them for specific games (that you both have installed on your iPhones or compatible devices).

Tip
As you explore the Game Center app and the Game Center service, you'll learn about new multiplayer games that you can experience through the service with other people. You'll also be able to view the high scores and achievements of your online friends, as well as total strangers.

Depending on the game you're playing, you can have Game Center match you up with a total stranger to compete against, day or night. While the games themselves and the Game Center service take precautions to help you hide your identity from strangers, you are given the opportunity in many cases to chat live with your opponents. Thus, you can reveal details about yourself and your location at your own discretion.

As you're browsing the App Store and looking at game descriptions, provided on the Details tab of each game's Info screen, the Game Center logo and title appear in the Information section if the game is Game Center compatible. As an example, if you refer to Figure 17-2 earlier in the chapter, you'll see that Angry Birds has the Game Center logo displayed.

How to... Adjust the Restrictions on the iPhone to Keep Your Kids Safe

If you're concerned about your child accessing Game Center and communicating with strangers, you can set up restrictions related to Game Center that will prevent them from using the app altogether or, if you want to allow them to use the app, prevent them from playing games against and communicating with anyone other than their existing online friends—in other words, no strangers.

To set up these restrictions, launch Settings, tap the General option, and then tap the Restrictions option. At the top of the Restrictions screen, tap the Enable Restrictions button, and then create a four-digit passcode. It's important that you, as the adult (parent), remember this passcode. It should be different from the password used to unlock your iPhone if you have the Passcode Lock feature active. If you forget the Restrictions-related passcode, you could find yourself locked out of various apps and prevented from using certain functions on your own iPhone.

Once you have turned on Restrictions, you'll see under the Allow heading a list of apps, each with a virtual On/Off switch. When you turn the switch to Off for a particular app, a child or unauthorized person will be unable to access or use that app without first entering the proper passcode. (On the Restrictions screen, you can also prevent other people from installing or deleting apps from your iPhone or accessing specific types of content.) Near the bottom of the Restrictions menu screen within Settings, you'll see the Game Center heading, which allows you to turn on or off the user's ability to play multi-player games and/or add online-based friends when experiencing Game Center.

Under the Allowed Content heading, you are given a handful of options that allow you to control which music, podcasts, movies, TV shows, books, and apps someone is allowed to access based on the age appropriateness ratings created by Apple and other entertainment industry ratings. For example, you can prevent a child from watching a Rated-R movie or watching a TV show episode that's rated TV-14 or TV-MA. You can also block in-app purchases and determine how often someone will need to enter an Apple ID password in between making any purchases from the App Store, iTunes Store, iBookstore, or Newsstand.

(Continued)

When it comes to restricting games, from the Restrictions menu screen within Settings, there is not a Games-specific option. However, tap on the Apps option under the Allowed Content heading to block all apps that have a specific rating or type of content. Keep in mind, some apps are offered within the Entertainment category, as opposed to the Games category, so this option protects your child from being exposed to all unsuitable app-related content.

As you scroll down the Restrictions screen, from the options listed under the Privacy heading, you can turn on or off access to specific apps that contain personal data, such as Contacts, Calendars, and Reminders, and prevent unauthorized people from sending Tweets or Facebook status updates from your accounts.

Near the very bottom of the Restrictions screen are options that relate directly to Game Center. You can turn on or off the ability for someone to play all multiplayer games on your iPhone (without the proper password), or prevent your kids from adding online Game Center friends (potential strangers) and then conversing with them.

While the Passcode Lock feature that's built into iOS 6 is designed to prevent unauthorized users from accessing your iPhone altogether, you can use the Restrictions options to allow people to use your iPhone but prevent them from accessing specific types of apps, content, or data, based on how you set up and customize the various Restrictions options.

PART V

Extend the Capabilities of Your iPhone

18

Find and Install Additional Apps

HOW TO...

- Access and acquire apps from the App Store
- Understand the difference between free apps, paid apps, and apps that offer in-app purchases
- Find and install "must have" optional apps from Apple
- Discover additional ways to use your iPhone that'll improve your life

As you know, the iPhone 5 comes bundled with iOS 6, the latest and most powerful operating system ever created for an Apple mobile device. In conjunction with iOS 6, your iPhone also comes with a handful of powerful apps preinstalled. One of these apps is called App Store, and you can use it to access Apple's online App Store directly from your iPhone. In the App Store, you can find, acquire, install, and update additional apps for your iPhone.

Thousands of third-party app developers have created in total more than 500,000 different apps for the iPhone, all of which can be found in the App Store. To access the App Store, your iPhone must have access to the Internet via a Wi-Fi connection or 3G/4G connection. You'll also need to establish an Apple ID account, if you haven't already done so, and link a credit card or debit card account to the Apple ID account in order to pay for your app purchases.

 For help setting up and managing an Apple ID account, see Chapter 2.

Everything you purchase through the App Store, iBookstore, and the iTunes Store, for example, is tracked via your Apple ID. Ultimately, you'll want to link all of your Macs and iOS mobile devices to the same Apple ID account so that you can share purchased content freely among them.

As an iPhone user, you can obtain apps only from the App Store— using either the App Store app on the iPhone itself or the iTunes software on your primary computer.

As new apps and accessories are constantly being developed and released for the iPhone 5, there's never a shortage of new, interesting, innovative, and engaging ways you can use your iPhone to enhance various aspects of your life, or to help you handle various tasks in a more efficient manner—all while keeping you connected to the world around you.

Based on what you do for a living or the responsibilities you juggle in your everyday life, by exploring what's offered in the App Store, you'll discover new ways you can use your iPhone and inexpensively add useful new features and functionality to this already powerful device.

Discover New Apps in the App Store

The fastest and easiest way to find new apps and install them onto your iPhone is to use the App Store app preinstalled on your iPhone. If you've been using an older-model iPhone and have recently upgraded, you'll discover that the design of the App Store app has been revamped with iOS 6.

 Instead of using the App Store app on your iPhone to download apps from the App Store, you always have the option to use the iTunes software on your primary computer (a PC or Mac) to access the App Store, download apps to your computer, and then transfer them to your iPhone using the iTunes Sync process, described in Chapter 4. Using iCloud, you can also download apps you've already purchased from the App Store to your iPhone,

On the iPhone's Home screen, tap the App Store app icon to launch the App Store app. You will be connected automatically to the online-based App Store, assuming your iPhone can connect to the Internet.

Displayed along the bottom of the main App Store screen (shown in Figure 18-1) are five icons: Featured, Charts, Genius, Search, and Updates. The following sections explain how to use these icons (except Updates) to browse the App Store and discover new apps for your iPhone. (The Updates icon is covered later in the chapter, in the section "Keep Your Apps Up to Date.")

Quickly Locate a Specific App Using Its Name or a Keyword

If you already know the exact name of the app you're looking for, or believe you can find the type of app you're looking for using a keyword search, tap the Search icon at the bottom of the App Store screen. Then, enter in the blank Search field at the top of the screen the name of the app, if you know it, or a keyword or search phrase for the type of app you're looking for (such as "PDF reader" or "Sudoku").

FIGURE 18-1   The main Featured screen of the App Store app on the iPhone

Tip   If you're looking for an app that's offered by a store or business you frequent often, such as Starbucks, JetBlue Airlines, or Target, enter the store or business name into the Search field to see if a proprietary app for that store or business is available.

Tap the Search button (displayed as part of the virtual keyboard) to initiate the search and display the search results in the center area of the screen (shown in Figure 18-2). Tap one search result to see a Preview screen for that app, such as the example shown for Angry Birds Free in Figure 18-3. To view a detailed description for the app, tap the app's title or graphic icon to open its Info screen. To quickly acquire the app from the Preview screen, tap the Price button (which is labeled Free in Figure 18-3).

Note   When looking at an app's Preview screen or Info screen, the Price button displays the purchase price of the app. If the app is free, the button says Free. If you've already purchased the app and it's installed on your iPhone, the Price button says Open. Or, if you've purchased the app but it's not yet installed on your iPhone, the Price button says Install.

Search field —

FIGURE 18-2 Use the App Store's Search feature to quickly find an app by entering its name or a keyword associated with it.

FIGURE 18-3 After performing a search, the App Store will provide at-a-glance previews of apps that meet your search criteria.

Browse the App Store's Featured Offerings

Instead of using the App Store's Search feature to find a particular app or to seek out a specific type of app, you can browse the App Store's featured offerings. Begin by tapping the Featured icon in the bottom-left corner of the App Store screen (refer to Figure 18-1).

The Featured section of the App Store includes a handful of banner ads for specific apps, as well as app listings under the New and Noteworthy section. Use your finger to swipe from right to left (or left to right) along the icons displayed below any heading to see the newest apps being showcased. You can also tap the See All option (to the right of the headings) to see listings for all apps in that section. Tap the listing for any app to view a detailed Info screen for that app.

Like any well-organized store, the App Store sorts apps by categories. To search for apps based on a particular category, tap the Categories button in the upper-left corner of the Featured screen of the App Store (refer to Figure 18-1). You can then narrow down your search to apps that fall into one of 22 categories (shown in Figure 18-4), which include:

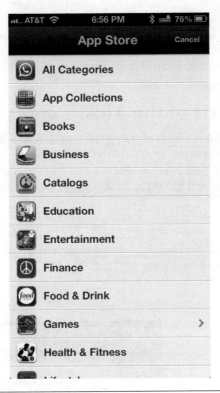

FIGURE 18-4   Tap the Categories button on the Featured screen of the App Store to browse for an app that falls into a particular category.

- Books
- Business
- Catalogs
- Education
- Entertainment
- Finance
- Food & Drink
- Games
- Health & Fitness
- Lifestyle
- Medical
- Music
- Navigation
- Newsstand
- Photo & Video
- Productivity
- Reference
- Social Networking
- Sports
- Travel
- Utilities
- Weather

 When you tap either the Games category or Newsstand category, a menu of subcategories appears.

Tap the category of your choice, such as Business. The Featured screen is replaced by a list of apps that fall into the category you've selected, with the category name at the top of the screen (shown in Figure 18-5). The apps are displayed under the New, What's Hot, Paid, and Free headings. You can either scroll horizontally to view the app listings under each heading, or tap the See All option associated with a heading. Again, tap the listing of any app to view a detailed Info screen for that app.

View Charts of the Most Popular Apps

By tapping the Charts icon at the bottom of the App Store screen (refer to Figure 18-1), you can view a series of charts that showcase the bestselling or most popular apps. By default, when you tap the Charts icon, you see a list composed of apps from all categories. Displayed are three headings (shown in Figure 18-6), Paid, Free, and Top Grossing.

The Paid list includes best-selling paid apps from all categories, the Free list includes the most popular free apps from all categories, and the Top Grossing list includes the most popular apps that generate the highest revenue as a result of their purchase price and/or in-app purchases (a concept that'll be explained shortly). You can either scroll horizontally to view the app listings under each heading, or tap the

FIGURE 18-5 After you tap an app category, you see a list of the apps available from the App Store in that category. Shown here are Business apps.

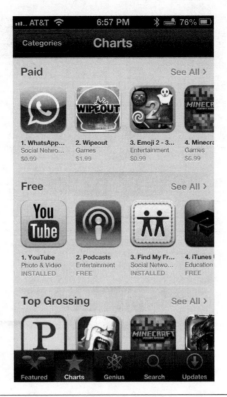

FIGURE 18-6   When you tap the Charts icon, you see headings for three separate lists (Paid, Free, and Top Grossing) of bestselling and popular apps.

See All option associated with a heading. Tap the listing of any app to view a detailed Info screen for that app.

To view a list of the top charts featuring apps from a specific category, tap the Categories button in the upper-left corner of the Charts screen and then select a specific category, such as Business, Entertainment, or Games.

A new set of category-specific Paid, Free, and Top Grossing charts will be displayed. To the right of the New and Noteworthy heading, for example, tap on the See All option. Figure 18-7 shows the top Paid apps in the Entertainment category. As you're looking at any chart, use your finger to scroll down the chart. The app in the number one position is the current bestselling or most popular app. You can keep scrolling down to view listings for up to 300 apps within a particular chart.

The lists of apps you see when you tap the Charts icon in the App Store change constantly and are regularly updated based on what your fellow iPhone users are purchasing and acquiring.

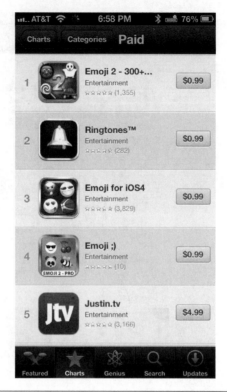

FIGURE 18-7 Choose an app category (in this case, Paid Entertainment apps) to see an up-to-date list of bestselling or popular apps that fit into that category.

Rely on the Genius to Help You Find Apps

Anytime you make an app purchase from the App Store, details about your purchase are recorded and associated with your Apple ID account. As a result, when you tap the Genius icon at the bottom center of the App Store screen (refer to Figure 18-1), the App Store quickly analyzes all of your past purchases and then recommends apps you may be interested in.

 As you scroll through the App Store Genius recommendations, you can enhance its accuracy in the future by tapping the Not Interested button for any apps that do not appeal to you.

Learn All About an App on the App's Info Screen

Every app listing in the App Store includes the name of the app, the category it falls into, its price, and a graphic logo or icon. When you tap a listing, a much more detailed Info screen for that particular app is displayed.

At the top of each Info screen (an example of which is shown in Figure 18-8) is the app's title, its logo/graphic icon, the category in which it is listed, its average star-based rating, the number of ratings it has received (the number in parentheses), and its Price button. Just below this information are three tabs, labeled Details, Reviews, and Related. The Details tab is the default selection and thus is discussed first.

Get All the Details About an App

Under the Details tab, you'll first see multiple sample screenshots from the app. You can scroll horizontally to view all of the featured screenshots. Look at the app's

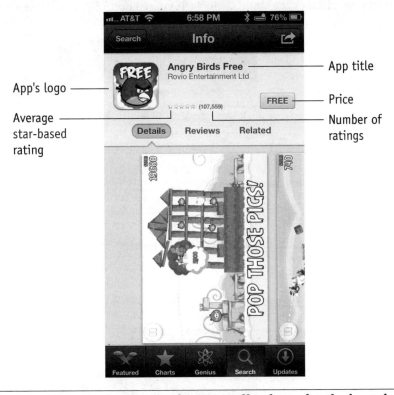

FIGURE 18-8 The top of an app's Info screen offers basic details about the app, including its title, category, price, and average star-based rating. In this example, a free app is shown.

screenshots to get a preview of its menu structure, user interface, and the quality of the graphics it offers, as well as some of its key features. The screenshots depict what the app will look like when it's running on your iPhone.

Scroll down the Info screen and you'll find a more detailed, text-based description of the app in the Description section. The app's description is written by the app's developer or publisher and is designed to persuade you to purchase or acquire the app.

Displayed below the Description section is the Information section (shown in Figure 18-9). Here, you'll see full details about the app, such as its seller, the category in which it's listed, the date it was last updated, its version number, its file size (which indicates how much internal storage space the app itself requires on your iPhone), its rating, and the system requirements to run the app.

If the app's developer has released multiple updates for the app, you'll also see a section called What's New, which outlines new features recently added to the app.

The Requires field is important to look at. While all apps sold from the App Store are for iOS devices, some are designed exclusively for the iPhone or exclusively for the iPad. Others require a specific version of the iOS operating system. Some apps are "hybrid" (also referred to as "universal apps") and will run on either an iPhone or an iPad. The Requires field lists the app's basic system requirements so that you can determine whether it's compatible with your iPhone 5 (or other devices you own).

FIGURE 18-9 The Information section of an app's Info screen provides more details about the app.

Did You Know?

Hybrid Apps Work Perfectly on Both the iPhone and iPad

Apps that are designed to run on both the iPhone and iPad, and automatically adjust for the respective screen sizes of the devices, are referred to as hybrid apps. If you see a tiny plus sign graphic displayed in the upper-left corner of an app's Price button, that indicates it's a hybrid app, as opposed to an iPhone- or iPad-specific app that only runs on that particular device. As noted, you can also determine which iOS devices an app will function on by looking at the Requires field in the Information section of the app's Info screen. If you have an iPhone and an iPad that are linked to the same Apple ID account, look for hybrid apps that will run flawlessly on both devices.

Although all iPhone apps also run on the iPad, some iPad-specific apps won't run on the iPhone, so if the Requires field in an app's Info screen lists only iPad, don't purchase the app for your iPhone.

All iPhone-specific apps will run on an iPad in their native size, in an iPhone-size window displayed in the middle of the iPad's screen. Often, these apps are locked in a single orientation, either portrait or horizontal. You can tap the small, circled 2X icon in the bottom-right corner of your iPad to double the size of the window, but this often reduces the clarity of the screen images.

Most, but not all, iPhone-specific apps also work flawlessly on the iPod touch, as long as the app does not require the actual phone functions of the iPhone. All iPod touch apps work on the iPhone.

Below the Information section is an option labeled Developer Info. Tap this option to view other apps offered in the App Store by the same developer. You can also tap the Version History option to see details about the various versions of the app that have been released in the past. If applicable, below the Version History option will be a Privacy Policy option. This information relates to the third-party developer's policies.

Note   Some apps include a Top In-App Purchases option in the Information section. This can give you information, for example, about prices for magazine issues or subscriptions. It can also give a parent a warning about the potential for a child to run up a huge credit card bill by buying game add-ons. This option is discussed in more detail later in the chapter.

Read Reviews for an App Before Acquiring It

The App Store allows customers to review apps in two different ways. Once you acquire an app, you can give it a star-based rating. You can rate an app using between one and five stars, with five stars representing the best possible rating. When you tap the Reviews tab in an app's Info screen (shown in Figure 18-10), you'll see a chart that graphically shows how many one-, two-, three-, four-, and five-star ratings that particular app has received, plus the total number of ratings.

Thus, if an app has received dozens, hundreds, or even thousands of four- or five-star ratings, you know it's probably a well-designed app that people truly like. However, if the app has received an abundance of one-, two-, or three-star ratings, this is a good indication that the app does not live up to expectations, may contain bugs, or has some type of issue that people don't like.

 In addition to giving an app a star-based rating, if you have Facebook integration turned on in your iPhone, you have the option to tap the Like button to share details about the app with your online friends and let them know you enjoy it.

As you're looking at the Reviews tab of an app's Info, scroll down to view the text-based App Store Customer Reviews that have been written about the app. These are more detailed reviews written by your fellow iOS device users. By reading a handful

FIGURE 18-10 The star-based rating chart shows you how many one-, two-, three-, four-, and five-star ratings a particular app has received to date.

of reviews for an app, you can quickly learn what's good and bad about the app based on other people's firsthand experiences using it.

If an app has received no star-based ratings or detailed reviews, or if the reviews are not unanimously positive or negative, you may need to acquire the app and try it for yourself to determine if it'll meet your needs. In this case, if a free trial version of the app is available, install it and try it out before you decide whether to acquire the paid version of the app.

 Displayed in conjunction with the App Store Customer Reviews for an app are two command buttons, Write A Review and App Support. To write and publish your own online review of the app and include a star-based rating for it, tap the Write A Review button. To access more information about the app and visit the app developer's own webpage, tap the App Support button; the Safari app launches and transfers you directly to the app developer's website. When you return to the App Store app, you'll be able to pick up exactly where you left off.

The App Store contains more than 500,000 different apps that are iPhone compatible. As a result, for every task the iPhone can be used for, chances are you'll discover at least several apps that offer similar functionality.

Find Related Apps

As you're looking at an app's Info screen, tap the Related tab to view app listings for other apps that offer similar functionality. Once you tap on the Related tab, you will see additional app listings. Tap on any listing to view additional information about the related app.

Acquire an App from Its Info Screen

If you decide to acquire and install an app as you're viewing its Info screen, tap the Price button. If it's a paid app, the Price button will turn green and the words Buy App will be displayed (shown in Figure 18-11). If it's a free app, the Price button will turn green and the words Install App will be displayed. Tap the Buy App button or Install App button to confirm your purchase.

When prompted, enter your Apple ID password. The app will then download and install onto your iPhone. If it's a paid app, the credit card or debit card account you have linked to your Apple ID account will be charged immediately. If you're acquiring a free app, you will still be prompted for your Apple ID, but you will not be charged for the app.

 If you have credits remaining from a redeemed iTunes Gift Card, the app purchase will be subtracted from the balance. Using iTunes Gift Cards is a great way to budget your iTunes purchases. A credit/debit card is still required, but it won't be charged as long as you have a balance from the iTunes Gift Card.

FIGURE 18-11 To purchase an app, tap its Price button, and then tap the Buy App button.

Once the app is installed, an icon for it appears on your iPhone's Home screen. To launch the app, tap its app icon. Depending on the file size of the app and how your iPhone is connected to the Internet, it will take anywhere from a few seconds to several minutes for an app to download and install.

 Some apps have a very large file size associated with them. As a result, they can't be downloaded and installed using a 3G/4G Internet connection. In such cases, you'll need to either use a Wi-Fi connection from your iPhone to download the app, or acquire the app using the iTunes software on your primary computer and then perform an iTunes Sync to transfer the app to your iPhone.

Discover the Difference Between Paid and Free Apps

The App Store is chock full of optional apps that can dramatically expand the capabilities of the iPhone. Some apps are free, while others are paid apps. A growing number of apps also now incorporate in-app purchases in some manner.

> **How to...**
>
> ## Install Already Purchased Apps
>
> When you purchase an app, details about the purchase get linked to your Apple ID account. As a result, you can then download and install the app on all of your iOS devices that the app is compatible with and that are linked to the same Apple ID account. So, if you have an iPhone, iPod touch, and/or an iPad, you can purchase a hybrid app once but install and use it on all three devices without having to repurchase it.
>
> If you've purchased a hybrid app on your iPad, for example, that also works on your iPhone, and you want to install it on your iPhone as well, you can preset the App Store app to automatically download and install all newly acquired apps on your iPhone, regardless of which device they were purchased on.
>
> To do this, launch Settings from the Home screen and tap the iTunes & App Stores option. Scroll down the iTunes & App Stores screen (shown here) and turn on the Apps virtual switch under the Automatic Downloads heading.
>
> You can also access a complete list of all iPhone-compatible apps you've ever purchased from the App Store (including apps purchased from your primary computer, an older iPhone model, or another compatible iOS device linked to the same Apple ID account) by launching the App Store app, tapping the Updates icon in the bottom-right corner of the screen (refer to Figure 18-1), and then tapping the Purchased tab. From the list of already purchased apps that's displayed, tap the iCloud icon associated with an app to download and install the app on your iPhone for no additional fee.

Acquire Free Apps

There are several types of free apps. Some are fully functional apps that the developer has chosen to distribute for free, with no strings attached. However, there are also three other types of free apps:

- **Free "demo" apps with limited functionality**   These are scaled-down or demo versions of paid apps. They often have some of their key features locked, or they expire after a predetermined period. The free demo app is offered to give you a hands-on look at what the company's full-featured paid app can do, and entice you to buy it.
- **Advertising-supported apps**   These are fully functional apps, but as you use them for whatever purpose they're designed for, you'll see display banner ads pop

up on the screen, which is how the app developer makes money. In exchange for being able to use the app for free, you must simultaneously view advertising messages.

- **Free apps that require in-app purchases to fully function** These are apps that are initially distributed for free, but require in-app purchases to unlock features, functions, or content. For example, if it's a game, you may be able to play the basic game for free, but you will need to pay to unlock optional game features, power-ups, or special levels. If the app is for a digital newspaper or magazine, the core app used to read the publication's content will be free, but you'll need to make in-app purchases to pay for each issue of (or a subscription for) the publication.

 When you make an in-app purchase, you need to provide your Apple ID password. The fee will be immediately charged to the credit card or debit card account you have linked to your Apple ID account. If you have an iTunes Gift Card credit associated with your Apple ID account, the purchase price of the in-app purchase will be deducted from that credit.

 Each time you use an app, if you make multiple in-app purchases, you may only be prompted to enter your Apple ID once. To prevent unauthorized in-app purchases, you can completely turn off in-app purchases, or you can change how frequently you require the Apple ID password to be reentered. See "Adjust the Restrictions on the iPhone to Keep Your Kids Safe" in Chapter 17 for details.

Acquire Apps by Paying for Them

The price of paid apps varies from $0.99 up to $19.99 (or more). This is a one-time purchase price for the app. Once you acquire it, you own the license to use it and can install it on all of your compatible iOS devices that are linked to the same Apple ID account. All future updates for the app that are issued by the app's developer are also free.

 Keep in mind, it is becoming more and more common for paid apps to also offer in-app purchases. When in-app purchases are offered (and are either optional or required), information about these options, including their prices, will be listed in the app's Info screen when you visit the App Store. Look for the Top In-App Purchases option (shown in Figure 18-12) and tap it for details.

Keep Your Apps Up to Date

Every so often, an app's developer will release a revised version of an app that offers new features, enhanced functionality, and/or bug fixes. Once you initially acquire an app, all future updates for that app are available for free, but you'll need to manually install them onto your iPhone.

FIGURE 18-12 An app's Info screen includes a Top In-App Purchases option if the app offers optional or required in-app purchases.

The Quality of an App Can't Be Determined by Its Price

It's important to understand that the quality of an app is not directly related to its price. There are many free and low-cost apps (priced under $1.99), for example, that are as powerful and as useful as much more expensive apps. There are also some high-priced apps that are loaded with bugs or that offer very poor user interfaces, are difficult to use, or don't offer the functionality you'd expect.

Instead of relying on an app's price to determine its usefulness and quality, access the app's Info screen and read the text-based description in the Description section, take a look at its sample screenshots, and invest a few minutes to read the reviews and look at its star-based ratings.

As a general rule and to ensure ongoing compatibility, periodically check to make sure your iPhone is running the most current version of all apps, along with the latest version of the iOS operating system.

To determine if updates or new versions of apps already installed on your iPhone are available, launch the App Store app from your iPhone and tap the Updates icon in the lower-right corner of the screen (refer to Figure 18-1). If all of your apps are up to date, a message that says, "All Apps Are Up To Date" is displayed. If updated versions of one or more apps are available for download, they'll be listed on the Updates screen. At this point, you can tap the Update button for each app that's listed, or install updates for all of the apps that are available by tapping the Update All button.

When you download and install an app update, it automatically replaces the older version of the app. The download and installation process will take anywhere from several seconds to a few minutes, depending on the file size of the app and how your iPhone is connected to the Internet.

While you can manually check for updates at any time, a Badge will appear on the App Store app's icon on your Home screen when and if app updates become available. The number displayed in the Badge indicates how many apps require an update.

From the Updates screen of the App Store app, you can download and install updates to any optional apps you've added to your iPhone. Whenever Apple releases an update to the iOS operating system, the update includes the latest versions of the preinstalled apps that come bundled with the iPhone (including Contacts, Calendar, Reminders, Safari, Mail, Phone, Camera, Photos, and so forth).

To determine if Apple has released an update to the iOS 6 operating system, launch Settings and tap the General option. Next, tap the Software Update option. If your iPhone is running the latest version of iOS 6, a message that says "Your software is up to date" will be displayed. Otherwise, you'll be prompted to download and install the iOS update, which will probably require that your iPhone be connected to the Internet using a Wi-Fi connection and external power source. All updates to the iOS operating system are free.

Obtain Apple's Own 'Must Have' Apps That Are Optional

As you know, iOS 6 comes bundled with over a dozen apps developed by Apple that allow the iPhone to perform a wide range of tasks right out of the box (refer to Chapter 5 for a complete list). In addition to the apps that come bundled with iOS 6, Apple offers a handful of optional apps that the company developed in-house, and that can further expand the functionality of your iPhone.

Many of these Apple apps are free, and most offer seamless integration with core iOS 6 functions, iCloud, and the preinstalled iPhone apps. The following is a brief summary of some of the optional iPhone apps Apple has developed that are considered "must have" by many iPhone users. All of them are available at the App Store.

- **Apple Store**   This free app (shown in Figure 18-13) allows you to purchase products directly from Apple.com, as well as access information about any local Apple Store. For example, wherever you happen to be, if you need technical assistance with your iPhone, you can use this app to find the closest Apple Store, and then make an appointment with an Apple Genus directly from your phone to avoid a long wait once you get to the Apple Store. You can also purchase a product from your iPhone and pick it up at the closest Apple Store (in the United States only).

 To set up an appointment with a Genius at an Apple Store, launch the Apple Store app, tap on the Store icon (displayed near the bottom of the screen), and then tap on the Genius Bar option and follow the on-screen prompts.

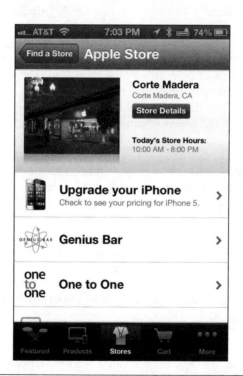

FIGURE 18-13   The Apple Store app allows you to shop from Apple.com for Apple computers, mobile devices, and accessories, or find the closest Apple Store to where you are and book an appointment with an Apple Genius.

Note Free and unlimited in-person support from an Apple Genius (at any Apple Store around the world) is offered to all iPhone 5 owners for 90 days after the purchase of a new iPhone, or for two years if you purchase AppleCare+ in conjunction with your iPhone.

- **Cards**   This free app is used to design and create customized greeting cards that Apple then prints and mails to the recipient on your behalf. Using the professionally designed card templates, you can incorporate your own digital photos and/or message. The printed cards look as nice as any greeting card available at a store, but the Cards app enables you to fully customize the card's design and message for a more personal touch. A $2.99 per card fee applies for a card sent to a location in the United States, but this includes postage. For $4.99 per card, which also includes postage, Apple will have your card sent anywhere in the world.
- **Find Friends**   Utilizing the GPS and Location Services functionality that's built into iOS mobile devices, this free app allows you to share your exact location with your approved friends and, at the same time, see their exact locations (as long as they're using an iPhone, iPad, or iPod touch that's connected to the Internet). The app is highly customizable and allows you to turn on and off various privacy settings.
- **Find My iPhone**   In conjunction with its free iCloud service, Apple allows you to track the exact location of your iMac(s), MacBook(s), and/or iOS mobile devices that are connected to the Internet and that have the Find My [Insert Device Name] functionality activated. This app allows you to pinpoint the location of any of your devices or computers on a map, and then access certain functionality to protect your data if the device has been lost or stolen. Once the Find My iPhone, Find My Mac, or Find My iPad feature is activated, in addition to using this app, you can track the whereabouts of each device by visiting www.iCloud.com/#find and entering your Apple ID and password using any computer or device that can connect to the Internet.
- **GarageBand**   You can compose and record music using this powerful app, as well as create custom ringtones for your iPhone. The iOS version of GarageBand ($4.99) is fully compatible with Garage Band for the Mac (sold separately).
- **iBooks**   This free app allows your iPhone to serve as a feature-packed and customizable e-book reader, and gives you access to Apple's own iBookstore, which offers one of the world's largest selections of paid and free e-books that are formatted to be read on the iPhone's screen. The free iBooks app also allows you to view PDF files that are stored on your iPhone. See Chapter 16 to discover how to use your iPhone to acquire and read e-books, as well as how to make your iPhone compatible with Kindle or Nook e-books.

Note While the iBooks app is optional and does not come preinstalled with iOS 6, the Newsstand app does come bundled with the iPhone. This app also allows you to access iBookstore in order to subscribe to or purchase issues of newspapers and magazines that are available in digital form. In some cases, the Newsstand app is also used to read those digital publications. However, some publications have their own free apps that you can find and download via the Newsstand app.

- **iPhoto**   This optional app ($4.99) greatly enhances the capabilities of your iPhone when it comes to viewing, organizing, editing, enhancing, printing, and sharing digital photos that are taken with or stored on your iPhone. This app (shown in Figure 18-14) is far more powerful than the Photos app that comes bundled with iOS 6, and is fully compatible with iCloud's Photo Stream and Shared Photo Stream features.

See Chapter 11 to learn more about how to use the Camera app to take pictures using your iPhone, and then how to use the Photos app to manage your photos.

- **iTunes U**   While you can purchase a tremendous amount of audio and video content from Apple's iTunes Store, Apple has also teamed up with some of the world's leading educational institutions, educators, business leaders, scientists, museums, and philanthropic organizations to offer literally thousands of online classes, workshops, and lectures—all of which are available for free, as is the iTunes U app (shown in Figure 18-15). Educational and personal enrichment

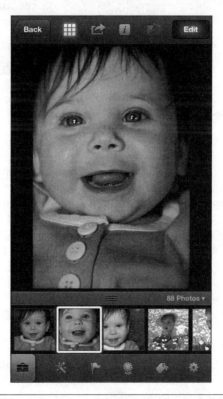

FIGURE 18-14   If you'll be using your iPhone to take and share photos, iPhoto is a "must have" app.

FIGURE 18-15 iTunes U is an incredibly vast and underpublicized resource that's available for free to all Mac and iOS device users.

programs are available for all age and education levels, and all take advantage of free e-books, text files, audio files, video, and other interactive multimedia content to present a vast and ever-growing selection of content relating to literally thousands of different topics and areas of interest.

- **Keynote** Similar in functionality to Microsoft PowerPoint, Keynote ($9.99) is a feature-packed app that allows you to create and present visually compelling digital slideshow presentations directly from your iPhone. The app is fully compatible with the Keynote app for the Mac (sold separately), as well as with PowerPoint files.

- **Numbers** Similar in functionality to Microsoft Excel, Numbers ($9.99) is a powerful spreadsheet management application that is compatible with both the Numbers app for the Mac (sold separately) and Excel files.

- **Pages** While the Notes app comes preinstalled on your iPhone, the optional Pages app ($9.99) offers full word processing functionality. Documents can be imported from or exported to your primary computer (a PC or Mac). Pages (shown in Figure 18-16) is fully compatible with the Pages app for the Mac (sold separately), as well as with Microsoft Word.

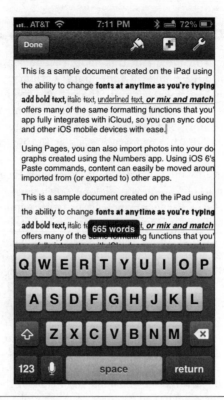

FIGURE 18-16   The Pages app is one of several apps that give you full word processing capabilities and the ability to create, view, edit, print, and share Microsoft Word–compatible documents on your iPhone.

Like many of the apps that come bundled with iOS 6, the optional Pages, Numbers, and Keynote apps (which are referred to as the iWork for iOS apps) are all fully iCloud compatible, and can automatically sync your documents and files with your PC or Mac. However, for the automatic file syncing feature to work, you must have an iCloud account set up, and you must turn on the iCloud function for each app. To do this, after you have installed Pages, Numbers, and/or Keynote on your iPhone, launch Settings and tap the Pages, Numbers, or Keynote option (one at a time). Then, turn on the Use iCloud virtual switch. Do this for each of the iWork for iOS apps you have installed.

Discover Additional Ways to Use iPhone Apps to Improve Your Life

By exploring the App Store, you'll discover apps that allow you to perform all sorts of tasks that can help you become more productive, better manage your finances,

How to... **Install the Official Facebook and Twitter Apps**

As mentioned throughout this book, Facebook and Twitter functionality is built into iOS 6 and fully integrates with many of the apps that come preinstalled with your iPhone. Thus, if you have an active Facebook or Twitter account, you can compose and publish Facebook status updates and/or compose and send tweets directly within many different apps that have a Share button or feature, such as Notification Center, Photos, and Safari.

However, if you want to fully manage your Facebook account and/or Twitter account from your iPhone, you'll need to download and install the free official Facebook app and/or Twitter app. You can acquire these apps from the App Store, or you can download, install, and configure them directly within Settings. To do the latter, launch Settings and scroll down to the Twitter and Facebook options. First, tap the Twitter option and then tap the Install button near the top of the Twitter screen. Then, tap the Settings button in the upper-left corner of the screen and tap the Facebook option. This time, tap the Install button displayed on the Facebook screen.

You also need to activate Facebook and/or Twitter integration on the Facebook and Twitter screens within Settings by tapping the Add Account option and then entering your existing username and password for each account. This only needs to be done once.

Then, once you've downloaded and installed the official Facebook and/or Twitter apps, you'll need to enter your account username and password, this time directly into each app when prompted.

effectively juggle a wide range of responsibilities, become more organized, gather and share information, capture and share stunning photos or videos, entertain yourself, communicate more efficiently, expand your knowledge and skill set, and, of course, make and receive phone calls.

But all of that is just the beginning. By combining your iPhone with other cutting-edge equipment and accessories, what's possible using your iOS mobile device dramatically increases in ways you might not have realized were even possible—and until recently were not.

Use Your iPhone with Other Gadgets and Technology

The following is just a sampling of useful and cutting-edge ways you can use your iPhone 5 as much more than a typical smartphone that's simply capable of making and receiving calls, surfing the Web, communicating via text messages, and allowing you to access your e-mail. When used in conjunction with other gadgets, accessories, and cutting-edge technologies, your iPhone can dramatically improve many aspects of your personal and professional life.

Simultaneously Display What's on Your iPhone's Screen on an HD Television

Using optional cables, your iPhone can connect directly to an HD TV set or monitor, or to an LCD projector, allowing you to share what's on your iPhone's screen with groups of people. However, when you use your iPhone's AirPlay feature in conjunction with an optional Apple TV device ($99, www.apple.com/appletv) connected to your home theater system and a wireless network, you can wirelessly stream photos, music, videos, TV show episodes, movies, presentations, and other multimedia content from your iPhone to your HD TV set with ease.

Using your iPhone with Apple TV, you can begin watching a TV show episode or movie on your iPhone while on the road, and then continue watching uninterrupted the same programming on your home theater system when you get home by tapping one icon. Or, you can stream the digital photos you shot with the camera that's built into your iPhone to your TV set and view them in stunning HD resolution as stand-alone images or as an animated slide show with custom slide transitions and the background music of your choice.

Let Your iPhone Help You Stay Healthy and Fit

Your iPhone can communicate with other technological devices if it connected to them either via a cable or wirelessly via Bluetooth, AirPlay, or Wi-Fi. When it comes to your personal health and fitness, there are pedometers, scales, blood pressure monitors, and workout machines that can be used in conjunction with specialized iPhone apps to help you monitor your health, track your fitness or diet progress, and become a more physically fit person.

For example, Apple has teamed up with Nike to offer the Nike + iPod Sport Kit ($29, http://store.apple.com/us/product/MA365LL/F/nike-ipod-sport-kit). When used with compatible Nike shoes (sold separately) and the special sensor and app that come with the product bundle, your iPhone will serve as a personal workout coach that provides you with real-time feedback as you work out or exercise at home, at the gym, or even outdoors.

Meanwhile, Withings offers a body scale ($129.95, www.withings.com) that can communicate with a specialized iPhone app wirelessly to track your body weight, your body mass index (BMI), and your lean and fat muscle mass. Or, if for medical or fitness purposes you need to monitor your blood pressure, Withings offers the Withings Blood Pressure Monitor ($129), which also communicates with a specialized iPhone app and allows you to measure, track, graph, and share your blood pressure data.

Tip You'll discover literally hundreds of apps in the App Store that can help you stay fit, eat healthy, plan and stick to a diet, research health-related information, or serve as a personalized fitness, workout, and/or exercise coach. You'll find these apps by browsing the Health & Fitness category and the Medical category in the App Store.

Automate Your Home and Maintain Control from Your iPhone

The iPhone can also communicate wirelessly with many of the latest home thermostats, home security cameras, and home alarm systems, as well as with special adapters that connect to your electrical outlets and allow you to remotely turn on and off appliances and lights, for example.

The Nest Learning Thermostat ($249, www.nest.com) allows you to control the climate within your home from anywhere via your iPhone, while Belkin's WeMo adapters and app ($49.99 to $99.99 each, www.belkin.com/wemo) allow you to control electrical appliances or lights.

ADT (www.adtpulse.com), Xfinity Home from Comcast (www.comcast.com/homesecurity/index.htm), and many other companies that provide home security systems now offer specialized apps that allow you to control their systems remotely from your iPhone.

Depending on the system and monitoring service provider, you'll be able to use your iPhone from just about anywhere to activate or deactivate your home's alarm system, open and close a garage door, lock or unlock your home's front door, turn on and off lights, adjust the temperature in your home, and even view a live security camera feed.

Keep Tabs on Your Baby, Pet, or Home While You're Away

If you're the parent of an infant, you're probably familiar with the concept of a baby monitor. When a specialized baby monitor from iBaby Labs ($199.95, www.ibabylabs.com/ibabymonitor) or Stem Innovation ($129.95, www.steminnovation.com) is used with a specialized app on your iPhone that's connected to the Internet, you can watch your child from anywhere, in real time, with full-color video and sound that gets streamed directly to your iPhone's screen.

Now, whether your baby is asleep in their nursery or bedroom while you're elsewhere in the house, or you leave your child with a nanny or babysitter while you're at work or enjoying a night out, an instant, real-time view of your child is always only a few screen taps away.

The baby monitors offered by iBaby Labs and Stem Innovation also work perfectly for monitoring your pet(s) while you're away from home. To use either of these devices with your iPhone, the video cameras/monitors must be able to connect to the Internet within your home.

Present Professional-Quality Presentations Virtually Anywhere

You already know that you can use the Keynote app, for example, to create and present visually stunning and professional-quality digital slide presentations from your iPhone. And, using specialized cables that are available from Apple Stores and Apple.com, for example, you can connect your iPhone directly to an HD TV set or LCD projector.

However, if you want to give presentations virtually anywhere, without having to worry about lugging around a lot of audio/video equipment, Brookstone offers the

Connecting Your iPhone to External Speakers Is Easy

Many companies offer external speakers that can connect to your iPhone either using a cable or via a wireless Bluetooth or AirPlay (Wi-Fi) connection. Brookstone (www.brookstone.com), for example, offers several different external speakers, some of which are battery powered and portable, while others are designed for in-home or office use.

Jawbone is another company that offers high-quality, yet extremely portable, battery-powered speakers designed for use with the iPhone. These speakers connect wirelessly to the iPhone using a Bluetooth connection ($199.99–$299.99, http://jawbone.com/speakers/).

A growing number of speaker manufacturers, including Denon, Bowers & Wilkins, JBL, and iHome, now support Apple's wireless AirPlay technology built into your iPhone. To learn more about this technology, visit www.apple.com/airplay.

HDMI Pocket Projector ($299.99, www.brookstone.com/hdmi-pocket-projector). This is a battery-powered, ultra-small, LED lamp projector that projects images up to 60 inches diagonally (including digital slide presentations or video) from your iPhone in 1080p high definition onto any wall or movie screen. The projector's built-in battery lasts for about two hours per charge or can be plugged into any AC outlet when in use. The device itself measures just 3.9" w × 3.8" d × .89" h and weighs half a pound.

If your presentation or video includes music, sound, or prerecorded narration, you can play it through your iPhone's built-in speaker or, by using AirPlay or Bluetooth, stream it to any compatible wireless speaker(s). You also have the option of using a cable to connect external speakers to your iPhone using its headphone jack.

Scan, Organize, and Share Documents, Notes, or Sketches While On the Go

In the App Store, you'll find several stand-alone apps, such as Scanner Pro ($6.99) or NeatCloud (http://store.neat.com/NeatCloud.html), that allow you to use your iPhone's built-in camera as a personal and portable scanner. When used with text-recognition technology that's built into some of these apps, you can snap a photo of a paper-based document and then edit, view, store, print, or share the document from your iPhone. Other apps allow you to create PDF files from "scanned" documents and/or annotate those files as you view them.

There are also several battery-powered and portable scanners that work in conjunction with the iPhone and specialized apps running on it, such as the Doxie Go scanner from Apparent ($199, www.getdoxie.com).

If you're accustomed to writing down all of your notes, lists, memos, and ideas, using a pen on a pad of paper, Moleskine offers a solution that works flawlessly with your iPhone. By teaming up with the developers of Evernote, which is a powerful note taking and information organization app for iOS mobile devices (as well as for Macs and PCs), Moleskine now offers the Moleskine Evernote Smart Notebooks ($24.95–$29.95, www.moleskineus.com/evernote-smart-notebooks.html). These are high-quality notebooks that allow you to write or draw on regular paper using your favorite writing instrument. Each page of the notebooks, however, features small dots imprinted on them that work with the special scanner app and allow you to quickly snap photos of the notebook pages and import your notes or drawings from the printed page into the Evernote app. Once imported into the app, the notes or drawings can be viewed, annotated, organized, achieved, printed, and/or shared with ease.

The small dots printed on the pages guide your writing but are light enough that they disappear from the "scanned" image, so it appears you have a plain, white background.

Control a High-Tech Toy

As kids, most of us enjoyed playing with remote control cars. Well, several companies have taken this concept to a more technologically advanced level and offer remote control cars, helicopters, hovercrafts, and other toys that can be wirelessly controlled using the iPhone. You'll find many of these toys available from Brookstone (www.brookstone.com). They range in price from around $30 to around $300, and are perfect for kids, teens, and adults.

Process Credit Card Transactions Anywhere

Several companies make it easy and inexpensive for just about anyone to be able to accept and process credit card payments virtually anywhere using the iPhone. This is ideal for a wide range of people, from small business operators, consultants, and freelancers who don't want the complexity and costs of a merchant account with a major credit card company, to occasional sellers who simply want to offer a convenient means of payment, such as artisans and crafters who sell their creations at craft shows, people who periodically hold yard sales, and high school students who babysit or do lawn work for their neighbors.

Square, Intuit, and PayPal each offer a tiny credit card reader that attaches to the top of the iPhone via its headphone jack. Then, once you set up the custom iPhone app and link it to your checking account or savings account, you can easily accept credit card payments for a very low fee, and have the funds deposited directly into your bank account within 24 hours.

Unlike other types of credit card (and debit card) merchant accounts, with the Square credit card processing option, for example, there are no annual contracts, account setup fees, or monthly fees. You simply pay a flat, 2.75 percent per-transaction fee (or a flat $275 per month fee, with no transaction fees whatsoever). The company provides the card swiper and the iPhone app for free.

Using a credit card processing solution from Square (www.squareup.com), Intuit (http://payments.intuit.com), or PayPal (www.paypal.com/webapps/mpp/merchant), you can set up an account within minutes and begin accepting credit card payments for products or services from anyplace your iPhone can connect to the Internet via a 3G/4G or Wi-Fi connection.

Tip Before you sign up with a company to be able to accept credit card payments using your iPhone, make sure you understand all of the fees you'll be responsible for. While Square, Paypal and Intuit charge no hidden or extra fees, other companies charge a monthly service fee, plus a per-transaction fee and/or a percentage of the sale amount.

Dramatically Enhance the Capabilities of Your iPhone's Built-in Camera

Your iPhone 5 has two powerful and high-resolution cameras built in, and when they're used with the Camera app (or another, third-party photography app), you can take great digital photos anytime and anywhere. And if you're serious about photography and want to be able to take even better photos using your iPhone, you have a variety of options. For example, there are photography apps that allow you to add special effects and photo enhancements to your images while you're taking them or immediately afterward.

However, if you want to step up to the professional level, there are optional photography accessories for the iPhone that are designed for those who want to snap even better quality photos, without compromising the portability and convenience of using the iPhone (or having to carry around a separate point-and-shoot or digital SLR camera).

The OlloClip is an optional, three-in-one photo lens that clips onto your iPhone (over its existing camera lens) to provide a more versatile fisheye, macro, or wide-angle lens when it's needed. When not in use, the OlloClip ($69.95, www.olloclip.com) can be stored in your pocket or purse. It works with all of your favorite photography apps, including the Camera app.

The iPro Lens System ($199–$299, www.iprolens.com) is an external lens system that comes with a specially designed iPhone case and handheld tripod. The lenses attach to the iPhone in front of the phone's existing camera lens to offer additional versatility. You can utilize a wide-angle, fisheye, or 2X optical zoom lens with this system.

Note When shopping for the OlloClip or iPro Lens System, make sure you purchase the iPhone 5 version of the product, as each is also available for the iPhone 4/4S.

Did You Know?

Your iPhone Can (or May Soon Be Able to) Interact Directly with Your Car

Car manufacturers have taken note of the iPhone's popularity and have begun developing innovative ways a car itself can communicate wirelessly with an iPhone, giving the driver the ability to remotely unlock doors, start the ignition, check a car's tire pressure or oil, and monitor other car functions directly from the iPhone. This functionality is being built directly into some new vehicles, and is separate from the functionality afforded by installing an optional hands-free car kit in your vehicle to make and receive calls on your iPhone without being distracted while driving. Chapter 7 offers additional information about optional Bluetooth headsets and hands-free car kits that you can (and should) use in conjunction with your iPhone while you're driving.

Take Better Control over Your Favorite Action and Arcade-Style Games

Whether you play video games on a Nintendo Wii, Xbox 360, or PlayStation 3, or enjoy experiencing these games in the arcade, the one thing these gaming experiences have in common is the joystick or controller pad used to control the action on the screen.

While your iPhone allows you to tilt the device itself and tap on the screen to help control the action, several companies offer optional joystick controllers that connect directly to the iPhone to give you maximum control when experiencing your favorite action or arcade-style games.

For example, the Joystick-It Arcade Stick for iPhone ($8.99, www.thinkgeek.com/product/e8f5/) attaches to the iPhone's touch screen using a suction cup. The Fling Mini ($24.95, http://tenonedesign.com/flingmini.php) offers a two-joystick option that also quickly attaches to the iPhone's touch screen.

Tip   Using the search phrase "iPhone joystick" on Google or Yahoo!, for example, you'll find a handful of other gaming accessories for the iPhone that offer joystick functionality and/or a more authentic arcade-style gaming experience.

Program Your TiVo from Anywhere

If you have a newer-model TiVo digital video recorder connected to your TV set and it has access to the Internet, you can use it in conjunction with the free TiVo app on your iPhone to not only turn your iPhone into a remote control for the TV (and TiVo), but also program your TiVo and schedule recordings from virtually anywhere. Similar functionality is also available from some other digital video recorders offered by Direct TV and cable TV providers.

19

Protect Your iPhone

HOW TO...

- Use a protective film on your iPhone's screen
- Choose the perfect case
- Decide if you need AppleCare+ or other iPhone insurance

Chances are, when you purchased your iPhone 5, you agreed to a two-year service contract with a wireless service provider, such as AT&T Wireless, Verizon Wireless, or Sprint PCS. Because you agreed to the long-term contract, the price of the iPhone 5 was subsidized, meaning that you paid a fraction of the iPhone's full retail price. If, however, your iPhone 5 gets lost, stolen, or damaged, unless you pre-purchase AppleCare + and/or third-party insurance for your iPhone, you could wind up having to pay upward of $500 to $800 to replace your iPhone (or at the very least, several hundred dollars to repair it).

 With a $49 per claim deductible, AppleCare+ offers coverage to repair a damaged iPhone, but it does not cover loss or theft of the phone. For this type of coverage, you'll need third-party insurance, which is discussed later in this chapter. AppleCare+ coverage lasts for two years and allows for up to two product repairs or replacements. You must purchase AppleCare+ at the same time you purchase your new iPhone 5, or within 30 days of the phone's purchase.

While it's impossible to protect your iPhone 5 against every possible mishap, you can take steps to prevent costly repairs and loss. For example, for a small investment, you can start by protecting the iPhone 5's screen, which is probably the most fragile part of the device, with a clear protective film. You can also encase the entire body of the iPhone with a similar clear film, or cover the phone's back with a skin.

Next, you can invest in a durable case for the iPhone, which will come in handy when you're not using the phone by protecting it if it gets dropped or crushed, for example. Plus, a case that somehow securely connects to your belt, briefcase, purse, messenger bag, or backpack can help prevent the iPhone from getting lost or stolen.

Note Aside from accidently dropping the iPhone on the floor, one of the most common mishaps people experience is spilling liquid on the phone, or dropping it into a toilet, bathtub, lake, or swimming pool. There are specialized cases available that offer protection against liquid, as well as kits you can purchase in order to attempt to revive an iPhone that's been submerged in water. Again, this is a situation where having AppleCare+ or third-party insurance protection would come in handy and save you a fortune.

Select a Clear Protective Film for the iPhone's Screen

A variety of companies offer custom-cut, clear protective films that can be applied directly over the iPhone's screen. The majority of these protective films are made from an extremely thin and durable, military-grade material that is very easy to clean. These protective films help to prevent the screen from getting cracked or damaged, plus help to reduce fingerprint smudges and glare.

As you begin shopping for a protective film for your iPhone's screen, you'll discover that all of them are crystal clear and extremely thin, but that some are very smooth to the touch while others offer a slight texture that helps to keep your finger from slipping around the screen. Which type you choose is a matter of personal preference.

Some of the protective films also provide protection against glare and actually help to improve the screen's clarity in certain lighting situations, while others offer an added level of privacy that prevents someone from looking over your shoulder and seeing what's on your iPhone's display.

For a good-quality protective film that covers the iPhone 5's entire screen but keeps the phone's camera lens, Home button, and speaker fully accessible, plan on spending anywhere from $14.95 to $29.95. These films are designed to be kept on the iPhone permanently, but they can be removed in seconds and won't leave any sticky residue on the screen.

Note Most of the protective films are so thin, once they're installed they're barely detectible, allowing you to still use any case, cover, or accessory for your iPhone. Even if you opt to not use a case or cover with your iPhone, a protective film is one layer of protection you should not forego.

If you want to purchase a protective film and install it onto your iPhone's screen yourself, you can purchase one from an office supply or consumer electronics store, such as Staples, Office Max, Best Buy, Radio Shack, Target, or Wal-Mart, or you can order one from an online store. You can install many of these films yourself in about 15 minutes. The following are a few companies that manufacture and sell these protective films online:

- Body Guardz   www.bodyguardz.com
- iSkin   www.iskin.com
- Phantom Skinz   http://phantomskinz.com
- Tru Projection   www.truprotection.com/films.html
- Wrapsol   www.wrapsol.com
- Zagg   www.zagg.com/invisibleshield

If you opt to apply your own protective film on your iPhone, carefully follow the directions that are provided so that you avoid accidently creasing the film, getting dirt stuck on the side of the film that attaches to the iPhone's screen, winding up with air bubbles between the screen and the film, or improperly lining up the perfectly sized and shaped film when applying it onto the screen.

Caution   The application instructions for some protective films require that you spray the screen or film with a little bit of water as you initially apply them, and then highly recommend waiting 24 hours before turning on and using the iPhone. To avoid accidently damaging your iPhone, read and follow the application instructions carefully, or have a professional install the protective film for you.

If you want to purchase a protective film from a company that will apply it for you, visit almost any mall in your area and look for a cell phone accessories or phone repair kiosk. There are also kiosk-based companies, like Ghost Armor (www.ghost-armor.com/locations.php), that do nothing but sell protective films for high-tech gadgets, and will apply one for you while you wait. This option will cost a bit more, but it'll save you some time and potential frustration.

3M Offers Protective Films That Also Provide Privacy

3M offers several different iPhone protective film covers that offer scratch protection, antiglare protection, and/or privacy protection. The antiglare and scratch protective films are crystal clear and similar to what many other companies offer. However, 3M's privacy protection screens are unique.

The 3M privacy screens for the iPhone (priced around $20; http://solutions.3m.com/wps/portal/3M/en_US/3MScreens_NA/Protectors/Shop_Products) are made from a proprietary and patented material that allows you to look directly at the iPhone's screen and view what's displayed on it perfectly, but if someone looks over your shoulder or attempts to glance at your phone's screen from the side, for example, all they'll see is a dark, blank screen. This is useful if you're on an airplane, bus, or train, for example, where strangers surround you and you want or need privacy as you read information displayed on your iPhone's screen.

Apply a Custom "Skin" to Encase the Entire iPhone

An alternative to applying a thin, clear protective film over your iPhone 5's screen is to apply either a clear or imprinted "skin" over the iPhone's entire housing. Obviously, the portion of the skin that covers the screen will be clear. However, the rest of the skin can be imprinted with any design, any graphic, or even your own digital photo. By covering the entire iPhone in a skin, not only is the screen protected, but you can help prevent scratches and other damage to the phone's back and sides.

 You also have the option to use a clear protective film on the front of your iPhone and a separate, imprinted skin on the back. For less than $20, GelaSkins (www.gelaskins.com/create), for example, allows you to have your favorite, full-color digital photo imprinted on an iPhone skin. This gives your iPhone a truly customized look.

Most skins are made from a durable, military-grade material that resists tearing and scratching, but some are made of a durable vinyl that is also extremely thin. Like the stand-alone protective screen films, once they're applied to your iPhone, you can still use the phone with any case or cover. You'll find a handful of companies selling skins for the iPhone 5 on the Internet.

Some of these companies include

- DecalGirl   www.decalgirl.com
- GelaSkins   www.gelaskins.com
- SkinIt   www.skinit.com
- Slickwraps   www.slickwraps.com
- Zagg   www.zagg.com

 When shopping for a skin, be sure to purchase one that's custom cut and shaped specifically for the iPhone 5, to ensure a proper fit and maximum protection for the device.

Choose the Perfect Case or Cover for Your iPhone

An iPhone case or cover can take the form of a plastic hard-shell casing, a padded sleeve, or a holster, for example. In fact, you'll find iPhone 5 cases come in a wide range of colors, shapes, and styles and are made from many different types of materials. Using a case with your iPhone not only adds another level of protection and a barrier against dirt and potential damage (if the phone is dropped, for example), but can also provide a sense of style to your iPhone.

Cases and covers are available wherever cell phone accessories are sold, including the Apple Store. However, some of the really nice, hand-crafted, and/or designer cases need to be ordered online.

When choosing a case or cover, focus on how you'll be using your iPhone, how you'll transport it around with you, and how much protection you believe it needs based on how you'll use it. Then, choose a design that meets your needs. As you begin case shopping, you'll find many designed specifically for the iPhone 5, as well as others that are generic and designed to house almost any smartphone model.

The final consideration should be the stylishness and quality of the case. Be sure to pay attention to the durability of the materials the case is made from, as well as the overall craftsmanship and the quality of the zippers, clasps, clips, or hooks that it incorporates. For example, if you're buying a case that will clip onto your belt, purse, or messenger bag so that you have easy access to your iPhone, make sure that clip is extremely strong and attached well to the case itself (so it will not break or snap off).

 The price of an iPhone case is not an indication of its quality, durability, or craftsmanship. There are some very inexpensive cases that are well made, and some higher-priced cases that are extremely poorly designed or that offer little protection to your iPhone. If you're shopping in a retail store, you can see the case and determine its quality firsthand. If you're shopping online, however, pay attention to the reputation of the seller and the product reviews other customers have written about the product.

Plan on spending anywhere from $29.95 to $200 for an iPhone case. The following is a small sampling of companies that offer iPhone cases that can be ordered online:

- Brookstone   www.brookstone.com
- Incase   www.goincase.com
- Incipio   www.incipio.com
- Levenger   www.levenger.com
- Saddleback Leather   www.saddlebackleather.com/Belt-Pouch
- Sena Cases   www.senacases.com
- Smythson of Bond Street   www.smythson.com/us/technology/phone-cases.html
- Speck Products   www.speckproducts.com/iphone-case.html
- Twelve South   http://twelvesouth.com/products/bookbook_iphone
- Waterfield Designs   www.sfbags.com/products/iphone-cases/iphone-cases.php

 Many popular fashion and fashion accessory designers also offer designer iPhone cases, including Coach, Louis Vuitton, Marc Jacobs, Kate Spade, Michael Kors, Juicy Couture, and Gucci.

In addition to housing just the iPhone 5, you'll find cases that offer separate compartments for cash, IDs, business cards, and credit cards, or that also allow you to carry around your corded ear buds/headphones. Some cases are designed to house

Did You Know?

Some iPhone Cases Have a Battery Pack Built In

If you're a heavy iPhone user and don't have time in the middle of your day to recharge the phone's battery, but you rely on it, and can't afford for the battery to go dead, there are a variety of external rechargeable battery packs available that can double or triple the battery life of your iPhone.

Some of these external batteries are actually built into iPhone cases, so not only will your iPhone stay protected, it'll also remain charged for extended periods. These case/battery pack combos add a little bit of extra weight and thickness to the iPhone, but they provide that extra power that's necessary to keep your iPhone going when it's most needed.

Mophie (www.mophie.com), for example, offers a line of thin but durable hard iPhone cases with a rechargeable battery built in that will double your iPhone's battery life. Incipio (www.incipio.com), Incase (www.goincase.com), and Brookstone (www.brookstone.com) also offer cases with built-in battery packs. Cases that include a battery pack start in price at just under $100.

Meanwhile, Sol Marketplace offers a solar-powered rechargeable battery that's built into a rugged plastic case for the iPhone (www.solmarketplace.com/products/SoL-Hybrid-Power-Pack.html).

the iPhone at all times, even when it's in use, while other designs require that you remove the iPhone from the case in order to use it.

Before choosing a cover that remains on the iPhone 5 at all times, make sure it offers a perfect fit and gives you full access to the iPhone's touch screen, Home button, volume buttons, power button, and headphone jack, and make sure that it does not block the camera lenses, speakers, microphone, or Lightning connector port.

Because the iPhone 5 offers a slightly different shape, size, and design than earlier models, it will take some of the third-party case manufacturers several months to begin offering iPhone 5 versions of their cases and covers. By early-to-mid 2013, a vast selection of iPhone 5 cases will no doubt be available, but for the first few months after the iPhone 5's release, the selection will likely be limited.

Discover the Benefits of Investing in AppleCare+

If you lead a normal, active lifestyle and keep your iPhone with you most of the time, accidents do happen, and without proper protection, repairing damage to your iPhone can get costly. Knowing this, Apple offers its AppleCare + program ($99 for two years), which must be purchased within 30 days of acquiring a new iPhone.

Without AppleCare + coverage, Apple offers new iPhone 5 users 90 days' worth of unlimited free technical support (including in-person help from an Apple Genius), and one year of basic coverage for manufacturing defects related to the iPhone. This free coverage, however, does not cover accidental damage you inflict on the phone.

When you purchase AppleCare + for your iPhone, which is available wherever the iPhone is sold (as well as from Apple Stores and Apple.com), it includes two full years of unlimited in-person or telephone technical support, as well as two years' worth of coverage against manufacturing defects and accidental damage you may inflict on your phone.

 If you accidently damage the iPhone, crack the screen, or drop it in water, for example, assuming you have AppleCare+, you will be charged a service fee of $49 per incident to repair or, if necessary, replace the phone. The AppleCare+ program allows for up to two separate incidents within the two-year period.

With AppleCare + , if you have questions about how to use your iPhone or need help accomplishing a specific task, you can make an appointment at any Apple Store to meet in person with an Apple Genius, or you can call Apple's toll-free AppleCare support phone number to receive assistance (800-APL-CARE).

Unlike virtually every other computer and consumer electronics manufacturer on the planet, within the United States, Apple offers superior technical support from knowledgeable, friendly, well-trained, and U.S.-based personnel (Apple Geniuses) who speak fluent English. If you use Apple's telephone-based technical support, at most you'll wait on hold for just a few minutes to speak with a technical support representative.

 What AppleCare+ does not cover is the loss or theft of an iPhone. If you want this type of coverage, you'll need to invest in third-party phone insurance.

Evaluate Third-Party iPhone Insurance Options

The wireless service providers in the United States that support the iPhone, including AT&T Wireless, Verizon Wireless, and Sprint PCS, all offer their own iPhone insurance programs. However, these are typically extremely costly, offer limited coverage, or require you to pay a high deductible to get the phone repaired or replaced.

Several independent companies, however, offer more comprehensive insurance policies for the iPhone 5 that provide between one and three years of coverage. Some of these policies cover the loss or theft of the iPhone, in addition to accidental damage. Be sure to read the fine print of the policy being offered before you purchase it to determine exactly what coverage is offered.

While third-party iPhone insurance offers coverage against accidental damage, and in some cases theft or loss of the iPhone, it does not offer any technical support whatsoever.

Starting at about $50 per year, two companies that offer third-party iPhone insurance are SquareTrade (www.squaretrade.com) and Worth Ave. Group (www.worthavegroup.com/iphone-insurance), the latter of which includes coverage against loss or theft of the device. Keep in mind, you'll typically need to purchase third-party insurance within 30 days of purchasing your iPhone 5 in order to receive coverage

iPhone insurance covers one iPhone (based on its serial number) and is not transferrable between phones. So, if you purchased AppleCare+ or other insurance for your iPhone 4 or iPhone 4S, for example, you'll still need to purchase AppleCare+ and/or third-party insurance for your iPhone 5.

Discover What to Do if Your iPhone Gets Damaged

The number of "creative" ways people manage to accidently damage or destroy their iPhone is vast. For those who believe, "Oh, that could never happen to me. I am very careful when using my phone," think again. At some point, you're probably going to trip and drop the iPhone (while texting and walking, for example) or spill liquid on it, or it's going to get knocked off a desk, fall out of your pocket and hit the ground, or get crushed because you accidently sit on it. You'll be surprised (and probably amused) to discover how common it is for people to accidently drop their iPhone in a toilet, swimming pool, or lake, for example.

If you damage your iPhone, regardless of whether or not it's covered by AppleCare+, take it into an Apple Store and have the extent of the damage diagnosed by an Apple technician, and then determine what options you have to repair it through Apple. In some cases, the Apple Store will be able to offer you a new or refurbished iPhone at the subsidized price, as opposed to the full retail price, even if you're in the middle of your two-year service contract.

Two of the most common types of iPhone damage people experience are a cracked screen or water damage. Without having AppleCare+ or other insurance, plan on spending $150 or more to have Apple repair a broken screen, for example. There are independent iPhone repair businesses at local malls or that you can send your iPhone into, but repair costs will still be significant, depending on the type of damage you've inflected on your iPhone.

If you need to repair an iPhone that suffers from water damage, Dry-All (www.dry-all.com) offers a repair kit ($49.99) specifically for this that allows you to do the repair yourself.

If you're somewhat technologically savvy, you can order an iPhone repair kit online and attempt to perform the repair yourself, using the parts, tools, and directions supplied with the kit. This can save you money, but you do run the risk of doing something wrong and causing additional damage. Attempting to repair the iPhone yourself could result in voiding all warranties from Apple.

To find and purchase a do-it-yourself iPhone repair kit, access an Internet search engine, such as Google or Yahoo!, and enter the search phrase "iPhone repair kit" or "iPhone replacement screen," for example. These kits cost anywhere from $25 to $100, depending on the type of damage you need to repair. Companies like iFixYouri.com (www.ifixyouri.com/23-iphone-repair-kit) and Mission Repair (www.missionrepair.com) offer kits for repairing a cracked screen or a broken back panel.

Strategies for Replacing a Lost, Stolen, or Damaged iPhone

Depending on the circumstances, it might not make financial sense to have a damaged iPhone repaired, especially if you don't have AppleCare + or other insurance for it. Or, if you've lost the phone or it's been stolen, you'll discover that without the proper insurance, you'll need to replace the iPhone by buying a new, full-priced iPhone (assuming you're somewhere in the middle of your two-year service agreement with your wireless service provider). Again, this can cost between $500 and $800.

To help reduce the financial blow associated with replacing an iPhone, you have a few options, including:

- Sell your broken iPhone (and/or your older-model iPhone) to a company that will pay anywhere between $100 and $300 for the device, depending on its condition. Companies like Gazelle (www.gazelle.com/iphone), The iPhone Antidote (www.iphoneantidote.com), and NextWorth (http://nextworth.com) will pay cash for used iPhones, regardless of their condition. Some consumer electronics stores will also buy older-model or broken iPhones and give you cash or store credit for them.
- Purchase a used or reconditioned iPhone to replace your lost or stolen iPhone 5. You can typically find a used iPhone 4 or iPhone 4S for $200 to $300 (or less) that's in full working condition. For at least six months after the initial release of the iPhone 5, finding a used or reconditioned iPhone 5 might be a challenge, but they too may be available from companies like Gazelle, The iPhone Antidote, or NextWorth.

    You can visit any Apple Store or a store operated by your wireless service provider and ask if they have any reconditioned iPhones in stock. These phones come with a warranty, but are priced lower than a brand new iPhone. For example, AT&T Wireless (www.att.com/shop/wireless/devices/refurbishedphones.html) and Verizon Wireless (www.verizonwireless.com/b2c/device/preowned) have special webpages set up to sell refurbished smartphones, including iPhones. The GameStop chain of retail stores (www.gamestop.com/collection/gamestop-refurbished-iPhone) also buys used iPhones and sells refurbished iPhones.

You also have the option to buy a used iPhone or sell your existing (broken or older-model iPhone) yourself using eBay.com or Craigslist.org. Make sure to fully disclose the condition of your iPhone when you advertise it.

Troubleshoot iPhone Problems

Just like a computer, your iPhone 5 is a highly technical and advanced piece of equipment. And, as can happen with all types of consumer electronics, things can go wrong with your iPhone 5. The good news is, Apple has devised ways to quickly fix the most common problems associated with using an iPhone.

Fix Common iPhone-Related Problems

There are several common types of problems you may encounter when using an iPhone, the most common of which is a dead battery. If your iPhone suddenly turns off, or refuses to power up, chance are its battery is dead. Don't forget, you have to keep the iPhone's battery charged in order for it to keep working.

 Get into the habit of charging your iPhone every night and/or while it's sitting idle at your desk, for example. You can also invest in an external battery pack and/or a car charger so that you can keep your iPhone's battery charged while you're on the go.

In this situation, plug the iPhone into an external power source for a few minutes, and then try turning the iPhone back on by pressing the Power (Sleep/Wake) button on the top of the phone (while the phone is still connected to the external power source).

If this doesn't work, try pressing and holding down the Home button and the Power (Sleep/Wake) button simultaneously for several seconds. This should cause the Apple logo to appear and the iPhone to power on and boot up.

Let's take a look at solutions to other common problems.

 Periodically, check to make sure your iPhone is running the most current version of iOS 6 and that you have the most recent version of each app you're using installed. See "Keep Your Apps Up to Date" in Chapter 18 for details on how to check both.

What to Do if Your iPhone Gets Lost or Stolen

In this situation, you have good options if you have turned on the Find My iPhone feature in advance of the incident. To do this (before the iPhone is lost or stolen), launch Settings, tap the iCloud option, and then turn on the Find My iPhone virtual switch. You need to do this only once.

Now, if the iPhone gets lost or stolen, use any computer or device with an Internet connection and visit www.iCloud.com/#find. Log in to this website using your iCloud username and password (which is typically your Apple ID and password).

Assuming the iPhone is turned on and connected to the Internet, the iCloud website will display a detailed map that pinpoints the exact location of your device. You'll then have several options for managing the iPhone while you're in the process of retrieving it:

- If you lost your iPhone, by using the Find My iPhone feature at the iCloud website, you can have your lost iPhone generate a tone so that you can more easily discover where you left it.
- If your iPhone was stolen (or you lost it and are concerned a stranger may have found it), you can lock down your iPhone by turning on the Passcode Lock feature (see Chapter 3) and/or opt to remotely erase everything from your iPhone. Command icons for these options are displayed when you use the Find My iPhone feature.

 If you have another iOS mobile device, such as an iPad, you can use the free Find My iPhone app to pinpoint the location of your iPhone, Mac(s), or other iOS mobile device and perform these same tasks by visiting www.iCloud.com/#find.

What to Do if Your iPhone Gets Damaged

In this situation, if you've followed the advice offered in Chapter 19 and purchased insurance for your iPhone, either Apple's optional AppleCare+ extended coverage or third-party insurance from a company like Worth Ave. Group or SquareTrade, you can have your iPhone 5 repaired or replaced (assuming you submit your claim during the coverage term). A $50 deductible may apply. With no insurance, the cost to repair a damaged iPhone can be several hundred dollars, or much more if it needs to be replaced.

Once an iPhone is physically damaged, take it to an Apple Store or authorized Apple service center to have them diagnose the problem and determine what's involved to repair it.

What to Do if Your iPhone Starts Acting Sluggish

If your iPhone begins acting very sluggish, you may have too many apps running in the background. To fix this common problem, enter Multitasking mode by pressing the Home button twice. Then, place and hold your finger on any app icon until they all start shaking. Now, one at a time, tap the negative sign "–" icon associated with each app icon to close the corresponding app.

When you close an app from within Multitasking mode, the app stops running in the background, but this does not delete the app from your iPhone. Once you shut down all apps that don't need to be running, your iPhone will probably begin running again normally. If not, reboot the iPhone by pressing and holding the Home button and the Power (Sleep/Wake) button at the same time for about 15 seconds. The screen will turn off and then turn back on. You'll see the Apple logo appear. At this point, remove your fingers from the Home and Power buttons and allow the iPhone to reboot. Doing this will not erase anything from the iPhone.

Sometimes, simply powering off the iPhone and then turning it back on will fix the problem. To turn off the iPhone, press and hold the Power (Sleep/Wake) button until you see the Slide To Power Off slider. Swipe your finger from left to right across this slider. The iPhone will shut itself down. To turn the iPhone back on and reboot it, press and hold just the Power (Sleep/Wake) button for several seconds. The Apple logo will appear on the screen. Between 15 and 45 seconds later, your iPhone will be ready to use.

What to Do if Your iPhone Won't Make or Receive Calls

Should you experience a situation where your iPhone will not allow you to make or receive calls, make sure the phone is turned on and not in Airplane mode (refer to Chapter 2 for details about Airplane mode). You should see the signal strength indicator and the name of your wireless service provider displayed near the top-left corner of the screen.

If no signal bars are displayed in the signal strength indicator, you are not close enough to a cell tower, meaning your iPhone is out of range from your wireless service provider or not in a coverage area. Thus, you'll need to change your location in order to pick up a viable signal.

If you're out of your wireless service provider's range, you have the option to turn on the iPhone's roaming feature from within Settings. However, you will incur hefty roaming charges for making or receiving calls while roaming. To do this, launch Settings, select the General option, and then tap the Cellular option.

What to Do if Your iPhone Can't Access the Internet

If your iPhone can't access the Internet, make sure you're within a 3G or 4G (LTE) wireless data coverage area. You will see the icon for 3G, 4G, or LTE displayed to the immediate right of the cellular signal strength indicator (in the top-left corner of the screen). If you're not within a wireless data coverage area, you'll need to connect your iPhone to the Internet using a Wi-Fi connection, if available.

If a Wi-Fi signal is too weak for your iPhone to connect to it, try moving closer to the wireless Internet router, or select a different Wi-Fi hotspot or wireless network to connect to.

Dealing with Other iPhone-Related Problems

When dealing with almost any iPhone-related problem, chances are you'll discover a solution at Apple's website. Visit https://expresslane.apple.com/Issues.action and choose the iPhone category. If you don't find a solution to your problem, use the Search field in the upper-right corner of the screen to enter keywords related to your problem.

For the first 90 days you own your iPhone (or for two years if you've purchased AppleCare+), you have unlimited access to Apple's technical support services by phone. Call (800) APL-CARE to speak with a technical support representative. When calling AppleCare, you'll need to provide your iPhone's serial number. See Chapter 19 for more information about AppleCare+.

 To access your iPhone's serial number, launch Settings, tap the General option, and then tap the About option. Scroll down to the Serial Number heading, where you'll find your iPhone's serial number displayed.

Yet another option is to visit any Apple Store and make an in-person appointment with an Apple Genius. You can make a free appointment online from Apple's website, or by using the free (and optional) Apple Store app, or by dropping into an Apple Store in person. If you show up to an Apple Store without an appointment, expect a long wait to receive one-on-one technical support, especially during busy periods.

 If you experience problems using a third-party app, access the listing for that app in the App Store and locate the developer's website. In some cases, you can make contact with an app's developer from directly within an app.

Try to Prevent Problems, but Be Prepared if Any Arise

As a general rule, you should get into the habit of creating and maintaining a full backup of your iPhone (using the iTunes Sync or iCloud Backup process, discussed in Chapter 4). Then, if something does go wrong with your iPhone, you always have the option to restore your important data, apps, and system preferences from a backup.

To help protect your iPhone from damage, invest in a thin protective film for the screen and a sturdy case for the phone, as described in Chapter 19. Also, turn on the Find My iPhone feature.

You should also take advantage of your free iCloud account and automatically back up and sync app-specific data for Contacts, Calendar, Reminders, Notes, Safari, and Mail with your iCloud account. Doing this ensures your most important data is always stored "in the cloud," as well as on your iPhone.

If you use an online service other than iCloud to sync your other app-specific data for Contacts and Calendar, for example, only sync your data with that one service, not with both Google and iCloud, Yahoo! and iCloud, or a Microsoft Exchange–compatible service and iCloud. Otherwise, you could wind up with duplicate entries.

Then, if you experience a problem with your iPhone, you can always access your app-specific data by visiting www.iCloud.com and using the online versions of the Contacts, Calendar, Reminders, and/or Notes apps. You can also access and manage your iCloud e-mail account, as well as files and documents synced with iCloud using the Documents & Data feature (in conjunction with apps like Pages, Numbers, and Keynote).

How to...   Restore Your iPhone to Factory Settings

Once your app-specific data is synced with iCloud, you can restore it to your existing iPhone (or to a new/replacement iPhone) should a problem arise. In certain situations, you may be instructed by an Apple Genius or Apple Technical Support specialist to erase and reset your iPhone and return it to its factory settings, before you restore your information.

Before doing this, make sure you have backed up all of your app-specific data using iCloud and have used the iCloud Backup feature (or have used the iTunes Sync feature to back up your entire iPhone and all app-specific data). Then, if you need to reset your iPhone, launch Settings, tap the General option, scroll down to the Reset option, and tap the Erase All Content And Settings option. Once you confirm your decision, your iPhone will erase and reset itself. When it turns back on, it will be in the state it was in when you purchased it and took it out of the box for the first time.

In the future, if you upgrade from your iPhone 5 to a newer model and want to give your iPhone 5 to someone else (or sell it), you will definitely want to restore it to its factory settings before you transfer ownership.

Index

Symbols and Numbers

! (exclamation point), 328
+ = key, 45
"." Shortcut, 51
3D map views, 297, 299–300
3G/4G connections
    Dictation and, 75
    multitasking capabilities
      and, 124
    selecting service provider and
      service plan, 15–16
    Siri and, 63
    troubleshooting iPhone,
      469–470
3M protective films, 459
4-inch screen, 6–7
4+ rating, 410
9+ rating, 410
12+ rating, 410
17+ rating, 410
123 key, 45

A

A6 processor chip, 10
aA icon, 240, 400–402
abbreviations in text messages, 351
ABC key, 45
Accept Cookies, 256
accepting calls
    in FaceTime app, 338–339
    in Phone app, 165–172
accounts
    Apple ID account. See Apple ID
      account
    iCloud, 142–143

setting up existing e-mail to
    work with Mail app, 217–220
activation
    automatic Siri, 127
    iPhone 5, 20–24
Add Bookmark screen, 247
Add Calendar, 312–313
Add Call, 182–183
Add Contact, 192
Add Event, 314–317
Add Field, 196–199
Add New Address, 196–197
Add To Favorites, 192
Add To Home Screen, 244
Add To Reading List, 245
Address Bar, 236–237
addresses
    in Contacts, 188
    creating new Contact entry,
     196–197
admission tickets, 382–383
Adobe Flash, 235–236
ADT Security, 452
advertising-supported apps,
  441–442
ages and game suitability, 409–411
AIM (AOL Instant Messenger), 352
Airplane mode
    setup and configuration, 31–32
    troubleshooting iPhone, 469
AirPlay
    iPhone as home theater
     system, 356
    preinstalled iOS apps, 122
    streaming photos and video, 277
    using Music app with external
     speakers, 377, 379

watching video content with
    Videos app, 381–382
AirPrint
    from Mail app, 228–229
    preinstalled iOS apps, 122
    printing notes, 330
    printing photos, 285
    sharing photos and videos, 280
alarms
    customizing list items, 326–327
    customizing Notification
     Center, 41
    home automation apps, 452
Albums
    Complete My Album
     feature, 376
    Music app, 374–375
    navigating with Photos app,
     273–275
    shopping for music in iTunes,
     358–362
Alerts
    calendar notifications, 320
    creating new events, 315–316
    customizing Notification
     Center, 35–42
    functionality from Lock
     screen, 135
    Messages app and, 347
    personalizing sound and
     vibration, 146–147
All Contacts, 189–190
All Inboxes
    defined, 222
    refreshing, 225
    VIP list, 230
Allow Access When Locked,
  127–128

Allow Calls From option, 168
Allowance, 362
Allowed Content, 423–424
Always Bcc Myself, 221
anatomy of iPhone 5, 6–8
Angry Birds, 412–413
annotating text as you read, 399
Answer button, 165–166
answering incoming calls
   with FaceTime, 338–339
   with Phone app, 165–172
AOL
   setting up existing e-mail to
      work with Mail app, 217–220
   syncing Contacts with, 212–215
AOL Instant Messenger (AIM), 352
Aperture 3, 280
app icons
   calendar notifications, 320
   custom folders for, 136–137
   rearranging Home screen,
      132–136
   removing apps from folders,
      137–138
App Store
   additional apps, 116
   alternatives for video
      conferencing, 345
   app Info screen, 435–440
   discovering new apps, 428–434
   Game Center, 108
   games. *See* games
   iMovie app, 272, 274
   improving life with apps,
      449–456
   optional Apple apps, 444–449
   organizational apps, 308
   other Web browsers, 257
   overview, 427–428
   paid vs. free apps, 440–442
   photography related apps,
      287–288
   preinstalled iOS apps, 101–102
   syncing purchased content
      with iCloud, 90–92
   unofficial Facebook and
      Twitter apps, 260
   updates, 442–444
   word processor apps, 329
App Support, 439
Apple
   importance of integration,
      99–100

look back at iPhone's past, 5
   optional apps, 444–449
   Siri, 62
   troubleshooting iPhone, 470
Apple ID account
   App Store, 427
   auto-syncing purchased
      content with iCloud, 91
   buying apps from Info screen,
      439–440
   iCloud account and, 142
   magazines and newspaper
      subscriptions, 405
   paying for content in
      iTunes, 362
   purchasing e-books from
      iBookstore, 395
   reinstalling apps, 139
   Restore from iCloud Backup, 29
   setting up FaceTime, 356–358
   setting up Messages, 347
   setup and configuration, 25–26
   syncing Bookmarks, 246
Apple Store
   app, 445
   bringing in damaged
      iPhone, 464
   importing contacts, 188
   setting up existing e-mail to
      work with Mail app, 218
   troubleshooting iPhone, 470
Apple TV, 356, 451
AppleCare +, 462–463
AppleCare support
   setting up existing e-mail to
      work with Mail app, 218
   troubleshooting iPhone, 470
applying protective film, 459
appointments in Apple Store, 445
apps
   Apple ID account, 26
   Calendar. *See* Calendar app
   Camera app. *See* Camera app
   Contacts. *See* Contacts app
   customizing app-specific
      settings, 154–155
   customizing Notification
      Center, 35–42
   deleting, 138–140
   finding and accessing Contacts
      data, 207
   iCloud integration, 13
   iMovie, 274

iPhone 5 anatomy, 6
iPhoto, 279
   launching with Siri, 66–67
   magazines and newspaper,
      403–405
   managing wireless service
      plan, 16–18
   Notes. *See* Notes app
   other Web browsers, 257
   Phone app. *See* Phone app
   photography related apps,
      287–288
   Photos app. *See* Photos app
   preinstalled. *See* preinstalled
      iOS apps
   printing photos, 285
   privacy settings, 152–153
   reasons to choose iPhone 5,
      11–12
   Reminders. *See* Reminders app
   running multiple and
      switching between, 59–61
   Share button, 95–96
   for sharing data and files,
      94–95
   syncing and backing up app-
      specific data with iCloud,
      142–146
   syncing data, documents, files
      and photos with iCloud, 90
   virtual keyboard and, 44
   while Contact labels are so
      important, 194
Artists, 374–375
Ask Before Deleting, 221
asking questions of Siri, 74
AT&T Wireless
   multitasking capabilities
      and, 124
   selecting service provider and
      service plan, 14–18
Atomic Web Browser, 257
Audible, 370
Audio Source
   Speaker option, 161–162
   while call in progress, 182
audiobooks, 369–370
authors, 393
Auto-Capitalization
   composing and sending
      outgoing e-mail, 233
   virtual keyboard options, 49

Auto-Correction
    composing and sending
        outgoing e-mail, 233
    Notes app, 333
    virtual keyboard options, 50
Auto-Enhance, 278
Auto Flash, 270–271
Auto-Hyphenation, 387
auto-rotation lock, 61–62
AutoFill, 255–256
Availability field, 316

B

baby monitoring apps, 452
backing up
    app-specific data with iCloud,
        142–146
    being prepared, 470–471
    deleting apps, 139
    iCloud app, 121
    Restore from iCloud Backup, 29
    Restore from iTunes Backup,
        29–30
Backspace key, 46
backup files
    creating and maintaining
        iPhone, 80–86
    setup and configuration, 23–24
Badge App Icon, 40–41
Badges
    calendar notifications, 320
    new voicemail, 174
Banners
    calendar notifications, 320
    customizing Notification
        Center, 40
    functionality from Lock
        screen, 135
    Lock screen, 41–42
    Messages app and, 347
battery power
    battery packs in iPhone
        cases, 462
    charging battery, 20
    iPhone 5, 6
    Maps app usage, 290
    shooting video and, 272
    troubleshooting, 467
    Wi-Fi and, 33
Bcc field, 232
Belkin's WeMo adapters and
    app, 452

birthdays
    adding to calendar, 315
    adding to Contacts, 199
Block Pop-Ups, 257
Bluetooth
    customizing iPhone 5, 151
    external keyboards, 55
    FaceTime and, 344
    reasons to choose iPhone 5, 11
    Silicone Keyboard, 55
    using Music app with external
        speakers, 379
    wireless headsets, 163–164
Blurb, 388
body scale, 451
Bookmarks
    adding location to, 302
    interacting with text from
        Table of Contents, 399–400
    manually setting as you
        read, 398
    Safari, 245–251
    Safari's Share options, 245
    syncing e-books with
        iCloud, 397
Bookmarks Bar, 247–248
books. *See* e-books
Books, 393
Both Margins Advance, 387
Brightness & Wallpaper, 129–132
Brookstone
    case/battery packs, 462
    HDMI Pocket Projector, 356,
        452–453
    portable keyboards, 55
    remote control toys, 454
browsers
    Adobe Flash and, 235–236
    other than Safari, 257
    Safari. *See* Safari
    Safari app, 115
bus icon, 292–293
businesses
    adding to Contacts with Maps
        app, 200–201
    viewing in Maps app, 301–302
buying content in iTunes. *See*
    purchasing content in iTunes

C

cable TV, 365–366
Calculator, 102–103

Calendar app
    accessing with Siri, 317–318
    adding, editing and deleting,
        312–313
    introduction, 307–308
    keyboard layout in, 45
    manually enter new events,
        314–317
    Notification Center and,
        318–320
    overview, 309–312
    preinstalled iOS apps, 103–104
    Siri and, 69
    syncing with Facebook app,
        258–259
    view, edit and delete events, 317
    views, 312
Calendar field
    creating new events, 316
    customizing Notification
        Center, 41–42
Call Back, 175
Call Forwarding, 184–185
call-in-progress screen, 166–167
Call of Duty: Black Ops Zombies,
    413–414
Call Waiting, 171–172, 184–185
caller ID
    answering incoming calls, 165
    customizing Phone app, 184
calls
    with FaceTime app. *See*
        FaceTime app
    initiating with Siri, 64–66
    making with Phone app. *See*
        Phone app
    troubleshooting iPhone, 469
Camera app
    become familiar with
        cameras, 264
    Location Services, 152
    overview, 263–264
    preinstalled iOS apps, 104–105
    shooting photos with, 265–271
    shooting videos with, 272–273
Camera Roll Album
    navigating with Photos app,
        273–275
    shooting photos, 267
    shooting video, 272
    uploading to Photo Stream, 283

cameras
  apps which enhance, 455
  capturing screenshot, 59
  FaceTime app, 343
  iPhone 5 anatomy, 6–7
  reasons to choose iPhone 5, 9
  using as scanner, 453–454
Caps Lock, 51
car icon, 292–293
car interaction apps, 456
car stereo, 162
card games, 419–420
Cards app, 288, 446
cases, 14, 460–462
Categories button
  in App Store, 431
  in iBookstore, 395
Cc field, 232
Change Voicemail Password,
  184–185
charging battery
  iPhone 5 setup, 20
  troubleshooting iPhone, 467
Charts tab
  in App Store, 432–434
  in iTunes, 359
Check Spelling
  composing and sending
    outgoing e-mail, 233
  virtual keyboard options, 51, 52
Chess Free, 414–415
children's games
  Game Center Restrictions,
    423–424
  ratings, 409–411
Choose Audience screen, 244
Clear Cookies and Data, 256
Clear History, 256
clear protective film, 458–459
Clock app
  defined, 105–106
  managing with Siri, 74
cloud-based file-sharing services,
  92–93. See also iCloud
Collections, 389–391
colors
  changing calendar, 313
  choosing iPhone 5, 13–14
.com key, 238
commands
  Albums screen, 274–275
  call-in-progress screen, 166–167

Contacts app, 191–192
controlling Music app with
  Siri, 71
FaceTime app, 343
fine-tuning Siri's performance
  through practice, 74–75
iBookstore, 393–394
iOS 6 features, 122
Maps app, 296
Maps app views, 298–299
Music app, 373–374
Share button, 240–245
Siri, 65
Company, 192
compatibility requirements for
  apps, 436–437, 442–444
Complete My Album, 376
Complete My Season, 376
Completed list, 322
Compose Message, 348
composing outgoing e-mail,
  231–234
computers
  downloading apps to, 428
  iTunes Sync backup, 81
  sharing photos and videos, 280
  shopping at iBookstore, 393
  streaming photos and video
    to, 277
  syncing Contacts with iCloud,
    211–212
conference calls
  with FaceTime. See FaceTime
    app
  participating in, 182–184
  Phone app features, 160
configuration. See setup and
  configuration
Configure, 375
Contacts app
  accessing Maps from, 304
  adding contacts from Maps
    app, 200–201
  adding contacts from Phone
    app, 201–203
  adding location to, 302
  adding new entries, 192–199
  adding pictures to entries, 200
  answering incoming calls, 165
  assigning custom ringtones,
    148–150
  calling with Siri, 65–66

composing and sending
  outgoing e-mail, 232
creating and initiating calls
  from Favorites, 176–178
customized database, 188–192
editing existing entries,
  203–206
finding and accessing data,
  206–209
finding and calling people, 180
initiating FaceTime calls, 340
keyboard layout in, 48–49
Maps app and, 294
Messages options, 349
overview, 187–188
preinstalled iOS apps, 106
sharing data manually, 209–211
sharing photos with, 285
syncing with Facebook app,
  258–259
syncing with iCloud, 211–212
syncing with other services,
  212–215
voicemail info, 174–175
while call in progress, 182
Cook, Tim, 290
cookies, 256
Copy
  annotating text as you read, 399
  Safari's Share options, 245
corded headsets, 163
cost. See also prices
  paid vs. free apps, 440–442
  of purchasing, renting,
    streaming content, 371–372
  of ringtones, 370
country, 20, 22
coverage
  maps, 16
  troubleshooting, 469
covers, 14, 460–462
creating
  lists in Reminders, 322–324
  new note from scratch, 331–333
credit card apps, 454–455
Crop, 279
Current Location
  in Maps app, 292
  pinpointing, 296
custom skins, 460
customizing
  Contacts app, 188–192

e-book appearance, 400–402
each item in a list, 326–329
iBooks app, 386–388
keyboard shortcuts, 52–54
Mail app, 220–222
mailbox, 223
Music app controls, 375
Notification Center, 35–42
Phone app settings, 184–185
Playlists, 378
Safari, 255–257
customizing iPhone 5
    app icons on Home screen,
        132–136
    app-specific settings, 154–155
    Bluetooth accessories, 151
    custom app folders on Home
        screen, 136–137
    deleting apps, 138–140
    overview, 125
    Passcode Lock feature, 126–128
    personalizing sound and
        vibration, 146–150
    privacy settings, 151–153
    removing apps from folders,
        137–138
    Spotlight Search, 140–141
    syncing and backing up app-
        specific data with iCloud,
        142–146
    wallpaper for Lock and Home
        screens, 128–132

D

damaged iPhones, 464–466, 468
data sharing. See sharing data
data syncing. See syncing
Date, 199
date-time alarm, 326–327
Day view, 309–310
deactivating Siri, 75
Decline button
    defined, 165–166
    rejecting FaceTime calls,
        338–339
Default Account, 221
Define, 399
deleting
    Albums, 275
    apps, 138–140
    Bookmarks, 250
    calendar events, 317

calendars, 312–313
content from Reading List, 253
customizing Mail app, 221
e-mail drafts, 233–234
entries from Contacts, 205
incoming e-mails, 229–230
items from list, 325
in Library screen, 388–389
listings from Favorites, 178
lists in Reminders, 322–324
photos, 276, 278
photos from Photo Stream,
    283–284
text message conversations, 351
voicemail, 175–176
demo apps, 441
Department, 198
Description
    for apps, 436
    in e-mail accounts, 218
Details
    apps, 435–437
    customizing to-do items
        from, 326
    for Movies, 364
    Reminders app, 321, 323
    viewing e-book, 396
Developer info, 437
Diagnostics, 27
Dial Assist (On/Off), 185
dialing with Siri, 64–66
Dictation
    functions, 75–76
    iPhone 5 interaction, 8
    outgoing e-mail, 232
    preinstalled iOS apps, 121–122
    in Reminders, 329
    vs. Siri, 43
dictionary, 333
digital admission tickets with
    Passbook, 382–383
digital cameras. See cameras
digital music
    enjoying with Music app,
        373–376
    shopping for music in iTunes,
        358–362
digital photos. See photos
directions
    getting from Siri, 71, 304
    interacting with Location
        Services, 302

turn-by-turn, 291–297
Do Not Disturb
    customizing Notification
        Center, 37–38
    sending calls to voicemail,
        168–169
    silencing iPhone 5, 33
documents
    syncing with iCloud, 88–92
    syncing with iTunes, 87–88
Documents To Go Premium –
    Office Suite, 329
Done button, 76
Doodle Jump, 415–416
double-tap, 56
downloads
    App Store. See App Store
    content to Reading List,
        251–252
    custom ringtones, 150
    from iTunes. See iTunes app
    Shared Photo Stream, 286
    syncing purchased content
        with iCloud, 90–92
Doxie Go scanner, 453
Drafts, 233–234
driving
    car interaction apps, 456
    with headphones, 163
    speakerphone feature, 162
Drop Pin, 298
Dropbox, 92–93
Dry-All, 464
DVR apps, 456

E

e-book reader. See iBooks app
e-books
    Info screen, 395–397
    reading with iBooks app,
        397–402
    shopping at iBookstore, 392–395
e-mail. See also Mail app
    composing, sending and
        reading with Siri, 68
    creating new Contact entry, 196
    e-mailing books, 393
    Messages options, 349
    notes from iBooks, 400
    sending using Contacts, 188
    setting up to work with Mail
        app, 217–220

e-mail (cont.)
    Share Contact, 209–211
    sharing photos and videos, 280–281
EarPods
    adjusting Music volume, 376
    FaceTime and, 344
    options for speaking on phone, 163
    reasons to choose iPhone 5, 11
    using for games, 408
editing
    Bookmarks, 248
    calendar events, 317
    calendars, 312–313
    existing Contacts, 203–206
    in Library screen, 388–390
    lists in Reminders, 322–324
    messages, 349
    photo editing apps, 288
    in Photo Stream, 284
    with Photos app, 273–279
    Shared Photo Stream, 284, 287
    specific lists, 325
    video with iMovie, 274
emoticons, 351
Enable Caps Lock, 51
encryption, 83
End
    answering incoming calls, 171
    defined, 166
    in Maps app, 296
    while call in progress, 182
End Locations, 291–297
Ends, 314–315
enhancing photos, 273–279
entertainment, multimedia. See multimedia entertainment
Entertainment Software Rating Board (ESRB) rating system, 411
entertainment system, 4
episodes of TV shows, 366–368
erasing iPhone, 471
ergonomics of iPhone 5, 9
ESRB (Entertainment Software Rating Board) rating system, 411
ETA (estimated time to arrival), 295
events
    adding new to calendar manually, 314–317
    defined, 309
    scheduling with Siri, 69

    viewing, editing and deleting, 317
Evernote app, 93, 308, 454
Excel, 448
exclamation point (!), 328
external keyboards, 43–44, 55
external speakers, 377, 379

F

face-detection feature, 267
Facebook
    adding pictures to Contacts, 200
    Chat, 352
    Instagram, 261
    installing app, 450
    integrating events in Calendar app, 312
    integrating in Contacts, 199
    Notification Center screen, 35–36
    preinstalled iOS apps, 107, 119–120
    reasons to choose iPhone 5, 11–12
    Safari and, 258–259
    Safari's Share options, 242–244
    sharing photos and videos, 280–283
    unofficial apps, 260
    updating with Siri, 74
FaceTime app
    accepting calls, 338–339
    activating with Siri, 65
    alternatives for video conferencing, 345
    call-in-progress screen, 167
    initiating calls, 339–342
    initiating calls from Phone app, 181
    initiating from Contacts, 191
    initiating from Messages, 349
    introduction, 335–336
    participating in calls, 342–345
    preinstalled iOS apps, 107
    using for video conferencing, 336–338
    while call in progress, 182
FaceTime camera
    iPhone 5 anatomy, 6
    overview, 264
factory settings, restoring iPhone to, 471

family service plans, 15
fast-forwarding voicemail, 175
Favorites
    adding contacts to, 192
    creating and initiating calls from, 176–178
    initiating FaceTime calls, 340–342
Featured tab
    in App Store, 430–432
    in iTunes, 359
fees for credit card apps, 454–455
Fetch, 226
Fetch New Data, 226
file sharing
    cloud-based file-sharing services, 92–93
    with online-based apps, 94–95
    syncing data, documents, files and photos with iCloud, 88–92
    syncing data, documents, files and photos with iTunes, 87–88
file syncing
    between computer, network and iPhone, 93
    with iCloud, 88–92
    with iTunes, 87–88
Find Friends app, 446
Find My Friends app, 74
Find My iPhone app
    optional apps, 446
    preinstalled iOS apps, 108
    recovering lost/stolen phone, 468
finger gestures, 54, 56
First, 192
fitness apps, 451
flagging e-mail
    defined, 228
    with Mail app, 229
    view single listing, 224
flash
    Camera controls, 266
    HDR mode and, 270
    shooting photos, 270–271
    taking better photos, 268
Flash and Safari, 235–236
flick, 56
Flickr.com, 280
Flight Control, 416–417

Fling Mini, 456

Flyover view, 299–300

folders
custom app, 136–137
moving e-mails, 230
organizing Bookmarks, 249
removing apps from, 137–138

fonts
changing in Notes app, 333
customizing e-book
appearance, 401

forecasts, 72–73

forwarding
with Mail app, 228–229
from Messages, 350

framing your shots, 268

Fraud Warning, 257

free apps
most popular, 432–434
vs. paid apps, 440–442

free e-book samples, 388, 395–396

free e-books, 395

free music, 359

free podcasts, 371

Freedom Pro Keyboard, 55

From, 232

front-facing camera, 264

Fruit Ninja, 417

Full Justification, 386–387

functions
custom keyboard shortcuts,
52–54
Dictation, 75–76
external keyboard, 55
Home button, 57–62
interaction, 76–77
Multi-Touch display, 54, 56
overview, 43–44
Siri. *See* Siri
virtual keyboard, 44–49
virtual keyboard options, 49–52

G

Game Center
overview, 421–423
preinstalled iOS apps, 108
Restrictions, 423–424

games
Angry Birds, 412–413
Call of Duty: Black Ops
Zombies, 413–414

Chess Free, 414–415
control apps, 456
Doodle Jump, 415–416
Flight Control, 416–417
Fruit Ninja, 417
Game Center, 421–423
Game Center Restrictions,
423–424
Infinity Blade II, 418
Monopoly, 418
NYTimes Crosswords, 418
overview, 407–409
Pac-Man, 418–419
suitable for people of all ages,
409–411
VIP Poker, 419–420
Words with Friends, 420–421

GarageBand app, 446

Gelaskins, 460

Genius
customizing Playlists, 378
defined, 369
helping you find apps, 434
making appointment in Apple
Store, 445–446
troubleshooting iPhone, 470

Genres, 363

geo-tagging photos and videos,
279–280

Ghost Armor, 459

Gift Cards
buying apps with, 439
paying for content in
iTunes, 362

globe icon, 244

gloves, 56

Google
data and file sharing with,
94–95
setting up existing e-mail to
work with Mail app, 217–220
social networking apps, 261
syncing Contacts with, 212–215

GoToMeeting, 345

GPS (global positioning systems)
Maps app. *See* Maps app
third-party map apps, 305–306
tracking location, 24

grammar, 76

Greeting, 174

Grid, 266

grouping Contacts, 204

H

hands-free iPhone operation,
64, 162

handwriting notes, 308

HD TV, 451

HD video, 264

HDMI Pocket Projector
iPhone as home theater
system, 356
presentation apps, 452–453

HDR (high dynamic range)
shooting mode, 266, 270

headphone jack, 7

headphones. *See also* EarPods
vs. headsets, 163
reasons to choose iPhone 5, 11

headsets
options for speaking on phone,
163–164
using for games, 408

health apps, 451

high dynamic range (HDR)
shooting mode, 266, 270

Highlight, 399

History
customizing Safari, 256
in iTunes, 362
Phone app, 179–180
viewing browser, 245

history of iPhone, 5

holding calls
defined, 56
while call in progress, 171–172

holding phone to ear, 161

home automation apps, 452

Home button
functions, 57–62
iPhone 5 anatomy, 6–7

Home Page, 196

Home screen
custom app folders on, 136–137
customizing wallpaper, 128–132
iPhone 5 anatomy, 6–7
launching Camera app
from, 265
Phone app, 160
rearranging app icons, 132–136
Safari's Share options, 244
setup and configuration, 27–28
while call in progress, 167

Home Sharing, 379

home theater system, 356
Hulu Plus, 366
hybrid apps, 437
Hybrid Map View, 299

I

iBaby Labs, 452
iBooks app
    customizing from Settings,
        386–388
    defined, 446
    Library screen, 388–391
    overview, 385–386
    preinstalled iOS apps, 108–109
    reading e-books with, 397–402
    shopping at iBookstore, 392–397
    viewing PDF files, 402–403
iBookstore
    accessing, 389
    iBooks app, 108
    overview, 385–386
    shopping for books in, 392–397
    syncing purchased content
        with iCloud, 90–91
iCloud
    accessing Contacts with, 204
    Apple ID account, 26
    backing up with, 470–471
    creating and maintaining
        backup, 83–85
    customizing Mail app, 222
    defined, 5
    downloading past iTunes
        purchases, 370–371
    Find My iPhone app, 468
    installing purchased apps, 441
    iPhone 5 and, 13
    iTunes content, 362
    optional apps and, 449
    Photo Stream, 267
    preinstalled iOS apps, 121
    reasons to choose iPhone 5, 11
    Reminders app, 324
    Restore from iCloud Backup,
        29, 86
    sharing calendars, 313
    sharing photos and videos, 280
    syncing and backing up app-
        specific data with, 142–146
    syncing Bookmarks, 245–246,
        250–251

syncing bookmarks, 397
syncing Calendar, Reminders,
    and Notes, 308
syncing data, documents, files
    and photos with, 88–92
syncing Notes, 329–330
syncing photos with Photo
    Stream, 283–287
syncing with iBooks, 387–388
syncing with iMovie, 274
iCloud account
    setting up, 142–143
    setting up existing e-mail to
        work with Mail app, 217–220
    shopping in iTunes, 357
iCloud Tabs, 253–254
icons
    Albums screen, 274–275
    app. *See* app icons
    e-mail icons, 224–226
    globe icon, 244
    in Maps app, 292
identifier in FaceTime, 337
ignoring calls
    Decline button, 165–166
    while call in progress, 171
images, 228. *See also* photos
iMessage
    introduction, 336
    Messages app and, 347–348
    overview, 346–347
iMovie, 272, 274
importing contacts, 187–188
in-app purchases, 442
In Notification Center, 38
Inbox
    accessing e-mail from, 224–226
    viewing contents, 222
Incase, 462
Incipio, 462
incoming calls
    answering, 165–172
    managing, 172–176
Increase Quote Level, 221
Infinity Blade II, 418
Info
    app, 435–440
    Contacts, 190–192
    e-books, 395–397
    editing Contacts, 203–206
    finding games ratings, 409–411

interactive Contacts fields,
    208–209
    in iTunes, 359–362
    for locations, 302–303
    for Movies, 364, 366
    Top In-App Purchases, 442–443
    for TV shows, 367–368
    voicemail, 175
Insert Photo Or Video, 232
Instagram, 261
Instant Message, 199
instant messaging. *See* Messages
    app
insurance
    AppleCare+, 462–463
    third-party, 463–464
    what to do if phone is
        damaged, 468
integration
    new iPhone functions, 117–118
    preinstalled apps, 99–100
interaction
    Contacts, 208–209
    with iPhone 5, 8
    iPhone 5 functions, 76–77
    Multi-Touch display, 54, 56
internal storage capacity, 14
international roaming
    answering incoming calls, 165
    maps apps and, 306
Internet
    connection. *See* Wi-Fi
        connection
    surfing with Safari. *See* Safari
    troubleshooting iPhone that
        can't connect, 469–470
Intuit app, 454–455
Invitations, 317
Invites, 315
iOS 6
    customizing iPhone 5. *See*
        customizing iPhone 5
    Dictation feature, 75–76
    FaceTime and, 335
    functionality from Lock
        screen, 134–135
    getting to know iPhone 5, 4–5
    preinstalled apps. *See*
        preinstalled iOS apps
    reasons to choose iPhone 5, 11
    setup and configuration, 27
iPad apps, 437

iPhone 5
anatomy of, 6–8
battery life, 6
choosing, 12
color, 13–14
customizing. *See* customizing
iPhone 5
getting to know, 3–6
as home theater system, 356
iCloud, 13
interaction, 8
new features, 9–12
preinstalled apps. *See*
preinstalled iOS apps
protection. *See* protecting your
phone
setup and configuration. *See*
setup and configuration
storage capacity, 14
troubleshooting, 467–471
wireless service provider and
service plan, 14–18
iPhoto app
Camera app and, 104–105
defined, 447
editing features, 279
sharing photos and videos, 280
iPod touch, 437
iPro Lens System, 455
iStabilizer Flex tripod, 287
iTunes app
vs. App Store, 428
cost of purchasing, renting,
streaming content, 371–372
custom ringtones, 150
discovering the rest of, 368–371
iBookstore and, 393
iCloud integration, 13
Music app, 111–112
overview, 357–358
preinstalled iOS apps, 108
purchasing or renting movies,
362–366
purchasing TV shows, 366–368
Restore from iTunes Backup,
29–30, 86
searching, 368
shopping for music in, 358–362
syncing purchased content
with iCloud, 90, 92
watching video content from,
380–382

iTunes Genius. *See* Genius
iTunes Match, 92, 373
iTunes Sync
backing up, 81–83
sharing photos and videos, 280
syncing data, documents, files
and photos with, 87–88
iTunes U app, 371, 447–448
iWork, 13

J

jacks, 7
JavaScript, 257
Jawbone, 163–164
Job Title, 198
Joby GorillaMobile Tripod, 287
Jot! Whiteboard app, 308
Journals, 279
Joystick-It Arcade Stick for
iPhone, 456

K

Keyboard Clicks
defined, 47
turning off, 148
keyboards, 43–44. *See also* virtual
keyboard
Keynote app
keypad
dialing from, 180–181
while call in progress, 182
keyword search of App Store,
428–430
Kogeto Dot lens, 287

L

Label, 193–197
landscape mode
auto-rotation lock, 61–62
Camera app, 265
FaceTime app, 344
Notes app, 332
using Safari in, 237–238
virtual keyboard and, 44
watching videos in, 381
language, 20–21
Last, 192
layout
Contacts, 209
rearranging app icons, 132–136
LED flash, 270–271

lenses for iPhone cameras, 287, 455
Library
iBooks app, 388–391
in Newsstand, 403–404
quickly returning to, 395
lighting, 268
Lightning connector port
iPhone 5 anatomy, 7
reasons to choose iPhone 5,
9–10
Lightning to USB Cable, 81
Link Contacts, 203–204
LinkedIn, 261
links in Safari, 256
list management. *See* Reminders
app
List Results, 298
List view, 309–310
Lists screen, 321–322
Live Nation app, 383
Load Remote Images, 221
Location screen, 203
Location Services
creating alarms for list
items, 327
fine-tuning Siri's performance
through practice, 75
geo-tagging photos and videos,
279–280
interacting with, 302–304
overview of Maps, 289
preinstalled iOS apps, 119
privacy settings, 152
reasons to choose iPhone 5, 12
setup and configuration, 23
tracking location, 24
turning on before using Maps
app, 290–291
Wi-Fi and, 33
locations
getting from Siri, 71
Time Zone Support, 320
Lock screen
accepting FaceTime calls, 339
answering calls from, 169–171
calendar notifications, 320
customizing Notification
Center, 41–42
customizing Passcode Lock
feature, 126–128
customizing wallpaper, 128–132
functionality from, 134–135

Lock screen *(cont.)*
  Home button functions, 57–58
  launching Camera app
    from, 265
  Sleep mode, 30
  unlocking, 125–126
  using Music app from in
    Multitasking mode, 376–377
loss of phone
  AppleCare+ and, 463
  third-party insurance, 464
  what to do, 468

M

Macs. *See also* computers
  Bookmarks Bar, 247–248
  Home Sharing feature, 379
  syncing Contacts with iCloud,
    211–212
  syncing iPhone, 107
magazines, 403–405
Mail app
  accessing e-mail from inboxes,
    224–226
  adding sender to VIP list,
    230–231
  composing and sending
    outgoing e-mail, 231–234
  composing, sending and
    reading e-mails with Siri, 68
  custom mailbox, 223
  customizing, 220–222
  customizing Notification
    Center, 41
  deleting incoming e-mails,
    229–230
  flagging e-mail/marking as
    unread, 229
  moving e-mails to mailbox or
    folder, 230
  overview, 217
  preinstalled iOS apps, 109–110
  reading e-mails, 226–228
  replying and forwarding,
    228–229
  Safari's Share options, 240–241
  sending e-mail using
    Contacts, 188
  setting up existing e-mail to
    work with, 217–220
  staying connected wherever
    you are, 234

switching between e-mail,
    222–223
  viewing inbox contents, 222
  VIP e-mails, 224
Mailboxes
  moving e-mails, 230
  reading and managing
    incoming e-mails, 222
  switching between e-mail
    inboxes, 222–223
making calls
  Phone app, 176–181
  VIP option, 224
managing
  magazines and newspaper
    subscriptions, 405
  Notes app, 333
  Reminders app, 324–325
  schedule with Calendar app.
    See Calendar app
Maps app
  accessing from Contacts, 304
  adding contacts from,
    200–201, 203
  changing view, 297–300
  Contacts and, 188
  Location Services and Siri,
    290–291
  overview, 289–290
  preinstalled iOS apps, 110–111
  Siri and, 71, 304–305
  third-party map apps, 305–306
  turn-by-turn directions,
    291–297
  viewing map of any location,
    301–304
Mark as Unread, 228, 229
Match service, 373
Medical apps, 451
meeting scheduling with Siri, 69
mega-pixels (MP), 264
Mercury Web Browser, 257
Merge Calls, 183
Messages app
  alternatives to, 352
  Contacts and, 188–189
  iMessage service and, 347–348
  initiating FaceTime calls, 342
  initiating from Contacts, 191
  Notes app and, 332
  overview, 345–347
  preinstalled iOS apps, 111

Safari's Share options, 240, 242
sending and receiving text
    messages, 348–352
  Share Contact, 209, 211
  sharing photos and videos, 280
  Siri and, 67–68
micro-SIM chip, 19
micro-SIM port, 7
microphone
  activating Siri, 64
  composing and sending
    outgoing e-mail, 232
  Dictation feature, 75–76
  reasons to choose iPhone 5, 10
Microphone key, 46
Microsoft Excel, 448
Microsoft Exchange
  data and file sharing with,
    94–95
  setting up existing e-mail to
    work with Mail app, 217–220
  syncing Contacts with, 212–215
Microsoft Hotmail
  setting up existing e-mail to
    work with Mail app, 217–220
  syncing Contacts with, 212–215
Microsoft OneNote app, 308
Microsoft PowerPoint, 448
Microsoft Word, 448–449
Middle, 198
missed calls, 180
mobile phone numbers, 195
Moleskin app, 454
monitors, 451
Monopoly, 418
Month view, 309–311
Mophie, 462
More
  iTunes app, 368–371
  Music app, 374–375
Move
  in Library screen, 388–389
  moving e-mails, 230
Move And Scale, 131–133
movies
  purchasing or renting in
    iTunes, 362–366
  querying Siri about, 69–70
MP (mega-pixels), 264
Multi-Touch display
  getting to know iPhone 5, 3
  interaction functions, 54, 56

reasons to choose iPhone 5, 9
multimedia entertainment
  with iTunes. *See* iTunes app
  Music app, 373–379
  overview, 355–357
  Passbook app, 382–383
  Videos app, 380–382
multiplayer games
  defined, 411
  overview, 421–423
  setting Restrictions, 423–424
Multitasking bar
  Home button functions, 58
  music controls and rotation
    lock, 61–62
  new iOS 6 features, 123–124
  running and switching
    between apps, 59–61
Multitasking mode
  FaceTime app, 344
  sluggish iPhone, 468–469
  using Music app from Lock
    screen, 376–377
  while call in progress, 167
Music app, 373–379
  Home button functions, 57–58
  music controls and rotation
    lock, 61–62
  preinstalled iOS apps, 111–112
  Siri and, 71–72
music in iTunes. *See* iTunes app
mute
  FaceTime app, 343
  Ring/Silent switch, 148
  silencing iPhone 5, 33
  while call in progress, 182
My Photo Stream, 283–287
My Verizon Mobile app, 18
myAT&T app, 17
MyScript Memo app, 308

N

Named List, 321–322
names, contact, 192
navigation. *See also* Maps app
  Albums screen, 273–275
  commands, 237
  turn-by-turn directions,
    291–297
NeatCloud, 453
Nest Learning Thermostat, 452
Netflix, 366

networks
  setup and configuration, 20,
    22–23
  syncing data between
    computer, iPhone and, 93
New and Noteworthy, 430
New Contact
  adding to Contacts, 192–199
  keyboard layout in, 48–49
new iPhone setup and
  configuration, 24–28
New Message, 231–234
newspapers, 403–405
Newsstand app
  defined, 446
  overview, 386
  preinstalled iOS apps, 112–113
  reading magazines and
    newspapers, 403–405
  syncing purchased content
    with iCloud, 90–91
Nickname, 198
Nike + iPod Sport Kit, 451
noise cancellation, 11
Not In Notification Center, 38
notes
  annotating text as you read,
    399
  Moleskin app, 454
Notes app
  creating new note from
    scratch, 331–333
  introduction, 307–308
  managing, 333
  managing with Siri, 73
  overview, 329
  preinstalled iOS apps, 113
  useful features, 329–331
Notes field
  creating new Contact entry,
    199
  creating new events, 316
  customizing list items, 329
Notification Center
  Calendar app and, 318–320
  Do Not Disturb feature,
    168–169
  Mail app and, 234
  Messages app and, 347
  personalizing sound and
    vibration, 146–148
  preinstalled iOS apps, 118–119

reasons to choose iPhone 5, 11
  setup and configuration, 34–42
Numbers app, 45, 448
NYTimes Crosswords, 418

O

OlloClip, 287, 455
online-based apps, 94–95
Online Content, 388
online storage space, 144–145
ooVoo, 345
open browser windows, 253
Open Links, 256
Opera Mini Web Browser, 257
organizational apps, 307–308. *See
  also* Calendar app; Notes app;
  Reminders app
Organize By Thread, 221
outgoing calls, 176–181
outgoing voicemail message, 174
Outlook, 211–212
Overview, 296

P

Pac-Man, 418–419
Pages app, 308, 329, 448–449
paid apps
  vs. free apps, 440–442
  most popular, 432–434
pairing Bluetooth devices with
  iPhone
  Bluetooth headsets, 164
  customizing iPhone 5, 151
Panorama shooting mode, 266–
  267, 269–270
Passbook app
  customizing Lock screen,
    127–128
  digital admission tickets with,
    382–383
  preinstalled iOS apps, 113
  reasons to choose iPhone 5, 12
Passcode Lock
  customizing, 126–128
  incoming calls and, 170
passwords
  Apple ID account, 25
  changing voicemail, 184
  iCloud account, 142
  Passcode Lock feature, 126–128
  setting up existing e-mail to
    work with Mail app, 218

paying for content from iTunes, 362
Paypal app, 454–455
PDF files
    iBooks app and, 391
    viewing with iBooks, 402–403
pedestrian icon, 292–293
Personal Hotspot, 15–16
personalizing sound and
    vibration, 146–150
pet monitoring apps, 452
Phone app
    adding contacts from, 201–203
    answering incoming calls,
        165–172
    conference calls, 182–184
    customizing Notification
        Center, 39, 41
    customizing with Settings,
        184–185
    FaceTime and, 337
    initiating call with Siri, 64–66
    launching, 159–160
    making calls, 176–181
    managing incoming calls,
        172–176
    options for speaking, 161–164
    other options while engaged in
        call, 181–182
    preinstalled iOS apps, 113–114
Phone field
    creating new Contact entry,
        192–193
    labeling, 194–195
phone numbers, 337–338
Phonetic First Name, 197–198
Phonetic Last Name, 198
Photo Stream
    Albums command, 274
    defined, 267
    syncing photos with, 283–287
photography related apps, 287–288
Photon Flash Video Player &
    Private Web Browser for Flash
    Video, 257
photos
    adding to Contacts, 200
    Camera app, 104–105
    inserting into e-mail, 232–233
    saving from Mail app, 228
    sending in Messages, 349
    sharing, 280–287

shooting with Camera app,
    265–271
syncing with iCloud, 88–92
syncing with iTunes, 87–88
Photos app
    Camera Roll Album, 267
    editing video, 272
    geo-tagging photos and videos,
        279–280
    overview, 263–264
    preinstalled iOS apps, 113–114
    switching between Camera app
        and, 266
    viewing, editing and
        enhancing photos with,
        273–279
    wallpaper for Lock and Home
        screens, 130–132
Photoshop Elements, 280
phrase shortcuts, 52–54
Picasa, 280
pinch finger motion
    defined, 56
    zooming in Camera app, 267
    zooming in Maps, 300
pixels, 264
Places
    Albums command, 274
    geo-tagging photos and videos,
        279–280
playing music. *See* Music app
playing video, 381–382
playing voicemail, 174
Playlists
    customizing, 378
    in Music app, 373–375
Pocket Projector
    iPhone as home theater
        system, 356
    presentation apps, 452–453
podcasts, 371
pop-up blocking, 257
portable keyboards, 55
portrait mode
    auto-rotation lock, 61–62
    Camera app, 265
    FaceTime app, 344
    Notes app, 332
    Panorama shooting mode, 267,
        269–270
    virtual keyboard and, 44
Power

answering incoming calls, 166
capturing screenshot, 59
fixing sluggish iPhone, 469
iPhone 5 anatomy, 7–8
rebooting, 58
states for iPhone 5, 30–34
PowerPoint, 448
Prefix, 197
preinstalled iOS apps
    additional features, 122–124
    AirPlay, 122
    AirPrint, 122
    App Store, 101–102
    Calculator, 102–103
    Calendar, 103–104
    Camera, 104–105
    Clock, 105–106
    Contacts, 106
    Dictation, 121–122
    exploring iPhone 5, 101
    Facebook, 107, 119–120
    FaceTime, 107
    Find My iPhone, 108
    Game Center, 108
    iBooks, 108–109
    iCloud, 121
    iTunes, 108
    Location Services, 119
    Mail, 109–110
    Maps, 110–111
    Messages, 111
    Music, 111–112
    Newsstand, 112–113
    Notes, 113
    Notification Center, 118–119
    overview, 99–100
    Passbook, 113
    Phone, 113–114
    Photos, 113–114
    Reminders, 115
    Safari, 115
    Share button, 120
    Siri, 118
    Stocks, 116
    syncing with older Macs, 107
    Twitter, 116, 119–120
    Videos, 116
    Voice Memos, 116
    Weather, 117
preinstalled wallpaper graphics,
    129–130
presentation apps, 452–453

previewing
  apps, 429–430
  in Mail app, 220–221
  movies, 364
  songs in iTunes, 360
prices
  app quality and, 443
  App Store, 429
  Bluetooth headsets, 163–164
  cases and covers, 461
  custom ringtone, 150
  in iBookstore, 395
  iMovie app, 274
  iPhoto app, 279
  iTunes music, 359
  online storage space, 144–145
  paid apps, 442
  photography accessories, 287
  of protective film, 458
  of purchasing, renting,
    streaming content, 371–372
  storage capacity, 14
  third-party map apps, 306
printing
  with AirPrint. See AirPrint
  from Mail app, 228–229
  Maps app, 298
  from Notes app, 330
  notes from iBooks, 400
  photos, 285
  Safari's Share options, 244
Priority, 328
privacy
  with 3M protective films, 459
  browser history and, 245
  customizing iPhone 5, 151–153
  customizing Safari, 256
  Privacy Policy, 437
Profile field, 199
profiles in Game Center, 421–422
proofreading
  Dictation messages, 76
  Siri messages, 67
protecting your phone
  AppleCare+, 462–463
  cases and covers, 460–462
  overview, 457–458
  protective film, 458–459
  skins, 460
  third-party insurance, 463–464
  what to do if phone is
    damaged, 464–466

protective film for iPhone, 458–459
public transportation directions,
  292–293
Public Website, 286
punctuation
  dictating with Siri, 68
  in Dictation, 76, 77
purchased content
  in iBookstore, 394
  Purchased Books, 390
  syncing with iCloud, 90–92
purchasing apps
  in App Store, 442
  from Info screen, 439–440
purchasing content in iTunes
  costs of, 371–372
  movies, 362–366
  TV shows, 366–368
purchasing protective films,
  458–459
purchasing used iPhones, 465–466
Push, 226
pushpins, 302

Q

querying Siri, 69–70
QuickOffice Pro, 329

R

radiation, 161
Raise to Speak, 127
rating
  apps, 437–439
  game suitability, 409–411
  songs in iTunes, 361
Reader, 239–240
reading
  e-books with iBooks app,
    397–402
  e-mails, 226–228
  messages with Siri, 68
  newspapers and magazines,
    403–405
Reading List
  defined, 251–253
  Safari's Share options, 245
rear-facing camera, 264, 266
rearranging app icons, 132–136
reboot, 58
receiving text messages, 348–352
Recents list

adding to Contacts, 201–202
  FaceTime, 341–342
  Phone app, 179–180
reconditioned iPhones, 465–466
recording video, 272–273
Red Eye Reduction, 278–279
refreshing inbox, 225
refurbished iPhones, 465–466
region, 20, 22
Related
  in App Store, 439
  in iBookstore, 396–397
  in iTunes movies, 366
  in iTunes music, 359–361
Related People
  Contacts and Siri, 189
  creating new Contact entry, 199
Remind Me Later
  functionality from Lock
    screen, 135
  Phone app, 173
Reminders app
  customizing each item in a list,
    326–329
  introduction, 307–308
  managing and viewing lists,
    324–325
  overview, 321–322
  preinstalled iOS apps, 115
  Siri and, 73
  using with Notification
    Center, 319
  view, search, create, edit and
    delete lists, 322–324
remote control, 456
remote control toys, 454
renting content
  vs. buying or streaming,
    365–366
  costs of, 371–372
repair kits for iPhones, 464–465
Repeat
  creating new events, 315
  customizing list items, 327
Repeated Calls, 168
Reply with Message
  customizing Phone app,
    184–185
  functionality from Lock
    screen, 135
  Phone app, 172
replying with Mail app, 228–229

reporting problems with Maps app, 303
Requires, 436–437
resetting iPhone, 471
resolution
  of iPhone cameras, 264
  reasons to choose iPhone 5, 9
restaurants, 69–70
Restore from iCloud Backup
  defined, 86
  setup and configuration, 23, 29
Restore from iTunes Backup
  defined, 86
  setup and configuration, 23, 29–30
restoring to factory settings, 471
Restrictions
  Game Center, 423–424
  privacy settings, 151, 153
reverse pinch, 56
Reviews
  in iBookstore, 397
  in iTunes, 361
  for locations, 303
  for Movies, 364
  reading app, 437–439
  for TV shows, 367
rewinding voicemail, 175
Ring/Silent switch, 148
  iPhone 5 anatomy, 7–8
ringtones
  buying from iTunes, 370
  customizing contacts, 196
  customizing Notification Center, 41
  personalizing sound and vibration, 146–150
roaming, 165, 306
Rotate, 278
rotation lock, 61–62
Route, 293–296

S

Safari
  Bookmarks, 245–251
  customizing from Settings, 255–257
  History, 245
  iCloud Tabs feature, 253–254
  latest version of, 236–239
  other browsers, 257

overview, 235–236
preinstalled iOS apps, 115
Reader feature, 239–240
Reading List feature, 251–253
Share button, 240–245
social networking apps and, 257–261
switching between open browser screens, 253
syncing with iCloud, 143
samples of e-book, 388, 395–396
Satellite Map View, 299
saving
  Bookmarks, 248
  content to Reading List, 251–252
  e-mail drafts, 233–234
  photos, 279
scanner apps, 453–454
Scanner Pro, 453
scheduling, 308. See also Calendar app
Scrabble, 420
screen, 6–7. See also Multi-Touch display
screenshot, 59
Scroll, 402
Search Engine, 255
searching
  App Store, 428–430
  Contacts, 188
  e-books, 399, 402
  for games, 411
  iBookstore, 393–394
  for information with Siri, 74
  iTunes app, 368
  lists in Reminders, 322–324
  with Safari, 237
  with Siri, 254
  Spotlight Search, 140–141
seasons of TV shows
  Complete My Season feature, 376
  purchasing in iTunes, 366–368
security, 452. See also protecting your phone
selling broken iPhones, 465
sending e-mail, 231–234
sending text messages
  from Contacts, 191
  with Messages app, 348–352
serial number, 470

service plans. See wireless service plans
Settings
  Calendar app, 320
  changing fonts, 333
  customization with. See customizing iPhone 5
  customizing iBooks app, 386–388
  customizing Mail app, 220–222
  customizing Phone app with, 184–185
  customizing Safari, 255–257
  deactivating Siri, 75
  Facebook, 258–259
  Game Center Restrictions, 423–424
  keyboard shortcuts, 52–54
  Messages app, 347–348
  Twitter, 259–260
  virtual keyboard options, 49–52
setup and configuration
  activation, 20–24
  Airplane mode, 31–32
  charging battery, 20
  Notification Center, 34–42
  overview, 19
  restore from iCloud Backup, 29
  restore from iTunes Backup, 29–30
  set up as new iPhone, 24–28
  silencing, 33–34
  Sleep mode, 30–31
  turning on/off Wi-Fi, 32–33
shaking icons
  creating app folder, 136
  deleting apps, 138
  removing apps from folders, 137
Share button
  in iBooks, 399
  in iBookstore, 397
  in iTunes, 361
  for Movies, 366
  Notes app, 332
  in Photo Stream, 284
  preinstalled iOS apps, 120
  sharing, 95–96
  sharing photos and videos, 280–282
  for TV shows, 367–368
  using Safari, 240–245
Share Contact, 192, 209–211

Share widget, 35, 39
Shared Photo Stream
    sharing photos and videos, 280
    showcasing photos, 284–287
sharing data
    calendars, 313
    with cloud-based file-sharing
        services, 92–93
    iCloud app, 121
    locations, 303
    with Mail app, 109
    manually with Contacts app,
        209–211
    with Messages app, 349
    notes, 330
    with online-based apps, 94–95
    photos and video, 280–287
    privacy settings, 152–153
Shift key, 45
shooting photos, 265–271
shooting videos, 272–273
shopping
    for books at iBookstore, 392–397
    for music in iTunes, 358–362
shortcuts, keyboard, 52–54
Show, 220
Show All Calendars, 312
Show All Purchases, 387–388
Show/Hide Traffic, 298
Show My Caller ID, 184–185
Show To/Cc Label, 221
Show Traffic button, 295
shutter button
    activation, 265
    shooting video, 272
Signature
    composing and sending
        outgoing e-mail, 232
    customizing Mail app, 221
silencing iPhone 5, 33–34. *See also*
    mute
SIM PIN, 185
single-player games, 411
single songs in iTunes, 358–362
Siri
    accessing Calendar app with,
        317–318
    asking questions, 74
    Calendar app, 69
    Contacts and, 189
    customizing access from Lock
        screen, 127

deactivation, 75
    vs. Dictation, 43
    finding and accessing Contacts
        data, 207–208
    fine-tuning performance
        through practice, 74–75
    Home button functions, 58–59
    initiate call with, 64–66
    initiating FaceTime calls, 342
    iPhone 5 interaction, 8
    launching apps, 66–67
    Location Services, 152
    Maps app, 71
    Maps app and, 304–305
    Messages app, 67–68
    Music app, 71–72
    overview, 62–64
    Phone app features, 160
    preinstalled iOS apps, 118
    querying, 69–70
    reasons to choose iPhone 5,
        11–12
    Reminders app, 73, 325
    searching for information, 141
    searching Web with, 254
    setup and configuration, 26–27
    stock prices, updating
        Facebook, sending Tweets, 74
    turning on before using Maps
        app, 290
    using with Phone app, 178
    weather, 72–73
    while Contact labels are so
        important, 194
Sketch Pad 3 app, 308
skins, 460
SkyDrive, 92–93
Skype, 345
Sleep mode
    accepting FaceTime calls, 339
    customizing Notification
        Center, 41–42
    setup and configuration, 30–31
Sleep/Wake button
    answering incoming calls, 166
    iPhone 5 anatomy, 7–8
Slideshow Play, 277
sluggish iPhone, 468–469
social networking apps
    Facebook. *See* Facebook
    Safari and, 257–261

sharing photos and videos,
    280–283
    Twitter. *See* Twitter
Sol Marketplace, 462
Songs
    in iTunes, 360
    in Music app, 374–375
sorting Contacts, 209
sound personalization, 146–150
SoundNote app, 308
Sounds, 47
Space key, 46
speakerphone, 161–162
speakers
    iPhone 5 anatomy, 7
    iPhone as home theater
        system, 356
    using Music app with external,
        377, 379
    while call in progress, 182
speaking on phone, 161–164
spell checker
    Notes app, 333
    virtual keyboard options, 51, 52
Spinning Top Adventure, 408–409
sports, 69–70
Spotlight Search
    customizing iPhone 5, 140–141
    finding and accessing Contacts
        data, 206–207
    Home button functions, 57
Sprint PCS, 14–18
Sprint Zone app, 18
Square app, 454–455
SquareTrade, 464
Standard Map View, 299
star-based ratings
    for apps, 437–439
    vs. game ratings, 411
    songs in iTunes, 361
Start Locations, 291–297
Starts, 314–315
states for iPhone 5, 30–34
status of e-mail, 224–226
Stem Innovation, 452
Stern, Howard, 5
Still In Theaters, 366
Stocks
    getting from Siri, 74
    preinstalled iOS apps, 116
    widget, 35
stolen phone. *See* theft of phone

Storage & Backup, 84–85
storage space
    choosing iPhone 5, 14
    iCloud Backup, 29
    purchasing additional iCloud, 144–145
    shooting video and, 272
streaming content
    AirPlay app, 122
    vs. buying or renting, 365–366
    costs of, 371–372
stylus, 56
Subject, 232
subscriptions to magazines and newspapers, 405
Suffix, 198
support
    Apple Genius, 445–446
    AppleCare+, 462–463
    setting up existing e-mail to work with Mail app, 218
    Time Zone Support, 320
surfing the Internet. See Safari
Swap, 183
swipe, 56
symbols, 45
Sync Bookmarks, 387
Sync Collections, 387, 390
syncing
    app-specific data with iCloud, 142–146
    Bookmarks, 245–246
    Bookmarks with iCloud, 250–251
    Calendar app, 103–104, 309
    with cloud-based file-sharing services, 92–93
    contacts with Contacts app, 187–188
    Contacts with iCloud, 211–212
    Contacts with other services, 212–215
    creating and maintaining iPhone backup, 80–86
    data and files between computer, network and iPhone, 93
    iCloud and iMovie, 274
    iCloud integration, 13
    notes, 329–330
    with older Macs, 107

photos with Photo Stream, 283–287
Playlists, 378
purchased apps, 441
Reminders app, 321
Restore from iTunes Backup, 29–30
Share button, 95–96
syncing data, documents, files and photos with iCloud, 88–92
syncing data, documents, files and photos with iTunes, 87–88
VIP list information, 231

T

Table of Contents, 400–401
talk time, 15
tap, 54
Tap To Post, 39
Tap To Tweet, 39
termination fee, 15
text
    customizing e-book appearance, 400–402
    increasing/decreasing size of, 240
text-based directions, 297–298
text editor. See Notes app
text messages. See also Messages app
    Contacts and, 188–189
    Reply with Message button, 172
    selecting service provider and service plan, 15
    using Siri and Messages app, 67–68
theft of phone
    AppleCare+ and, 463
    third-party insurance, 464
    what to do, 468
Theme, 401
third-party apps
    alternatives for video conferencing, 345
    alternatives to Messages app, 352
    availability of digital content, 100

cloud-based file-sharing services, 92–93
    maps apps, 305–306
    for organization, 308
    syncing Contacts with, 212–215
    troubleshooting iPhone, 470
    unofficial Facebook and Twitter apps, 260
third-party insurance, 463–464
three-dimensional map views, 297, 299–300
tickets, 382–383
Time, 5
Time Zone Support, 320
TiVo app, 456
to-do lists. See Reminders app
To field
    e-mail, 231–232
    messages, 349
tones
    customizing Notification Center, 41
    personalizing sound and vibration, 146–150
Top Authors, 393
Top Charts, 393
Top Grossing apps, 432–433
Top In-App Purchases, 442–443
touch screen. See Multi-Touch display
Touch To Return To Call bar, 168
tracking location, 24
traffic, 295
transaction fees, 454–455
transmission
    Airplane mode, 31–32
    Sleep mode, 30–31
tripods, 287
troubleshooting iPhone problems, 467–471
TTY (text telephone)/TDD, 184–185
turn-by-turn directions, 291–297
TV
    displaying iPhone screen on, 451
    subscription services, 365
Twitter
    installing app, 450
    integrating in Contacts, 198–199
    Location Services, 152

Notification Center screen, 35–36

preinstalled iOS apps, 116, 119–120

reasons to choose iPhone 5, 11–12

Safari and, 259–260

Safari's Share options, 242–243

sending tweets with Siri, 74

sharing photos and videos, 280–283

unofficial apps, 260

U

U app, 371, 447–448

undeleting voicemail, 176

unlimited data plans, 16

unlocked iPhone 5, 19

unsent e-mails, 233–234

updating apps, 436, 442–444

updating iPhone, 467

URLs

Add Bookmark screen, 247

creating new events, 316

entering in Safari, 236

website extension key, 238

Use Cellular Data, 256–257

used iPhones, 465–466

usernames

iCloud account, 142

using FaceTime, 337–338

V

vacations, 315

.vcf format, 192, 210–211

Verizon Wireless, 14–18

Version History, 437

Vibrate mode

vs. Do Not Disturb, 168, 170

silencing iPhone 5, 33

vibration

customizing Contacts, 196

personalizing iPhone, 146–150

video

built-in camera features, 264

Camera app and, 104–105

Camera app controls, 265–267

inserting into e-mail, 232–233

sending in Messages, 349

sharing, 280–287

shooting with Camera app, 272–273

video conferencing. *See* FaceTime app

video geo-tagging, 279–280

Videos app

overview, 380–382

preinstalled iOS apps, 116

views

3D map, 297

calendar event, 317

changing Maps, 297–300

List, Day and Month, 309–311

lists in Reminders, 322–324

one calendar at a time, or multiple simultaneously, 312

PDF files with iBooks, 402–403

Photos app, 273–279

specific lists, 324–325

viewing map of any location, 301–304

VIP e-mails, 224

VIP list, 230–231

VIP Poker, 419–420

virtual keyboard

abbreviations and emoticons, 351

custom shortcuts, 52–54

customized for Safari, 238

iPhone 5 interaction, 8

Multi-Touch display, 55

in Notes app, 331–332

options, 49–52

overview of functions, 44–49

voice control. *See* Siri

Voice Memos, 116

voice recognition, 62

voicemail

changing password, 184

Do Not Disturb feature, 168–169

managing, 173–176

volume

activating shutter button, 265

adjusting call, 170

adjusting Music app, 376

FaceTime app, 344

iPhone 5 anatomy, 7–8

personalizing sound and vibration, 146

silencing iPhone 5, 33–34

W

walking directions, 292–293

wallpaper, 128–132

water damaged iPhone, 464

weather

customizing Notification Center, 39

Notification Center screen, 35–36

preinstalled iOS apps, 117

Siri and, 72–73

web browsing. *See* Safari

websites

creating new Contact entry, 196

entering URLs, 236

extension keys, 238

Week view, 309–312

Welcome, 20–21

Wi-Fi connection

for content downloads, 355

creating and maintaining iCloud backup, 83

Dictation and, 75

FaceTime and, 335–336, 344

iTunes Wireless Sync backup, 81–83

Maps app, 290

Messages app and, 346

multitasking capabilities and, 124

reasons to choose iPhone 5, 11

setup and configuration, 20, 22–23

Siri and, 63

troubleshooting iPhone, 469–470

turning on/off, 32–33

when using iTunes, 357

wide-band audio technology, 11

Windows, 211–212

wireless headsets, 163–164

wireless networks, 20, 22–23

Wireless Provider Services, 185

wireless service plans

iPhone protection, 457

Maps app usage, 290

Messages app and, 347

participating in conference calls, 184

selecting, 14–18

wireless service providers
  accessing voicemail, 173
  choosing iPhone 5, 14–18
  multitasking capabilities
    and, 124
  Phone app use and, 160
  troubleshooting iPhone that
    won't make calls, 469
  Wireless Provider Services
    feature, 185
wireless speakers, 379
Withings, 451
Word, 448–449
word processing
  apps, 308, 329

Notes app, 113
Words with Friends, 420–421
workout apps, 451
world clock, 106
Worth Ave. Group, 464

X

Xfinity Home from Comcast, 452

Y

Yahoo!
  data and file sharing with,
    94–95
  setting up existing e-mail to
    work with Mail app, 217–220

  syncing Contacts with, 212–215
Yelp!
  integration with Maps app, 301
  interacting with Location
    Services, 302–304
YouTube app, 258

Z

zooming
  in Camera app, 267
  in Maps app, 300
  Multi-Touch interaction, 56

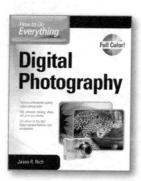